Praise for Iris Chang and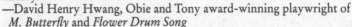

"Comprehensive, beautifully written, fi... ...sis—the definitive book on Chinese Am... ...Iris Chang places today's Chinese Ame... ...U.S. history."
       —David Henry Hwang, Obie and Tony award-winning playwright of
       M. Butterfly and *Flower Drum Song*

"A major drama . . . Chang's book is crammed with telling stories not only from the mining camps and Chinatowns of America but from Chinese villages and cities. Chang has found a great subject, and her stories are well worth reading."   —*The Washington Post Book World*

"Valuable for the mirror it holds up to the United States . . . Chang's timely book deserves to be read in homes and schools because it documents well the struggles of one ethnic group to win its rightful place alongside others."
                                                    —*St. Louis Post-Dispatch*

"Tells the story thoroughly and with confidence . . . vital to our history. To understand who we are in the early twenty-first century one must know who we were and how we got here. Iris Chang's book tells one important part of the American story comprehensively."   —*Los Angeles Times*

"As a chronicle of the timeless battle for civil liberties, the book is high, panoramic drama."   —*The Oregonian* (Portland)

"Informative, thought-provoking and entertaining."   —*AsianWeek*

"May be the definitive history of the Chinese experience in this country."
                                            —*The Atlanta Journal-Constitution*

"Both a sweeping view and personal stories of what it means to be Chinese in the United States . . . [told] in clear, rich prose."   —*San Jose Mercury News*

"[An] engrossing account of Chinese-American struggles and triumphs. . . . Chang, perhaps the best young historian working today, combines exhaustive research with sheer writing ability to fashion a unique history that has the potential to reach a wide audience."   —*Ft. Worth Star-Telegram*

"If you are hungry for the history of the American experience, *The Chinese in America* is a must-read. We are fortunate to have the incomparable Iris Chang tell this important and timely story."
                            —James Bradley, author of *Flags of Our Fathers*

"A remarkable narrative . . . an epic that flows effortlessly and sweeps the reader along for an informative, fascinating and emotional ride. . . . This book is not just for Chinese Americans but also for all newly arrived immigrants and conscientious citizens that care to appreciate the deficiencies of the American democracy."   —George Koo, Pacific News Service

ABOUT THE AUTHOR

Iris Chang graduated with a degree in journalism from the University of Illinois at Urbana-Champaign and worked briefly as a reporter in Chicago before winning a graduate fellowship to the writing seminars program at The Johns Hopkins University. Her first book, *Thread of the Silkworm*, told the story of Tsien Hsue-shen, father of the People's Republic of China's missile program. Her second, the international bestseller *The Rape of Nanking*, examined one of the most tragic episodes in World War II. Her third and last book was *The Chinese in America*, an epic history spanning 150 years. As one of America's leading young historians, Iris Chang received numerous honors, including the John T. and Catherine D. MacArthur Foundation's Program on Peace and International Cooperation Award, the Woman of the Year Award from the Organization of Chinese Americans, and honorary doctorates from the College of Wooster in Ohio and California State University at Hayward. Her work appeared in many publications such as *Newsweek*, *The New York Times*, and the *Los Angeles Times*, she was featured on numerous television and radio programs, and she lectured widely. She died in November 2004.

THE
CHINESE
IN
AMERICA

A NARRATIVE HISTORY

IRIS CHANG

PENGUIN BOOKS

THIS BOOK IS LOVINGLY DEDICATED TO
MY PARENTS

PENGUIN BOOKS
Published by the Penguin Group
Penguin Group (USA) Inc., 375 Hudson Street, New York, New York 10014, U.S.A.
Penguin Group (Canada), 90 Eglinton Avenue East, Suite 700, Toronto, Ontario, Canada
M4P 2Y3 (a division of Pearson Penguin Canada Inc.)
Penguin Books Ltd, 80 Strand, London WC2R 0RL, England
Penguin Ireland, 25 St Stephen's Green, Dublin 2, Ireland
(a division of Penguin Books Ltd)
Penguin Group (Australia), 250 Camberwell Road, Camberwell, Victoria 3124, Australia
(a division of Pearson Australia Group Pty Ltd)
Penguin Books India Pvt Ltd, 11 Community Centre, Panchsheel Park,
New Delhi – 110 017, India
Penguin Group (NZ), 67 Apollo Drive, Rosedale, North Shore 0632, New Zealand
(a division of Pearson New Zealand Ltd)
Penguin Books (South Africa) (Pty) Ltd, 24 Sturdee Avenue, Rosebank,
Johannesburg 2196, South Africa

Penguin Books Ltd, Registered Offices: 80 Strand, London WC2R 0RL, England

First published in the United States of America by Viking 2003
Published in Penguin Books 2004

9 10 8

Copyright © Iris Chang, 2003
All rights reserved

THE LIBRARY OF CONGRESS HAS CATALOGED
THE HARDCOVER EDITION AS FOLLOWS:
Chang, Iris
The Chinese in America: a narrative history / Iris Chang
p. cm.
Includes bibliographical references and index
ISBN 0-670-03123-2 (hc.)
ISBN 978-0-14-200417-3 (pbk.)
1. Chinese Americans—History   I. Title.
E184.C5C444 2003
973'04951—dc21   2002044858

Printed in the United States of America
Designed by Nancy Resnick

Except in the United States of America, this book is sold subject to the condition
that it shall not, by way of trade or otherwise, be lent, resold, hired out, or otherwise
circulated without the publisher's prior consent in any form of binding or cover other
than that in which it is published and without a similar condition including
this condition being imposed on the subsequent purchaser.

The scanning, uploading and distribution of this book via the Internet or via any
other means without the permission of the publisher is illegal and punishable by law.
Please purchase only authorized electronic editions, and do not participate in
or encourage electronic piracy of copyrighted materials. Your
support of the author's rights is appreciated.

CONTENTS

INTRODUCTION

The story of the Chinese in America is the story of a journey, from one of the world's oldest civilizations to one of its newest. The United States was still a very young country when the Chinese began arriving in significant numbers, and the wide-ranging contributions of these immigrants to the building of their adopted country have made it what it is today. An epic story that spans one and a half centuries, the Chinese American experience still comprises only a fraction of the Chinese diaspora. One hundred fifty years is a mere breath by the standards of Chinese civilization, which measures history by millennia. And three million Chinese Americans are only a small portion of a Chinese overseas community that is at least 36 million strong.

This book essentially tells two stories. The first explains why at certain times in China's history certain Chinese made the very hard and frightening decision to leave the country of their ancestors and the company of their own people to make a new life for themselves in the United States. For the story of the emigration of the Chinese to America is, like many other immigration stories, a push-pull story. People do not casually leave an inherited way of life. Events must be extreme enough at home to compel them to go and alluring enough elsewhere for them to override an almost tribal instinct to stay among their own.

viii   Introduction

The second story examines what happened to these Chinese émigrés once they got here. Did they struggle to find their place in the United States? Did they succeed? And if so, how much more difficult was their struggle because of the racism and xenophobia of other Americans? What were the dominant patterns of assimilation? It would be expected that the first-arriving generations of Chinese, like the first generations of other immigrant groups, would resist the assimilation of their children. But to what degree, and how successfully?

This book will also dispel the still pervasive myth that the Chinese all came to America in one wave, at one time. Ask most Americans and even quite a few Americans of Chinese descent when the Chinese came to the United States, and many will tell you of the mid-nineteenth-century Chinese laborers who came to California to chase their dreams on Gold Mountain and ended up laying track for the transcontinental railroad.

More than one hundred thousand Chinese laborers, most from a single province, indeed came to America to make their fortunes in the 1849-era California gold rush. But conditions in China were so bad politically, socially, and economically that these émigrés to California represented just a small part of the single biggest migration out of that country in history. Many who left China at this time went to Southeast Asia or elsewhere. Those who chose America were relying on stories that there was enough gold in California to make them all rich quickly, rich enough to allow them to return home as successes, and the decision to leave their ancestral homeland was made bearable only by the promise they made themselves: that no matter what, they would one day return. But most stayed, enduring prejudice and discrimination, and working hard to earn a living, and their heritage is the many crowded Chinatowns dotting America from San Francisco to New York. Of their descendants, however, very few are still laborers or living in Chinatowns; many are not even recognizably Chinese because, like other immigrant groups, their ancestors intermarried. If we restrict the definition of Chinese American to only full-blooded Asians with an ancestral heritage linking them to China, we would exclude the many, many mixed-race descendants of Chinese immigrants.

This is just the beginning of the story. In terms of sheer numbers, the majority of Chinese in America probably have no forty-niner ancestors; they are, as I am, either part of later waves or children of those who arrived here more than a century after the gold rush. Life in China had changed dramatically over those one hundred years and sent a second, very different wave of immigrants. After the 1949 Communist revolution, many bureaucrats, professionals, and successful businessmen realized that their futures were not in China. They packed their belongings, often in extreme haste, and left the land of their ancestors. My own parents and grandparents belonged to this group of refugees. For some the destination was America, for others it was Hong Kong, but for most people, such as my family, the next stop would be Taiwan. These émigrés were devoted anti-Communists who longed to return to their homeland. Indeed, many Nationalist legislators considered themselves the official ruling body of China, now forced by wartime expediency to occupy a temporary capital on an offshore island. However, their children were different. For many young Chinese in Taiwan in the 1950s and 1960s, nothing was more prestigious or coveted than a scholarship to a top American university. The Nationalist government in Taiwan imposed a restriction on those who wanted to study in the United States—they had to be fluent in English.

Thus making up the second major wave of Chinese coming to America were not just the anti-Communist elites but their most intellectually capable and scientifically directed children. Like many of their peers, my parents came to the United States on scholarships, obtained their doctoral degrees, and later became professors. And across the country, their friends—doctors, scientists, engineers, and academics—shared the same memories and experiences: a forced exile from the mainland as children, first in Taiwan and then in the United States.

Most of these newest émigrés did not find their way to the old Chinatowns, other than as tourists, but instead settled in the cities and suburbs around universities and research centers. Because they saw themselves as intellectuals rather than refugees, they were concerned less about preserving their Chinese heritage than with casting their lot with modern America, and eventual American citizenship. It is in connection with these immigrants, not surprisingly, that the term "model minority" first appeared. The term refers to an image of the Chinese as working hard, asking for little, and never complaining. It is a term that many Chinese now have mixed feelings about.

Not all of those who arrived here during the mid-twentieth-century second wave were part of this success story, however. Many entered not as students but as political refugees, and often they did end up in American Chinatowns, only to be exploited as cheap labor in factories and restaurants. The arrival of these two disparate contingents in the 1950s and 1960s created a bipolar Chinese community in America, sharply divided by wealth, education, and class.

The story does not end here either. A third wave entered the United States during the last two decades of the twentieth century. Interestingly, this large wave encompassed Chinese of all socio-economic groups and backgrounds, who arrived as Sino-American relations thawed and as the People's Republic of China (PRC) began its rocky transition from a pariah communist state to a tenuously connected capitalist one.

Although the three waves came at different times and for different reasons, as Chinese Americans they shared certain common experiences. In the course of writing this book, I discovered that the Chinese in general brought distinctive cultural traits to America—such as reverence for education, hard work, thriftiness, entrepreneurship, and family loyalty—which helped many achieve rapid success in their adopted country. Many Chinese Americans, for example, have served an important "middleman minority" role in the United States by working in occupations in which they act as intermediaries between producers and consumers. As economist Thomas Sowell has noted, middleman minorities typically arrive in their host countries with education, skills, or a set of propitious attitudes about work, such as business frugality and the willingness to take risks. Some slave away in lowly menial jobs to raise capital, then swiftly become merchants, retailers, labor contractors, and money-lenders. Their descendants usually thrive in the professions, such as medicine, law, engineering, or finance.

But as with other middleman minorities, the Chinese diaspora generally found it easier to achieve economic and professional success than to acquire actual political power in their adopted countries. Thus the Chinese became, in the words of historian Alexander Saxton, "the indispensable enemy": a people both needed and deeply feared. Throughout history, both the U.S. government and industry have sought to exploit Chinese labor—either as raw muscle or as brain power—but resisted accepting the Chinese as fellow Americans. The established white elite and the white working class in the United States have viewed the Chinese as perpetual foreigners, a people to be imported or expelled whenever convenient to do one or the other. During an economic depression in the nineteenth century, white laborers killed Chinese competitors and lobbied politicians to pass the Chinese Exclusion Act. Later, in the twentieth century, the United States recruited Chinese scientists and engineers to strengthen American defense during the Cold War, only to harbor suspicions later that some Chinese might be passing nuclear secrets to the PRC.

The great irony of the Chinese American experience has been that success can be as dangerous as failure: whenever the ethnic Chinese visibly excelled—whether as menial laborers, scholars, or businessmen—efforts arose simultaneously to depict their contributions not as a boon to white America but as a threat. The mass media have projected contradictory images that either dehumanize or demonize the Chinese, with the implicit message that the Chinese represent either a servile class to be exploited, or an enemy force to be destroyed. This has created identity issues for generations of American-born Chinese: a sense of feeling different, or alien, in their own country; of being subjected to greater scrutiny and judged by higher standards than the general populace.

Another important theme has been the struggle of Chinese Americans for justice. A long history of political activism belies the myth that Chinese Americans have stood by and suffered abuse as silent, passive victims. Instead, from the very beginning, they fought racial discrimination in the courts, thereby creating a solid foundation of civil rights law in this country, often to the benefit of other minorities. But with the passage of the Chinese Exclusion Act, large-scale Chinese immigration ceased entirely for eighty years, and at one point the ethnic Chinese population in the United States dwindled to only a few tens of thousands of people. Only new legislation in the middle of the twentieth century permitted the second and third waves of Chinese immigrants to arrive, forcing these newcomers to start almost from scratch as they built their own political coalitions. But build them they did.

The stories in this book reveal the ever precarious status of the Chinese community in America. It has historically been linked to the complex web of international politics, and more recently to the relationship between two of the world's great powers, the United States and China. When Sino-American relations are excellent, the Chinese Americans benefit as goodwill ambassadors and role models, serving as cultural and economic bridges between the two countries; but when Sino-American relations deteriorate, the Chinese Americans have been vilified as enemies, traitors, and spies—not just in the United States, but in mainland China. To describe the vulnerability of his people, one Chinese American aptly called them "an egg between two big plates."

Throughout history, some Chinese immigrants and even their American-born children adopted the naïve and misguided notion that if things turned sour for them in the United States, they could always "go back to China." But as some would learn the hard way, to do so could be dangerous: during the Korean War and the Cultural Revolution, a number of returning Chinese were persecuted in mainland

China because of their former association with the United States. Ronald Takaki, an ethnic studies professor at the University of California at Berkeley, once called the Chinese and other Asian Americans "strangers from a different shore." I propose to take this a step further. At various times in history, the Chinese Americans have been treated like strangers on *both* shores—a people regarded by two nations as too Chinese to be American, and too American to be Chinese.

When I was in junior high school in the early 1980s, a white classmate once asked me, in a friendly, direct manner, "If America and China went to war, which side would you be on?" I had spent all of my twelve years in a university town in Illinois and had never visited either mainland China or Taiwan. Before I could even answer the first question, she continued, "Would you leave and fight for China? Or try to support China from the U.S.?" All I could think of at that moment was how disastrous such a scenario would be for the Chinese American population, who would no doubt find themselves hated by both sides. I don't remember my exact response, only that I mumbled something along the lines that, if possible, I would try to work for some kind of peace between the two countries.

Her question, innocently put, captures the crux of the problem facing the ethnic Chinese today in America. Even though many are U.S. citizens whose families have been here for generations, while others are more recent immigrants who have devoted the best years of their lives to this country with citizenship as their goal, none can truly get past the distinction of race or entirely shake the perception of being seen as foreigners in their own land. Not until many years later did I learn that this very question has been posed to numerous prominent ethnic Chinese throughout American history, ranging from a brilliant aeronautics professor to a political candidate for Congress. Indeed, the attitudes and assumptions behind this question would later drive much of the anti-Chinese antagonism I have had to describe to make this book an honest chronicle of the Chinese experience in the United States. My classmate unwittingly planted the seed in my psyche that grew into this book.

But it was not until the mid-1990s, when my husband and I moved to the San Francisco Bay Area, that I really became interested in the history and complexity of the Chinese American population. I learned about a nonprofit organization that would later be known as the Global Alliance for Preserving the History of World War II in Asia, whose mission was to educate the world about the unrecognized wartime horrors committed by Japan in the Pacific theater. For the first time in my life, I met Chinese Americans who were not simply academics or scientific professionals, but committed activists, driven by idealism I had seen only in organizations such as Amnesty International and the American Civil Liberties Union. These Chinese Americans, working with leaders of other ethnic groups, were outspoken on a wide range of human rights abuses around the globe. Learning from them led me to write *The Rape of Nanking*, about the rape and massacre of hundreds of thousands of Chinese civilians in the former capital of China.

As I toured the United States and Canada giving talks on the subject, I encountered vibrant Chinese American communities that I had not even known existed. The people I met ranged from descendants of transcontinental railroad workers to new immigrants studying here on scholarships, from illiterate factory workers to Nobel laureates at leading universities, from elderly survivors of Japanese wartime atrocities to baby girls adopted by white parents. I had the privilege of talking with several Chinese Americans whose work had transformed entire industries or intellectual disciplines, such as David Henry Hwang, the Tony Award–winning playwright of *M. Butterfly;* David Ho, a preeminent medical researcher whose antiviral drugs have helped thousands of AIDS victims; and David Chu, head of the Nautica fashion empire.

Soon I learned that all across the United States, Chinese American groups were busy organizing to talk about themselves, their history, and their future, and to make their presence heard in American society. The Autry Museum of Western Heritage in Los Angeles was preparing a huge exhibit about the Chinese in America. A new museum of Chinese American history was scheduled to open also in Los Angeles. The Chinese community in San Francisco was lobbying for better preservation of the poetry written on the walls of Angel Island, where newly arrived Chinese immigrants were detained and interrogated during the early decades of the twentieth century. Chinese American researchers were demanding full access to the immigration case files stored in the National Archives in San Bruno, California. And new ethnic magazines geared toward younger Chinese and Asian Americans, such as *A, Monolid, Face,* and *Jade,* proliferated. It seemed to me there was a big, exciting story to be told.

At first, I feared the subject might too broad, but I couldn't let go of the idea of exploring the history of my people. Moreover, I believed I had a personal obligation to write an honest history of Chinese America, to dispel the offensive stereotypes that had long permeated the U.S. news and entertainment media. Saturday morning cartoons flattened the Chinese into buck-toothed, pigtailed caricatures, with slanted dashes for eyes. Elementary school libraries were still carrying racist, out-of-date textbooks, with images and descriptions of the Chinese eating meals of fermented snails with long, claw-like fingernails. Hollywood films depicted Chinese men as bowing sycophants, spies, or crime kingpins; Chinese women as sex toys or prostitutes. The lack of strong Chinese American role models in popular culture—or even of realistic images of Chinese Americans as diverse and multifaceted human beings—bothered me deeply. People tend to perform at a level society expects of them, not their actual potential, and I imagined there must have been many young Americans of Asian descent who suffered a crisis of confidence as a result of coming to see themselves as they thought others saw them. But worse, I also knew that, based on my knowledge of the literature on genocide, atrocities are more likely to occur if the perpetrators do not see their victims as real people. The first, essential, step toward getting a population to visit torture and mass murder on a group is to dehumanize the group, to reduce them to alien *things.* This is what those books, films, and television programs were doing; they were far from depicting the kinds of fascinating, complex, accomplished people I knew.

There is nothing inherently alien about the Chinese American experience. In the end, the Chinese shared the same problems as all other immigrants—universal problems that recognized no borders: The eternal struggle to make a living and provide their children with food, shelter, and a good education. The exhaustion of striving to sustain cherished values in a changing world. The loss of a place once called home. And yes, the initial reluctance of all people in a new land to drop their cultural habits and risk new associations—only to discover, years later, that they have already done so.

If the Chinese American story is a journey, then the writing of this book has been a journey for me as well: one that has taken me deep into a voluminous body of records, including oral histories, autobiographies, Chinese-language newspapers, diaries, court transcripts, immigrations records, and more, all showing the vast range of experiences of a people that have truly helped shape America. Ultimately, in this book, I try to show the Chinese Americans as they really were and are: real, and diverse, flesh-and-blood individuals in search of a dream. All I ask of the reader is to look past ethnicity and see the shared humanity within us all.

Note on usage and spelling

Most names of places and other Chinese terms in this book are spelled according to the Hanyu Pinyin system. Exceptions have been made for certain Cantonese terms, or the more familiar Wade-Giles term by which a person, place, organization, event, etc., may be known. In the Chinese system of naming, the family name precedes the person's given name. This practice has been followed except for those individuals who have adopted the Western system (given name followed by family name) or are better known by the Western version of their names.

CHAPTER ONE

The Old Country: Imperial China
in the Nineteenth Century

"A journey of a thousand miles begins where you are standing," says an old Chinese proverb. And so the story of the first wave of Chinese emigration to the United States properly begins not in nineteenth-century America but rather in the world these immigrants left behind.

Perhaps no country exudes a greater air of mystery to Westerners than China. It is remote (from the West, at least), and it is vast. The territory of China today (almost 3.7 million square miles) comprises the third largest country in the world. Though it only just surpasses the size of the continental United States, its diversity is breathtaking. Its borders stretch from the mountains of Siberian Russia to the Himalayas of India, from the densely populated coastal lands that border the Yellow, East China, and South China Seas to the almost uninhabitable Gobi Desert of north-central China, then farther west to the isolated plateaus of Central Asia.

China's true grandeur, however, is not vested in its size or distance, but in its age—five thousand years of continuous civilization and intact practices and traditions. The Chinese state is considered by many historians to be the oldest functioning organization on earth. It is also the world's most populous country. China is home to more than one billion people—fully one-fifth of humanity.

. . .

In the mid-nineteenth century China was still an imperial state, ruled by the surviving members of the Qing dynasty. The Qing, originally from Manchuria, a region north of China, had held power for two hundred years, but that power was waning. Monumental changes were about to take place that would transform not only the lives of people inside China, but also their entire relationship to the world beyond China's borders.

Westerners of the time, when they thought of China, imagined a genteel and exotic land filled with quaint pagodas, curved stone bridges, and lotus blossoms—images popularized by the paintings and poetry and observations of the handful of writers, missionaries, travelers, and merchants who had come there. But few outsiders who traveled in China could understand the language or the culture around them. While most noted—accurately—that it was a culture in whose bedrock was respect for social, economic, and family traditions—the culture that also invented paper and printing, rocketry and gunpowder, and introduced to the West exquisite foods, silks, and spices—the real China was far more complicated.

Few visitors were able to travel the length and breadth of the country, so they failed to grasp how dramatically the geography itself shifted, and along with it, cultural customs that were often in great conflict from region to region. Within the boundaries of this one nation were divisions as dramatic as you would find crossing border after border in Europe.

In western China, a remote area encompassing more than half of the nation's territory, in a shifting landscape of deserts, rugged mountains, and grassy valleys, lived some of the many ethnic minorities of China, most notably the Mongols and the Tibetans. In the desert were scattered oasis cities on what was once called the Silk Road, along which Marco Polo traveled in the thirteenth century to find marvels so dazzling, so magnificent, that when he put together a record of his travels Europeans thought it all a creation of his imagination. Over the steppes, nomads roamed about on horseback, or tended sheep, a fiercely independent, rugged people, skilled at hunting and warfare.

In the southwest corner was Tibet itself, with its villages and towers of stone, desolate and hauntingly beautiful structures, built into the sides of cliffs. Tibetans crossed some of the local gorges by rope bridge—nothing more than a single plaited cable of bamboo. (Snapping a wood cylinder around the sagging rope, a Tibetan traveler would slide halfway across the abyss with his or her feet dangling, then shimmy hand over hand up to the other side.) Very few people or sights here would fit the silk-and-pagoda stereotypes that so many Westerners held (and hold). In fact, some inhabitants would have distinctly southern European or Arabic features and wear Middle Eastern garments and jewelry.

Moving west to east, a visitor could follow one of two rivers: the famous Yangtze River of south China, or the Yellow River of the north, both flowing from the highlands of Tibet to the sea. The significance to Chinese civilization of these two rivers rivals that of the Nile to Egypt; the area between them was the heart of China, a region of fertile farmland, fed with silt, webbed together by lakes, rivers, and canals. Millions of Chinese depended on the rivers for their survival, but one of them, the Yellow River, was known as China's "sorrow" for its unpredictable floods of yellow, muddy water that all too frequently surged beyond the river's course, swirling through or even drowning entire villages.

Dominating the north-central area of China was the Gobi Desert, and to the northeast Manchuria and the Great Khingan Range. Some of the vast, flat stretches of land were covered with wheat and millet; other areas were overcultivated into desert. In the winter, icy gusts buffeted the plains, and many farmers chose to live in earth-walled villages, or in caves deep within the steep cliffs of mountains.

Not so farther south. Here the air turned humid and balmy, and the fields, flooded with water and webbed by stone pathways, sparkled in the sun like shards of mirror. Spread throughout these fields was the classic beauty of the Chinese countryside: the bamboo and willow groves, the silver lacework of canals between towns. Farmers tended lush mulberry groves used for the cultivation of silkworms, and in the nearby villages teams of women boiled cocoons in vats of water, spinning long, delicate threads to be woven into lustrous fabrics. There were graceful pavilions, monasteries, and curved dragon bridges, teahouses nestled in wooded, mist-shrouded hills, spas built over natural hot springs, with people soaking in the water—all the trappings of a sophisticated society.

Yet over all these diverse regions, each with its own ethnic tradition and history, ruled one all-controlling, coherent authority, maintained by one of the oldest bureaucracies on earth. One significant element of this formal cohesion was language. Out of a welter of dialects in China, only one written language had emerged. About the time that Hannibal crossed the Alps in Europe, the first emperor of China mandated an official script of three thousand characters, and these pictographs (which, unlike the letters of Western alphabets, are not phonetic) became the basis of the modern Chinese vocabulary. This universal set of characters made it possible for an official to travel from one end of China to the other, bearing official documents that could be read by all educated people in each region, even if they spoke different tongues. A centralized state using such a uniform written language could exercise effective control over a diverse population speaking very different dialects, despite the fact that most people seldom traveled far from their home villages and had little personal interaction with the rulers and their officials. Also aiding the institutionalization of the Chinese civil service was a system of imperial examinations exploited by the Qing dynasty in the seventeenth century. As China moved into modern times, this bureaucracy managed to exercise at least some control over three very different populations: the China of the inland, the China of the elite, and the China of the coast.

Inland China in the mid-nineteenth century was filled with dirt-poor families. At that time, most people in China, 80 to 90 percent of them, lived in the countryside as peasants, serving as the nation's raw muscle. Their costumes rarely varied—in south and central China the men wore baggy cotton trousers, sandals of leather or grass, and broad-brimmed hats to protect their faces from the sun. Their lives followed an endless cycle dictated by the seasons: pushing plows behind water buffalo to break the soil and prepare the seed bed; planting rice seedlings by hand in ankle-deep water, stepping backward as they progressed from row to neat row; scything the rice stalks at harvest, then threshing them over a hard earth floor—in short, lives spent, generation after generation, in nonstop, backbreaking labor.

The work was mind-numbing, but ingenuity was often evident, as when peasant farmers devised a complex system of irrigation to flood or drain the fields. They built special equipment, water wheels and water mills, to harness the forces of nature. In the countryside you might see a peasant pedaling away on a treadmill field pump, as if putting in time on a modern stationary exercise bicycle. Foreigners who visited China in the mid-nineteenth century marveled at the ingenuity of these contraptions, and at the remarkable economies they helped produce.

No group in China worked harder for so little than the peasants. In the typical rural village, people slept on mats on dirt floors, their heads resting on bamboo pillows or wooden stools. They ate a spare but nutritious diet: rice and vegetables, supplemented by fish and fowl, which they cooked over a wok-shaped boiler. An armload of fuel warmed and fed a dozen people. Hardly anything was wasted; even their night soil would later be used to fertilize the fields. In times of famine, people had little more than a bit of rice to sustain them. To survive hard times, some ate tree bark or even clay. Rice was by no means the only crop the peasants grew, but it evolved into China's main food staple because of its nutritional value and ability to sustain a huge population. Rice could be harvested more frequently than wheat, and its system of cultivation far predated historical Chinese civilization.

Most lived and died without gaining more than a dim comprehension of the world beyond their own village. If a peasant traveled, it was usually only over dirt roads to a nearby market town to purchase or sell goods. Along the way, he might encounter his countrymen bumping along on horseback, by wheelbarrow, or on foot. A common sight during his journey would be the baggage porter accompanying a wealthier traveler or merchant. With bamboo poles balanced over their shoulders, weighed down on both ends with other people's luggage, these men served the public as beasts of burden. At night, they stayed in hostels that resembled stables in their crudeness, where they washed themselves with filthy communal rags and collapsed into sleep on an earthen floor.

Few peasants would ever see any member of the class who actually ruled their lives, as they often lived thousands of miles away. In mid-nineteenth-century China, the center of power could be found in the capital city of Beijing—the nerve center of the nation, in the far north of the country—where a handful of bureaucrats and their civil servants could alter the destinies of large parts of the population with the stroke of a pen.

Everywhere in the city stood silent monuments to power. Surrounded by acres of marble, darkened by the shadow of three domes, the Temple of Heaven humbled the visitor who came into its presence. But far more intimidating was the Forbidden City, the ancient home to generations of emperors. Constructed in the fifteenth century, this city within a city has earned its place in the pantheon of the world's great architectural masterpieces. Within the Forbidden City was a Chinese vision of paradise on earth. A breathtaking array of art—dragons of marble, lions of bronze, gilded gargoyles carved into balustrades—guarded a gigantic maze of palaces and pavilions, gardens and halls. A series of arches stretched from the edges of Beijing to this imperial labyrinth, and everything in the Forbidden City complex, right down to the last courtyard, converged upon the imperial throne, reflecting the belief that the entire world radiated out from the royal seat of China and its emperor: the son of heaven, the core of the universe.

North of Beijing was the Great Wall of China, the longest structure on earth. The Great Wall took many generations to build, and its purpose was simple: to protect the Han, who were the dominant ethnic population, from foreign incursion. For more than a thousand miles, it wound a serpentine path from east to west over mountains and the Mongolian plateau, a concrete expression of the Chinese resolve to repel all outsiders. Han rulers—the Ming dynasty—had controlled the empire for three centuries, during which time the wall had successfully kept out the barbarians from the north. But in 1644, nomads from Manchuria—the Manchus—fought their way past the barrier and conquered the Han people.

The new Manchu rulers might have been seen as barbarians by the Han, but they were swift, effective, and savvy conquerors, and they seized Beijing for their own. Moving into the Forbidden City, they established their own ruling line, the Qing dynasty, and declared their own capital in Beijing. They quickly adopted the habits of the previous Chinese ruling class and exploited its infrastructure, its vast system of laws and bureaucrats, though they added their own refinements to the system. To enforce the subjugation of the Han people, they mandated that all Han men wear long, braided queues as a badge of their humiliation (to shave one's head was considered a sign of treason). Eager to guard their status as a privileged class, they outlawed intermarriage between Han and the Manchu. They also forbade Han migration to Manchuria, for as a minority population they wanted their own region within China to which they could safely retreat in case they were ever ousted from power.

But the most effective weapon in the Manchu arsenal was the imperial examination system, which used civil service tests as a mechanism of social order, forcing all aspiring officials to write essays on ancient Chinese literature and philosophy. Three tiers of examinations—local, provincial, and national—determined entrance into and promotion through the Chinese civil service bureaucracy. These tests created the illusion of meritocracy, of a system in which power and prestige were achieved not through lineage but through individual hard work and the rigors of learning. The examination process itself as well as its subject matter, converging with the Chinese respect for tradition and the Confucian emphasis on education, contributed to the development and maintenance of the culture's reverence for education.

Children were told that "ministers and generals are not born in office"—they had to earn their way to the top. Like many motivational stories told to children, however, this one was not entirely true. Only certain groups were allowed to take the tests (women were entirely excluded from the process), and elite families had resources to hire the best tutors to prepare their sons for the examinations, giving wealthy test takers an enormous advantage over the sons of the poor. Most Chinese villages had special schools and tutors for the children of prosperous peasants and landlords.

In addition, as designed, defined, and dictated by the Manchus, the examination system had the nefarious result of creating a society in which the Han constantly competed against each other for favor with their rulers. More significantly, the system suppressed rebellion until the nineteenth century. The memorization and mastery of Chinese classics served as a safe outlet for the nation's most ambitious, talented young men, encouraging them to direct their youthful energies into scholastic competition rather than openly questioning and challenging the system. The imperial exams soon became more potent than any military force, as the people themselves embraced this instrument of their own oppression.

Further, the system bred a sense of entitlement that turned the most talented sons of the Han Chinese, who should have been their leaders, into agents of the oppressor group. The very purpose of Qing hierarchy was to divorce the most talented from the masses from which they came. Passing the first test transformed a young man into a local magistrate, and even at the lowest level of government, he would enjoy the prerogatives of lifetime job security and exemption from torture, as he ascended to a world that severed him from his people. Once an official was in the system, it was impossible to get him out. The system gave him no incentive to serve the commonweal, because most of his tasks could be relegated to clerks who would interface with the suffering masses. The imperial exam system encouraged officials to think of their current position as merely one step on the ladder to the next, and to spend their days dreaming of passing the next exam.

Meanwhile, such men often ruled their districts like totalitarian despots. Virtually no redress could be taken against any official who broke the law, because he *was* the law. A Chinese magistrate could, with no threat of retaliation, accuse a peasant of banditry, throw him in jail, take his property, and even execute him if he proved a troublesome prisoner. If he lusted after a girl in the village, he could coerce her father to surrender her to him as one of his concubines. So absolute was his power that a Chinese man once told a Western observer, "I would rather be mayor in China than President of the United States."

Only a small percentage of Chinese officials lived in the capital. Local officials who passed the first test could be found dispersed in villages throughout the empire, and those who passed the second might ascend to a middle, provincial level, such as the mayoralty of a city. The coveted places in Beijing usually went to a select few who passed the third and final test. There, the Qing regime promptly organized them further into nine grades, easily identified by their garments. Each dignitary wore a flowing silk robe embroidered with the insignia of his office and a cap tipped with a button or globular stone, the color of which indicated his title. Commoners immediately recognized these officials not only by their costume, but also by the luxury of their vehicles and the size of their entourage. Considering themselves too lofty to walk, imperial bureaucrats traveled by carriage or sedan chair and felt compelled to descend to earth only when summoned to court in the Forbidden City, where the rarefied atmosphere made it clear that each individual, even a noble, was utterly insignificant and totally dispensable in the presence of the imperial family.

The coastal cities were the only places in China that looked out to the world beyond its borders, across the ocean. Shanghai, Canton, and Hong Kong, as ports, naturally were built not only near the sea but on or near major rivers that started deep within China's interior. They served as hubs of international trade and commerce, where products from inland China, such as silks, teas, and porcelains, were shipped out internationally. With the constant arrival of overseas vessels and the interaction with foreign merchants and explorers, the port cities of China, as those elsewhere in the world, were more cosmopolitan, more progressive, and less locked in cultural traditions than the rest of the country. While Beijing emphasized respect for status above all, the Chinese along the coasts were usually more concerned with making money.

The influences of overseas merchants, the conduct of business, and the daily contact of their residents with foreign ideas and foreign people made these cities more difficult for the Chinese state to control than the rest of the country. One place in particular was notorious for its independence: Canton, the capital of Guangdong province and one of the oldest port cities in China. As early as the seventh century, merchants from across the globe—Arabic, Persian, Jewish, and Indonesian—had come there to trade. A millennium later, in the seventeenth century, Canton began a powerful legacy of anti-Manchu subversion: descendants of the founding Ming dynasty emperor, working from strongholds in Canton and other cities along the southern coast, waged furious resistance against their new rulers, a campaign that lasted for years before they were overwhelmed, captured, and executed. The local people, however, bitterly resented their new masters and established secret societies with the goal of one day overthrowing the Qing.

Yet they readily accepted another form of inequality. Money was king on the coast, and the rich lived almost like royalty. In the business districts of Shanghai during that era, the merchants in their prosperous shops with red signs engraved with gold calligraphy operated abacuses as fast as people today handle calculators. The wealthiest owned mansions with inner courtyards and manicured gardens. Stepping inside one of these upper-class homes was like entering a museum: a world of carved mahogany furniture and stained-glass lanterns, of private libraries and art collections, filled with lacquer, gold, and jade. The families of these merchants dined on porcelain dinnerware, with ivory and silver chopsticks. The women, too, served to dazzle—their bodies gleaming in brocade *chipao* gowns, their hair elaborately coiffed, their crippled feet (bound since childhood to fulfill the demands of fashion) snug in tiny, satin-embroidered shoes—as if to personify their roles as precious objects of art in their homes.

Just outside these mansions lay terrible poverty. Indeed, the social distance between merchant and coolie, or unskilled laborer, in these coastal cities was almost as great as that between official and peasant in inland China. During a famine in Shanghai in the late 1840s, the poor literally died in the streets at the doorsteps of the rich. Many begged piteously for soup-kitchen tickets that entitled them to the ladlefuls of rice gruel that were dispensed as acts of charity by wealthy merchants.

Nonetheless, the areas closer to the sea also supported a working class of small entrepreneurs. In the province of Guangdong, boatmen, peasants, and small merchants mixed in a way that rarely happened inland, sparking an important part of the economy. Along Guangdong's Pearl River drifted floating villages of junks, whose occupants handled cargo, or fished for a living, and these water-borne communities amassed the experience that comes with constant travel. Some natives of Guangdong worked the land, which was so poor that it bred a certain resourcefulness. Since the province was hilly and cursed with sandy soil, many rural families sought other ways to survive, such as producing handicrafts or working as middlemen merchants. And because Guangdong derived a certain energy from its port cities, such as Canton, many villages supported a thriving professional class, complete with doctors, artisans, real estate speculators, and teachers. It was this class of entrepreneurs who were the most eager to travel abroad.

The Chinese had once been adventurous and robust world travelers, and, at the peak of the Ming dynasty, long before the Manchu invasion, had launched from the coast several voyages of world exploration. Unfortunately, in the mid-fifteenth century, an emperor suspicious of the pressures for change introduced by these returning travelers abruptly shut down the naval expeditions, believing the Chinese people would do better to curb their wanderlust and tend to the graves of their ancestors. This marked the beginning of a long period of self-imposed isolation. During the early years of the Qing dynasty, the Manchu conquerors, fearing that Chinese overseas would ally themselves with rebel forces in the tropical Chinese island of Taiwan to plot the overthrow of the government, kept this anti-emigration policy in place. The penalty was death by beheading. Of course, once they had left the country, émigrés who flouted the law were obviously out of the reach of the government, so the law provided that any magistrates who assisted them were to be executed. Bureaucrats who captured people attempting to leave the country were rewarded with merit points that could lead to promotions.

But the law proved difficult to enforce. Despite the threat of execution, millions of Chinese, mostly from the coastal areas, left the country during the Qing dynasty to seek better lives elsewhere. In fact, the nineteenth century saw perhaps the greatest single exodus from China that the country had ever experienced in its history.

The nineteenth century also saw China's decline as a world power. Centuries earlier, the Chinese had earned international admiration and respect as the most powerful civilization in the world, wealthier than all other countries, vastly more sophisticated than the societies of medieval Europe. China not only surpassed in area the greatest expanse of the Roman Empire, but lasted longer as well. But by the 1800s the nation had finally fallen prey to its own isolation. The Industrial Revolution vaulted many European countries far ahead of China in technological development. This almost fatal failure to keep pace would soon result in China's humiliation by Western powers.

The West had received a bewildering array of contradictory reports of the decline. Some nineteenth-century travel writers from Europe or the United States saw the problems but preferred to dwell on the glories of the Chinese past, still extolling China as a land of imperial splendor, steeped in Confucian wisdom, a near-utopian society in which millions of people lived and worked together in peace and harmony. Yet other Western visitors in China began to reach very different conclusions, waking up at last to the filth, violence, and poverty in which so many lived. The truth, of course, reflected aspects of both versions, but the important new element was that the Qing dynasty was about to collapse under the weight of its own corruption. The government was bloated, increasingly inefficient and ineffective at controlling a growing and restless population.

Part of the problem lay with the personal extravagance of the Manchu ruling class. The Qing created an elite welfare state for their own people, for instance granting military stipends to each Manchu boy at birth. The original intent of the policy was to bind these boys to future service as soldiers, but later this stipend grew into an entitlement for all Manchu men, whether they served as soldiers or not. Corrupt rule allowed the Manchus to indulge in dissolute lives that contributed little to the public good, yet were impervious to challenge. In this setting, it was easy for the ruling class to accustom themselves to living beyond their means. During the eighteenth and nineteenth centuries, gross mismanagement of state funds almost emptied the coffers of the Qing treasury. In 1735, when Qian Long became emperor of the Qing dynasty, the imperial government owned some 60 million *liang* of silver; subsequent excessive spending sent China on such a downward spiral that by 1850, 115 years later, the reserves had dropped to only nine million *liang*.

Meanwhile, the Chinese population had more than doubled. In 1762, only about 200 million people lived in China, but a long period of internal peace caused the number to soar to 421 million by 1846. Inevitably, overcrowding caused shortages of arable land, which led to higher rents for tenant farmers, and greater concentrations of wealth among landowners. And what grew on the land wasn't enough to feed everyone. Even during the best harvests, China had to import extra rice from abroad. In the province of Guangdong, the soil could yield only enough food to feed one-third of its people. Soon, people across China took matters into their own hands. Farmers chopped down entire forests on mountains near major rivers, denuding the land in hopes of growing more crops. The result was soil erosion, causing serious floods, which in turn brought famine and epidemics, killing tens of millions of people.

European imperialist appetite worsened the misery. For years, the West had tried unsuccessfully to break into the enormous Chinese market. Merchants scoured the world for goods such as fur pelts to sell to China, but the Qing scorned most of their products, and treated the foreign merchants with contempt, dictating where they could live and do business. By the early nineteenth century, however, British smugglers had opened the market wide, though not with legitimate trade goods like food or cloth, but by introducing a dangerous and highly addictive drug. Opium, harvested from the British colony of India, cut a wide swath through every class: from socialites seeking release from boredom to coolies who wished to ease the pain of heavy loads. Whether they smoked opium through a pipe or sucked it in tablet form, heavy addicts fell into a near-comatose stupor, gradually decaying into living skeletons. Demand spiraled, and imports of the drug soared from 33,000 chests in 1842 to 46,000 chests in 1848 to 52,929 in 1850, draining the Qing dynasty of its silver. (A chest contained 130 to 160 pounds of opium.) Millions of Chinese were wasting away, slowly dying from the poison.

The Chinese government tried desperately but unsuccessfully to stop the trade. In 1839, the Qing emperor appointed a special commissioner, an official named Lin Zexu, to end the drug traffic. In Canton, Lin confiscated 20,000 chests of opium—a British stockpile weighing more than three million pounds—and ordered the narcotic to be dissolved in fresh lime and water and flushed out to sea. In response, the British government launched a series of attacks against

China to exert what they believed to be their right to foist a dangerous drug onto another country. Using this as a long-awaited excuse to break through China's closed barriers, British forces invaded one port city after another—Canton, Amoy, Ningpo, Shanghai, Nanjing (Nanking)—until the Chinese finally capitulated. In 1842, the Qing government signed the Treaty of Nanking, which forced the country to open its ports to international trade, pay massive indemnities, and continue to allow the open importation of opium. The British established concessions at Amoy and Shanghai, and turned a rocky island into the colony of Hong Kong. They also joined France and other European nations in creating a system of extraterritorial privilege, whereby certain European powers were given their own jurisdictions within the port cities. Within these "concession" areas, Europeans were above Chinese law, and native Chinese were relegated to second-class citizenship in their own country.

Reports later emerged of white foreigners swaggering through Chinese port cities like petty dictators. A young American bank teller boasted that if a Chinese man failed to make room for him on the street, he would strike him down with his cane: "Should I break his nose or kill him, the worst that can happen would be that he or his people would make complaint to the Consul, who might impose the fine of a dollar for the misdemeanor, but I could always prove that I had just cause to beat him."

Unfair treaties with the West also wreaked havoc in the countryside, when the Qing government shifted the burden of indemnities to the peasants, forcing them to pay increased taxes. The peasants were already slaves to the land, living a hand-to-mouth existence, owing heavy rents and the cost of supplies to their landlords. They already suffered horrid consequences for every disaster beyond their control (if they endured crop failure from unexpected weather or floods, they were always held personally accountable, while relief money sent by the central government lined the pockets of the local elite). Now, with the burdens of these new treaties put on the already sagging shoulders of the poor, large numbers of peasants found themselves thrown even deeper in debt. Many had no choice but to sell all their possessions—their plows, their oxen, even their own children—to pay down the debt. If they could not pay, rent collectors and local officials had the power to arrest them, beat them, or throw them into jail.

A Chinese prison was the last place anyone wanted to go. Conditions for the incarcerated in China exposed the depths of cruelty of the Qing dynasty. People were caged like animals, left in filth, dying from disease. Men were often left chained to decaying corpses, forgotten by the wardens. A mobile version of jail was the *cangue*, a cage in which the victim would be paraded before jeering crowds in the streets. A small opening cut into the bars at the top permitted the prisoner's head to be drawn up for display to the crowds; each rough jostle would throw his neck against the jagged edges.

A desperate citizenry finally turned to violence. Nineteenth-century China roiled with rebellions, unprecedented in scale, and tens of millions of people died in the upheavals. The most serious one, known as the Taiping Rebellion, erupted in 1850 under the leadership of Hong Xiuquan, an ambitious young man from Guangdong province. A rural schoolteacher, Hong had tried repeatedly to pass the district-level imperial examination as his route to gentility. After failing the test several times, he suffered a mental breakdown and came to believe he was the son of God and the younger brother of Jesus Christ. An impassioned speaker, he started proselytizing, recruiting tens of thousands of followers, most from the bottom tier of Chinese society: homeless peasants, unemployed fishermen, charcoal burners off the streets. Some, however, were people with formidable military or technical skills, such as bandits, pirates, and former soldiers, as well as miners who knew how to handle explosives. Drifting north from Guangdong, the group moved from one city to another, seizing weapons and recruiting more people for their army.

Sadly, the biggest losers of this rebellion were the peasants. Marauding Taiping troops swept through the countryside, stripping fields of all food. And when the Manchu government eventually crushed the movement, they took vengeance on millions of innocent country people, many whom had had nothing more to do with the rebellion than the fact that they had watched it happen.

This and several subsequent rebellions over the next decade left the population devastated and the land ravaged. People who had farmed in one place for decades, or even centuries, found they could no longer support their families. They roamed the country in search of farmland and better jobs, to escape civil warfare and the tax collector. With starvation or soldiers at their heels, many Chinese were willing to defy authority, because they risked death even if they stayed put and did nothing. Some chose to leave the country entirely. During the nineteenth century, millions of Chinese moved abroad to southeast Asia, the West Indies, the Philippines, New Zealand, Australia, Africa, and the Americas. Even the Qing ban on migration to Manchuria could not prevent northern Chinese peasants, attracted by the region's sparse population and open spaces, from slipping in illegally.

Nowhere was the urgency to leave greater than in the province of Guangdong. In 1847, the region experienced a credit crisis when British banks cut off funding to warehouses along the Pearl River. For more than a year, trade within the province halted almost completely, and a hundred thousand laborers found themselves unemployed. It was just about this time that some began to hear stories of the incredible wealth of a land across the sea—a land called *Gum Shan,* or "Gold Mountain."

"Gold Mountain" was California. When gold was discovered there in 1848, a Chinese resident in California wrote a letter to share the news with one of his friends in the Canton region. Soon the region was buzzing with excitement, and people could talk of nothing else. If only they could get to Gold Mountain, perhaps all their problems would be solved.

Most people in Guangdong had only a dim concept of American life; almost no one had actually met anyone from America, or any Westerner. They heard rumors that white missionaries kidnapped and ate Chinese children, and reports of strange-looking foreigners, blue-eyed barbarians with red hair. There were hazards abroad—but stronger than the fear of the unknown was the opportunity to make money and salvage a living. Along with tales of barbarous deeds, the Chinese heard stories of a land glittering with wealth—all you had to do was walk around and pick the nuggets of gold up from the ground. Of course, these stories were no different from those that had enticed other adventure seekers to the mines in California, and later to Alaska, from all over the world. Greed is a powerful antidote to fear and an ancient inducement to adventure. Christopher Columbus, after all, found America while looking for El Dorado—a paradise of gold—in the Indies.

The promise of gold electrified the imaginations of the impoverished Chinese. It ignited hopes among poor people that they could go away for a brief period of time, then return wealthy enough to enjoy a new status among fellow townsmen. Perhaps a handful of gold was all they would need to break from the grind of daily life: to establish a small business, to purchase the land that would free them from the tyranny of rents, to build a house that would engender respect, to hire tutors for their children so they could pass the tests and become mandarins—in short, to achieve the wealth, power, and status that had been denied them solely by dint of their low birth.

Frenetically, men in the Canton region prepared to leave. They borrowed money from friends and relatives, sold off their water buffalo or jewelry, or signed up with a labor agency that would front them the money for passage in exchange for a share of their future earnings in America. All of this, of course, was illegal, but officials could easily be bribed to look the other way.

While the community willingly accepted the idea that the young men who left for Gold Mountain might be gone for many months, if not years, perhaps they knew it was important to cement each man's

ties to his home village. To remind him that the purpose of his trip
was to earn money to bring back home, they usually married him off
to a local woman and even encouraged him to father a child in the
months or even weeks before he left. This step—the creation of a new
family—carried a dual purpose: it would obligate him to send back
remittances, and would also ensure the preservation of the ancestral
bloodline.

A Cantonese nursery rhyme of the era, a simple ditty, expressed
the collective longings of entire families:

> *Swallows and magpies, flying in glee:*
> *Greetings for New Year.*
> *Daddy has gone to Gold Mountain*
> *To earn money.*
> *He will earn gold and silver,*
> *Ten thousand taels.*
> *When he returns,*
> *We will build a house and buy farmland.*

That, at least, was the plan.

CHAPTER TWO

America: A New Hope

America in the twenty-first century gleams for many hopeful immigrants; this was no less the case 150 years ago. Less than a century after its colonial rebellion, the young and vibrant country broadcast to the world a raw new culture not necessarily locked into old ways—certainly it contrasted sharply with the ancient mores enforced by petrified bureaucracies in China and Europe. To thousands worldwide who found themselves desperately trapped, without money, property, job, or future, this land of wide-open spaces, seemingly infinite resources, and unsettled territories (ignoring, of course, the long tenure of Native Americans) held out the promise that here was a place where a person could walk away from his or her past and begin again, reinvent himself or herself and give that new self a better life.

Few other countries offered such simple luxury of space—land enough for all, the stories said! Only 23 million people lived in the mid-nineteenth-century United States, compared to 430 million in China, a country similar in physical size: in short, one American for almost twenty Chinese. Only 15 percent of the U.S. population lived in towns of more than 2,500 people. The vast majority lived on small farms or in hamlets, mostly east of the Mississippi River. A person could walk for days in most areas along the East Coast, the most densely populated region in the country, and never lose sight of the woods. And west of the Mississippi stretched largely unpopulated land as far as the eye could see, a sight unmatched in any other temperate zone on the planet.

Compared to Europe's great cosmopolitan centers, American cities were tiny in size and provincial in character. More than one million lived in Paris, more than two million in London. By contrast, a mere six cities in the United States had more than 100,000 people, and only one—New York—held more than half a million citizens. Even New York, America's largest metropolis, was hardly what we think of today as urban: in what is now midtown Manhattan, families reared chickens in their yards, while in Brooklyn, hogs and cattle strolled down village streets.

Long before the first wave of Chinese reached California, America had fired the dreams of the poor of Europe, with most coming from the British Isles, others from France, Germany, Italy, and eastern Europe. As the nineteenth century approached its midpoint, more than one million Irish immigrants in flight from their country's potato famine arrived on America's shores. To escape the weight of British oppression, the unreasonable rents and taxes levied upon them, and the religious discrimination to which they were subjected in their own land, the Irish had been coming in a constant trickle for decades. But now there was an extra urgency in their migration; almost half the immigrants arriving in America in the 1840s were Irish, to whom America meant more than new opportunity. It meant survival, a chance to escape from the ever-present hunger that had left thousands of their countrymen dying in the streets.

There was in fact no one "America" to be reached in the mid-nineteenth century. The eastern, populated, half of the country was sharply divided into two separate social and economic spheres, soon to be at war with each other. The northeastern states had the largest cities and held most of the country's industrial development. European immigrants could usually find work in northern factories, which offered jobs, albeit usually for paltry wages, especially for children. The South was dominated by a vast agricultural system that was sustained in large part by the work of slaves. Neither region held great opportunities for self-starting entrepreneurs; to start a business usually required capital, which few immigrants had in sufficient quantity, or land, which proved surprisingly difficult to acquire and farm.

The economic hazards of the immigrant's "fresh start" were usually matched by prejudices that hemmed in new arrivals no matter where they landed. Racism ran deep, coupled with a class prejudice that, at least in the South, stigmatized a man who engaged in trade, or the farmer who worked his own land, without slaves. Often illiterate and malnourished, small planters were derided by the plantation elite and endured conditions which, while certainly better than those of black field hands, were worse than those of house slaves in the stately homes of the plantation owners. Ironically, in the 1830s less than one-third of the white population in the South owned a single slave.

Although immigrants might find greater opportunities in the New World than in their own lands, those who came expecting an easy life and quick riches would be sorely disappointed. Statistics paint an often grim picture of life in mid-nineteenth-century America for both citizens and new arrivals. The life expectancy there was not much higher than in China, and in certain populations it was significantly lower. A white person born in the United States in 1850 could expect to live, on average, to age thirty-nine—only about four years longer than the typical Chinese man in Beijing. For a black American, it was about a decade and a half less, twenty-three. Infant mortality rates were so high that, looking back, we wonder how families of that time could bear so painful a loss with such regularity: white families buried one infant for every five born; black families, one in three. Only half of all black babies survived their first year of life. Epidemics regularly swept through American cities, due to poor sanitation, drainage, and hygiene—sometimes as simple a matter as having no source of fresh water.

American industrial working conditions were also harsher than those experienced in many parts of the world. In New England factory towns, dark clouds billowed incessantly from tall chimneys, with layers of gray smoke hovering over the towns and surrounding countryside day and night. In metal- and wood-product manufacturing plants, workers choked on air filled with soot and sawdust. Northeastern businessmen built hundreds of textile mills, where low-paid, mostly female spinners, or "spinsters," as they were called, transformed southern cotton into cloth for curtains, bed linens, and garments. Breathing lint and dust through ten- and twelve-hour shifts, many never married and died early from bronchitis and tuberculosis.

Eager for more land, and with it, they hoped, opportunity, Americans moved deeper into the interior of the great continent. The migration westward gathered its greatest steam in the early nineteenth century as settlers began to strike out through the Ohio and Missouri valleys, settling a region now called the Midwest but then considered the edge of civilization.

Gradually, these Americans adjusted to their new lives "out west." Dotting a landscape of tree stumps were a few whitewashed cabins faced with rough-hewn shingles. Some dwellings were even more simple: a hastily constructed log cabin or a sod hut of prairie turf, its doors built from wood packing crates. What would later grow into the grand cities of the American Midwest were then nothing but muddy outposts, often with more livestock than people walking their streets. Nearly everything had to be done by hand and took great physical effort. As they converted prairie into planting field, farmers struggled with grass roots so old and stubborn that steel plows were needed to overturn the soil. Their wives spent hours in household drudgery, washing the family's clothing, preparing meals, dipping candles, making soap out of lye, churning butter. Even though textile mills and sewing machines mass-produced clothes in the East, most women of the Midwest still made their garments by hand: combing wool, spinning yarn, weaving cloth, then stitching with thread and needle. Work defined even recreation, as families organized their social lives around communal labor, such as corn husking, flax making, and quilting.

Although the middle of the country remained relatively sparsely populated during the early- to mid-nineteenth century, many farmers began to feel more and more penned in with the arrival of each new family. What "crowded" meant to them might startle a city dweller today, and the urge to go westward never abated. One man decided to leave Illinois because "people were settling right under his nose"— twelve miles away.

The 1840s saw a significant rise in the number of families venturing westward from the Midwest to settle the Great Plains, that plateau between the Mississippi River and the Rocky Mountains that stretches from Canada in the north to Texas in the south. They journeyed by covered wagon over unbroken stretches of prairie inhabited by enormous buffalo herds, following the wheel marks of other pioneers before them, across flat seas of grass all the way to a horizon that never seemed to change.

This expansionism was reinforced by a swelling sense of national chauvinism regarding the United States' right to dominate the continent. During the 1840s, the federal government threatened war with Canada over the northern border of Oregon, declared war on Mexico, and then forced its southern neighbor to cede large western territories that would become the states of California and New Mexico. Journalist John L. O'Sullivan coined the phrase "Manifest Destiny" to describe the prevailing, though arrogant, belief among Americans that the entire expanse of the continent belonged to them, as if preordained by Providence. In the next three decades, a quarter of a million Americans crossed the nation from east to west.

The most adventurous pioneers pushed across the plains to California, all the more swiftly after news of the discovery of gold there in 1848 spread across the world. To reach the West Coast, pioneers had to cross first the Rocky Mountains and then the Sierra Nevada by wagon or stagecoach, relying on guides and scouts to lead them through traversable passes. In fact, so treacherous was this journey that some who were intent on reaching California opted instead for one of two indirect routes, each thousands of miles longer than the direct one. The first was to sail all the way around South America, a sea voyage of more than ten thousand miles. The second was a combination of land and sea routes: booking an ocean voyage to Central America, crossing by land to the Pacific Ocean, then proceeding by ship north up the West Coast.

For the Chinese headed for California from across the Pacific, the greatest threat would come not from the harshness of nature, but from the cruelty of fellow humans and the racism endemic to their beloved "Gold Mountain." When the founding fathers of the United States "ordained and established" a Constitution intended, in the words of its preamble, to "establish justice . . . and secure the blessings of liberty to ourselves and our posterity," they excluded blacks from those blessings and saw no place in their society for the people living on the land before the arrival of Europeans. As the white population expanded and moved westward, both the federal and various state governments waged a campaign against those Native Americans whose usefulness as trading partners had ended. In the early nineteenth century, the U.S. government used its military superiority to force Native Americans to sign treaties ceding, tract by tract, the richest part of the land to whites, and then banished them to desolate reservations. The tacit process of extermination took even more direct and brutal forms. In California, the state legislature at one time offered bounty hunters a fee for each Indian scalp turned in. Eventually murder, hunger, heartbreak, and disease had their desired effect. In 1790 there were almost four million American Indians, but by 1844, fewer than thirty thousand remained east of the Mississippi, a much more manageable inconvenience for the white man.

Yet, by the mid-nineteenth century, some of the oppressed groups in America were starting to find their voices. Working women organized strikes, some violent, smashing through eastern factories with brickbats and stones. They demanded access to education. The era saw the first woman graduate of a medical school, and the first medical school for women established in Pennsylvania. A few daring women abandoned their confining corsets and petticoats for a new style called "bloomers," baggy, gownlike pants that allowed them a new freedom of movement that did not expose them to the charge that they were flashing views of their legs as they went about active lives. In 1848, the first American convention to discuss women's rights convened in Seneca Falls, New York, launching the female suffrage movement. The delegates issued a manifesto modeled after the Declaration of Independence, demanding that the legal right to own property, pursue education, and vote be extended to women. In the coming decades, the most oppressed population—the enslaved blacks—would see their cause taken up across the country. Inspired by the words of Harriet Tubman and Sojourner Truth, American abolitionists forced their fellow citizens, many far removed from those states where it was practiced, to face the evil of slavery. In 1852 Harriet Beecher Stowe published *Uncle Tom's Cabin*, an anti-slavery book that focused the world's attention on that horrendous institution.

Although the Chinese came from the most populous nation on earth, at the time of the gold rush perhaps fewer than fifty of them lived in the continental United States. This tiny population included merchants, former sailors, and a handful presented to the American public as sideshow curiosities. Their limited number made them highly marketable commodities in a country captivated by the mystery and exoticism of the East. Afong Moy, the first recorded Chinese woman in America, came to New York City in 1834 as part of a cultural exhibit. Museums in New York and Brooklyn displayed the sixteen-year-old Moy in a life-size diorama, seated on an oriental latticework chair, wearing a silk gown and slippers, as if she were a rare zoological specimen. Audiences watched with fascination as she ate with chopsticks, counted in Chinese and did computations on her abacus, and minced about on her "monstrously small" four-inch-long bound feet. A few years later, a second Chinese woman, starring as a museum showpiece under the aegis of American circus pioneer Phineas T. Barnum, attracted twenty thousand spectators in only six days. A "double-jointed Chinese dwarf Chin Gan" also appeared before huge crowds in America. But the most successful performers were Chang and Eng Bunker, the eponymous Siamese twins, who shared a liver and a five-inch ligament of flesh connecting their torsos. Even though the Bunker twins gained wide renown for their deformity, which reinforced the popular image of all Asians as freaks of nature, they should be remembered today for their formidable entrepreneurial skills and ingenuity in self-promotion—and, possibly even more significant, their ability to find acceptance in America.

The story of these twins contains elements of the American Horatio Alger legend. Born in 1811 in Siam (today Thailand), sons of a poor ethnic Chinese fisherman, their bizarre appearance was so disturbing to their fellow countrymen that the authorities considered condemning them to death. Later, a British trader discovered the twins and persuaded their family to send them on a world tour, starting in 1829, for a fixed monthly salary. When their contract expired on their twenty-first birthday, the twins went into business on their own. For the next seven years, they made a fortune touring the United States and Europe, rubbing elbows with European royalty and the cream of Western society. In 1839, the twins visited Wilkesboro, North Carolina, and, falling in love with the region, decided to retire from show business and live there permanently. Wholeheartedly adopting southern culture, they ran their own plantation, complete with thirty-three black slaves, and established themselves as two of the wealthiest men in the county. Though legally nonwhites could not become naturalized U.S. citizens under a 1790 statute, the twins managed, nonetheless, to establish themselves as U.S. citizens in their new community, adopting "Bunker" as their official surname to honor one of their friends. The Bunkers also married two local white women and fathered twenty-one children between them. (During the Civil War, two of their eldest sons enlisted in the Confederate army the moment they came of age.)

The Bunkers might have been tolerated, but were also protected by their world fame and especially by their great wealth. Their neighbors seemed to have viewed them as friends and contributors to the community; being only two, not an immigrant group, they posed no threat to established ways. Their ownership of black slaves reinforced the notion that, however odd they looked, they were of one mind with their fellow plantation owners. Had they been forced to endure the brutal realities of being industrial wage-earners or small farmers in nineteenth-century America, they might not have been so kindly disposed toward those who lived so splendidly off the labor of others.

Such was the America the first wave of Chinese immigrants entered. If the Chinese were not part of the focus of the debate on racial politics, it was probably because there were simply too few of them to arouse much fear and suspicion. Their time would come.

CHAPTER THREE

"Never Fear, and You Will Be Lucky": Journey and Arrival in San Francisco

Americans are very rich people. They want the Chinaman to come and make him very welcome. There you will have great pay, large houses, and food and clothing of the finest description. You can write to your friends or send them money at any time and we will be responsible for the safe delivery. It is a nice country, without mandarins or soldiers. All alike; big man no larger than little man. There are a great many Chinamen there now, and it will not be a strange country. China god is there, and the agents of this house. Never fear, and you will be lucky.

—A nineteenth-century circular translated into the Chinese language, posted in the Canton region by a Hong Kong brokerage office

Flush with hope, dazzled by tales of immediate riches, the Chinese who dreamed of what they would find in California were not warned that many grave dangers lay between Guangdóng and Gold Mountain. For the unsuspecting, the first danger—and perhaps the worst—lay waiting just a few miles away, in Guangdong's own busy port city, Canton.

In Chinese the term *k'u-li* literally means "hard strength." Foreigners living in China often employed it to describe household help or menial Chinese laborers, but the term would take on a different coloration in the 1840s, when European capitalists experienced labor shortages on colonial plantations in regions like South America and the Caribbean. With the help of unscrupulous Chinese recruiters, or crimps, as they were called, a devil's bargain was struck to replace African slave labor with Asian slave labor. Coastal cities, such as Amoy, Macao, Hong Kong, and Canton, served as major ports where men were bought and sold as human traffic. When the practice finally ended in the 1870s, following an investigation by the imperial Qing government, an estimated three-quarters of a million Chinese men had been either decoyed into or physically abducted and then sold into slavery, in what became known as the "coolie" trade.

The Chinese crimps used a variety of methods to fill their quotas. Men in debt, men imprisoned after clan fights, and men eager for work to avoid starvation all served as ideal candidates for entrapment, but for naïve youths arriving in coastal cities fresh from the villages, the danger of entrapment was greater still. Some victims were lured into teahouses, regaled with stories of fortunes to be made overseas, and deceived into signing labor contracts for work in South America. When persuasion failed, the crimp resorted to outright abduction, and a British consul observed that even in broad daylight men could not leave their houses "without a danger of being hustled, under false pretenses of debt or delinquency, and carried off a prisoner in the hands of crimps, to be sold to the purveyors of coolies at so much a head, and carried off to sea, never to be heard of."

Once a person had fallen into the hands of coolie traders, it was almost impossible to escape. The victims were locked in filthy, disease-ridden receiving stations, or barracoons, which the Chinese called *zhuzi guan* (literally, "pig pens"). Because of its squalor, this trafficking in human bodies was also referred to as "the buying and selling of piglets." In one *zhuzi guan* at Macao, slave traders beat gongs and set off fireworks to hide the frantic cries for help. In Amoy, they stripped the men naked and stamped their chests with letters indicating their destination—for instance, "P" for Peru, or "S" for the Sandwich Islands (Hawaii)—then herded the prisoners onto ships and locked them in bamboo cages or chained them to posts. As with the African slave system, the more people a trader could cram into a vessel, the greater his profit for the voyage. During the African slave trade, approximately 15 to 30 percent died during capture or confinement along the African coast, and an additional 10 to 15 percent perished during the journey across the Atlantic Ocean. In the mid-1800s, the death rate of coolies in transit also hovered between 15 and 45 percent.

In 1873 and 1874, the Chinese government sent official delegations to South America to learn the fate of these coolies,* and the picture that emerged was shocking. Chinese slaves on the Cuban sugar plantations were made to labor twenty-one out of the twenty-four hours, and, fed only about three unripe bananas per meal, many quickly died from hunger and exhaustion. Those who survived a few years often bore scars from repeated whippings. Others (probably those who had tried to escape) had had their limbs maimed or lacerated. Suicides were not uncommon. Some slit their own throats, others ingested opium, still others jumped into wells and drowned.

An equally horrific situation existed in Peru, where the Chinese were put to work on the Chincha Islands. The islands provided a rich source of guano (bird droppings), which Peru exported as fertilizer to Europe and North America. The unfortunate Chinese sent to labor on the guano beds endured both blazing heat and the unbearable stench of fowl excrement. Those too weak to stand worked on their knees, picking out gravel from guano, and guards stood sentinel on the shores to prevent coolies from accessing the only means of freeing themselves from their misery—hurling themselves into the sea.

---

*The Chinese delegation to Cuba led to the signing of a 1879 treaty between China and Spain to end the coolie trade, and the delegation to Peru resulted in treaties that protected the rights of Chinese immigrants in that country, and permitted only immigration on a voluntary basis.

Fortunately, the vast majority of emigrants were able to protect themselves by working through responsible emigration brokers, called *k'o-t'ou* or *towkay*. While these brokers could hardly be characterized as Good Samaritans—viewed in their entirety, their actions were clearly exploitative—they did provide some protection to men eager to emigrate but ignorant about how to protect themselves against the dangers into which they might fall. Broker-sponsored émigrés to the United States were housed at a special inn (*hak-chan*) while awaiting embarkation, usually from the port cities of Hong Kong and Canton. In addition, during his client's sojourn in America, the emigration broker would make sure that mail, remittances, and news would travel from the émigré to his family back home.

For those eager lacking the funds, a credit-ticket system evolved. Chinese middlemen would typically advance forty dollars in gold, and in exchange the émigré assumed debt and a monthly interest rate of about 4 to 8 percent, which he could take up to five years to repay. Or the emigrant might agree to work for a set period of time as an indentured laborer, in exchange for the debt's repayment by his employer.

The Pacific Ocean crossing was grueling and hazardous. The amount of time it took to reach California varied, depending on weather conditions and whether the journey was made by junk, boat, or steamer. During the gold rush it took between four and eight weeks to travel by steamer from Canton to San Francisco, and the cost of the trip ranged from about forty to sixty dollars. Steerage conditions, already appalling before 1848, grew worse as shipmasters and Chinese entrepreneurs competed for business by driving down ticket prices and making up for it through increased volume. Passengers brought their own bedding, which they spread on wooden bunks below deck, each bunk often only seventeen inches above the one underneath. Those with the cheapest tickets would take turns sleeping. The food was at best unfamiliar to the passengers and at worst inedible, and was rendered more unpalatable by the accompanying stink of body odor and freight. "The food was different from that which I had been used to, and I did not like it at all," one passenger complained. "When I got to San Francisco I was half starved because I was afraid to eat the provisions of the barbarians." Disease was prevalent. In 1854, the *Libertad* arrived in San Francisco after eighty days at sea with 180 Chinese—one-fifth of all those who had set out—dead from fever or scurvy. Ship captains routinely threw the dead overboard, and it was not unusual for Chinese passengers to take up collections to prevent this practice and to ensure that the bones of the dead would be returned to their ancestral land.

Did the émigrés spend the lonely nights on board these ships regretting their decision, wondering if they would survive the journey? Or did they set aside their very real fears, and focus instead on the future? And if the latter, what did they imagine the future would hold in store for them? Would San Francisco be another Canton? Or perhaps Hong Kong? And the Americans? What would they be like? Would they welcome the Chinese to their country, as all the emigration posters had suggested they would? Or would the Americans resent them and perhaps try to fleece them, or worse, kill them?

What were the shipboard dreams dreamt in 1849 by young men on their way to America, at a time when America represented a new start for so many? How many of these young men would have those dreams fulfilled? The records tell us less than we would like to know about these first shiploads of Chinese to America. But they do tell us something: for the Chinese, as for every other immigrant group, America may have seemed a stop on a journey back to wealth and position in the homeland. But for a surprisingly large number, it would be a one-way trip. While America surely transformed some of these impoverished émigrés into wealthy returnees, it turned many more into something else—hyphenated Americans, Americans who would always remember their homelands as a treasured past but find in America their future.

When the ship carrying the first group of Chinese headed for

Gold Mountain docked in San Francisco, after months at sea, the first impression must have been unforgettable. By the shore near the docks, the émigrés would see hundreds of square-rigged vessels drifting vacant, abandoned by their owners, would-be gold hunters from Central America, for the authorities to deal with.

Before the gold rush, San Francisco had been a desolate area of sand dunes and hills. Discovered by the Spanish in 1769, the area had served as a presidio, a military post, with little more than a chapel and some brush and tule huts, and for almost a century, it lay relatively untouched by civilized men. Then, in 1848, gold was discovered at Sutter's Mill near the Sacramento River.

Thousands of gold hunters descended on San Francisco, a great natural port, on their way to Sutter's Mill. When the first prospectors arrived, they threw down planks as makeshift bridges between the wharves; these planks soon became city streets. Beyond the wharves sprawled hundreds of canvas tents and wooden shacks, connected by dirt roads that melted into mud swamps with each rainfall. Residents tottered over temporary sidewalks created from garbage dumped into the mire; one precarious path was made from sacks of flour, stoves, tobacco boxes, and even a grand piano. To build shanties and stores, they ripped apart the seagoing vessels they found rotting at the docks.

Between 1848 and 1850, this sleepy village of five hundred people exploded into a boom town of thirty thousand, roughly the size of Chicago. By 1851, when the Chinese began arriving by the thousands, it was one of the largest cities in the United States. But it exhibited none of the respectability of the older, staid communities of the East Coast. San Francisco was a roaring frontier town—boastful and ambitious, shameless in its filth and greed. It made no effort to hide its excesses or sins. Rowdy young men roamed the streets, determined to spend their gold as fast as they found it. The first two-story buildings in San Francisco were not churches, city halls, or courthouses, but hotels and casinos, and by 1853 the city enjoyed 46 gambling halls, 144 taverns, and 537 places that sold liquor. So dizzying was the pace of growth that within only a few years the newly rich had moved from their shacks to luxurious, palatial establishments, gorging on twenty-course dinners served to them on gold-plate dishes.

As in many gold rush towns, those who profited most handsomely were not just the miners, but those who supplied them with essential goods and services. Fortunes were made in small businesses, most started by former prospectors themselves, who reaped unheard-of profits selling food, equipment, and clothing. Eggs fetched a dollar apiece, and an 1848 price list showed a pound of butter selling for six dollars, a pair of boots for a hundred. Anticipating the needs of miners for rugged wear, Levi Strauss made pants out of denim tent canvas and created an empire. Those who provided domestic help, such as laundering clothes, also prospered. The granddaughter of one forty-niner recalls a local washerwoman wearing a shawl with a diamond brooch "worthy of an Empress."

Women were scarce in San Francisco. Most prospectors were single, or chose not to bring their wives and children to this raw frontier. In a town with only one woman for every dozen men, the mere rumor of a female newcomer was enough to empty saloons and hotels, causing a stampede to the docks. In this respect, San Francisco hardly differed from the entire state: census reports show that 92 percent of California was male, and 91 percent were fifteen to forty-four years of age. Wrote one California pioneer woman, "Every man thought every woman in that day a beauty. Even I have had men come forty miles over the mountains, just to look at me, and I never was called a handsome woman, in my best days, even by my more ardent admirers."

With these demographics, brothels inevitably flourished. Some enterprising women in San Francisco charged more than a hundred dollars a night—the equivalent of the price of a house, or about a year's wages in other parts of the country. Entrepreneurs in the world's oldest profession rode furiously on horseback from camp to camp, trying to fit as many clients as possible into their schedules.

In a city of young men on the make, violence was the rule in the settling of disputes. Rogues of all kinds—cutthroats, charlatans, professional gamblers—naturally gravitated toward a city where no one questioned your past, where no authority checked your records. No court or police system existed until 1850, no California land office until 1853. Inevitably, then, disputes over property and land titles were most often settled by force, the decision often going to the disputants less averse to or more adept at using fists, pistols, or knives. Since the city was populated mainly by aggressive, ambitious men who had braved disease, robbers, frozen mountain passes, and the desert to make the journey, it is not surprising that during the early 1850s, San Francisco witnessed an average of five murders every six days.

Without a government in which the people had confidence, mob rule prevailed, often in the form of public hangings, in particular scapegoating foreigners without sufficient evidence. For a while, San Franciscans—who created the "Committee of Vigilance" in 1851—tended to blame all crimes on arrivals from Australia, viewing them as rabble from a penal colony. The vigilantes thought nothing of stringing up suspicious characters, defying and even intimidating whatever little public authority existed—on one occasion abducting and holding hostage a California state supreme court justice.

Strangely enough, however, a progressive element also thrived in San Francisco. The city drew not only criminals and capitalists, but also intellectuals, attracted like the others not only by the opportunity for quick wealth but also the romance of adventure. By 1853, the community supported a dozen newspapers and a strong subculture of writers. It soon boasted more college graduates than any other city in the country. Despite its rough-hewn beginnings, San Francisco swiftly became the most cultured city on the West Coast, where even callused, weather-beaten gold prospectors could be seen attending theater performances. The presence of intellectuals fostered a certain tolerance in the city, a fascination for anything different, even as just under the surface ran a current of barely restrained hair-trigger tempers and murderous rage.

It was against this backdrop—a weird juxtaposition of greed and violence on one hand and an avid curiosity about new ideas and experiences on the other—that the first wave of Chinese made their appearance in the American West. If San Francisco did not initially resist their arrival, perhaps it was because almost everyone in San Francisco had come from somewhere else. By 1853, more than half of the San Francisco population was foreign-born, and in a city united by the single, driving obsession to make money, only one color seemed to matter: gold.

This would change.

CHAPTER FOUR

Gold Rushers on Gold Mountain

The gold rush was born out of the sense among people living bleak lives of interminable desperation, Chinese or otherwise, that here at last was a chance to change the unchangeable—to wrench themselves out of the endless and demeaning routine of their daily existence and maybe catapult themselves into another class entirely. People more conservative in outlook might regard with contempt those who would invest all they had in such pie-in-the-sky hopes, and China had always been a land where the conservative outlook—respect for one's elders, one's betters, one's rulers—was highly revered. But wherever the future was the dimmest, there, too, would be found people most eager to grab at this last chance at a better life, a chance that according to rumor had already led some few to great riches.

Like the thousands of others who had come to San Francisco to find their fortunes, the Chinese quickly set out for the gold fields. During the early 1850s, some 85 percent of the Chinese in California were engaged in placer mining. Over the next months and years, they wandered the western wilderness, sometimes walking hundreds of miles in response to news of fresh discoveries. They soon replaced their Chinese silk caps or straw hats with cowboy hats and their hand-stitched cotton shoes for sturdy American boots. But along with their blue cotton shirt and broad trousers, they retained one vestige of Qing tradition: a long, jet-black queue that swayed gleaming down their backs.

The daylight hours of a gold miner's life were spent bent over a stream panning for gold. He might live in a primitive tent, a brush hut, an abandoned cabin, or a shack hastily slapped together from scrap lumber and flattened kerosene cans. The Chinese gold miners, not surprisingly, stayed to themselves, even when it meant that twenty to thirty Chinese miners had to cram themselves into a space hardly large enough to "allow a couple of Americans to breathe in it," as one *San Francisco Herald* correspondent reported. Then again, another contemporary writer, J. D. Borthwick, described a Chinese mining camp he visited as "wonderfully clean." After glimpsing the evening rituals of the Chinese, he wrote, "a great many of them [are] at their toilet, getting their head shaved, or plaiting pigtails." In a hectic time and place, on an almost mad mission, when most men had neither time nor energy to spare for the threshold requirements of civil society, many Chinese maintained strict standards of personal hygiene.

The Chinese also established a reputation for hard work. "They are quiet, peaceable, tractable, free from drunkenness," Mark Twain wrote in admiration. "A disorderly Chinaman is rare, and a lazy one does not exist." They further astounded white observers with their creative use of nature's laws of physics, particularly their astonishing ability to balance heavy burdens on long poles. Describing one miner's descent into a gulch with a sack of rice, two large rolls of blankets, two hogsheads, several heavy mining tools, a wheelbarrow, and a hand-rocker all swinging from his pack-pole, the editor of the *Madisonian* wrote, "It was a mystery how that Chinaman managed to tote that weary load along so gracefully, and not grunt a groan."

A few Chinese prospered through sheer luck, finding enough gold in a single day to last them a lifetime. When one group discovered a forty-pound nugget, they prudently chiseled it into small pieces to sell along with their gold dust, because many small nuggets would ensure both that each man received his fair share and that the find would not draw unwanted attention to the group. Two Chinese miners who had never earned more than two dollars a day stumbled upon a 240-pound nugget worth more than $30,000, a considerable fortune during that era. Like most gold rushers of the time, the Chinese chased after rumors of new findings, wherever such rumors might take them. In 1856, a few Chinese ventured out of California into the Rocky Mountains and the Boise Basin of Oregon Territory (now southern Idaho), where friendly Shoshone and Bannock Indians led them to placer beds so rich in gold that their deerskins soon bulged with nuggets.

Other Chinese prospered not just by luck or hard work, both of which were always needed, but by resourceful use of technology. The Chinese introduced the water wheel to American placer mining. This device, modeled after irrigation techniques used by rice paddy farmers back home, allowed them to pump and sluice water from the river, which was then used to wash gravel from gold. The pumping method was not only derived from Chinese agriculture, but from generations of experience from tin miners in Guangdong, who had originally acquired their knowledge from Chinese miners in Malaysia.

Still other Chinese benefited from the fact that they were willing to work as a group. When a group of Chinese miners working in northern central California realized that a rich vein lay underneath the riverbed, they agreed to work together to build a dam across the Yuba River to expose the gold. In Utah Territory, another group of Chinese dug an irrigation ditch from the Carson River to Gold Canyon, which made mining possible in that desert region and greatly impressed the Mormons living there.

At night, a lively bachelor culture sprang up in these scattered mining camps. The miners formed bands and played Chinese music with instruments brought over from their homeland. Not everyone enjoyed their performances: in 1851, one writer compared the local Chinese orchestra to the "wailings of a thousand lovelorn cats, the screams, gobblings, braying and barkings of as many peacocks, turkeys, donkeys and dogs."

The miners also gambled—gambling being possibly the greatest Chinese vice in the American West. ("About every third Chinaman runs a lottery," Twain remarked.) In gambling shacks, loud, excited groups of Chinese bet on dice, lots, and tosses of coin. A Montana editor complained about the noise, which began after dark: "We don't know and don't care how many years they claim to have been infesting the earth, and only wish they would go to bed like decent people and stop playing their infernal button game of 'Foo-ti-hoo-ti,' so a fellow can get a nap."

Still, the Chinese mining life was very similar to all life in the American West—rough and lawless. An English-Chinese phrase book, published in San Francisco, reflected their experience through its selection of what a Chinese prospector needed to be able to say in English:

> He assaulted me without provocation.
> He claimed my mine . . .
> He tries to extort money from me.
> He falsely accused me of stealing his watch.
> He was choked to death with a lasso, by a robber.
> She is a good-for-nothing huzzy [sic].

As always, everywhere, absent any effective rule of law, the rule of brute strength prevailed, posing a special threat to those less aggressive or poorly armed. Gangs of thugs roved through the countryside, relieving unwary Chinese prospectors of their gold. One of the most notorious was led by Joaquin Murieta, a young Sonoran whose gang would descend on a Chinese camp, round up the miners, and tie their pigtails together. Slowly, deliberately, he and his men would torture them until someone disclosed where they had hidden their gold dust, at which point Murieta would slit their throats with a bowie knife. In May 1853, the state of California finally offered a $1,000 reward for Murieta's capture, dead or alive, to which the Chinese community contributed an additional $3,000. Two months later—by which time, according to some accounts, the price on his head had grown to $5,000—Murieta was reportedly ambushed by a posse and shot to pieces.

While in this instance the government of the newly created state of California came to the aid of all miners, including the Chinese, a year earlier it had revealed a xenophobic strain when it passed two new taxes directed against foreign miners. As popular sentiment dictated that gold in California should be reserved for Americans, in 1852 legislators proposed excluding the Chinese migrants, as well as gold rushers from Mexico, Chile, and France, from further work in the fields. The Chinese work ethic that so impressed Mark Twain had engendered special resentment among American miners, who had also come to California to change their luck, but discovered that in gold mining, as in most pursuits, luck favors the industrious. The Chinese, more dissimilar from Americans in appearance and cultural norms than other immigrant gold rushers, were singled out for particularly harsh criticism, and the Committee on Mines and Mining of the California state legislature declared that "their presence here is a great moral and social evil—a disgusting scab upon the fair face of society— a putrefying sore upon the body politic—in short, a nuisance."

A week after the assembly's declaration, Governor John Bigler went a step further, urging the legislators to impose heavy taxes on the Chinese "coolies" and stop the "tide of Asiatic immigration." In response, in 1852, the California legislature enacted two new taxes, the first to discourage other Chinese from coming to the United States and the second to penalize those Chinese already working the gold mines.

The commutation tax required masters of all vessels arriving in California to post a $500 bond for each foreign passenger aboard. Because the bond could be commuted with payment of a fee ranging anywhere from five to fifty dollars, most ship captains simply added the fee to the price of passage. The resulting revenue, extracted from the sweat of Chinese laborers, went to the largest California hospitals; although the Chinese ended up paying over half of all commutation taxes, they were barred from the city hospital in San Francisco.

The foreign miner's tax stipulated that no Chinese could work his mining claim unless he paid a monthly license fee in gold dust, a fee arbitrarily increased by the state of California over the next few years. Designed ostensibly for the "protection of foreigners," the loose way the law was written, and the way it was administered and enforced, effected the opposite. Some collectors backdated the effective date of a miner's license, obligating the miner to pay money he didn't even owe. Others pocketed money from miners and gave them bogus receipts, leaving the miners vulnerable to legitimate collection efforts later on. One tax collector wrote in his diary, "I had no money to keep Christmas with, so sold the chinks nine dollars worth of bogus receipts." The worst of the collectors used physical coercion to compel Chinese miners to pay the tax more than once a month: they tied the Chinese to trees and whipped them; pursued them on horseback, lashing at them with rawhide as they fled. Corruption aside, no law restrained the methods collectors could employ. "I was sorry to have to stab the poor fellow," one collector wrote, "but the law makes it necessary to collect tax, and that's where I get my profit."

The Chinese, however, had come to America with some experience in thwarting corrupt agents of an indifferent government. To evade the tax collector, they devised various warning systems, such as arranging for runners to sprint from one village to the next, alerting the inhabitants to the collector's approach. These stratagems were so effective that the government found it necessary to employ the services of Maidu Indians to track down Chinese miners who had fled without paying their taxes.

While these first two tax laws unfairly burdened the Chinese miners, the most damaging government action was a legal decision barring them from testifying against whites in court. In 1853, a grand jury in Nevada County indicted George W. Hall and two others for the murder of a Chinese man called Ling Sing. After three Chinese and one Caucasian testified on behalf of the prosecution, Hall was found guilty and sentenced to be hanged. Hall's lawyer appealed the verdict on the ground that Chinese testimony was prohibited under the state's Criminal Proceeding Act, which stated that "no black or mulatto person, or Indian, shall be permitted to give evidence in favor of, or against, any white person." In *People* v. *Hall,* the state supreme court reversed Hall's conviction on the grounds that "the evident intention of the act was to throw around the citizen a protection for life and property, which could only be secured by raising him above the corrupting influences of degraded castes." Further, in a bizarre decision illustrative of the absurd workings of the California jurisprudential mind of the time, Chief Justice Hugh Murray asserted that the Chinese were, in reality, Indians, because Christopher Columbus had mistaken San Salvador as an island in the China Sea. "From that time," he wrote, "down to a very recent period, the American Indians and the Mongolian, or Asiatic, were regarded as the same type of the human species."

Then, to shore up what he must have expected would be read as weak legal reasoning, Murray declared that even if Asians were not the same as American Indians, the word "black" should be understood to include all nonwhite races. Noting that the Naturalization Act of 1790 prohibited the Chinese and other nonwhites from becoming U.S. citizens, Murray further justified his decision as necessary for social stability: if the Chinese were admitted as witnesses in court, he said, the state would "soon see them at the polls, in the jury box, upon the bench, and in our legislative halls." Where would it all end?

In many criminal acts, the complaining victims are the principal if not the only witnesses, so denying them the right to offer in court their account of what occurred makes prosecution impossible. Before *People* v. *Hall,* many whites had physically expelled Chinese miners from the most desirable locations. Once white miners understood that they could now terrorize Chinese camps without fear of legal consequences—that the law had in effect immunized them—they simply posted signs warning the Chinese to leave the premises immediately. In 1856, the people of Mariposa County gave the Chinese ten days' notice to vacate the area: "Any failing to comply shall be subjected to thirty-nine lashes, and moved by force of arms." In El

Dorado County, white miners torched Chinese tents and mining equipment and turned back stagecoaches filled with Chinese passengers. As one scholar of the period has written, the ruling "opened the way for almost every sort of discrimination against the Chinese. Assault, robbery, and murder, to say nothing of lesser crimes . . . so long as no white person was available to witness in their behalf." This was the era that coined the term "a Chinaman's chance"—meaning not much of a chance at all.

Legalized persecution turned the Chinese into gold rush scavengers. Rather than compete directly with whites, Chinese prospectors picked over abandoned claims. From now on, most of those who succeeded would do so through a combination of patient toil and a frugal lifestyle, though more than a few resorted to ingenuity. One smart and determined man named Ah Sam bought a log cabin from six miners for twenty-five dollars. Past experience had told him that he might make a killing by washing the gold dust from the dirt floor. He left with $3,000 worth of gold dust, a nice return on his investment.

Eventually, Chinese miners took millions of dollars' worth of placer gold out of America. Within a few decades, some had returned to China, where they invested their wealth in farmland and became powerful landlords. Other stayed in the United States, living on money that lasted for another generation or two; family oral histories of Chinese Americans recount tales of dilettante ancestors sustained by their own fathers' earnings during the gold rush. There were even a few who, despite the extensive racial discrimination against Chinese gold miners, legal and otherwise, managed to become mining capitalists—staking their claims, hiring their own workers, expanding their operations into vast enterprises. One of the wealthiest in this class was a man called Wong Kee, who employed as many as nine hundred men in his mining company.

Gold Mountain dreams came true for a few, but many more Chinese immigrants found only heartbreak, failure, and loneliness. One man worked as a prospector from his arrival in America till his death many years later, yet died with only enough gold to pay for his funeral. Newspapers contained reports of failed Chinese prospectors who, rather than return home in disgrace, ended their misery by committing suicide. Between the two extremes of wealth and wretchedness lay the vast majority of Chinese immigrants, who, recognizing the odds against them, pragmatically turned their sights on San Francisco, the site of their arrival. One by one, they made the decision to forgo their mining stakes, staking out instead a piece of the town to call their own.

According to the noted historian Hubert H. Bancroft, the first ship to sail from Canton to San Francisco was the *American Eagle,* which landed in February 1848—a month after the discovery of gold at Sutter's Mill, but well before the news had reached China. Two Chinese men and one Chinese woman disembarked. That April, the *San Francisco Star* reported that "two or three 'Celestials' " (as the Chinese were called) had found employment in the city.* The mere fact that this appeared in a newspaper suggests that these three may have been the very first Chinese to take up residence in San Francisco.

As more Chinese arrived (according to one estimate, 325 Chinese arrived in California in 1849, and then 450 in 1850, although more than 90 percent quickly moved to rural mining camps), those who remained in the city clustered in a region centered on Sacramento and Dupont Streets, which soon grew into ten blocks bounded by California, Jackson, Stockton, Kearney, and Pacific Streets. Known as "little China," "little Canton," or the "Chinese quarter," this neighborhood eventually evolved into what we now call Chinatown. Like the rest of San Francisco, the area gradually filled in, from isolated shacks to congested city blocks. Some Chinese hammered shanties together using local materials, while others used prefabricated structures carved out of tree branches brought over from Hong Kong. Inside their shanties, the Chinese created a rough semblance of

---

*The nickname grew out of Chinese claims of being part of a celestial kingdom.

home. They built brick stoves and chimneys like those used in their homeland—a brick bench, or tin box packed with earth, constructed near a window or on a balcony to permit smoke to escape. They called San Francisco *Dai Fou*, literally, "Big City."

Ethnic grocery stores were not far behind. By the early 1850s, as one white observer noted, they were filled with tea, ham, dried fish, and duck. Vendors hawked fruits and vegetables from reed baskets suspended from bamboo poles, and small shopkeepers spread game meat on sidewalk mats. The area reeked of fish as Chinese fishermen who worked along the bay sold their catches to miners. They dried their fish on the ground and later sorted them into sacks, boxes, and barrels. Some were salted and heaped on top of gravel rooftops to cure in the sun.

The San Francisco Chinese community continued to expand. By 1851, more than 2,716 new immigrants had arrived on the shores of San Francisco, and by 1852 the number had jumped to more than twenty thousand, though for many of them San Francisco would be only their port of entry, as they wandered out into the gold fields. In addition, around this time, an increasing number of Chinese miners were also returning to San Francisco. Plenty of money could be made from serving their dietary preferences, and not surprisingly, a thriving business catering to various Chinese needs soon developed.

In most cultures, eating is a social as well as a nutritional experience. But food occupies an even more important place in Chinese culture, which for millennia has revered its cuisine as not just a biological necessity but an exalted art form. So it should come as no surprise that Chinese restaurants soon followed the Chinese miners. As early as December 10, 1849, the *San Francisco Daily Alta California* newspaper reported a gathering of some three hundred Chinese at the "Canton" restaurant on Jackson Street. Here, lonely immigrants had an opportunity to forget, if only for an evening, that they were thousands of miles from their families back home.

But the Chinese were not the only San Franciscans enjoying a home-cooked Chinese meal. Soon people of all nationalities were flocking to Chinatown to eat. Beckoning to sightseers with triangular flags of yellow silk, some of the first Chinese "restaurants" were little more than cheap dining cellars, where customers ate as much as they wanted for a dollar, spitting bones and gristle onto the floor. But soon more ambitious, upscale establishments appeared, lit by lanterns hanging from green and red balconies. Sitting in rooms filled with regal décor—wood screens imported from China, gas lamp chandeliers, marble and carved mahogany furniture—customers could enjoy rare delicacies such as bird's nest soup and shark's fin.

Chinese restaurants became so beloved by San Franciscans of all races that in short order they became a featured selling point to encourage Americans to visit the city. During this era, travel guides urged people to eat a Chinese meal in San Francisco, some referring to the food as Chinese "chow chows." In his 1851 memoir *Golden Dreams and Waking Realities,* miner William Shaw announced, "The best eating houses in San Francisco are kept by Celestials and conducted Chinese fashion. The dishes are mostly curries, hashes and fricasee served up in small dishes and as they are exceedingly palatable, I was not curious enough to enquire as to the ingredients."

Not all the dishes served, however, were traditional Chinese fare. According to gold rush folklore, a group of drunken white miners invaded a San Francisco restaurant late one evening, demanding service. On the verge of closing for the night, the Chinese proprietor prudently decided to feed them and avoid trouble. His cook stir-fried the table scraps in his larder—a melange of fried vegetables, meat, and gravy—and called it chop suey. The miners raved about this new Chinese delicacy, and soon people all over San Francisco were clamoring for it.

After their success in the food industry, the Chinese soon began to seek other ways to earn money. Many recognized that the path to riches lay, ironically, in domestic service. In those days before care-free fabrics, washing and ironing was difficult as well as tedious work, something most white men considered beneath their dignity. It was considered women's work, but few women could be found to help them. Many Californians during the gold rush era, both Chinese and white, shipped their laundry to Hong Kong to be cleaned, but the prices were exorbitant—twelve dollars for a dozen shirts—and the process took four months. Still, sending dirty linen to be washed in Asia was cheaper and faster than mailing it back east. Laundrymen in Honolulu soon captured the business by washing shirts for only eight dollars a dozen. Finally, Chinese men in San Francisco saw a market need and moved to meet it. The first Chinese laundryman in the city was Wah Lee, who washed shirts for five dollars a dozen and advertised his services in 1851 by hanging the sign WASH'NG AND IRON'NG.

The Chinese also opened curio stores, enticing white miners to trade gold dust for a variety of collectibles: porcelain vases, carved ivory and jade art, Oriental chess pieces, inkbrush scroll paintings, fans, shawls, and teapots. The modest shops advertised themselves with gaudy signboards and red ribbons, but in the grander establishments merchants installed glass windows in their storefronts and kept lavish shrines to bring them good luck: luxurious, gilded altars decorated with silk scrolls and ritual artifacts of worship.

By 1853, the Chinese had occupied most of Dupont Street, one of the best retail areas in San Francisco. Although the structures in that neighborhood were hardly exceptional (the *San Francisco Daily Alta California* noted they were "mere shells and tinder boxes, which could be fired by a single spark"), the location was excellent. As a group, the Chinese were mostly tenants, not homeowners, renting from white landlords who preferred the Chinese because of their willingness to pay more than Caucasians. For instance, one house that rented to a white man for $200 a month (an exorbitantly high figure at that time) went to a Chinese for $500 a month. On this street and others, a sophisticated Chinese business community soon appeared. By 1856, a Chinese directory called the *Oriental* listed thirty-three merchandise stores, fifteen apothecaries, five herbalists, five restaurants, five barbers, five butchers, three boarding homes, three wood yards, three tailors, two silversmiths, two bakers, one carver, one engraver, one interpreter, and one broker for U.S. merchants.

Not all of the Chinese settlers could read or write their own language, so this new community soon had need of professional writers. Some of the better-educated Cantonese picked up languages quickly, a few becoming fluent not only in English but also in Spanish. Most hired out as scribes, so illiterate Chinese could dictate letters to relatives back home. A few with journalistic skills published small ethnic newspapers in San Francisco and across the state. In 1854, the *Gold Hills News* became quite possibly the first Chinese newspaper published in the United States. Two years later, the *Chinese News* appeared in the northern California town of Sacramento, causing a local historian to later comment, "It is a little singular that the only paper ever printed in a foreign language in our city should have been a Chinese publication, particularly when we remember the considerable German and French elements in our population." If this historian had been aware of the Chinese respect for education, he might have been less surprised.

The Chinese émigrés also hungered for art and entertainment. In 1852, the first Chinese theater was constructed in San Francisco from a prefabricated kit. The building, with a pagoda as its edifice, housed an auditorium for a thousand people and a stage of embroidered panels and gilt walls, gleaming with pictures of men, animals, and sea monsters. Visiting troupes from Guangdong province performed Cantonese operas there, performances that could last for weeks, attended by both Chinese and curious whites. The actors sometimes narrated in minute detail the epic sagas of an entire dynasty, providing audiences with nightly entertainment; according to one observer, "two or three months are generally consumed before all the acts of a play are finished." At these performances, Chinese immigrants far from home could lose themselves in heroic stories of the past, forgetting for a short while their demeaning roles in everyday life and how far they had had to go to achieve their dreams.

White San Franciscans, watching the Chinese community expand and thrive, felt emotions ranging from awe and fascination to fear and hatred. Although details remain sketchy, the earliest Chinese in San Francisco seem to have received a warm welcome when they arrived—a mix of genuine excitement and curiosity. In 1850, when the Chinese colony numbered only a few hundred, the city fathers invited their participation in rites observing the death of President Zachary Taylor, assigning them a prominent place in the memorial procession. That year, Mayor John Geary and other city officials also honored the Chinese with a special ceremony, and when California became the thirty-first state in the union, the Chinese took part in the lavish celebrations. In May 1851, the *San Francisco Daily Alta California* went so far as to predict that the "China Boys will yet vote at the same polls, study at the same schools and bow at the same Altar as our own countrymen."

But as the Chinese population grew, so did consternation among certain whites. In April 1852, Governor John Bigler called for an exclusionary law to bar future Chinese immigration. Although ignored by the federal government, his request may have been the first expression by a public official of an emerging anti-Chinese sentiment. Infuriated or alarmed, or both, by Bigler's proposal, several Chinese in San Francisco published a long reply, defending their character and their ability to assimilate. "Many have already adopted your religion as their own, and will be good citizens," they wrote. "There are very good Chinamen now in the country, and a better class will, if allowed, come hereafter—men of learning and of wealth, bringing their families with them."

Such assimilation, however, was what some whites feared most. In 1853, the *San Francisco Daily Alta California* changed editors, and its tone swiveled from pro-Chinese to a virulently racist, pro-Bigler position. The Chinese, asserted a series of editorials, were "morally a far worse class to have among us than the negro. They are idolatrous in their religion—in their disposition cunning and deceited, and in their habits libidinous and offensive. They have certain redeeming features of craft, industry and economy, and like other men in the fallen estate, 'they have wrought out many inventions.' But they are not of that kin that Americans can ever associate or sympathize with. They are not of our people and never will be, though they remain here forever . . . They do not mix with our people, and it is undesirable that they should, for nothing but degradation can result to us from the contact . . . It is of no advantage to us to have them here. They can never become like us."

These sentiments echoed faintly in Washington. During this time, a few federal lawmakers began to express concern that the Chinese would not only remain in the United States, but would eventually demand their rights as Americans. Religious differences were cited as justification for exclusion. In 1855, for instance, William Russell Smith, a congressman from Alabama, raised the issue of excluding the Chinese from citizenship. "How long, sir, will it be before a million of Pagans, with their disgusting idolatries, will claim the privilege of voting for American Christians, or against American Christians?" he asked. "How long before a Pagan shall present his credentials in this Hall, with power to mingle in the councils of this Government?" Smith insisted that legislation eradicate such a possibility: "The American Party demands a law to prevent it."

In the 1850s, however, with the country working its way toward civil war, these discussions in Congress had little immediate impact on Chinese American daily life in California. For many Chinese, the right to suffrage or election to public office were the last things on their minds: their ambition lay not in becoming part of the governing class, but in earning a living. And the reality of the time was that the antagonism toward the Chinese on the West Coast was not broadly reflected in the corridors of federal power. Many in Washington saw the Chinese as a valuable source of manpower. Soon, when war came and coincided with grand plans to construct a transcontinental railroad, American capitalists eyed the industrious Chinese as labor for one of the most ambitious engineering feats in history.

CHAPTER FIVE

Building the Transcontinental
Railroad

From sea to shining sea. In the decade of the 1840s, Americans were consumed by this vision, articulated in the doctrine of Manifest Destiny, which proclaimed it the right and duty of the United States to expand its democratic way of life across the entire continent, from the Atlantic to the Pacific, from the Rio Grande in the south to the 54th parallel in the north. The country was feeling confident (during this decade, it acquired the territories of Texas, California, and Oregon), its population was increasing, and many wanted to push west, especially to California, made famous by gold and Richard Henry Dana's recounting of his adventures there, in *Two Years Before the Mast*.

Making the vision real, however, was dangerous and frustrating. The territory between the coasts was unsettled and there was no reliable transport or route. Crossing the continent meant braving death by disease, brigands, Native Americans, starvation, thirst, heat, or freezing. This was true especially for those headed straight to the gold hills of California, but the gold rushers weren't the only ones frustrated by the lack of a safe passage between the settled East and the new state of California in the sparsely populated West. Californians themselves were impatient at waiting months to receive mail and provisions. Washington, too, recognized the economic as well as political

53

benefits of linking the country's two coasts. In the West lay rich farmland waiting for settlement, gold and silver to be mined and taxed.
What was needed was a transcontinental railroad to move more people west and natural resources safely and profitably to major markets
back east.

There were only two overland routes west—over the Rockies or
along the southern route through Apache and Comanche territory—
both hazardous. It took longer, but was almost always safer, to get to
California from anywhere east of the Missouri by sea. This meant
heading east to the Atlantic Ocean or south to the Gulf of Mexico,
boarding a ship that would sail almost to the southern tip of South
America, passing through the Strait of Magellan, and heading back
north to California. The sea voyage could be shortened considerably
by disembarking on the eastern coast of Central America, traveling by
wagon across the isthmus, and then hitching a ride on the first steamer
headed north.*

The need for a transcontinental railroad was so strongly argued
that Congress, with the support of President Lincoln, passed legislation to finance the railroad with government bonds, even though the
country was already at war. Two companies divided the task of actual
construction. In 1862, the Central Pacific Railroad Corporation,
headed by the "Big Four"—Leland Stanford, Collis P. Huntington,
Charles Crocker, and Mark Hopkins—was awarded the contract to
lay tracks eastward from Sacramento, while its rival, the Union
Pacific, was awarded the path westward from Omaha, Nebraska,
which was already connected to the East through existing rail lines.
The goal was to meet in the middle, connecting the nation with a continuous stretch of railroad tracks from the Atlantic to the Pacific. The
Union Pacific's job—laying track over plains—was much easier, while
the Central Pacific had to go over steep mountains. The Central
Pacific engineers promised that the formidable physical obstacles

---

*Eventually, U.S. engineers would build the Panama Canal in the early twentieth
century.

could be overcome, and to a great extent, it was Chinese labor, and even, here and there, Chinese ingenuity, that helped make the transcontinental railroad a reality.

The first and largest challenge was figuring out how to cut a path through California's and Nevada's rugged Sierra Nevada, which stood as a final barrier to the West. The workers of the Central Pacific had the dangerous task of ramming tunnels through these mountains, and then laying tracks across the parched Nevada and Utah deserts. Some engineers, watching the project from afar, said this was impossible. In a major recruitment drive for five thousand workers, the Central Pacific sent advertisements to every post office in the state of California, offering high wages to any white man willing to work. But the appeal secured only eight hundred. Why toil for wages when an instant fortune was possible in the mines? Many men who did sign on were, in the words of company superintendent James Strobridge, "unsteady men, unreliable. Some of them would stay a few days, and some would not go to work at all. Some would stay until payday, get a little money, get drunk, and clear out." The company thought of asking the War Department for five thousand Confederate prisoners to put to work, but Lee's surrender at the Appomattox Court House ended the war and this plan.

Fortunately for the Central Pacific, Chinese immigrants provided a vast pool of cheap, plentiful, and easily exploitable labor. By 1865, the number of Chinese in California reached close to fifty thousand, at least 90 percent of them young men. In the spring of that year, when white laborers demanded higher pay and threatened to strike, Charles Crocker, the Central Pacific's chief contractor, ordered Superintendent Strobridge to recruit Chinese workers. The tactic worked, and the white workers agreed to return, as long as no Chinese were hired, but by then the Central Pacific had the upper hand and hired fifty Chinese anyway—former miners, laundrymen, domestic servants, and market gardeners—to do the hard labor of preparing the route and laying track. Many claimed the railroad did this as a reminder to the white workers that others were ready to replace them. Needless to say, this did not contribute to harmony between the whites and the Chinese.

Of course prejudice against the Chinese railroad workers did not start with the white laborers. Initially, Superintendent Strobridge was unhappy with their being hired. "I will not boss Chinese!" he roared, suggesting that the Chinese were too delicate for the job. (The Chinese averaged four feet ten inches in height and weighed 120 pounds.) Crocker, however, pointed out that a race of people who had built the Great Wall of China could build a railroad. Grudgingly, Strobridge put the Chinese to work, giving them light jobs, like filling dump carts.

To the surprise of many—but apparently not the Chinese themselves—the first fifty hired excelled at their work, becoming such disciplined, fast learners that the railroad soon gave them other responsibilities, such as rock cuts. In time, the Central Pacific hired another fifty Chinese, and then another fifty, until eventually the company employed thousands of Chinese laborers—the overwhelming majority of the railroad workforce. E. B. Crocker, brother of Charles, wrote to Senator Cornelius Cole (R-Calif.) that the Chinese were nearly equal to white men in the amount of work they could do and far more reliable. Leland Stanford, the railroad's president, and later the founder of Stanford University, praised the Chinese as "quiet, peaceable, patient, industrious and economical." (Stanford's position on the Chinese was governed by expedience. In 1862, to please the racist sentiments of the state, he called the Chinese in California the "dregs" of Asia, a "degraded" people. A few years later, he was praising the Chinese to President Andrew Johnson and others in order to justify the Central Pacific's mass hiring of Chinese. Later still—notably in 1884, when he ran for the U.S. Senate—he would ally himself with those who favored a ban on Chinese immigration.)

Delighted by the productivity of the Chinese, railroad executives became fervent advocates of Chinese immigration to California. "I like the idea of your getting over more Chinamen," Collis Huntington, one of the "Big Four" executives at the Central Pacific, wrote to

Charlie Crocker in 1867. "It would be all the better for us and the State if there should a half million come over in 1868."

The Central Pacific printed handbills and dispatched recruiters to China, especially the Guangdong province, to find new workers. It negotiated with a steamship company to lower their rates for travel. And, fortuitously for the Central Pacific, Sino-American diplomacy would create more favorable conditions for Chinese immigration to the United States. In 1868, China and the U.S. government signed the Burlingame Treaty. In exchange for "most favored nation" status in trade, China agreed to recognize the "inherent and inalienable right of man to change his home and allegiance and also the mutual advantage of free migration and emigration of their citizens and subjects respectively from one country to the other for purposes of curiosity or trade or as permanent residents."

The new Chinese recruits docked at San Francisco and were immediately transported by riverboat to Sacramento, and then by the Central Pacific's own train to the end of the laid tracks, which was a moving construction site. There they were organized into teams of about a dozen or so, with each team assigned its own cook and headman, who communicated with the Central Pacific foreman. The Chinese paid for their own food and cooked it themselves—they were even able to procure special ingredients like cuttlefish, bamboo shoots, and abalone. At night they slept in tents provided by the railroad, or in dugouts in the earth. At the peak of construction, Central Pacific would employ more than ten thousand Chinese men.

The large number of Chinese made white workers uncomfortable. As Lee Chew, a railroad laborer, later recalled in a spasm of national pride, the Chinese were "persecuted not for their vices but for their virtues. No one would hire an Irishman, German, Englishman or Italian when he could get a Chinese, because our countrymen are so much more honest, industrious, steady, sober and painstaking." Crocker explicitly acknowledged this work ethic. After recruiting some Cornish miners from Virginia City, Nevada, to excavate one end of a tunnel and the Chinese the other, he commented, "The Chinese, without fail, always outmeasured the Cornish miners. That is to say, they would cut more rock in a week than the Cornish miners did. And here it was hard work, steady pounding on the rock, bone-labor." The Cornish eventually walked off the job, vowing that "they would not work with Chinamen anyhow," and soon, Crocker recalled, "the Chinamen had possession of the whole work."

White laborers began to feel that Chinese diligence forced everyone to work harder for less reward. Crocker recalled that one white laborer near Auburn was questioned by a gentleman about his wages. "I think we were paying $35 a month and board to white laborers, and $30 a month to Chinamen and they boarded themselves," Crocker said. "The gentleman remarked, 'That is pretty good wages.' 'Yes,' says he, 'but begad if it wasn't for them damned nagurs we would get $50 and not do half the work.' "

Some white laborers on the Central Pacific whispered among themselves about driving the Chinese off the job, but when Charles Crocker got wind of this, he threatened to replace all the whites with Chinese. Eventually the white workers gave up, placated perhaps by being told that they alone could be promoted to the position of foreman. The more Chinese workers, the fewer whites in the labor force and the less competition for foreman positions among the whites. And foremen were paid several times the wages of a Chinese laborer.

In the process of laying the track across northern California, Nevada, and Utah, hundreds of men—Chinese, Irish, German, and others—cleared a path through some of the world's largest trees, some with stumps so deeply rooted that ten barrels of gunpowder were often needed to unearth them. It was dangerous work—work that loosened boulders, started landslides, and filled the air with flying debris. Even more dangerous was the work that began upon reaching the Sierra Nevada.

Ideally, the roadbed through the mountains would be tunneled through by heavy machinery. This machinery was unavailable, however, because it was expensive and difficult to transport (entire bridges would have had to be rebuilt for such machinery to reach the current site). Thus the Chinese were forced to chisel tunnels through the granite using only handheld drills, explosives, and shovels. In some places they encountered a form of porphyritic rock so hard it was impervious to frontal attack, even with gunpowder. Work proceeded, on average, seven inches a day, at a cost of as much as a million dollars for one mile of tunnel.

In the summer of 1866, to move farther faster, the railroad kept several shifts of men going day and night. Shoulder to shoulder, hour after hour, the Chinese railroad workers chipped away at the rock, breathing granite dust, sweating and panting by the dim flickering glow of candlelight, until even the strongest of them fainted from exhaustion.

Finally, to speed up the process, the Central Pacific brought in nitroglycerin. Only the Chinese—a people experienced with fireworks—were willing to handle this unpredictable explosive, pouring it into the tunnel through holes drilled in the granite. Countless workers perished in accidental blasts, but the Central Pacific did not keep track of the numbers.

Still the workers struggled on. One terrifying challenge lay at Cape Horn, the nickname for a three-mile stretch of gorge above the American River three miles east of Colfax, California, and fifty-seven miles east of Sacramento. Through much of the way, a flat roadbed had to be carved along a steep cliff, and a Chinese headman suggested to Strobridge that they employ an ancient method used to create fortresses along the Yangtze River gorges: they could dangle supplies down to the work site in reed baskets, attached to ropes secured over the tops of mountains.

Reeds were shipped out immediately from San Francisco to Cape Horn. At night the Chinese workers wove them into wicker baskets and fastened them to sturdy ropes. When everything was ready, workers were lowered in the baskets to drill holes and tamp in dynamite, literally sculpting the rail bed out of the face of sheer rock. The lucky ones were hauled up in time to escape the explosions; others, peppered with shards of granite and shale, fell to their deaths in the valley below.

Disease swept through the ranks of the exhausted railroad workers, but the Chinese fared better than whites. Caucasian laborers, subsisting largely on salt beef, potatoes, bread, coffee, and rancid butter, lacked vegetables in their diet, while the Chinese employed their own cooks and ate better-balanced meals. White workers succumbed to dysentery after sharing communal dippers from greasy pails, but the Chinese drank fresh boiled tea, which they kept in whiskey barrels or powder kegs suspended from each end of a bamboo pole. They also avoided alcohol and, "not having acquired the taste of whiskey," as one contemporary observed, "they have fewer fights and no blue Mondays." Most important, they kept themselves clean, which helped prevent the spread of germs. The white men had "a sort of hydrophobia," one writer observed, whereas the Chinese bathed every night before dinner, in powder kegs filled with heated water.

In the Sierras, the railroad workers endured two of the worst winters in American history. In 1865, they faced thirty-foot drifts and spent weeks just shoveling snow. The following year brought the "Homeric winter" of 1866–67, one of the most brutal ever recorded, which dropped forty feet of snow on the crews and whipped up drifts more than eighty feet high. Power snowplows, driven forward by twelve locomotives linked together, could scarcely budge the densest of these drifts. Sheds built to protect the uncompleted tracks collapsed under the weight of the snow, which snapped even the best timber. On the harshest days, travel was almost impossible; as horses broke the icy crust, sharp edges slashed their legs to the bone. They received mail from a Norwegian postal worker on cross-country skis.

Making the best of the situation, the Chinese carved a working city under the snow. Operating beneath the crust by lantern light, they trudged through a labyrinth of snow tunnels, with snow chimneys and snow stairs leading up to the surface. Meanwhile, they continued to shape the rail bed out of rock, using materials lowered down to them through airshafts in the snow.

The cost in human life was enormous. Snow slides and avalanches swept away entire teams of Chinese workers. On Christmas Day 1866, the *Dutch Flat Enquirer* announced that "a gang of Chinamen employed by the railroad . . . were covered up by a snow slide and four or five died before they could be exhumed. Then snow fell to such a depth that one whole camp of Chinamen was covered up during the night and parties were digging them out when our informant left." When the snow melted in the spring, the company found corpses still standing erect, their frozen hands gripping picks and shovels.

Winter was only one obstacle. Other conditions also affected the workers. Landslides rolled tons of soil across the completed track, blocking its access and often smothering workers. Melting snow mired wagons, carts, and stagecoaches in a sea of mud. Once through the mountains, the crews faced terrible extremes of weather in the Nevada and Utah deserts. There the temperature could plummet to 50 degrees below zero—freezing the ground so hard it required blasting, as if it were bedrock—or soar above 120, causing heat stroke and dehydration.

The Chinese labored from sunrise to sunset six days a week, in twelve-hour shifts. Only on Sundays did they have time to rest, mend their clothes, talk, smoke, and, of course, gamble.* The tedium of their lives was aggravated by the systematized abuse and contempt heaped on them by the railroad executives. The Chinese worked longer and harder than whites, but received less pay: because the Chinese had to pay for their own board, their wages were two-thirds those of white workers and a fourth those of the white foremen. (Even the allocation for feed for horses—fifty dollars a month for each—was twenty dollars more than the average Chinese worker

---

*Gambling was as addictive for Chinese railroad workers as whiskey among their white counterparts. Chinese gamblers left their mark on Nevada, where casinos credit the nineteenth-century Chinese railroad workers with introducing the game of keno, based on the Chinese lottery game of *pak kop piu.*

earned.) Worst of all, they endured whippings from their overseers, who treated them like slaves.

Finally, the Chinese rebelled. In June 1867, as the Central Pacific tottered on the brink of bankruptcy (Leland Stanford later described a two-week period when there was not a dollar of cash in the treasury), some two thousand Chinese in the Sierras walked off the job. As was their way in a strange land, they conducted the strike politely, appointing headmen to present James Strobridge a list of demands that included more pay and fewer hours in the tunnels. They also circulated among themselves a placard written in Chinese, explaining their rights. In retrospect, it is surprising that they managed to organize a strike at all, for there are also reports of frequent feuds erupting between groups of Chinese workers, fought with spades, crowbars, and spikes. But organize they did.

The Central Pacific reacted swiftly and ruthlessly. An enraged Charles Crocker contacted employment agencies in an attempt to recruit ten thousand recently freed American blacks to replace the Chinese. He stopped payments to the Chinese and cut off the food supply, effectively starving them back to work. Because most of them could not speak English, could not find work elsewhere, and lacked transportation back to California, the strike lasted only a week. However, it did achieve a small victory, securing the Chinese a raise of two dollars a month. More important, by staging the largest Chinese strike of the nineteenth century, they demonstrated to their current and future employers that while they were willing and easily managed workers, if pushed hard enough they were able to organize to protect themselves, even in the face of daunting odds.

Later, the railroad management expressed admiration at the orderliness of the strike. "If there had been that number of whites in a strike, there would have been murder and drunkenness and disorder," Crocker marveled. "But with the Chinese it was just like Sunday. These men stayed in their camps. They would come out and walk around, but not a word was said; nothing was done. No violence was perpetuated along the whole line."

The Chinese were certainly capable, however, of violence. As the railroad neared completion, the Chinese encountered the Irish workers of the Union Pacific for the first time. When the two companies came within a hundred feet of each other, the Union Pacific Irish taunted the Chinese with catcalls and threw clods of dirt. When the Chinese ignored them, the Irish swung their picks at them, and to the astonishment of the whites, the Chinese fought back. The level of antagonism continued to rise. Several Chinese were wounded by blasting powder the whites had secretly planted near their side. Several days later, a mysterious explosion killed several Irish workers. The presumption was that the Chinese had retaliated in kind. At that point, the behavior of white workers toward the Chinese immediately improved.

If relations were often tense between the Chinese and the Irish, there were also moments of camaraderie. In April 1869, the Central Pacific and Union Pacific competed to see who could throw down track the fastest. The competition arose after Charlie Crocker bragged that the Chinese could construct ten miles of track a day. (In some regions, the Union Pacific had averaged only one mile a week.) So confident was Crocker in his employees that he was willing to wager $10,000 against Thomas Durant, the vice president of Union Pacific. On the day of the contest, the Central Pacific had eight Irish workers unload materials while the Chinese spiked, gauged, and bolted the track, laying it down as fast as a man could walk. They broke the Union Pacific record by completing more than ten miles of track within twelve hours and forty-five minutes.

On May 10, 1869, when the railways from the east and west were finally joined at Promontory Point, Utah, the Central Pacific had built 690 miles of track and the Union Pacific 1,086 miles. The two coasts were now welded together. Before the transcontinental railroad, trekking across the country took four to six months. On the railroad, it would take six days. This accomplishment created fortunes for the moguls of the Gilded Age, but it also exacted a monumental sacrifice in blood and human life. On average, three laborers perished for every two miles of track laid, and eventually more than one thousand Chinese railroad workers died, with twenty thousand pounds of their bones shipped to China.* Without Chinese labor and know-how, the railroad would not have been completed. Nonetheless, the Central Pacific Railroad cheated the Chinese railway workers of everything they could. They tried to write the Chinese out of history altogether. The Chinese workers were not only excluded from the ceremonies, but from the famous photograph of white American laborers celebrating as the last spike, the golden spike, was driven into the ground. Of more immediate concern, the Central Pacific immediately laid off most of the Chinese workers, refusing to give them even their promised return passage to California. The company retained only a few hundred of them for maintenance work, some of whom spent their remaining days in isolated small towns along the way, a few living in converted boxcars.

The rest of the Chinese former railway workers were now homeless as well as jobless, in a harsh and hostile environment. Left to fend for themselves, some straggled by foot through the hinterlands of America, looking for work that would allow them to survive, a journey that would disperse them throughout the nation.

---

*Years later, some of the Chinese railroad workers would journey back to the Sierra Nevada to search for the remains of their colleagues. On these expeditions, known as *jup seen you* ("retrieving deceased friends"), they would hunt for old grave sites, usually a heap of stones near the tracks marked by a wooden stake. Digging underneath the stones, they would find a skeleton next to a wax-sealed bottle, holding a strip of cloth inscribed with the worker's name, birth date, and district of origin.

CHAPTER SIX

Life on the Western Frontier

By 1869, twenty years after the first Chinese workers stepped tentatively onto the piers at San Francisco harbor, tens of thousands of Chinese men were now living in America. Many were no longer young. Some had worked in the United States for more than a decade, some for close to two decades, and for too many of them, these years had been long, hard, and lonely, with scant respite and meager reward. At an age when most men relied on the companionship of wives and the joys of children to temper the harshness of life, these men were left to soldier on alone in a foreign land. Perhaps most tragic, unable to afford the fare back to China on any sort of regular basis, or just too embarrassed to return as failures, some learned only from letters how the sons and daughters they had sired before their departure for the United States had come of age. Had it been worth it?

Surely those who spent their lives drifting from job to job, never quite getting ahead, would answer no. Perhaps those who fared worst were the ones who continued to search for gold. A couple of decades after the discovery of gold, opportunity shifted from the lone prospector with a sieve, a pan, and a burro, to large corporations able to afford expensive machinery and battalions of cheap labor to extract gold deposits from hard rock quartz. If a Chinese stayed in mining, he most likely ended up a low-paid employee of a large organization in a wage system stratified by race (whites were paid seven dollars a day, the Chinese two dollars or less.) Working not only in quartz but in coal and quicksilver mines, some inhaled toxic mercury fumes from the quicksilver and grew deathly ill, becoming in due course "shaking, toothless wrecks." For such men, their early, youthful visions of an American El Dorado had vanished forever. The only vision that remained was the angel of death coming to them in an alien world.

While it is true that thousands of Chinese workers who came to America were simply used up and spit out, never catching hold of their piece of the American dream, this experience is neither the only one nor is it even the most typical. A lucky few found exactly what they had sought on Gold Mountain—some as prospectors but many more as industrious entrepreneurs—and, as planned, returned to Guangdong province, never to return to America. For this group, getting to America served as a means to an end. Their story, as least in terms of the Chinese in America, ended on a happy note. With their new affluence, some bought land in China, built country estates, and fulfilled their dreams of spending the rest of their lives as wealthy men of leisure. They had stories to tell their grandchildren of San Francisco and the California gold mines and perhaps of other parts of the American West Coast as well—a snapshot of Gold Mountain at one moment in time, destined to fade over the years.

A second group of workers did well enough in America to allow brief periodic returns to China, reconnecting with their families but always returning to America. For even at the reduced wages of a Chinese laborer in America of the mid-nineteenth century, the money they made changed the lives of their families back in China. And from this flowed a less well-known consequence of Chinese emigration to America.

At this time in the nineteenth century, one week's pay in America was equivalent to several months of wages in China. Thus, from the meager earnings of many Chinese in America emerged a new class of aristocrats in Guangdong province. Thanks to favorable exchange rates, as well as the willingness of their relatives in America to work long, hard hours, many "Gold Mountain families," as they had now become known, enjoyed a level of prosperity previous generations could only dream of. With those hard-earned foreign wages, they built family homes and summer vacation homes, hired tutors for their children and sent these children to universities. And soon a new mindset emerged and spread—with such rich relatives in America, why work at all?

In Toishan county, for example, where the remittances flowed the heaviest, the once austere Chinese work ethic all but disappeared within a couple of decades. One by one, formerly thrifty Gold Mountain wives who once maintained taut households, or who had painstakingly fashioned handicrafts to sell at the local markets, now delegated their manual tasks to servants. The sons, brothers, and nephews of Gold Mountain men, many of whom had once been industrious farmers, hired laborers to do the work for them, or even neglected their fields and irrigation systems entirely to import food from other regions. It was only a matter of time before Toishan would depend so heavily on foreign rice purchased by foreign remittances that a local wag noted, "when the ships occasionally cannot [sail,] fires in kitchens immediately stop burning." Within a few decades, Toishan, a region once renowned as one of the most entrepreneurial in China and which had supported itself in the mid-1850s, was fast becoming a welfare state, with family after family living on the back-breaking labor of a Chinese husband working round the clock half a world away.

Even more debilitating than the gradual loss of skills and drive was the acquisition of expensive tastes. For a growing number of Gold Mountain families, the pursuit of pleasure became an obsession. Women acquired rare artwork and jewelry, while men gambled away fortunes, smoked opium, and bought new concubines. A Chinese historian complained that the Toishan region, once "simple, reverential, and thrifty" because of its poor soil, changed drastically after so many of its young men went overseas to earn money: "In a flash, clothing and food tend toward Chinese American, the business of marriage becomes especially contentious, wasteful, and excessively extravagant."

While some families had the foresight to save, others spent recklessly. Because the flow of money from overseas seemed endless, there was no incentive to question these new lifestyles. Fortunately, not all this money was squandered on private indulgences. Many Gold Mountain families donated generous sums to create new schools, colleges, libraries, and other public works. By the late nineteenth century, a Toishan gazetteer commented that "various charities are everywhere," observing that vast sums of overseas money had funded local hospitals, lecture halls, orphanages, and land for the poor. But it also noted, "The customs of the people are gradually becoming wasteful. Capping ceremonies [a coming-of-age ritual in which a father honored his son on his twentieth birthday] and wedding banquets required the expenditure of several hundred gold pieces. Fields lie barren and infertile and cannot be restored to their original state."

And there was another problem, one of even greater concern. Just when the traditional Toishan personal and familial values, derived from Confucianism, were degenerating, social unrest increased. The mid-nineteenth century was a time of spontaneous uprisings congealing into outright rebellions in this part of China. One of those, the Red Turban rebellion, an outgrowth of the Triads' secret criminal network, plotted the overthrow of the Manchu government. For years, Triad bandits had been terrorizing rural villages, pressuring peasants to join their movement, extorting protection money from towns. Then in 1853, the local Triads, calling themselves the Red Turbans, ran amok in Guangdong, forcing villagers to arm and defend themselves. The Turbans were suppressed by the government two years later, with a bloody reprisal that beheaded some seventy-five thousand suspected participants.

Another bitter conflict was the Punti-Hakka feud, the roots of which predated even the founding of the Qing dynasty in 1644. In the thirteenth century, the Cantonese-speaking Punti had settled into richer, more fertile farms in the lowlands of Guangdong, while the Hakka—known as the "guest people" because they arrived later— were forced to move to poorer regions in the hills. Thus began a furious ethnic rivalry, in which the Puntis and the Hakkas fought not only over land, but also for government positions through the imperial examination system. The Hakkas performed so well on the tests that the Qing imposed strict quotas against them, which only increased their resentment. In the 1850s, in the aftermath of the Red Turban uprising, the hatred between the Puntis and Hakkas erupted into new violence. Villages that had armed themselves against the Red Turbans now had the weaponry to fight each other; between 1854 and 1867, clashes killed two hundred thousand people.

The money sent home from America apparently exacerbated the situation. Through most of the twenty years of mass Chinese emigration to America, the province of Guangdong roiled with banditry, as the unemployed came to believe China was so corrupt that no one could succeed by playing it straight. Looting, kidnappings, and armed robberies increased dramatically. The Gold Mountain families, now firmly entrenched as the local gentry, became a highly visible and tempting target, leading to an even greater demand for overseas money—to hire bodyguards, to purchase arms, to build fortresses and walls against invaders. Ironically, the peace and security that the Chinese émigrés sought to purchase for their families with hard labor in America became more elusive than ever.

This may explain why one group of Chinese emigrants to the United States returned to China with a very different purpose in mind. Some arrived home to encourage their sons, nephews, or brothers to join them in America, to assist in the running of successful businesses they had established there. For them, America, with all its racism and discrimination, remained a land of opportunity, if only in relative terms. Rather than looking back longingly at what they had left behind, they looked forward to a time when they might be able to bring all their family members to a new life in America. Yes, the

United States had its faults, and it was certainly not the welcoming haven the Chinese once thought it would be. But these men had crossed a line: with each visit to China, they became a little less wedded to their Chinese past and a little more to their American present. Their families recognized it even before they did. Anecdotes relate how baffled villagers watched the returning relatives drink coffee, wear American hats, or accidentally intermingle English with Chinese in casual conversation.

Only years later, looking back on old memories, did the workers themselves recognize how much they had changed. Huie Kin, who established a Protestant mission in New York, remembered that as a boy in Guangdong province he had heard that Caucasians were "red-haired, green-eyed foreign devils with . . . hairy faces," people who were "wild and fierce and wicked." Later, as an American of Chinese descent, he was amused at how wholeheartedly he had once believed these myths.

Even those Chinese who had not started out with such wild notions remembered their surprise at the little things. "[A]s we walked along the streets the Americans and their dress looked very funny to us, and we all laughed," one nineteenth-century Chinese émigré recalled of his first day in San Francisco. Some found it astonishing that white men wore close-fitting suits, since everyone knew that Chinese gentlemen preferred loose robes. "It was a long time before I got used to those red-headed and tight-jacketed foreigners," Yan Phou Lee noted in his autobiography, *When I Was a Boy in China*. " 'How can they walk or run?' " Meanwhile, others thought it hilarious that white women wore long, wide, flowing gowns that mopped up dirt from the streets. Zhang Deiyi, an interpreter for the 1868 Burlingame Treaty, noted with amusement the "barbarian women" with unbound feet, who enjoyed "trailing long skirts on the ground like the tails of foxes."

Other bizarre American customs provoked even greater amusement. What could be more absurd than people who ate with metal utensils instead of chopsticks, which made a "cacophony of dingdang noises" as they dined? And then there was the decidedly American tradition of shaking hands, which left Zhang Deiyi's wrist sore, and of exchanging cards and autographs, which was "a great bother." But perhaps nothing could compare with the kiss—the "ritual of touching lips together," as Zhang put it. A Chinese popular magazine was almost at a loss for words when trying to describe it to its readers. The way to kiss, the editors had heard, "requires making a chirping sound. Those who do not know how to translate say the sound is like a fish drinking water, but this is wrong."

Over time, however, the Chinese emigrants made the transition from Old World to New, such that there would come a point in each man's life when during a visit back to China, his own relatives would suggest that his behavior no longer seemed Chinese.

The completion of the transcontinental railroad in 1869 threw thousands of Chinese men out of work, work they needed not only to support themselves but also to provide the funds they had to send home. New work had to be found. Although they had proved themselves energetic and innovative workers, most traditional jobs remained closed to them solely because of their race. Nonetheless, the Chinese immigrants applied ingenuity and willing diligence to the problem and made their way by accepting opportunities that others found squalid or dangerous.

As the transcontinental railroad made it profitable to ship fresh produce to other regions in the United States, many of the swamps and valleys of California were turned into farmland, which in turn created a demand for farm labor. To exploit the situation, some of the more entrepreneurial Chinese arrivals established themselves as labor contractors. Their ability to speak Cantonese enabled them to recruit and manage large crews of migrant laborers, while their familiarity with American ways allowed them to cut a good deal for themselves with the white farmers.

These Chinese middlemen collected at both ends, charging the

Chinese workers fees for finding them jobs and charging the farmers for placing workers. The middlemen also charged the Chinese for the provisions they needed. While we do not know if they actively recruited new workers from China, or simply used the pool of laid-off railroad employees, we do know that they served a real, necessary function by acting as the gateway between capital and labor. Many white landowners were eager to use Chinese labor because it was both inexpensive and self-sufficient. Under contracts worked out with the farm owners, for instance, the Chinese farmhands did their own cooking or paid for the services of a professional cook. They also slept in their own tents or under the open sky. Before long, they dominated the ranks of field labor: in 1870, only one in ten California farm laborers was Chinese; by 1884, it was one in two; by 1886, almost nine in ten.

These Chinese formed the backbone of western farm production. They sowed crops, plowed the soil, and ended up producing about two-thirds of the vegetables in California. Thanks to Chinese sweat, fruit shipments soared—from nearly two million pounds in the early 1870s to twelve million a decade and a half later. As the Chinese poured into farm work, grain swiftly surpassed mining as the largest source of revenue for the state. By the 1870s, California had become the wheat capital of the United States.

All these contributions paled, however, compared to the Chinese reclamation of the Sacramento–San Joaquin delta. Every spring, the Sacramento and San Joaquin Rivers, the two major rivers in California, flooded their common delta for hundreds of square miles. The rotting tules, or bulrushes, decayed into a rich, fertile layer called peat, but to exploit this nutrient-rich soil, farmers had to drain, clear, and plow the delta as well as construct numerous levees and dikes to protect crops from future floods. Because horse hooves sank straight into the slushy bottom, humans were needed to complete these tasks, but few white men wanted to wade knee- or sometimes waist-deep in these mosquito-infested swamps. Only the Chinese were willing to do what was needed—to work in the muck, slashing their knives through miles of rotten tules, and build by hand a series of gates, ditches, and levees to create a giant labyrinthine network of irrigation channels.

The exact number of Chinese who died from disease, infection, or overwork as they restored five million acres of boggy delta swampland was not recorded. Some landowners valued Chinese life less than that of their animals; in the flood of 1878, as Chinese workers, covered with mud and weighted down with sandbags, struggled to shore up levees, some farm owners dispatched boats upriver to rescue their stock but left the Chinese behind to scream at passing ships for help. But we do know what the Chinese did for the landowners: they not only reclaimed the land, an achievement that would have been impossible without their stubborn dedication to the task assigned them, but they also invented the "tule shoe" during the project, so that horses could be used in this environment. And after their work was done, a surveyor estimated that the land, which the owners had purchased from the federal government for as little as two or three dollars an acre, the land on which the Chinese had worked for about ten cents per cubic yard of soil moved, was now worth seventy-five dollars an acre. The combined value of Chinese labor on the railroads and tule swamps, two projects essential to California's growth, ran in the hundreds of millions.

The sea also provided work opportunities for the Chinese, though its dangers rivaled or even surpassed the brutality of the delta reclamation. Some Chinese labor contractors cut a new kind of deal with the salmon-canning factories of the Pacific Northwest, in which the canneries paid contractors for the volume of work produced, while the contractor paid the laborers a fixed wage. The incentives of such an arrangement ensured a negative outcome. The Chinese labor contractors became harsh taskmasters, and conditions in the canning industry grew notoriously bad. The horror of the job began even before arrival at the work site. On board vessels sailing to Alaska, the Chinese received no water for washing, so their living quarters swarmed with lice and fleas; when inspecting the "Chinatown" section of his vessel one shipmaster wore rubber boots as protection against parasites. By the early 1880s, canneries in the region employed more than three thousand Chinese, who labored under such shocking conditions that Rudyard Kipling, visiting one such cannery, wrote, "Only Chinese men were employed in the work, and they looked like blood-besmeared yellow devils, as they crossed the rifts of sunlight that lay upon the floor." One observer remarked that the scene in a cannery was "not so much like men struggling with innumerable fish as like human maggots wiggling and squirming among the swarms of salmon."

There were two ways the middleman could increase his profit—pay the workers a minimal sum, and force them to work faster. A Bureau of Fisheries investigator reported that the contractors drove workers "as with the whip," noting that "the work of canning exceeds in rapidity anything I have ever seen, outside the brush-making establishment in the East."

Their speed was indeed stunning. One Chinese Columbia River butcher could behead and debone up to two thousand fish, or eighteen tons, a day. History does not record how many Chinese men, reduced to the level of human machinery, died from accidents or disease in canneries of the Northwest. Decades later, the invention of a fish-butchering machine reduced the need for workers from dozens to only two operators. In a twisted acknowledgment of the enormous work capacity of these immigrants, the manufacturer named it "the Iron Chink."

Not all Chinese entrepreneurs succeeded by exploiting their compatriots. Many had grown up within or near villages along the Guangdong coastline, or along the Pearl River, and they saw opportunities in the rich California coastal waters. The nets of Chinese fishermen were cast all along the West Coast, from the state of Oregon to Baja California. Hundreds of Chinese moved to Monterey, California, building cabins on the beach, laying abalone meat on rooftops and railings to dry.

They failed, however, to anticipate the strength of the white fishing lobby. Just as white miners had convinced the state of California to impose special taxes on their Chinese competitors, so did white fishermen succeed, in 1860, in getting the government to impose a special four-dollar-a-month fishing license on the Chinese.* In addition, throughout the 1870s other immigrant groups—Greeks, Italians, and Balkan Slavs—organized to force through legislation limiting the size of Chinese nets, and thereby their catch. At one point, in 1880, California decided to withhold fishing licenses from aliens ineligible for naturalization, which meant, of course, all Chinese and only Chinese. Although the courts later declared this regulation unconstitutional, while the cases were pending, the impact devastated the Chinese fisheries.

At this same time, another very different entrepreneurial trend was developing among the Chinese in America. They were becoming increasingly an urban population. To earn their living, some decided to service the needs of local farm workers and miners by creating tiny Chinatowns in rural California communities, such as Sacramento (called *Yee Fou,* or "Second City"), Stockton (*Sam Fou,* or "Third City), Marysville, and Fresno. Others gravitated toward Los Angeles, formerly a way station for prospectors, a ranch town supplying wagons, equipment, and beef. Los Angeles, a lawless city, teemed with gamblers and prostitutes, and the Chinese moved there to open their own casinos and stores. Still others moved to fast-growing cities in the Pacific Northwest, like Tacoma, Portland, and Seattle, where they ran restaurants and laundries as well as businesses to assist the fishing industry. None of these Chinese communities, however, could compare in size or importance to the San Francisco Chinatown, which by 1870 was home to almost a quarter of all of the Chinese in California.

A Chinese man returning two decades after entering through the port of San Francisco in 1849 would not have recognized the city.

---

*This license fee was repealed in 1864.

During the gold rush, San Francisco had been a filthy jumble of rough frame buildings, shacks, and tents, its beaches strewn with suitcases, trunks, and shovels. But the new San Francisco, the San Francisco of the 1870s, was tall, handsome, dignified. Muddy wagon trails had given way to paved streets that wended their way from the harbor up into the hills; along them rose stately buildings of stone and brick, designed in Gothic, Italian, and other classical architectural styles. Where unshaven, unkempt miners in plaid shirts and denim trousers had once roamed, there now walked refined, serious men in broadcloth suits and top hats, emerging from banks, hotels, and offices. One immigrant who had remembered San Francisco as "narrow, revoltingly dirty, its squares filled with filth and the remains of animals," was astounded to find it "no longer recognizable . . . a great and beautiful city."

But this transition, miraculous and sudden to the eyes of an outsider, had not been easy at all. The gold rush boom had been followed by bust times, poverty, and a series of devastating fires. Fortunately for San Francisco, local entrepreneurs always found methods to turn disaster into profit. The smoldering piles of scrap iron left by the periodic infernos led to the beginning of the city's foundry industry, which supplied much-needed metal supplies for ship repairs and quartz mining equipment. Then, once the transcontinental railroad was finished, factories sprang into being, churning out goods of all kinds for export across America. Some processed food for the rest of the country—they milled wheat into flour, or salted and packaged meat. Others shipped out nonperishable products like tobacco and textiles. By the 1870s, San Francisco had grown into one of the major manufacturing centers in the United States.

The Chinese in San Francisco adapted to this change. Though Chinese vegetable peddlers continued to walk the streets with baskets suspended from each end of a shoulder pole, and Chinese washermen, numbering in the thousands, still controlled the city's laundries, many others entered the new world of mass production. Most of those who made the transition did so as workers. By 1870, the Chinese constituted nearly half the labor force in the city's four major industries: shoes and boots, woolens, cigars and tobacco, and sewing. Moreover, they represented about 80 percent of the workers in woolen mills, and 90 percent of the cigar makers in San Francisco.

But now, for once in America, their employers were likely to be Chinese. And something else was also new for the Chinese immigrants. In China, those who engaged in trade had been traditionally reviled, relegated to the bottom of a Confucian-defined social hierarchy that valued the scholar, the official, and the farmer, but not the merchant. But in the United States, financial success in business was worshipped. This new attitude would have far-reaching consequences, both within the Chinese community and outside it.

By the 1870s, San Francisco had five thousand Chinese businessmen, many of whom were highly successful and posed to local whites a formidable economic threat. In 1866, these Chinese had owned half the city's cigar factories, and by 1870, eleven out of twelve slipper factories, most of which employed Chinese labor almost exclusively, were in Chinese hands. This elite of five thousand included vendors and middlemen in agriculture, the retail sector, and hydraulic quartz mining, as well as the labor contractors. Unafraid to flaunt their wealth and success, many lived in opulent apartments in San Francisco gleaming with crystal, porcelain, and ivory, staffed with servants. Their lives were a far cry from those of their employees, fellow Chinese who lived and worked in tenement factories, rolling cigars, sewing shirts, making boots and slippers. For these piecemeal laborers, the line between work and home often disappeared. "It is no uncommon thing to find in an apartment fifteen feet square three or four branches of business carried on, employing in all at least a dozen men," one observer wrote of the world of the San Francisco Chinese worker. "In apartments where the ceiling is high, a sort of entresol story is fitted up, and here a dozen are to be seen engaged in various avocations, eating and sleeping upon and beneath their work benches or tables."

Just as thousands of European immigrants endured atrocious conditions in the ghettos of New York, so did many Chinese cope with expensive, substandard housing in San Francisco. To save rent, they packed into crowded rooms where virtually every inch of space was used. J. S. Look, a Chinese émigré who arrived in the city during its manufacturing era, recalled that "there were so many of us that we had to sleep on the floors as there were not enough beds in Chinatown for the people that lived there."

Because many Chinese could not afford furniture, they used crates found on the street as tables and cabinets. Because beds were scarce, they slept in shifts, or nailed bunks to the wall, one above another, like shelves, until their apartments resembled army barracks. The most unfortunate lived in squalid underground cellars where, one observer noted, "scarcely a single ray of light or breath of pure, fresh air ever penetrates. These rooms are filled with bunks like the rooms for passengers on ships and steamers, and by the dim, flickering light of a little oil lamp the poor wretches who den there crawl into their miserable couches." When contemplating how they were able to tolerate such conditions, two factors must be kept in mind. The first is that their sacrifices were providing better lives for their families back home. The second is that many no doubt believed their discomfort to be temporary and refused to see the conditions in which they found themselves as the long-term reality of their lives.

The new economics of Chinatown—the elaborate terracing of wealth and position—soon found expression in an informal but all-encompassing power structure. At the foundation was a tier called the clans, who addressed the basic daily needs of Chinese laborers, such as housing. One level up, the clans of each district were organized into civic associations. Finally, at the pinnacle, ruled six powerful district associations, at the time known as the Chinese Six Companies, and later as the Chinese Consolidated Benevolent Association of America. The Six Companies anointed themselves the supreme power in Chinatown, with the ostensible purpose of resolving disputes, protecting members, and guarding the welfare of the entire community. So powerful were they that before the first Chinese consulate appeared in the city during the 1870s, the Six Companies served as

unofficial ambassadors of China, acting as the voice of the Qing imperial government in the United States.

The Six Companies had evolved out of the need of the emerging
Chinese business elite for order. The white man's government had
demonstrated that its mission was to suppress, not protect, Chinese
interests. Chinese businessmen may have organized their own guild in
San Francisco as early as 1849, and certainly by 1850 a number of
immigrants from Guangdong had formed the Kong Chow Association, literally, "Pearl River Delta," one of the first Chinese American
organizations in America. When tensions arose between Cantonese
people of different dialects and districts, the association split into two
groups, which became the first two of the Six Companies. Later, four
additional organizations appeared in the 1850s, with offices in prominent neighborhoods in San Francisco.

The Companies' influence on a new Chinese worker began the
moment he arrived at the docks. Representatives would be there to
load the new arrival's luggage onto a wagon and bring him into
Chinatown, ostensibly to find him food, lodging, and work, but also
to make sure he joined one of the associations, explaining that his
dues would be more than offset by the social services the Six
Companies provided. The Six Companies did in fact provide services.
In San Francisco they created a safety net for the Chinese workers,
lending them money when necessary and helping out when they were
sick. They settled disputes between members, opened a Chinese-
language school, maintained a Chinese census, and channeled remittances for their members back to their home villages through the
district associations.

Their services extended into the spiritual realm as well, supporting joss temples, which were places of peace and meditation. During
that era, a Chinese émigré could identify a house of worship by the
tinsel on its balcony or the dragon figures on its balustrades. Stepping
inside, he could ponder his fate in darkness, inhaling the aroma of
burning incense, listening to prayers chanted to the music of gongs
and drums. The décor within the temple—the idols sculpted from

wood or plaster, the red and gold calligraphy, the glass lanterns filled with oil, the carved art from Chinese myths—transported the worshipper into a world that seemed to transcend both America and China.

The Six Companies also lavished attention on funerals, which could be huge, almost theatrical productions. Beginning typically at the home or store of the deceased, a Buddhist priest in a satin robe would chant prayers, and bang his bell and cymbals. Then a procession would head for Lone Mountain Cemetery, where each of the Six Companies had fenced off its own area. Along the route, white-clad mourners would weep and toss strips of brown paper, symbolizing copper coins needed for the passage to heaven. The entrance to the graveyard lot was usually marked by a canopy, beyond which lay a brick furnace, table, and headboard with Chinese characters. There, friends would burn paper near the body—Chinese messages, paper servants, paper money—gifts for the deceased in the afterworld that disappeared with his spirit in flame and smoke. Instead of the corpse being buried, the flesh would later be scraped off and the bones laid out to dry in the sun before being bundled into white muslin and shipped back to China. The return of these bones represented a final act of patronage, a commitment by the Six Companies to protect their members and send them back safely to their home villages, even after death.

While the Six Companies had their dark side—their social system may have unintentionally reinforced the image of the Chinese as foreigners, not melting-pot Americans—the real threat to Chinese émigrés came from a very different group: those who belonged to the secret societies known as the tongs.

Tong members tended to be outcasts who either lacked clan ties or had been expelled by their associations. They modeled themselves after the Triad societies in China, an underground fraternity in Guangdong province dedicated to the overthrow of the Manchu government. Representing the interests of the poor and the oppressed, the Triads drew into their ranks legions of impoverished peasants, embittered tenant farmers, people who had failed the civil service examinations—in general, those angry enough at the system to organize against the landlords and the imperial Qing elite. They invented elaborate initiation ceremonies, passwords, and coded hand signals, and swore blood oaths to pledge eternal brotherhood: "Tonight we pledge ourselves before Heaven that the brethren in the whole universe shall be as if from one womb, as if begotten by one father, as if nourished by one mother, and as if they were of one stock and origin."

But unlike the Triads, the tongs had no clear political motives driving their actions, and very quickly they became involved in the extremely lucrative business of importing thousands of Chinese women and girls to America to service the Chinese bachelor population. Most of these women did not come by choice but were forced into degradation.

Prostitution and enslavement had a long history in China. In times of famine, a Chinese family on the brink of starvation might sell the youngest daughter to keep the other members of the family alive. The Qing dynasty officially sanctioned the practice, noting that the survival of one in ten families depended on a daughter's being prostituted. Of course, many parents did not sell their daughters outright but nevertheless sealed their destiny by selling them as *mui tsai*, a Cantonese term for "little sister." As children, *mui tsai* worked as indentured servants for another family, ostensibly to be freed by marriage at age eighteen. While a fortunate few might be treated kindly, many others were abused, raped, and sold into brothels. Some *mui tsai* ended up in America to service the army of Chinese male laborers who had no prospects for female companionship in a white world.

Because they tended to be illiterate and born into the poorest levels of Chinese society, most of these women left no memoirs. Several poignant stories survive as oral histories, however, recorded by missionaries and journalists. Ho-tai remembered that her mother had been determined not to sell her, even though the family faced starvation and "death was all around them." But one night, when her mother was away from home, her father sold her for several pieces of silver. As she sailed away, she caught one last glimpse of her frenzied mother, "her dress open far below her throat, her hair loose and flying, her eyes swollen and dry from over-weeping, moaning pitifully, stumbling in the darkness, searching for the boat but it was gone."

Lilac Chen, a former prostitute, recalled that her father gambled away all his money, leaving the family destitute. When Lilac was six years old, her father told her he was taking her to see her grandmother, whom she adored. She eagerly boarded the ferry, but then felt something was amiss: "Mother was crying, and I couldn't understand why she should cry if I go see Grandma. When I saw her cry I said, 'Don't cry, Mother, I'm just going to see Grandma and be right back. [Then] that worthless father sold me on the ferry boat. Locked me in a cabin while he was negotiating my sale." Lilac kicked and screamed, but when she was finally let out her father had disappeared and she was on her way to America.

Some women were deceived by pimps who bamboozled unsuspecting girls and their families with stories of the incredible wealth and leisure to be enjoyed in the United States. One nineteen-year-old girl, Wong Ah So, agreed to emigrate when a stranger posing as a rich laundryman offered to take her to Gold Mountain as his bride. On the journey she was thrilled that she was headed for a "grand, free country, where everyone was rich and happy." Upon arrival in San Francisco, however, Wong was horrified and heartbroken to learn that she would be forced to work as a prostitute.

Western authorities at the treaty ports were charged with detecting and preventing such trafficking in women and children, but pimps easily bribed their way through the inspection process. During the journey, traffickers coached women to give proper answers on arrival, ordering them to memorize key phrases in case they were interrogated by officials seeking to ascertain whether they had traveled to the United States of their own free will. Some traffickers warned the women that if they failed to answer correctly, they would be locked up and left to rot in a "devil American prison." Quick-witted girls managed to escape their fate by creating a commotion upon arrival, either on the ship or the docks—shrieking for help, crying that they had been kidnapped, begging passersby to save them. Thus a few were rescued and later given passage back to China, but most of the new arrivals had no chance to win either freedom or sympathy, especially in the early years of San Francisco's rough-hewn, male-dominated frontier society.

Gripped by terror and confusion, these young women were locked in barracoons, stripped and inspected, and then auctioned off to the highest bidder, their sale price determining their place in the city's hierarchy of prostitution. Though California was not officially a slave state, it tolerated the sale of female flesh during the antebellum period; slave auctions of Chinese women were held openly and brazenly on the docks, before large audiences that included police officers. By the 1860s, however, a stricter code of morality disapproved of such public transactions. The auctions didn't stop but simply moved to Chinatown and then indoors—for instance, to a Chinese theater or even a Chinese temple. At these auctions, the youngest and most beautiful were usually sold as mistresses or concubines to Chinatown's wealthy elite—merchants, tradesmen, and business owners. Relatively speaking, they were the lucky ones, though as property they had no rights and could be sold or disposed of at whim. Other women—the next tier—were acquired by exclusive "parlor houses," where, elegantly dressed and perfumed, they were expected to entertain men in luxurious apartments of teak, bamboo, and embroidered silks. Most girls ended up in low-class brothels, or "cribs," tiny shacks no larger than twelve by fourteen feet, facing dim, narrow alleys and sparsely furnished with a washbowl, a bamboo chair, and a bed. These *loungei* (literally, "woman always holding her legs up") were forced to service, often in rapid succession, laborers, sailors, and drunks for as little as twenty-five cents each, drawing in customers with their plaintive chants: "Two bittee lookee, flo bittee feelee, six bittee doee!"

Chinese prostitutes shipped to mining camps on the western frontier were deterred from escape by the wilderness itself. One woman fleeing from her master in Nevada was later found half-dead in the hills, with both feet frozen and requiring amputation. In the hinterlands, they faced an even greater male-to-female ratio than in San Francisco's Chinatown. They also endured insults and abuse from white miners, who called them "Chiney ladies," "moon-eyed pinch foots," and "she-heathens."

At the same time, the prostitute-trafficking tongs were battling incessantly among themselves for control over territory and profits. Before such a war would erupt, the tongs often contrived a public excuse for the pending hostilities, such as a slap in the face or a stolen prostitute. In outbursts of Chinese tong warfare on the western frontier, some prostitutes were kidnapped and held for ransom; others died in the crossfire between rival gangs. In one notorious case, tongs seized four women in the Comstock Lode; only one victim was found alive—nailed shut inside a crate that had been shipped from San Francisco to Reno.

By the 1860s, the tongs almost entirely controlled the sex trade, leaving little room for independent operators. For prostitutes on the lowest level, there was no respite from work: many were doubly exploited by San Francisco brothel owners, who leased them out to local garment factories to sew by day, then sold their bodies by night. There was no respite from abuse: most were routinely beaten with clubs, threatened with pistols, burned with red-hot pokers. If they failed to make enough money, the madam "beats and pounds them with sticks of fire-wood, pulls their hair, treads on their toes, starves them and torments and punishes them in every cruel way." One prostitute had acid thrown in her face by a Chinese actor who resented having to share her with other men. Some women chose to escape their unbearable lives by committing suicide, often by swallowing opium or flinging themselves into San Francisco Bay.

For some Chinese women taken into prostitution, the only escape was death. Those who tried other methods found themselves up against a corrupt system comprising not only the tongs and their network of opium dealers and gambling houses, but also the police, the

courts, and even the Six Companies. Since prostitution was so lucrative—in 1870 the average brothel employed nine women, each of
whom brought in an average net annual profit of $2,500 (compared
with the $500 average annual income of the Chinese male laborer)—
the tongs jealously guarded their golden-egg-producing property, hiring "highbinders"—associations of Chinese thugs—to monitor the
women. They also paid $40 in insurance for every Chinese prostitute
brought into the United States, as well as weekly or monthly fees to
hire special policemen for surveillance. Brothel owners forced women
to sign contracts penalizing them if they fell ill or were unable to perform their duties because of menstruation or pregnancy, virtually
guaranteeing deeper bondage for these women. The following agreement is typical:

> Yut Kum consents to prostitute her body to receive company
> to aid Mee Yung for the full time of four years. When the time
> is fully served, neither service nor money shall be longer
> required. If Yut Kum should be sick fifteen days she shall
> make up one month. If she conceives, she shall serve one year
> more. If during the time any man wishes to redeem her body,
> she shall make satisfactory arrangements with the mistress
> Mee Yung. If Yut Kum should herself escape and be recov-
> ered, then her time shall never expire. Should the mistress
> become very wealthy and return to China with glory, then
> Yut Kum shall fulfill her time, serving another person.

By the 1870s, horrified Christian activists, mostly middle-class
white Protestant women, established rescue homes for Chinese
women. San Francisco had two sanctuaries: the Women's Missionary
Society of the Methodist Episcopal Church, established by Reverend
Otis Gibson, and the Presbyterian Mission Home, founded by the
Woman's Occidental Board. Soon a stream of prostitutes began slipping away from their cribs to beg admission. To bring them back, the
brothel keepers sent emissaries to the mission, asking to interview the

former prostitutes for just a few minutes. If an interview was granted, they would cajole the women, then threaten them if they refused to return, frightening them to tears. On occasion, the brothel owners even sent their attorneys with writs of habeas corpus.

To protect the women, the mission took to hiding them wherever they could—between folding doors or under floorboards. One resident of the Presbyterian Mission Home recalled how the tongs would "search the whole house, even dig into our rice bins to see if we put any [prostitutes in] there!" They harassed the director, Donaldina Cameron, by smashing the mission's windows and planting sticks of dynamite on doorsills and against the foundation.

But the courageous Cameron would not be stopped in her cause. Beginning in the late nineteenth century, she struck upon a new, even more aggressive strategy. Rather than wait for the women to find her, she went looking for them. With the help of the police, she began paying daring surprise visits to bordellos, first ascending to the rooftops of adjoining buildings, crossing to the bordello's rooftop, then climbing in through the building's skylights. In an attempt to thwart this latest assault, the tongs established a sophisticated system of alarm bells to warn brothel operators of approaching police. Not surprisingly, these heroic efforts drew considerable press attention to Chinatown's criminal element and greatly contributed to the demise of Chinese prostitution on the West Coast. In 1942, the Presbyterian Mission Home was renamed the Donaldina Cameron House to honor her life and work. Through her efforts and those of others it is said that eventually an estimated fifteen hundred Chinese women were rescued.

What did those women do afterward who were rescued or had broken free on their own? As surprising as it may seem, some went on to become madams and brothel owners themselves, using their own experience to exploit other Chinese women. The most famous was Ah Toy. She was possibly the first Chinese prostitute in America, a woman who had migrated "to better her condition," mostly likely of her own free will. Arriving from Hong Kong in early 1849, she began her career as a *loungei* in an alleyway shanty. Soon she became San Francisco's most successful Chinese courtesan, owning a brothel in a prestigious neighborhood and enjoying near-celebrity status. At the peak of her popularity, Asian and white men alike lined up for blocks and paid an ounce of gold just to "gaze upon the countenance of the charming Ah Toy," as one man breathlessly put it. Part of her success derived from both her strong will and genius for self-promotion. The Chinese crime syndicates could not control her; she successfully fought the tongs that tried to extort money from her. Men who cheated her (such as one who paid her with brass filings instead of gold) found themselves hauled into court. Her name appeared constantly in the local newspapers. And unlike most women in her profession, Ah Toy lived a long life. She reportedly ended her days peacefully and died three months short of her hundredth birthday.

Then there was the case of Suey Him, first sold at age five by her father for a piece of gold, and then again at age twelve for three handfuls of gold. For a decade she worked as a prostitute, until she wed a poor Chinese laundryman who loved her. For eight years they scraped and saved to buy her freedom from the brothel keeper. But later her husband fell ill and died, forcing her back into the profession. This time, however, she returned as a capitalist, importing some fifty girls from China to work for her. She worked as a madam until she converted to Christianity and freed all her girls.

Other former prostitutes, however, joined mainstream society in substantial numbers as wives and mothers. (This is evident from statistics indicating that while the total number of Chinese women in the United States decreased during the 1870s, those keeping house grew from 753 in 1870 to 1,145 in 1880.) Many former prostitutes married Chinese laborers, and a few married Caucasians. The union of Polly and Charlie Bemis is one of the most famous love stories of the American West; it inspired the 1981 novel *Thousand Pieces of Gold* by Ruthanne Lum McCunn and a 1991 feature film of the same name starring Rosalind Chao and Chris Cooper.

Originally known as Lalu Nathov, Polly Bemis was born in 1853 to an impoverished farm family in China. After a severe crop failure and a raid on the village by outlaws, her father was forced to sell Polly to the outlaws for two bags of seed. Resold in the United States for $2,500, she became the slave and concubine of Hong King, a Chinese saloon owner in Warren, Idaho, until Charlie Bemis won her in a poker game. An educated man from a prominent New England family, Bemis granted Polly her freedom. She soon repaid his kindness: when a miner shot Bemis in the face, Polly performed surgery with a razor blade to save his life. After his recovery, Bemis asked her to marry him, and they spent the rest of their lives as ranchers at the bottom of a canyon on the Salmon River in Idaho. Polly Bemis, who used her knowledge of Chinese herbs to nurse sick children, became a much-beloved neighbor in the community.

Yet other women were never able to escape the world of prostitution. There are stories of women rushing into marriage to escape the brothel, only to discover themselves wedded to a new pimp. Their desperation for a better life made them easy prey for unscrupulous men with no qualms about forcing them back into the sex trade. Some former prostitutes married honest, loving men, only to be abducted by gangsters in their husbands' absence. According to Donaldina Cameron, highbinders would hunt down and kidnap these married women even after they had moved to remote rural villages.*

In time, those who unable to leave the profession became outcasts, scorned by Chinese and whites alike. When they grew old and sick, many were treated like human refuse and simply thrown out onto the streets. The hospitals of the American West would not help

---

*Even women who had not been prostitutes were treated by the tongs as property, without rights of their own. In Seattle, a Chinese widow who turned down several proposals of marriage from tong members received an ultimatum: "She would either have to marry one of them men or go back to China," a neighbor recalled. "This woman came over to me and cried. She said she did not want to go back to China. Her children had been born here and she wanted to stay in the country." The tongs forced her to return anyway.

them—white San Francisco physicians lobbied to exclude Chinese prostitutes from the hospitals—and few could afford the services of Chinese herbalists. Clan associations and the Six Companies established nursing facilities for former prostitutes, but they were tiny, dark, squalid rooms furnished with a few straw mats, referred to by some as "death-houses." A visitor to one of these facilities described entering through a low door into a room dimly lit by a Chinese nut-oil lamp, and finding "stretched on the floor of this damp, foul-smelling den . . . four female figures . . . victims of the most fearful . . . loathsome disease."

And what of those Chinese women who came to America as wives? In China, society mandated that a married woman's life centered on the family, serving them from cradle to grave. According to one school of ancient Chinese philosophy, the "Three Obediences" dictated that she first obey her father, then her husband after marriage, and finally her eldest son when widowed.

Because the average worker could not afford to support a family in the United States, most Chinese women emigrants who were not prostitutes were wives of merchants. Most had grown up in modest but respectable families in small villages near Canton. They tended to be middle-class, because upper-class families would not allow their daughters to marry outside China, and because many Chinese merchants in the United States considered working-class women beneath them.

Having been raised in a protected, insular household, the typical merchant's wife had never ventured far beyond her village until journeying to the United States. Even more problematic was the fact that the middle and upper classes in China practiced the nine-hundred-year-old tradition of bandaging a young girl's toes under the ball of her foot, reducing the foot to a length of five or even three inches. Reflecting the same impulse as the Western fashion of warping the female ribcage with corsets, foot-binding existed primarily to symbolize a family's wealth and power, advertising its ability to support a nonworking, purely ornamental human being.

For many of the wives, home in the United States was nothing more than a gilded prison, where they were jealously guarded as treasured possessions. Some Chinese immigrant women could easily count the number of times in their lives they had ever stepped outdoors. "My father traveled all over the world," one Chinese American remembered, "but his wife could not go into the street by herself." Only during holidays were some permitted to venture out, accompanied by a chaperone. A merchant's wife in Butte, Montana, recalled, "When I came to America as a bride, I never knew I would be coming to a prison . . .":

> I was allowed out of the house but once a year. That was during the New Year's when families exchanged New Year calls and feasts. We would dress in our long-plaited, brocaded, hand-embroidered skirts. These were a part of our wedding dowry brought from China. Over these we wore long-sleeved, short satin or damask jackets. We wore all of our jewelry, and we put jeweled ornaments in our hair.

> The father of my children hired a closed carriage to take me and the children calling. Of course, he did not go with us, as this was against the custom practiced in China. The carriage would take us even if we went around the corner, for no family women walked. The carriage waited until we were ready to leave, which would be hours later, for the women saw each other so seldom that we talked and reviewed all that went on since we saw each other.

> Before we went out of the house, we sent the children to see if the streets were clear of men. It was considered impolite to meet them. If we did have to walk out when men were on the streets, we hid our faces behind our silk fans and hurried by.

No doubt many Chinese men felt they had good reason to keep their wives under lock and key. The scarcity of women in the West and the violence of frontier society posed a very real danger of kidnapping or molestation in the streets. A bound-foot woman could neither run from assailants nor fend off attacks. Indeed, with several toes rotted away from foot-binding, she could hardly walk—or even remain standing—for an extended period of time. The annals of nineteenth-century California recount many stories of helpless Chinese women being thrown down into the mud, dragged by the hair, pelted with stones, their clothes and earrings yanked off.

So perhaps staying indoors was safer, though less than stimulating. One wife whiled away the hours playing cards with her servant, looking after her son, gossiping with neighbors, or hiring a hairdresser or a female storyteller to entertain her. In her essay "The Chinese Woman in America," Edith Maud Eaton, a Eurasian writer who used the pen name Sui Sin Far, offered a glimpse of these women's lives:

> Now and then the women visit one another. They laugh at the most commonplace remark and scream at the smallest trifle, they examine one another's dresses and hair, talk about their husbands, their babies, their food, squabble over little matters and make up again, they dine on bowls of rice, minced chicken, bamboo shoots and a dessert of candied fruits.

In contrast, other Chinese wives did not enjoy the luxury of idleness. Some belonged to the laboring class, toiling long hours like their husbands. In the late 1870s, a few could be found as domestics or in intensive labor industries as seamstresses, washerwomen, shirtmakers, gardeners, and fisherwomen. In family-run operations, like laundries or grocery stores, the line between business owner and laborer blurred, and wives were often compelled to work alongside their husbands to keep their businesses afloat.

Difficult as her life could be, the typical Chinese wife had more power in the United States than she could have achieved in her home village. First and most important, she had escaped the tyranny of her mother-in-law. In China, a daughter-in-law lived with her husband's family and endured her husband's mother's hazing until she gave birth to a son; bearing a male child validated her existence and earned her the respect of the family. Her power grew with each additional male child and climaxed when she became a mother-in-law herself, attaining the authority to perpetuate the tradition by bullying her sons' wives.

In the United States, Chinese families were nuclear, not multigenerational, and wives were usually freed from this hierarchical scheme of abuse. In addition, they lived in a country where women who worked were not stigmatized as they were in China. In their home villages, a working woman was often viewed with derision or pity, her employment a sign that her husband or family could not support her. But in the United States, some merchant wives passed their time doing needlework in the privacy of their own homes, earning thousands of dollars by mending clothes for Chinese bachelors. A few even opened their own tailor shops. The labor of these working women was valued by their families, because the money sent back home could spell the difference between life and death for relatives in China.

Perhaps most significantly, the Chinese emigrant wives also mothered a tiny population of American children. In 1876, the Chinese Six Companies estimated that a few hundred Chinese families lived in America, and perhaps one thousand Chinese children. In the long run, these infants, the first generation born in America, would enjoy more rights and privileges in the United States than their immigrant parents. Most were too young then to know that heated racial discussions were under way in Congress and across the country, negotiations about civil rights that would profoundly affect their future.

CHAPTER SEVEN

Spreading Across America

By the time of the 1870 census, 63,199 Chinese were living in the continental United States, 99.4 percent of them in the western states and territories, with a clear majority—78 percent—in California. 'It was only a matter of time before the Chinese emigrants crossed the Rocky Mountains, then the Missouri and Mississippi Rivers. Some found themselves clear across the country, on the Atlantic coast, while others, with the help of labor contractors, would end up in the American South. All of them would face a post–Civil War America grappling with the politics of race, and with the question of where certain ethnic groups would fit within a new social hierarchy.

One of the strangest episodes in the history of the Chinese in America concerned workers who signed labor contracts that in essence rendered them substitutes for former black slaves on postwar southern cotton plantations. Fortunately, it was a story with a reasonably happy ending for the Chinese. For while many southern plantation owners initially saw the arrangement as a match made in heaven—they had had heard wonderful reports about the industrious and cooperative nature of Chinese worker—they would quickly learn, however, that in addition to their diligence and accommodating nature, most Chinese workers understood a contract and expected its terms to be fully honored by both sides.

Relatively speaking, few Chinese laborers took field jobs in the South, for no one living in the country during the 1850s and 1860s could have been completely unaware of the consequences of slavery based on race. Southern plantation owners, accustomed to laborers who had no rights whatsoever, were unlikely to be beneficent, or even fair, employers, especially to people who had agreed to pick up the work of former slaves. These owners had lived most of their lives believing that the way to increase productivity was to have overseers whip grown men into total tractability. Why would they suddenly view a labor contract with a member of another race as an arrangement between parties sharing equal rights?

As it turned out, the Chinese in America would not acquiesce easily to white efforts to relegate them into a permanent underclass, in the South or elsewhere. In a culture that viewed blacks and Native Americans as having sprung from an inferior culture, the Chinese quickly recognized that anyone associated with these other two races was likely to be abused. In 1853, when a California judge barred a Chinese man from testifying against whites on the premise that the Chinese should be considered part of the same race as Indians and blacks, the Chinese community took greater offense at the comparison than at the exclusion. In an outraged letter widely circulated throughout the San Francisco business community, one Chinese merchant wrote that his people enjoyed thousands of years of civilization. How dare white Americans "come to the conclusion that we Chinese are the same as Indians and Negroes . . . these Indians know nothing about the relations of society; they know no mutual respect; they wear neither clothes nor shoes; they live in wild places and in caves." Not surprisingly, such attitudes aroused bitter resentment from other minority groups, who believed that the Chinese should not be exempted from the unfair treatment they endured from the white population. When the Grass Valley Indians in central California were being shunted onto reservations, King Weimah, their chief, pointedly objected to the Chinese remaining free in the United States while his own people were being rounded up and isolated from American society.

Until the Civil War, racial injustice was legally codified in most states, and only after the war did the ratification of the Fourteenth Amendment guarantee all citizenship rights, including the right to vote, to "all persons born or naturalized in the United States," while the Fifteenth Amendment guaranteed the right to vote regardless of race, color, or previous servitude. But during the post-Reconstruction era, southern states resorted to a variety of ruthless Jim Crow tactics, ranging from poll taxes to outright violence, to keep blacks away from the ballot box.

While southern racists were widely regarded in the North with righteous scorn, it should be noted that western politicians were equally unwilling to see the Chinese gain the right to vote. They feared, as California Republican senator Cornelius Cole warned, that "If the Chinese were allowed to vote," it would "kill our party as dead as a stone." Those who feared that the Chinese immigrants would start applying for naturalization, and once they had citizenship be guaranteed the right to vote, won a victory when in the 1870s Congress and a federal court decision withheld from the Chinese the right of naturalization, declaring them aliens ineligible for citizenship. But the Fourteenth Amendment, written to ensure that African Americans were given the full rights of citizenship, extended the right of birthright citizenship to all those born in the United States, and as a consequence to the American-born Chinese population as well. So while Congress denied Chinese immigrants the right to become naturalized citizens, the Reconstruction amendments precluded both the federal and state governments from denying American-born children their citizenship rights. It would be a distinction the Chinese would not ignore.

Before the 1870s, only a handful of Chinese had lived in the old South, a few working as physicians, and many more as merchants, storekeepers, or cooks. Some had made their homes in southern port cities such as Charleston and New Orleans. But with the end of the Civil War and the emancipation of the black slaves, southern planters, hearing of the exemplary work habits of the Chinese and knowing they had no rights of citizenship, wanted to use them as field hands. Unlike the ruling class in the West, which feared the Chinese as competition, white southerners had no difficulty with the idea of importing hordes of foreigners, in this case to pressure their former black slaves to return to field labor under conditions that had prevailed under slavery. "Emancipation has spoiled the Negro, and carried him away from the fields of agriculture," editorialized the *Vicksburg Times*. "Our prosperity depends entirely upon the recovery of lost ground, and we therefore say let the Coolies come, and we will take the chance of Christianizing them." No doubt, one of the first Christian traits they would have the Chinese learn was to turn the other cheek when abused. But clearly the intent was not to save the souls of the Chinese, but to use them as leverage against the emancipated blacks. A planter's wife wrote, "Give us five million of Chinese laborers in the valley of the Mississippi and we can furnish the world with cotton and teach the Negro his proper place."

To this end, the southern elite organized a conference to discuss strategy. In 1869, hundreds of delegates arrived in Memphis, Tennessee, for the nation's first Chinese labor convention. Tye Kim Orr, a Chinese Christian who had established a Chinese colony in British Guiana before moving to Louisiana, addressed the delegates in Memphis on the second day of the conference, assuring his audience that the Chinese were docile, obedient, and industrious—in short, a race amenable to easy exploitation. The conference whipped up considerable excitement in the press, especially with the appearance of Cornelius Koopmanschap, the country's best-known importer of Chinese workers, who had helped supply the Central Pacific Railroad with Chinese labor. He captivated his audience at Memphis by promising that the Chinese would be willing to move to the South from San Francisco for about twenty dollars a month, or from China on five-year contracts for as little as ten dollars a month.

Anticipating the prospect of a new South rising on the backs of coolie labor, the delegates agreed to raise a million dollars to further Koopmanschap's plans; they also appointed a committee to bring five hundred to one thousand Chinese immigrants to the South.

After the conference, the South went about actively recruiting Chinese labor. A few, brought from Cuba in 1866, were already working in sugarcane fields. To help lure more workers to the region, American clipper companies distributed handbills in south Chinese ports. "All Chinese make much money in New Orleans if they work," one of these asserted. "Chinamen have become richer than mandarins there." Some of the advertisements promised the Chinese that on their passage to the United States they would find "nice rooms and very fine food. They can play all sorts of games and have no work." The handbills urged the Chinese to hurry. "It is a nice country. Better than this. No sickness there and no danger of death. Come! Go at once. You cannot afford to wait. Don't heed the wife's counsel or the threats of enemies. Be Chinamen, but go."

These aggressive efforts netted the arrival of about two thousand Chinese in the South in 1869 and 1870. Some went to work on the plantations and shrimp farms of Louisiana. Others replaced black labor in the cotton fields of Mississippi and Arkansas. Still others toiled on railroads. In December 1869, some 250 Chinese men came as employees of the Houston & Texas Central Railroad. The following August, a thousand arrived in Alabama to build track toward Chattanooga.

By the middle of 1871, however, there appeared signs of serious conflict and, on both sides, disillusionment. On one plantation, the Chinese staged a strike to protest the whipping of a Chinese servant. On another, a Chinese labor gang attempted to lynch a Chinese agent who had given them false information about their life in the South. There were cases of plantation owners who shot and killed Chinese workers who rebelled against oppressive conditions.

The primary issue was that plantation owners, accustomed to absolute control over their workers, viewed their relationship with the Chinese as master and slave rather than employer and employee. In contrast, the Chinese considered their relationship to the planters as a capitalistic, not feudal, transaction and expected their employers to adhere to the terms of their contracts. Time had left the southern employers behind, and the Chinese laborers, unlike black slaves, now enjoyed decided advantages.

First, the Chinese worked under labor contracts and, to the dismay of the southern elite, proved to be shrewd and litigious negotiators. To spell out every detail of their contracts, they hired bilingual interpreters, men who served not only as translators but as surrogate agents and lawyers. Their job was to haggle over the terms of the contract, communicate worker grievances to employers, and secure new employment for their clients if they were dissatisfied with their jobs. When planters violated their contracts, the interpreters filed lawsuits on behalf of the Chinese.

Second, the Chinese in the South could sue or press charges against their employers. For example, in 1871, Chinese workers took their case to court after a skirmish with an overseer left one Chinese dead and two others wounded. The local judge not only permitted their testimony to be delivered in Chinese but later ruled in favor of the plaintiffs. In this respect, the Chinese enjoyed greater protection under the law in the South than in California, where state law specifically barred them from testifying against Caucasians.

Third, Chinese workers were protected by a postwar federal government deeply suspicious of southern efforts to exploit people on the basis of race. As early as August 1867, U.S. authorities halted Chinese labor recruitment in the South until they received testimonials and certificates from the Chinese stipulating that they had migrated to the South voluntarily and signed labor contracts of their own free will. This governmental vigilance made it difficult for southern plantation owners to hold Chinese workers in bondage.

For the southern oligarchy, the experiment with Chinese labor, begun with such high hopes, proved to be a disaster. Within a few years, most Chinese had walked away from their contracts and

accepted other jobs at better wages. Many gravitated toward cities like
New Orleans, where they opened their own stores. Some simply ran
away, and most planters lacked the resources to pursue them. By
1915, scarcely a single plantation still employed Chinese labor.

If the southerners thought that they could import Chinese labor to
discipline their former slaves, the North thought it could exploit
Chinese labor to discipline its white workers. The northern attempt
came during the "Gilded Age," as Mark Twain called it, a showy,
counterfeit epoch, its gilt veneer barely hiding underlying corruption.
It was a time when ruthless capitalists, known as "robber barons,"
ascended to positions of enormous power, not through exemplary
hard work à la Horatio Alger, but through wholesale bribery, collusion, and intimidation. It was an age of contrasts, of conspicuous consumption by the wealthy juxtaposed against a backdrop of deep
despair and disillusionment within the working class.

This yawning gap between rich and poor, which widened further
during the second half of the nineteenth century, was already apparent
during the Civil War, when men like J. P. Morgan, Andrew Carnegie,
John D. Rockefeller, and James Mellon eluded military service by
paying less privileged men to act as their substitutes. Many of the rich
grew richer selling shoddy equipment to the government for use by
the Union armies. Class differences grew more distinct in the postwar
era, especially during the presidency of U. S. Grant, a legendary Civil
War general but a spectacularly incompetent public official. In an
administration wracked by scandal, federal officials consistently protected the interests and ignored the excesses of those willing to pay
them off. The robber barons engaged in an orgy of confiscatory
expansion, first wounding and then gobbling up competitors, all with
the connivance of the courts and the help of the legislatures they purchased. Financiers and railroad moguls watered down stocks, used
strong-arm tactics to bully employees into submission, and bought
off federal, state, and city politicians to create their empires. Washing-

ton spent millions of taxpayer dollars to bail out Wall Street after a failed conspiracy by stock speculators to corner the gold market.

Against this background of greed, the frustration of the American worker mounted. Those who had loyally risked life and limb to fight in the Union armies were cast adrift after the war. Returning to crumbling, disease-ridden tenements in the cities, they had to compete with thousands of others for work, including even more desperate European immigrants—men and women willing to endure unhealthy and even dangerous conditions in factories for minimal wages. Others seeking work were farmers forced off the land when they found that they could afford neither the expensive equipment required to make agriculture profitable, nor the exorbitant shipping rates charged by powerful railroad monopolies. There were riots in the coal mines, strikes in mills and factories, accompanied by literal starvation in the streets. In an effort to defend themselves against their corporate employers, white employees started to organize unions to fight for decent working conditions and fair wages.

A new method of control had to be found quickly, a new source of labor that would demonstrate that union members were expendable, and eastern industrialists began to consider the Chinese as that source. In 1870 at North Adams, Massachusetts, the workers of a ladies' boot and shoe factory went on strike, demanding an eight-hour day, a wage increase, and the right to review the company's account ledgers. The owner, Calvin Sampson, fired them, but since the strikers belonged to the Secret Order of the Knights of Saint Crispin, the largest and possibly the most powerful union in the country, he was unable to hire replacement white workers. Still, Sampson rejected the demands of his workers, and after reading a newspaper article praising the efficiency of Chinese workers in a San Francisco shoe factory, he signed a three-year contract with the emigration firm of Kwong, Chong, Wing & Company under which seventy-five Chinese laborers would be sent east from the West Coast. Sampson was the first manufacturer in American history to transport Asians east of the Rockies to end a strike.

A crowd gathered at the North Adams train depot to gape at the arriving strikebreakers. Some spectators came out of sheer curiosity, as most New Englanders had never before seen an Asian person, but many were there to harass and even intimidate the Chinese. "A large and hostile crowd met them at the depot, hooted them, hustled them somewhat, and threw stones at them," *The Nation* wrote. Thirty police officers escorted the Chinese to the factory dormitories, where they were protected by locked gates and guards. Later, someone scrawled "No scabs or rats admitted here" on the factory wall, but no violence broke out.

Sampson's decision to hire Chinese labor proved a success. *Harper's New Monthly* reported that "there can be nowhere a busier, more orderly group of workmen." Within a few months, the Chinese were outperforming the Crispins, producing shoes at a brisker rate than the more experienced strikers had done. *Scribner's Monthly* pointed out that the Chinese "labored regularly and constantly, losing no blue Mondays on account of Sunday's dissipations nor wasting hours on idle holidays." The magazine estimated that the Chinese had saved Sampson $840 a week, or almost $44,000 annually, which, if applied to the rest of the shoemaking industry, would result in national savings of $3.5 million a year.

Widely reported in the press, the North Adams experiment inspired other East Coast capitalists to try Chinese labor. Three months after Sampson imported his Chinese workers, James B. Hervey, owner of the Passaic Steam Laundry in Belleville, New Jersey, brought Chinese laborers from San Francisco to replace his Irish female employees, whose frequent strikes were cutting into his profits. The arrival of these Chinese laborers panicked white workers throughout the eastern states. James Hervey received several threatening letters, one warning that he would be murdered if he did not fire his Chinese employees. When a cutlery factory in Beaver Falls, Pennsylvania, brought in more than a hundred Chinese, some of the town's citizens petitioned Congress, complaining that the use of Chinese labor "shows a manifest attempt to revive the institution of slavery."

Unreasonable panic at what tomorrow might bring was exactly the effect that many capitalists sought to instill in their white workers. Soon after Sampson's success in North Adams, a number of companies convinced striking white workers to return to their jobs—at a 10 percent wage reduction.

But the Chinese were not as docile as the white capitalists had expected. To Hervey's chagrin, his new Chinese workers turned out to be just as militant as the Irish women, and he complained the Chinese were becoming "more and more like their white neighbors." Eventually he lost his enthusiasm for Chinese laborers and in 1885 his assistant discharged all of them.

Hervey could not have foreseen that his decision would plant the seeds of future Chinatowns along the East Coast. Many of his former Chinese employees moved to New York City or to Newark, New Jersey, and from there wrote their relatives, inviting them to join them in opening laundries of their own.

Up to this time, the number of Chinese in New York had been tiny. Some, including former sailors who worked in a variety of occupations, from peddling and candy making to cigar rolling and operating their own boarding houses, had migrated directly from China to the East Coast. According to the 1880 census, 748 Chinese lived in Manhattan, a miniscule number for an urban center with more than 1.2 million people, yet still the largest Chinese community east of the Sierra Nevada. But within just a few years after Hervey let his Chinese workforce go, some two thousand Chinese laundries were operating in metropolitan New York.

The early history of the Chinese on the East Coast was not exclusively one of exploitation and strikebreaking. Early in the nineteenth century, a very different pattern had begun, eventually running parallel to the struggle for economic survival being played out by Chinese workers elsewhere in America. A handful of Chinese intellectuals were admitted to the eastern seaboard's great centers of learning, its preparatory academies and ivy-decked universities. The education these students acquired would later lend them a disproportionate influence on the futures of both the United States and China.

Christian missionaries were instrumental in opening the schools' doors to the Chinese. They not only held Sunday school classes to teach immigrant factory workers the English language, but also followed up by sponsoring programs to help Chinese youths attend eastern high schools and colleges. Even earlier, between 1818 and 1825, a generation before the arrival of the first gold rush Chinese in California, five Chinese youths had come to the United States to study at a mission school in Cornwall, Connecticut. One of the five, Ah Lum, would later become a translator for Commissioner Lin Zexu, who was renowned for burning stockpiles of British opium before the Opium Wars.

Perhaps the most famous nineteenth-century Chinese intellectual who enjoyed missionary patronage was Yung Wing. His story exemplifies the experience of the Chinese émigré scholar, who readily assimilates into American society but always struggles with his identity, especially as his desire to create a stronger China is thwarted by a growing sense of alienation from his people and his homeland.

Yung Wing was born in 1828 in the Chinese village of Nam Ping, a few miles away from the Portuguese colony of Macao. When he was seven, his father enrolled him in a new English missionary school in Macao. His parents, he later wrote, observed that "foreign intercourse with China was just beginning to grow," and anticipated that this might "assume the proportions of a tidal wave." In 1840, when his father died, leaving Yung Wing's mother with four children and no means of support, Yung's education came to an abrupt halt. To help his family, he hawked candy in the streets, labored in the rice paddies, and folded papers in a printer's shop. This might have been the pattern for the rest of his life had not a medical missionary, dispatched by his old school, invited him to study at the Morrison Education Society School in Macao. At Morrison, Yung was befriended by the Reverend S. R. Brown, the American founder of the school, who offered him and a few other students the opportunity to resume their education in the United States. In 1847, Yung and two other Chinese boys arrived on the East Coast and enrolled at the Monson Academy, a renowned preparatory school in southwestern Massachusetts.

In America, Yung resolved to acquire the knowledge he would need to help his homeland. The trustees of the academy offered to fund his college degree if he pledged to become a missionary after graduation, but Yung, both ambitious and stubborn in his convictions, refused to make that commitment. "I wanted the utmost freedom of action to avail myself of every opportunity to do the greatest good in China," he later wrote of his decision. "To be sure, I was poor, but I would not allow my poverty to gain the upper hand and compel me to barter away my inward convictions of duty for a temporary mess of pottage." Remarkably, he prevailed. Thanks to his friend Reverend Brown, Yung found several financial patrons in Savannah, Georgia, and with their support enrolled at Yale in 1850. There he impressed his peers by winning first prize in English composition during two collegiate competitions. In 1854, Yung successfully completed his studies and became the first Chinese graduate of a major American college.

He returned to China and, driven by a sense of his own destiny—and by a certain amount of self-importance—told his mother, "Knowledge is power and power is greater than riches. I am the first Chinese to graduate from Yale College, and that being the case, you have the honor of being the first and only mother out of the countless millions of mothers in China at this time, who can claim the honor of having a son who is the first Chinese graduate of a first-class American college. Such an honor is a rare thing to possess." But as he would soon learn, one man's American college degree was not enough to bring about massive reform in China.

Readjusting to life in China proved much more difficult than Yung Wing had expected. While living with a missionary in Canton, he witnessed firsthand some of the abuses and corruption of the Qing regime. In the summer of 1855 Yung saw the gory result of Manchu suppression of a local rebellion. The viceroy Yeh Ming Hsin had ordered the decapitation of seventy-five thousand people, most of them innocent, and Yung Wing lived only half a mile from the execution grounds. "But oh! What a sight," he recalled. "The ground was perfectly drenched with human blood. On both sides of the driveway were to be seen headless human trunks, piled up in heaps, waiting to be taken away for burial."

His idealism and independence of spirit, no doubt enforced by his exposure to American culture, made it almost impossible for Yung Wing to hold down a full-time job in China. To support himself, he worked first as a secretary to an American, then as a court interpreter in Hong Kong, but later claimed that the British attorneys had conspired to drive him out: "If I were allowed to practice my profession [in law], they might as well pack up and go back to England, for as I had a complete knowledge of both English and Chinese I would eventually monopolize all the Chinese legal business." After a short time, Yung left the snake pit of legal politics in Hong Kong to move to Shanghai, where he worked for the Imperial Customs Translating Department, only to resign again, after just four months. Disgusted by the systematic bribery at every level of the organization, he decided to leave public service altogether. Soon he became a successful tea merchant.

In 1863 he left his prospering tea business to help Tseng Kuo-fan, a powerful imperial viceroy, with industrial plans to mechanize China. He assisted Tseng in creating the Kiangnan Machine Works near Shanghai and journeyed back to the United States to purchase equipment for it. The viceroy was so impressed by the results Yung had achieved that he promised to help him realize his dream of a Western-style education for the Chinese. With the viceroy's support, Yung persuaded the Qing government to send Chinese students to the United States for advanced education and training.

Evolving into a cultural ambassador of sorts, in 1872 Yung became the deputy commissioner of the Chinese Educational Mission, the first officially sponsored exchange program between the two countries. While serving in this capacity he also became China's associate minister to the United States, one of the first official diplomatic links between the two countries. The Chinese Educational Mission brought 120 young Chinese males to America, to study at imperial expense, and these youths, ranging in age from ten to sixteen, boarded in private homes and enrolled in schools throughout New England.

The original plan, as formally proposed by two Chinese viceroys to the Qing court, was to have these boys study in the United States for about fifteen years, preferably at military academies such as West Point and the Naval Academy, and then to have them return to China by age thirty—"the best time to serve their homeland." But what the Qing government did not recognize until much later was that these American-educated students would be internally transformed. Instead of the students returning with Western knowledge that might help China, the reverse occurred: China lost some of its best and brightest minds to the United States.

It was only natural that youths transplanted to a new environment during the most formative years of their lives would be irrevocably changed by the experience. And in the case of the 120 mission students, the change would be profound. These Chinese wasted no time in adapting to New England life. They replaced their scholarly Chinese silken gowns and round caps for Western suits and blue flannel trousers. They tucked their queues out of sight under shirt collars, or sheared them off entirely. They played American sports* and went to parties, dances, and church socials. Many converted to Christianity. As their friendships with white Americans deepened, some, inevitably, dated and married white women.

In 1881, Qing officials abruptly shut down the educational mission, ostensibly because they were insulted by West Point's refusal to

---

*One Chinese student, Chung Mun-yew, became coxswain for the Yale varsity crew team, helping Yale defeat Harvard in 1880 and 1881 in races along the Thames River. Another student, Liang Tun-yen, led a Chinese baseball team to several victories.

consider Chinese applicants, but perhaps even more significantly because they rightly feared that the students were forsaking Chinese values for American ones. But in the end, it was impossible to hold back the currents of change. China's increased exposure to American concepts of freedom and democracy would eventually inspire future revolutionaries to bring about the Qing's downfall, and afterward, in the new Republic of China, the Chinese Educational Mission graduates would assume important positions in government, such as in the diplomatic service and the transportation, naval, and mining bureaus. Just as the Qing had originally intended, the students would bring back their Western knowledge to assist China*—though, ironically, their education would benefit the regime that supplanted the Qing. One student, Tang Guoan, would become the first president of the prestigious Qinghua College in Beijing, while another, Tang Shaoyi, would serve as the first premier of the Republic of China in 1912. A third student, Zhan Tianyou, would apply his training at Yale's Sheffield Scientific School to the design and construction of China's railroads, pioneering an entire industry in his homeland.

For many émigrés, the journey across the United States became a journey of the soul, during which they crossed the invisible line from being Chinese in America to becoming Chinese Americans. The story of their dispersing across America rather than returning to China is not so much a catalog of the jobs they held as a tale of the subtle changes within them, the gradual shifts in attitudes, the decisions to adapt their ancient, well-established culture in order to put down roots in the United States. This transformation occurred across class lines, from manual laborers to merchants to intellectuals. When the

---

*These graduates had the good fortune of witnessing the height of America's industrial and technological revolution during the nineteenth century: during the 1870s, the decade of the mission's existence, Alexander Graham Bell would invent the telephone, and Thomas Edison the phonograph and electric light bulb.

Chinese first came to America, virtually all of them settled in California and worked, either directly or peripherally, in the mining industry. Later, when they moved apart, dividing into smaller groups—and increasing the geographical distance between both individual Chinese people as well as between the subgroups—the change was accelerated, and was often more profound.

Compared to those in the western states, the Chinese communities in the South and Midwest were tiny. In many regions, there simply weren't enough Chinese to form their own Chinatowns, prompting the émigrés to interact more with people of different races. In southern cities, such as New Orleans, the limited number of Chinese made them less threatening to local whites, enabling them to escape the oppressive segregation inflicted on the African American population. The Chinese lived undisturbed with urban whites in southern boarding houses—though it should be noted that many of their neighbors were European immigrants, not native-born Americans. Similarly, in the Midwest, the Chinese did not live in concentrated ethnic neighborhoods like the Italians, Poles, or blacks. Instead, the Chinatown that evolved in Chicago served mainly as a social center for the Chinese spread throughout the city or in smaller towns nearby.

As with all immigration stories, the transformation within each traveler creeps up so gradually that it is difficult, if not impossible, to pinpoint the precise moment in his life when the ultimate change occurred. It usually starts small, such as the decision to use an Anglo name in the United States. (Late-nineteenth-century census data reveal that along the East Coast, some Chinese immigrants had adopted Western first names and even altered their last names.) But the revelation that the change is far more profound than a name scrawled on paper typically arrives during a visit to the ancestral homeland. In America, it is jarring even for people who have moved out of state to visit their hometown after an absence of only a few years. Cherished landmarks have disappeared, family members have aged, a once familiar town of friends is now filled with strangers. The Thomas Wolfe title, *You Can't Go Home Again*, conveys the sense of dislocation. The experience of returning home from another country can be even more startling.

Relatives and old friends are often just as shocked that the émigré is no longer the man who once lived among them. His new habits, his new values, the different way he carries himself, his occasional utterance of English in conversation, are viewed with suspicion. The experience of Lue Gim Gong is particularly instructive. In 1868, Lue left Toishan at the age of ten, first to work in San Francisco and later at the shoe factory in North Adams, Massachusetts. There he befriended Fanny Burlingame, a Sunday school teacher and cousin of the famous diplomat Anson Burlingame. Impressed by his intelligence, Fanny adopted him as her son. Upon her death he inherited $12,000 and two houses in Deland, Florida, in the center of the state's citrus region. In Florida he devoted his life to horticulture, creating the Lue Gim Gong orange, an award-winning orange that could withstand both frost and shipment over great distances without spoilage; the frost-resistant Lue Gim Gong grapefruit; a new kind of sweet apple; the cherry currant; and a greenhouse peach that could be cultivated to ripen before Thanksgiving. Though he achieved acclaim in the United States, Lue found himself in a kind of cultural limbo when he returned to visit his home village. His neighbors viewed him with animosity, baffled by his obsession with conducting agricultural experiments. When Lue pumped water uphill to sustain some orange trees, local farmers destroyed the grove, complaining that the trees blocked their *feng shui*, literally, "wind water," the practice of an ancient Chinese philosophy of design that seeks harmonious balance in the environment. To make matters worse, Lue's parents insisted on marrying him off at this point and selected a suitable bride for him. Against his wishes, his family proceeded with the wedding plans.

On the morning of the scheduled ceremony, Lue fled the village and headed back to the United States, never to return, leaving behind relatives so outraged that they struck his name from the family register—the social equivalent of an American family blotting out the name of a prodigal son from the family Bible.

For many Chinese, the decisive moment when they first recognized that their future lay in America, not China, came when they married outside their race. It was not uncommon for Chinese immigrants to wed non-Asian women in the South. "With few or no Chinese women available, the first and succeeding generations blended through intermarriage with previously recognized ethnic groups," notes historian Lucy Cohen, author of *Chinese in the Post–Civil War South* and herself a child of Chinese-Jewish intermarriage. She points out that marriage between whites and Chinese was more acceptable in the South than marriage between whites and blacks, largely because of the ambiguity of Chinese racial status: no scheme of racial classification had evolved for the Chinese, and as a result they became "a truly 'mixed nation.' "

Interracial marriage was also popular among Chinese intellectuals on the East Coast. Yung Wing married a Caucasian, Mary L. Kellogg, in 1875, and several students in his educational mission violated Chinese government regulations by marrying white women and settling permanently in the United States. (One reason the Chinese government terminated Yung Wing's Chinese Educational Mission was that many Qing officials disapproved of these interracial unions.) During the late nineteenth century, the city of New York also showed a discernible pattern of interracial marriage between Irish women and Chinese men.

Unlike other European immigrants, Irish women often migrated alone, without their families, and sometimes outnumbered Irish male arrivals two to one. It was natural, then, for these women to form relationships with those of an immigrant population that suffered a serious shortage of women. As early as 1857, *Harper's Weekly* took note of the marriages between Chinese cigar vendors and Irish apple peddlers in New York. By the end of the decade, the *New York Times* noted that most owners of Chinese boarding houses were married to either Irish or German women.

A great deal of racial antagonism is an expression of sexual anxiety. This goes back to humankind's earliest days, when tribal conflict often ended with the men of the victorious tribe carrying off the women of the defeated tribe. So it is not surprising that some newspapers took to depicting Chinese men as lascivious creatures preying on innocent, impoverished white girls. Such was the tone of warning underlying a *New York Times* article on December 26, 1873, which described a "handsome but squalidly dressed young white girl" in an opium den. The Chinese owner allegedly told the reporter, "Oh, hard time in New York. Young girl hungry. Plenty come here. Chinaman always have something to eat, and he like young white girl. He! He!"

More frequently, Chinese-white relationships were ridiculed rather than described portentously. In New York, the comedy of actor/theater manager Edward Harrigan featured stereotypical characters like Mrs. Dublin, the Irish washerwoman, and Hog-Eye, the Chinese laundryman. Store windows displayed mechanical toys of Chinese men dancing with Irish women. In March 1858, *Yankee Notions* ran a cartoon on its cover ascribing the following dialogue to a Chinese-Irish couple:

> MRS. CHANG-FEE-CHOW-CHY (the better half of the Celestial over the way): Now, then, Chang-Mike, run home and take Pat-Chow and Rooney-Sing wid ye, and bring the last of the puppy pie for yer daddy. And, do ye mind? Bring some praties of your mother, ye spalpeens. (To her husband) How be's ye, Chang Honey?

> CHANG-HONEY: Sky we po kee bang too, mucho puck ti, rum foo, toodie shee sicke.

Despite these caricatures, the Chinese-Irish marriages seemed to work well. When a *New York World* reporter told two Irish women they should be married to whites, not Chinese, one retorted that their Chinese husbands were as "white" as anyone, even "whiter" than most of their neighbors. Some Chinese husbands were studying English at night, to move up in American society. A writer for the

New York *Sun* described his visit to a Chinese clubhouse and his exchange with a "young and pretty Irish girl, scarcely over eighteen":

> "Today we had a nice dinner, chickens and such things, and the men and their wives are now smoking and drinking sour wine. The wives are all Irish girls. I'm married." "What, married to a Chinaman?" "Certainly," she answered proudly, "married two weeks today." Then laughing outright she went on to say that the Chinamen were all good "fellows," that they work hard, go to night school, and are devoted to their wives.*

Originally, many Chinese immigrants did not plan to fall in love with non-Chinese women. Take the example of Charles Sun, who arrived in California in 1878 and later moved to a small Illinois town to work for his cousin, a laundryman called Fook Soo. While delivering freshly washed clothes, Fook Soo met the daughter of a rich white family and maintained a secret, two-year romance with her. When she became pregnant he skipped town and returned to China to marry a native woman. Feeling compassion for his cousin's abandoned lover (her family immediately disowned her, then grudgingly took her back), Charles Sun offered her financial support, then marriage. Eventually they reared four children together. "It was hard for me to refuse her," he later told an interviewer. "She was so pitiful! I was really in love with her at that period already, even though I had no intention that I should marry a white woman . . . [or spend] my whole life in that little town."

Some Chinese men already had wives back in the old country, because their families had taken the precaution of marrying them off

---

*By 1882, the *Sun* would report that the Chinese "from the fashionable clubs of Mott and Park Street rode . . . in Chatham Square coaches, carrying a liberal supply of liquor and cigars . . . accompanied by their Irish wives, many of them young, buxom and attractive."

before they left for Gold Mountain. And no doubt some loved the Chinese wives they had left behind, and were loyal enough to send them regular remittance checks, year after year. But in time, some Chinese émigrés met other women in America, women who could easily compete for affection with the fading memories of those first wives back in China.

Having a relationship with a non-Chinese woman was often the tipping point in the assimilation process, the point where the émigré first started saying "back in China," rather than "back home." Some men who took American girlfriends, and even some who took new wives, continued to send funds back to their China families, and some didn't. The people in the home villages would carefully make note of this, for though they were thousands of miles apart, they kept tabs on their Gold Mountain men with newsletters and gazetteers. An unspoken agreement soon evolved. As long as the money kept arriving, the village would tolerate infidelity from the men, but not their wives. Even if they wed other women in the United States, the first wives were expected to remain "Gold Mountain widows" if the husband continued to support his children in China. However, if the money flow stopped, the reverse applied—the village was willing to look the other way if the wives chose to remarry.

As the Chinese dispersed across the United States, many left behind mixed-race children. Unfortunately, no systematic studies have traced the lives of these children; indeed, few reliable statistics exist on any of the early Chinese, let alone their descendants. California was the only state in the union to list the Chinese as a separate group in the 1860 U.S. census. In most states, the census counted only whites, blacks, and mulattos, and the Chinese were often classified as either "white" or "black."

Occasional glimpses of these children can be found in scattered newspaper and magazine accounts. "It is very curious to hear the little half-breed children running about the rooms and alternatively talking

Irish to their mothers and Chinese to their fathers," one New York reporter noted. And as these children grew older, they made their own choices about their identity. Some—perhaps most—passed for white and adopted the values of the local community, like the southern-born children of the famous Siamese twins Chang and Eng Bunker. But others embraced the Chinese half of their heritage, such as the two sons of Yung Wing, both of whom graduated from Yale, moved to China, and married Chinese women.

In the South, where Chinese men married white, black, Indian, or Creole women, the ethnicity of offspring was fluid. Their descendants chose to be "white" in certain settings, and "colored" in others; for them, race was not socially mandated, but was rather an individual choice. Lucy Cohen interviewed the grandson of a Chinese settler whose multiracial heritage permitted him access to stores with "Whites only" signs—but who also fit himself into the "Mexican/ Indian" category, so he could "pass for what he wants." Cohen also met the mixed-race granddaughter of a Chinese immigrant who recounted that some of her family members passed for white, either denying or forgetting their heritage, while others retained the memory of their Chinese ancestry. The granddaughter recalled the day her son was called a "nigger" by a distant relative who was even darker-skinned than he was. "That made me angry, and I told him: 'My daddy and your daddy are first cousins, you half-white b——. Our grandparents were Chinese and Creole."

What was the range or depth of emotions these descendants experienced as they came of age? Were some happy with their ability to defy racial pigeonholing—to be accepted by more than one ethnic group? Or were they tormented by a lifelong confusion over identity? Only hints of their feelings can be traced. One of the first to document the psychological turmoil of the mixed-race Asian in America was Edith Maud Eaton. Born in England in 1865, the daughter of a British father and a Chinese mother, Eaton grew up in Canada and later moved to the United States, where she wrote under the pseudonym Sui Sin Far. An early pioneer of Chinese American literature,

Eaton wrote not only about the struggles of the Chinese in the United States against white hostility, but also of her own conflicted feelings about being half-Chinese. Her books are a poignant blend of racial pride, celebration, and despair. In the autobiographical *Leaves from the Mental Portfolio of an Eurasian*, published in 1909, she wrote:

> I have come from a race on my mother's side which is said to be the most stolid and insensible to feelings of all races, yet I look back over the years and see myself so keenly alive to every shade of sorrow and suffering that it is almost a pain to live. Mother tells us tales of China. Though a child when she left her native land she remembers it well, and I am never tired of listening to the story of how she was stolen from her home. She tells us over and over again of her meeting with my father in Shanghai and the romance of their marriage. I glory in the idea of dying at the stake and a great genie arising from the flames and declaring to those who have scorned us: "Behold, how great and glorious and noble are the Chinese people!" Whenever I have the opportunity I steal away to the library and read every book I can find on China and Chinese. I learn that China is the oldest civilized nation on the face of the earth and a few other things. At eighteen years of age what troubles me is not that I am what I am, but that others are ignorant of my superiority.

"Why is my mother's race despised?" Eaton agonized, in a question that was to be shared by generations of other mixed-race children. "I look into the faces of my father and mother. Is she not every bit as dear and good as he? Why? Why?"

CHAPTER EIGHT

Rumblings of Hatred

R acial and ethnic tensions simmer just below the surface in virtually all multiethnic societies, but it usually takes an economic crisis to blow off the lid of civility and allow deep-seated hatred to degenerate into violence. When our livelihoods are at stake, when we are desperate, when families are uncertain where their next meal is coming from, when adults fear for the futures of their children, it is natural to ask why fortune has treated us so cruelly. And in these moments, we are all vulnerable to explanations that easily assign blame to some outside group. Perhaps it goes back to our primitive origins, when in threatening times our personal safety was best assured by sticking with our own tribe. But for whatever reasons, a general rule of history seems to be that the more people feel insecure about their own well-being, the more likely they will join with those of close affinity in striking out at some alien group.

In the 1870s, when America slid into a nationwide depression, the Chinese became that scapegoat, especially in regions where they clustered in the greatest numbers. During an earlier era of prosperity, some Chinese might have been lulled into a false feeling of security when they moved into white neighborhoods or signed contracts with white businessmen. But when the prosperity vanished, the Chinese had to face just how resented, even loathed, they were by their white neighbors and competitors.

Nowhere was that resentment greater than in the state of California, where all the ingredients for racial unrest came together. The gold disappeared and with it all those businesses that supported mining and prospecting. The railroad was complete and the men who had built it found themselves out of work. Thousands of ex-miners and discharged track laborers, white and Chinese, roamed the region in search of jobs. Even if the local economy been able to absorb these shocks, with the end of the Civil War came the end of the national manpower shortage. Now, former Union and Confederate soldiers were back home, eagerly looking for work, and some headed west, to the Golden State of California.

Before the war, the expense and inconvenience of intercontinental travel would have deterred all but the most resolute from reaching the West Coast, but the new railroad made it easy for job-seekers to come, disgorging a steady stream not only of Civil War veterans from the East and South, but of newly arrived immigrants from Europe. Even though cities like San Francisco and Los Angeles were growing rapidly, they did not have enough work for them all.

Worse, the transcontinental railroad did not bring the prosperity that many in California had hoped it would. While it did open eastern markets to western manufactured goods and some agricultural products, it also allowed shipment of inexpensive eastern products *into* California, which hurt local industries. The new factories in San Francisco were no match for the older, more established factories on the East Coast, and those who had traveled west to escape eastern sweatshops and mill towns, to seize new opportunities and build new lives, found instead mass unemployment and ruthless competition for jobs. Many of the competitors for these jobs were Chinese, and by the end of 1870 there were one Chinese and two whites for every job in San Francisco.

As would be expected, many California businessmen, eager to cut costs in hard times, hired the Chinese because they were usually willing to work longer hours for less than half the pay. Further exacerbating racial tensions, some businessmen also used the Chinese as strikebreakers, just as had been done on the East Coast. In 1870, a traveler reported, "In the factories of San Francisco they had none but Irish, paying them three dollars a day in gold. They struck, and demanded four dollars. Immediately their places, numbering three hundred, were supplied by Chinamen at one dollar a day."

For struggling Irish workers engaged in a strike to secure decent wages for themselves, it must have been galling to witness the sheer number of Chinese willing to serve as scabs. Of course, most Chinese were likely unfamiliar with the concept "scab," and in addition owed no allegiance or support to a union that would not have them as members. Nevertheless, the tensions between the two immigrant groups rose. In September 1870, the *Overland Monthly* published a humorous poem by the famous newspaperman, writer, and poet Bret Harte that depicted the growing animosity between the Irish and the Chinese. The verse was originally titled "Plain Language from Truthful James," but eventually came to be known almost exclusively as "The Heathen Chinee." It recounts a card game between two fictional characters: Ah Sin, a Chinese man, and William Nye, an Irishman. Even though Nye blatantly cheats with cards stuffed up his sleeves, he keeps losing to Ah Sin. Finally Nye, losing patience, shouts, "We are ruined by Chinese cheap labor!" and then assaults Ah Sin, knocking hidden cards out of the Chinese man's sleeves.

Which group did Harte intended to ridicule more, the Chinese or the Irish? If his poem depicted the former as crafty cheaters, it mocked the Irish as inept ones, forced to resort to violence after losing to the Chinese, even after excessive cheating. Whatever Harte's intention, "The Heathen Chinee" struck a chord deep within the American psyche and became the country's most popular poem in the 1870s. It was set to music and reprinted in virtually every newspaper in the county. Newsstands sold illustrated copies of the poem as pamphlets. The *New York Globe* published it twice, and in January 1871 the paper reported that hundreds of people had gathered to see a version of "The Heathen Chinee" displayed in a shop window: "In all our knowledge of New York nothing like this has ever been seen on Broadway." Bret Harte and Mark Twain even collaborated to bring "The Heathen Chinee" to the stage, under the title *Ah Sin*.

But underneath the laughter provoked by the poem was tremendous fear of the Chinese, especially in California. Everything about the Chinese—their physiognomy, their language, their food, their queues—struck many whites as bizarre, making it easy to demonize them. Large numbers of whites, seeing their livelihoods threatened by Chinese competition, began to feel as if the Chinese were somehow part of a giant, secret conspiracy to undercut the American working man. They complained, with some basis in fact, that the Chinese worked for less money, rarely spent what they had, and tended to keep their capital within the community, shopping at Chinese groceries and importing their food from China. They also believed that the Chinese who sent part of their money home to China were draining the country of its currency, its very lifeblood, while they ignored the larger contributions made by these Chinese in America. Anti-Chinese clubs soon flourished throughout California, pressuring officials in San Francisco to pass a series of municipal ordinances against Chinese residents, designed to drive them out of the city.

One was the 1870 Cubic Air law, which required lodging houses to provide at least five hundred cubic feet of open space for each adult occupant. On its face the law was not discriminatory, but it was flouted in poor white neighborhoods across the city while rigorously enforced in the Chinese section of San Francisco. City officials routinely arrested Chinese in the middle of the night, dragging them from bed and driving them "like brutes" into prison. Ironically, the local government violated its own cubic-air ordinance when it herded the Chinese into jail, where, as one newspaper noted, each Chinese enjoyed only twenty cubic feet of space. As an act of passive resistance, many refused to pay the fine, in essence staging jailhouse sit-ins. The San Francisco board of supervisors retaliated with the infamous "queue ordinance": each male prisoner who did not pay his fine would have his hair shaved within an inch of his scalp. This ordinance devastated the morale of the Chinese, for a shorn head in their homeland was a mark of treason and occasioned a complete loss of caste.

Another discriminatory measure was the 1870 "sidewalk ordinance," which made it a crime for anyone to walk through the city carrying over his shoulder a pole with baskets at each end. Of course this order was aimed at the Chinese, who were seen throughout the city delivering clean laundry in this manner. The city also required all laundries with a horse-drawn vehicle to pay a license fee of two dollars a quarter, those with two such vehicles four dollars a quarter, and those with *no* vehicles at all—as was the case with virtually all Chinese laundrymen, who delivered on foot—*fifteen dollars* a quarter. The clear intent of these laws was to damage, if not destroy, the Chinese laundry industry.

Chinese immigrants were especially vulnerable during this time because they could not vote. Although the Fifteenth Amendment guaranteed that "the right of citizens of the United States to vote shall not be denied or abridged by the United States or by any State on account of race, color, or previous condition of servitude," in 1870, the year the amendment was ratified, Congress deliberately withheld the right of the Chinese to naturalize, a necessary step to participation in elections, declaring that Asians were "aliens ineligible for citizenship." The American-born male children of Chinese immigrants could one day vote, because their birth on U.S. soil conferred automatic citizenship, but most were too young to cast the ballot, and there were too few of them to make a difference even if they could. Thus the adult Chinese population was locked out of the entire political process—taxed, but unable to elect those who passed laws governing their lives. White politicians had little incentive to address the needs and interests of the Chinese, because the Chinese could not express their gratitude or displeasure at the polls. And as anti-Chinese clubs appeared among white workers and grew in number and influence, no Californian could hope to be elected to office unless he shared, or pretended to share, anti-Chinese sentiments. Inevitably, such feelings, blatantly pandered to by political leaders, would flare into open violence, especially since the Chinese in California were barred not only from the ballot box, but from court witness stands as well.

On October 24, 1871, the Chinese in Los Angeles fell victim to mob violence following an episode of gang warfare. It was believed that the incident, known as the Chinese Massacre, started when two Chinese tongs battled over a beautiful Chinese woman. A white police officer, hearing gunfire in Chinatown, in a neighborhood known as Nigger Alley, approached the scene to investigate. Someone fired a shot at him, and the officer, wounded and bleeding, called out for help. Despite warnings from onlookers that "the Chinks are shootin'," a white man rushed out to assist him, and he was promptly killed in the crossfire. By this time a furious mob of several hundred men had gathered, eager to take revenge on the entire Chinese community. "American blood had been shed," one member later recalled in a letter. "There was, too, that sense of shock that Chinese had dared fire on whites, and kill with recklessness outside their own color set. We all moved in, shouting in anger and as some noticed, in delight at all the excitement."

With howls of "Hang them! Hang them!" the mob dragged innocent Chinese residents from their houses, gunned them down, lynched them in the streets. They looted houses in search of gold, cut holes in buildings at random and fired their pistols inside. As many as two dozen Chinese may have been murdered. A highly respected Chinese doctor, who begged in both English and Spanish for his life, ended up dangling from a noose, his money stolen and one of his fingers cut off by a mob impatient to steal the rings he wore. The rioters also seized a young boy, whose fate was described by journalist P. S. Dorney: "The little fellow was not above twelve years of age. He had been a month in the country and knew not a word of English. He seemed paralyzed by fear—his eyes were fixed and staring, his face blue, blanched and idiotic. He was hanged."

Public hatred for the Chinese, exposed in fits of blood lust and glee, intensified as the economy worsened from overspeculation. The failure of a major eastern banking house led to the Panic of 1873, which ignited the first great industrial depression in the United States. Factories on the East Coast and in the Midwest shut down, pushing more Americans westward in search of work.

To escape the bleak job prospects of the cities, some whites retreated to the countryside, hoping to work as small farmers, but there, too, they encountered Chinese competition, which, given the social and financial disruption of the time, was contorted to feed the notion that the Chinese were the tools of a giant conspiracy. During the construction of the transcontinental railroad, the U.S. government had granted the project some ten million acres, with the stipulation that the property later be sold to the people. Yet when the time came, individual tracts were offered only at outrageous prices far beyond the reach of the typical American family farmer. Instead, railroad moguls kept the land for speculation, selling plots to the wealthy, many of whom used teams of Chinese labor to develop them into arable land.

After the war, the industrial strength of America and its resources were increasingly controlled by monopolies, or trusts, managed by financiers who understood that reducing competition meant greater profits. Lacking the resources to fight the railroad monopolies, the land speculators, and other industrial giants, white Americans felt backed into a corner and lashed out at the Chinese. In San Francisco, white workers began to hold anti-Chinese demonstrations. Marchers carried placards with slogans like "WE WANT NO SLAVES OR ARISTO-CRATS" and "THE COOLIE LABOR SYSTEM LEAVES US NO ALTERNATIVES STARVATION OR DISGRACE" and "MARK THE MAN WHO WOULD PUSH US TO THE LEVEL OF THE MONGOLIAN SLAVE WE ALL VOTE." San Francisco businessmen who hired Chinese employees soon faced boycotts, arson, and physical intimidation.

In such emotionally driven conflicts, reason is often an early casualty. Some whites tried to blame a myriad of social problems on the Chinese, arguing that they filled American prisons, almshouses, and hospitals. The statistical reality was precisely the opposite: the

Chinese, so often singled out for discriminatory taxes, shouldered more than their share of the total tax burden, yet they were regularly turned away from hospitals and most other public institutions in San Francisco. According to Otis Gibson, a missionary in the city, in 1875 Chinese represented less than 2 percent of the patients at the San Francisco city and county hospital, while more than 35 percent of the patients had been born in Ireland. More significant, he wrote that in a single year, the number of European immigrants to the United States was than twice the number of Chinese who had entered the country in the previous twenty-five years. The United States also harbored more Europeans at public expense in hospitals, asylums, prisons, and other reform institutions than the average number of immigrants from China within a whole year. The anti-Chinese activists, he argued, were "chasing a phantom."

But none of this stopped the opponents of the Chinese from making outrageous claims. Some white doctors lent credibility to the anti-Chinese movement by suggesting that the Chinese brought inexplicable diseases to the United States. Back in 1862, Dr. Arthur Stout had published *Chinese Immigration and the Physiological Causes of the Decay of the Nation*, arguing that the Chinese posed a serious health hazard. In 1875, the American Medical Association even supported a study that attempted to measure the role of Chinese prostitutes in spreading syphilis in the United States—an investigation that turned up nothing unusual. The absence of hard facts, however, did not deter the president of the AMA from charging that "even boys eight and ten years old have been syphilized by these degraded wretches," or prevent a medical journal from publishing an editorial under the title "How the Chinese Women Are Infusing a Poison in the Anglo-Saxon Blood." If data could not be found to substantiate certain claims, doctors enthralled and inflamed by racial hostility heightened the public's terror by resorting to nonscientific, mythic images of the Chinese. As one historian observed, many experts from that era considered Chinese disease as "the result of thousands of years of beastly vices, resistant to all efforts of modern medicine."

Engulfed by such a tide of white hostility, some Chinese expressed regret at emigrating in the first place, but admitted that they lacked the resources to return to their homeland. Sensing a future bloodbath in their communities, they began to stockpile weapons, as if preparing for war. Pawnbrokers in San Francisco reported selling huge quantities of bowie knives and revolvers to Chinese customers. In 1876, one dealer in the city supplied sixty pistols to the Chinese community in a single day. Chinese businessmen, anxious for tensions to cool off for a while, began to warn their countrymen to stay away from the United States. On April 1, 1876, the Chinese Six Companies issued a manifesto:

> [The Chinese] expected to come here for one or two years and make a little fortune and return. Who among them ever thought of all these difficulties,—expensive rents, expensive living? A day without work means a day without food. For this reason, though wages are low, yet they are compelled to labor and live in daily poverty, quite unable to return to their native land . . . It is said that the six companies buy and import Chinamen into this country. How can such things be said? Our six companies have, year after year, sent letters discouraging our people from coming into this country, but the people have not believed us, and have continued to come.

For many Chinese, there was little they could do except hang tight and wait for things to get better. Instead, matters grew worse— much worse. In 1877, two unexpected events caused the stock market to plummet. The first was a severe drought that destroyed fruit, wheat, and cattle farms in the American West; the second was the sudden decline of Nevada's Comstock Lode, where the silver output was reduced to a third of its former level. San Franciscans, whom gold rush history had selected for their recklessness, were among the most aggressive stock speculators. When the financial markets crashed, many lost their entire life savings. Members of all classes—railroad tycoons, professionals, shopkeepers, clerks, domestics—were left heavily in debt or impoverished. During the winter of 1876, there were already some ten thousand unemployed men in the city; now more people roamed the streets, competing for what little work existed. As always in dire times, newcomers—bankrupt miners, former farm laborers, immigrants from Europe—drifted into the cities, desperate for a little income, angry and bewildered by the turn of events.

Against this backdrop of despair, an immigrant Irishman named Denis Kearney rose to power. Kearney, a young sailor, had invested heavily in mining stocks and lost everything in the crash. Bankrupt and embittered, he started haranguing whoever would listen in a huge vacant lot, known to locals as "the sandlots," near San Francisco's city hall. At first his audience consisted of a few vagabonds and stragglers, but when disgruntled workers took to gathering routinely at the sandlots at night, the crowds swelled to thousands. By the glow of bonfires and torches, sandlot orators stoked the anger of the crowds by showing just how, and by whom, their lives had been stolen from them. The method was conspiracy, and the thieves were the railroads, the corporate monopolies, and the Chinese.

A gifted demagogue, the thirty-one-year-old Kearney soon became a crowd favorite, prescribing violent solutions for those with the courage to take matters into their own hands. "Before I starve in a country like this, I will cut a man's throat and take whatever he has got," he announced. He urged workers to "tear the masks from off these tyrants, these lecherous bondholders, these political thieves and railroad robbers, when they do that they will find that they are swine, hogs possessed of devils, and then we will drive them into the sea." While making threats, he would strip off his coat, as if preparing for physical combat. He advocated the overthrow of the government and promised to lead a mob into city hall, where they would eliminate the police, hang the prosecuting attorney, burn the law books, write new laws for workingmen. He talked about lynching railway moguls and suggested exterminating the Chinese population by dropping balloons filled with dynamite over Chinatown. He apparently knew his psychology, ending his speeches with the rallying cry of "The Chinese must go!"

Social commentators found it ironic that the most visible spokesman of the anti-Chinese lobby was an Irishman, for only a generation earlier, in the 1840s and 1850s, Irish émigrés had faced the hysteria of the Know-Nothing movement. Help Wanted signs often carried the postscript "NINA," for "No Irish Need Apply." "A while ago it was the Irish," Robert Louis Stevenson observed in *The Amateur Emigrant.* "Now it is the Chinese who must go." Nonetheless, Kearney's antics turned him into an overnight celebrity. His fiery rhetoric and street theater were cathartic for thousands of frustrated laborers in California, many of them Irish, and in 1877 they formed the Workingmen's Party of California and elected Denis Kearney president.

Some Chinese immigrants had the misfortunate to arrive in San Francisco at the very peak of this hysteria. In an 1877 account, one observer painted a vivid picture of what the Chinese newcomers faced as they stepped off the docks. On their way to Chinatown, he said, the harassment they endured from whites was like "running the gauntlet among the savages of the wilderness": "They follow the Chinaman through the streets, howling and screaming after him to frighten him. They catch hold of his cue [sic] and pull him from the wagon. They throw brickbats and missiles at him, and so, often these poor heathen, coming to this Christian land under sacred treaty stipulations, reach their quarter of this Christian city covered with wounds and bruises and blood." During that dark era, Andrew Kan recalled, "When I first came, Chinese treated worse than dog. Oh, it was terrible, terrible . . . The hoodlums, roughnecks and young boys pull your queue, slap your face, throw all kind of old vegetables and rotten eggs at you."

The Chinese lived in fear, knowing they could be killed at any moment, quite likely with no punishment for the assailants. "We were simply terrified," Huie Kin recalled of San Francisco in the 1870s. "We kept indoors after dark for fear of being shot in the back.

Children spit upon us as we passed by and called us rats." Just to walk outdoors was to risk assault. J. S. Look had similar recollections. "I remember as we walked along the street of San Francisco often the small American boys would throw rocks at us," he said. In the evenings, "all the windows in the Chinese stores had to be covered at night with thick wooden doors or else the boys would break in the glass with rocks."

The small towns of California were getting to be as dangerous as the cities—perhaps even more so, because of their isolation. Threatened by the inexpensive labor provided by the Chinese, white workers began to burn down Chinese homes in central California and to torch the barns and fields of landowners who refused to discharge their Chinese field hands. On March 13, 1877, a group of armed white men broke into a cabin in Chico, California, where they shot to death five Chinese farm workers, then poured oil over the bodies and set them ablaze. One of the killers later confessed that he had acted under orders from the Workingmen's Party.

In July 1877, the mounting tension exploded into a full-fledged pogrom, perhaps the worst disturbance in the history of San Francisco. Ten thousand agitators gathered in the city to voice their support for an eastern railway strike that had spilled over into a nationwide labor rebellion. The meeting deteriorated into anarchy when an anti-Chinese club took center stage and whipped the audience into a frenzy of rage. With cries of "On to Chinatown!" they rampaged through the city, wrecking Chinese laundries, setting fire to Chinese buildings, and shooting Chinese bystanders in the streets. By morning, the National Guard had been summoned, backed by a militia of several hundred volunteers, but they could not stop the violence. The mob tried to burn the docks and the ships of the Pacific Mail Steamship company (for transporting thousands of Chinese immigrants to California), and even assaulted firemen attempting to extinguish the flames. Finally, with help from the United States Navy, four thousand volunteers fought the arsonists through a third day of riots, which left four dead and fourteen wounded.

Anti-Chinese feeling may have been the most evident in California, but it also swelled along the East Coast. During an 1877 strike of cigar makers in New York City, manufacturers exploited ethnic antagonism to keep their workers in line. Although the striking cigar makers included Chinese ("Even CHINAMEN," the *New York Labor Standard* declaimed, "have asserted their manhood in this strike and have risen to the dignity of the American trade unionists"), the manufacturers tried to destroy union solidarity by spreading rumors that they would import Chinese scabs. To that end, one employer hired a Chinese man just to walk in and out of his factory, the goal being to have picketers believe that Chinese strikebreakers had already arrived from San Francisco. Another manufacturer hired white men to masquerade as Chinese workers by wearing Chinese clothing and fake queues. Eventually, these ploys succeeded in pitting the strikers against each other. White laborers began to equate scabs with the Chinese: when a white family capitulated and returned to a tenement house to roll cigars, it was greeted with cries of "Chinamen!" The strikers also hanged a scab in effigy with the warning, "So we will serve every Chinaman."

Soon, laws were passed to make it difficult for the Chinese to find any work at all. They could still work for themselves, or for individually owned companies, but not, according to a new law passed after the second California constitution was ratified in 1879, for a corporation: "Any officer, director, manager, member, stockholder, clerk, agent, servant, attorney, employee, assignee, or contractor of any corporation . . . who shall employ in any manner or capacity . . . any Chinese or Mongolian is guilty of a misdemeanor. . . ." As a result of this hostility, many Chinese left the state in a mass exodus in 1880. Some who could afford the passage went back home to China; others traveled across the United States, migrating east over the Rockies by rail, headed for cities in Illinois, Ohio, Pennsylvania, New York, and New Jersey. These departures would continue for the next few decades.

Even this exodus, however, did not satisfy western politicians bent on purging the region of all Chinese presence. Some were determined to pass federal legislation prohibiting the Chinese from entering the United States at all. The anti-Chinese movement achieved a major victory when the Grant administration, under pressure from California politicians, modified the Burlingame Treaty of 1868, which had ensured open emigration from China. In 1879, during his highly publicized world tour, former president Ulysses S. Grant met with Chinese officials in Tientsin to discuss a possible three- to five-year ban on Chinese immigration to the United States. The Qing regime, at the time fearing a military attack from Russia and war with Japan, acquiesced to American demands for a new treaty. Signed the following year, it gave the United States the right to limit, regulate, and suspend Chinese immigration, though not to prohibit it absolutely. The door was now open for passage of a new law, one that would haunt the Chinese American community for generations—the Chinese Exclusion Act.

CHAPTER NINE

The Chinese Exclusion Act

In February 1881, a furious debate raged in the United States Congress when California senator John F. Miller, known for anti-Chinese sentiments, introduced a bill to bar Chinese immigration for the next twenty years. His arguments, intended to damn the Chinese with scorn and disgust, today read like a reluctant paean to the Chinese work ethic, conceding the substantial contributions the Chinese had already made to the building of the American West. Comparing the Chinese immigrants to "inhabitants of another planet," Miller argued that they were "machine-like . . . of obtuse nerve, but little affected by heat or cold, wiry, sinewy, with muscles of iron; they are automatic engines of flesh and blood; they are patient, stolid, unemotional . . . [and] herd together like beasts."

According to Miller, America belonged to white people and white people only. His vision of America was a land "resonant with the sweet voices of flaxen-haired children." Pleading with his colleagues to preserve "American Anglo-Saxon civilization without contamination or adulteration . . . [from] the gangrene of oriental civilization," Miller asserted that group discrimination on the basis of ancestry was natural and sensible. "Why not discriminate? Why aid in the increase and distribution over . . . our domain of a degraded and inferior race, and the progenitors of an inferior sort of men?"

Many of Miller's colleagues wholeheartedly agreed with him, but one senator from Massachusetts rose above the passion of the moment and tried to remind his colleagues of the larger issues involved. George Frisbie Hoar, a progressive-minded leader who had opposed slavery and championed the civil rights of workers, believed that excluding people on the basis of race rather than conduct made a mockery of the high ideals set forth in our own Declaration of Independence. Denouncing racism as "the last of human delusions to be overcome," a force that "left its hideous and ineradicable stains in our history," Hoar blasted the hypocrisy of America's race-baiting politicians: "We go boasting of our democracy, and our superiority, and our strength," he said. "The flag bears the stars of hope to all nations. A hundred thousand Chinese land in California and everything is changed . . . The self-evident truth becomes a self-evident lie."

Few agreed with Hoar, either in Congress or across the nation. His speech provoked condemnation from both the press and the political establishment. "It is idle to reason with stupidity like this," the *New York Times* proclaimed. The *New York Tribune* put Hoar in the class of "humanitarian half thinkers." Legislators from western states pointed out that many of the signers of the Declaration of Independence had owned slaves, and one Colorado lawmaker insisted that the Caucasian race "has a right, considering its superiority of intellectual force and mental vigor, to look down upon every other branch of the human family."

Despite popular support for the bill, President Chester Arthur vetoed it. He claimed the twenty-year ban was too long, but it seems clear that he feared the Qing government might respond to such a law by shutting Chinese ports to American trade. In a speech no doubt intended to fortify diplomatic relations with China, Arthur praised the contributions of the Chinese émigré workers in building the transcontinental railroad as well as in developing industry and agriculture, and he argued the bill's potentially adverse economic consequences. "Experience has shown that the trade of the East is the key to national wealth and influence," he said. "It needs no argument to show that the policy which we now propose to adopt must have a direct tendency to repel oriental nations from us and to drive their trade and commerce into more friendly lands."

The public swiftly retaliated against Arthur. Across the West the president was hanged in effigy, his image burned by furious mobs. Representative Horace Page, another Republican from California known for his anti-Chinese attitudes, immediately introduced a compromise bill that shortened the ban from twenty to ten years. In addition, under Page's bill Chinese laborers would be barred, but select groups of Chinese—merchants, teachers, students, and their household servants—would be permitted to enter the country.

Page's bill passed both houses of Congress. This time, President Arthur, doubtless fully sensitive to the response after his previous veto, did not oppose it. On May 6, 1882, he signed into law the Chinese Exclusion Act. Thus was enacted, as one scholar has put it, "one of the most infamous and tragic statutes in American history," one that would "frame the immigration debate in the years that followed and [result in] greater and greater restrictions on foreigners seeking refuge and freedom in the United States."

Far from appeasing the fanatics, the new restrictions inflamed them. Having succeeded in barring the majority of new Chinese immigrants from American shores, the anti-Chinese bloc began a campaign to expel the remaining Chinese from the United States. During a period of terror now known as "the Driving Out," several Chinese communities in the West were subjected to a level of violence that approached genocide.

For example, on September 28, 1885, delegates at a mass anti-Chinese rally in Seattle issued a manifesto to force all Chinese out of the Washington Territory by November 1. To warn the Chinese of the impending deadline, they formed two committees to deliver the message from house to house in the cities of Tacoma and Seattle. By the end of October, most Chinese laborers had left town, but many merchants, unwilling to abandon their goods, remained.

On the morning of November 3, 1885, hundreds of white men

held good on their promise in a giant raid against the Tacoma Chinatown. They kicked down doors, dragged the occupants outside, and herded six hundred Chinese to the Northern Pacific Railroad train station during a heavy rainstorm, where they kept them without shelter for the night. As a result, two men died from exposure and one merchant's wife went insane; the rest were rescued by the railroad, which transported them safely to Portland.

The secretary of war dispatched troops to Seattle, preventing, temporarily at least, another anti-Chinese pogrom. But it is difficult to assess which posed the greater threat to the Chinese, the mob or the troops. Some soldiers decided to collect a "special tax" from the residents of Chinatown, seizing cash from the people they were sent to protect. Others joined in mob activities, beating up several Chinese, cutting off one man's queue, pushing another down a flight of stairs, throwing still another into a bay.

The following February, months after the troops had left, white rioters in Seattle once again violently ousted the remaining Chinese from their homes. They dragged the Chinese from their beds, ordered them to pack, and marched them to a steamer bound for San Francisco. Even without an angry mob at their heels, most Chinese were anxious to leave town, but they lacked the funds to purchase steamship tickets. Some eighty Chinese who had the cash to pay for passage embarked immediately, while the rest, at least three hundred people, were left shivering on the docks, thronged by a crowd determined to prevent them from returning to their homes. The governor, Watson C. Squire, issued a proclamation ordering the mob to disperse, and volunteers were sworn in as policemen to protect the refugees from physical injury. When the Home Guard escorted the Chinese back to their old neighborhoods, a mob of two thousand rioters attacked them, resulting in gunfire that left one rioter dead and four wounded. After this fracas, President Grover Cleveland declared martial law and dispatched federal troops to Seattle.

In 1885, far worse occurred in a mining community in Rock Springs, Wyoming. The end of the silver boom had created a labor excess in the area, and white miners, unable to compete with the low wages the Chinese accepted, conspired to drive out their competition. Arming themselves with knives, clubs, hatchets, and guns, they headed for the local Chinatown, robbing and shooting the Chinese they met along the way. Once they reached Chinatown, they ordered the residents to leave within one hour. The Chinese quickly packed their belongings, but the white mob grew impatient and began torching shacks, shooting many of those who ran out to escape the fire and smoke. Some of the residents were forced back into the inferno, where they burned to death. Those who managed to escape hid in the mountains, where, exhausted from lack of sleep and food, some died from exposure or were eaten by wolves. Hundreds of stragglers were rescued by passing trains. In the end, the massacre claimed at least twenty-eight lives, and local authorities, unable to quell the riot, called in federal troops to protect the Chinese.

Outraged Chinese diplomats demanded proper action from the United States government, but Thomas Francis Bayard, the U.S. secretary of state, explained that Washington was not responsible for crimes committed in a territory. Later, the American government grudgingly paid $147,000 in indemnities to the Chinese for destroyed property, but failed to bring any of the murderers to justice. During this era, it should be noted, even Chinese diplomats were not safe from violence. In New York in 1880, Chen Lanbing, the Chinese minister to the United States (a position then equivalent to ambassador), was "pelted with stones and hooted at by young ruffians," according to the *New York Times*. The police stood by and laughed.

Then, in the Snake River Massacre of 1887, which the historian David Stratton calls "one of the worst, yet least known, instances of violence against Chinese," thirty-one Chinese miners in Hell's Canyon, Oregon, were robbed, killed, and mutilated by a group of white ranchers and schoolboys intent on stealing their gold and cleansing the region of their presence. A federal official who investigated the crime called it "the most cold-blooded, cowardly treachery I have ever heard tell of on this coast, and I am a California 49er.

Every one of them was shot, cut up, stripped, and thrown into the river." Apparently some body parts were kept as souvenirs; according to Stratton, "a Chinese skull fashioned into a sugar bowl graced the kitchen table of one ranch home for many years." After the state identified the murderers, only three were brought to trial—and all three were acquitted. A white rancher later commented, "I guess if they had killed thirty-one white men something would have been done about it, but none of the jury knew the Chinamen or knew much about it, so they turned the men loose."

Yet perhaps the most hurtful cut was still to come. These episodes of physical violence by local citizenry were followed by federal legislation that further restricted the lives of the Chinese.

Initially, the Exclusion Act had restricted only new Chinese immigration. But two years later, in 1884, Congress amended the act, now permitting only those Chinese laborers who had lived in the United States before November 1880—the date of the last treaty signed with China—the right to travel freely between the two countries. A special certificate was issued promising the émigré that should he leave, he would be guaranteed the right to return. So for those laborers who had arrived before this date, travel out of the country was still an option. But then in 1888, only a few years after amending the Chinese Exclusion Act, Congress broke the promise the United States had made to the earlier-arriving group by passing the Scott Act, which canceled all certificates granting Chinese laborers their right of reentry. Twenty thousand Chinese who had the misfortune to be out of the country when the legislation was enacted were unable to return, despite the previous guarantee from the United States government and the fact that many owned property and businesses here and had families here as well. At the very moment the law went into effect, some six hundred Chinese were on their way back to the United States with government-issued certificates granting them the right of reentry, yet they were not allowed to disembark.

The Chinese minister in Washington strongly protested the Scott Act with the U.S. State Department, which ignored him. As for the discriminatory intent of the act, President Cleveland made it clear that this was its purpose: the experiment of mixing the Chinese with American society had, he noted, proved "unwise, impolitic, and injurious." If the Chinese had any money owed to them in the United States, he added, they could collect it in the American courts, where "it could not be alleged that there exists the slightest discrimination against Chinese subjects."

Was Cleveland being disingenuous? Chinese émigrés immediately challenged the Scott Act in federal court. In *Chae Chan Ping* v. *United States*, a laborer (Chae Chan Ping) who had lived in San Francisco since 1875 and had obtained a legitimate return certificate before departing for China in 1887, was denied permission to disembark upon his return to California on October 7, 1888. His case went all the way up to the Supreme Court, which upheld the Scott Act, ruling that as the United States "considers the presence of foreigners of a different race in this country, who will not assimilate with us, to be dangerous to its peace and security, their exclusion is not to be stayed." Continuing in this vein, the highest court in the land labeled Chinese immigrants a people "residing apart by themselves, and adhering to the customs and usages of their own country." As such, the Chinese in America, the Court decided, were "strangers in the land."

Four years later, in 1892, the Exclusion Act expired, but if anyone had hopes that it would be allowed to die a quiet death, they were disillusioned. Under the Geary Act, which replaced it, Chinese immigration was suspended for another ten years and all Chinese laborers in the United States were now required to register with the government within one year, in order to obtain certificates of lawful residence. Any Chinese caught without this residence certificate would be subject to immediate deportation, with the law placing the burden of proof on the Chinese. The Geary Act also deprived Chinese immigrants of protection in the courts, denying them bail in habeas corpus cases.

Insulted, many Chinese residents refused to comply with the new law. A Chinese consul urged his countrymen not to register, and in cities like Los Angeles and San Francisco the Chinese community ripped up official registration notices. Three Chinese facing deportation under Geary took their case to the Supreme Court. In *Fong Yue Ting* v. *United States,* the Court decided that just as a nation had the right to determine its own immigration policy, it also possessed the right to force all foreign nationals to register. In 1895 the Supreme Court ruled in *Lem Moon Sing* v. *United States* that district courts could no longer review Chinese habeas corpus petitions, a decision that opened the door to all kinds of corruption and abuse by immigration authorities who assumed the unchecked power to bar or deport Chinese immigrants without fear of opposition from the courts.*

In this era of unchecked anti-Chinese passion, even Americans of Chinese descent found themselves subject to extralegal attempts to strip them of their rights—and their citizenship. John Wise, the collector of customs in San Francisco, would accept testimonials only from Caucasians to verify the U.S. citizenship of Chinese Americans. In an 1893 letter to a California lawyer, Wise boasted that his policy made it "almost next to impossible to prove the birth of a Chinese in this country as they never call in a white physician, and twenty years ago, no record of these births were [*sic*] kept."

In 1894, Wong Kim Ark, a twenty-one-year-old Chinese American born in San Francisco, visited his parents in China. Returning the following year, he was denied permission to reenter the country. Once again, despite two setbacks, the Chinese took their case to the courts. Filing a writ of habeas corpus, Wong Kim Ark argued that his

---

*The exclusionists expanded their reach beyond the continental United States into newly annexed territory. In 1898, the U.S. government applied the exclusion laws to the Chinese community on the Hawaiian islands. While the Hawaiians received U.S. citizenship upon annexation, the ethnic Chinese were required to apply for certificates of residence, even though many came from families who had lived on the islands for generations. These measures applied to the Chinese in the Philippines when it, too, became a U.S. territory in 1898.

native birth entitled him to the privileges of American citizenship. His case would also eventually reach the U.S. Supreme Court.

At stake was the very definition U.S. citizenship. Would the Supreme Court embrace the judicial principle of *jus soli* ("law of the soil"), whereby a person obtained citizenship simply by virtue of being born in America? Or would it turn to the racial principle of *jus sanguinis* ("law of blood"), by which the citizenship of a child would be determined by the citizenship of his or her parents? In theory, with the passage of the Fourteenth Amendment, the United States had embraced the right of birthright citizenship, but in practice, the government had failed to protect the full privileges of citizenship of blacks and Native Americans. Legally, the Wong Kim Ark affair forced the Court to determine whether nonwhites born in the United States would be entitled to U.S. citizenship on the same basis as that applied to whites or be relegated to a permanent foreign underclass.

To the credit of the Supreme Court, the majority opinion ruled on March 28, 1898, in Wong Kim Ark's favor, declaring that all children born in the United States are American citizens, even if their parents are ineligible for naturalization. In his dissent, Chief Justice Melville Fuller insisted that all Chinese, native or foreign born, should be ineligible for citizenship, because he believed that no matter where they lived, they owed their allegiance to the emperor of China. But Justice Horace Gray, speaking for the majority, declared, "The fact . . . that acts of Congress or treaties have not permitted Chinese persons born out of this country to become citizens by naturalization cannot exclude Chinese persons born in this country from the operation of the broad and clear words of the Constitution: 'All persons born in the United States, and subject to the jurisdiction thereof, are citizens of the United States.' "*

---

*The Wong Kim Ark case was only one of several important legal battles waged by the Chinese that would pioneer the field of civil rights law in the United States. Another landmark case, *Yick Wo* v. *Hopkins,* would set the standard for equal protection before the law. Between 1873 and 1884, the San Francisco board of super-

Although the Chinese community was relieved by this Supreme Court decision, victory in the courts did not always translate into a new respect for the Chinese community or for the Chinese in America as a people. To the contrary, by the turn of the century, a shameful series of local and federal acts reminded the Chinese that any court ruling, to have meaning, must have the support of local officials prepared to carry out its provisions.

In 1899, U.S. officials in Hawaii learned that a few people had died of plague in Hong Kong. Fearful that the disease had spread to Honolulu, they forbade the local Chinese from boarding ships headed for the continental United States. In addition, the board of health burned down a section of the city's Chinatown. Health officials in San Francisco followed their example, shutting down all Chinese-owned businesses and ordering all Chinese who wished to leave the city to submit to inoculation first. The illegality of these measures prompted a Mr. Wong Wai to sue the department of public health, a lawsuit he won in both the local district court and the court of appeals. In May 1900, the court ordered the San Francisco public health department to cease and desist, but officials persisted in their campaign by enlisting the support of the board of supervisors. Soon, in contravention of the

---

visors passed fourteen anti–Chinese laundry ordinances, one of which was a fire safety ordinance that mandated that all laundry owners in wooden buildings be licensed or risk heavy fines and six months of imprisonment. Since all of the Chinese laundries in the city were housed in wooden buildings, the Chinese viewed the ordinance as discriminatory, designed to cripple their livelihoods. When the board of supervisors rejected virtually every Chinese application for a license, the laundrymen protested by refusing to comply with the law and keeping their wash houses open. In 1885, the board refused to grant Yick Wo, a Chinese laundryman, a license to operate his business, even after he had secured city permits to prove that his building had passed the fire and health inspections. In response, the Chinese laundry guild filed a class action lawsuit that eventually made its way to the Supreme Court, which ruled that while the ordinance appeared to be "fair on its face and impartial in appearance," its enforcement was not. The high court concluded that any law applied in a discriminatory manner, whether to U.S. citizens or foreign aliens, was unconstitutional because it violated the Fourteenth Amendment.

legal order, Chinatown was cordoned off by the police, barricaded, and completely quarantined, while city officials talked about burning and razing it to the ground. It took the combined efforts of the Chinese Six Companies, their attorneys, the Chinese ethnic media, the local Chinese consul, and China's minister (ambassador) to the United States to break the quarantine and save the San Francisco Chinatown from total destruction.

It didn't help the Chinese cause that, just at this time, the Boxer Rebellion was developing in China. Calling themselves "The Boxers United in Righteousness," gangs of impoverished Chinese peasants, blaming foreigners for China's economic ills, besieged and slaughtered white Christians and Chinese converts in northern China as well as white missionaries and diplomats in Beijing. While China's ills were by no means solely attributable to the influence of foreign powers, the Opium Wars early in the nineteenth century had certainly disrupted the country's economy and led to the granting of special economic rights to Great Britain and broad concessions to various other foreign powers in China. It took a combined military force of several Western nations to crush the rebellion, and afterward the Qing government agreed to pay massive indemnities in gold. Even though the Chinese émigrés in the United States had nothing to do with the rebellion, the strain on Chinese-American relations was bound to hurt them. Before the Boxers, the Chinese ambassador could be counted on to argue the case of the Chinese community with Washington. Now, with a weakened China—in effect, a nation that had become almost a subject nation—there was no one with any clout to plead for them.

Nonetheless, the Chinese continued to protest the American policies that targeted them. "We helped build your railroads, open your mines, cultivated the waste places, and assisted in making California the great State she is now," one group of petitioners would write to the president of the United States. "In return for all this what do we receive? Abuse, humiliation and imprisonment. We ask that these things be changed, and that we be treated as human beings instead of outlaws."

But nothing changed, either in the West or in Washington, D.C. When the Geary Act expired in 1902, Congress passed yet another exclusion law, this time extending the period of exclusion indefinitely and continuing to deny naturalization to the Chinese already in the United States. In 1904, Ng Poon Chew, founder of *Chung Sai Yat Po,* San Francisco's first Chinese-language daily newspaper, described what it felt like to be Chinese in America: "all Chinese," he wrote, "whether they are merchants or officials, teachers, students or tourists, are reduced to the status of dogs in America. The dogs must have with them necklaces"—here Chew is referring to the residence certificates—"which attest to their legal status before they are allowed to go out. Otherwise they would be arrested as unregistered, unowned dogs and would be herded into a detention camp."

In 1905, just when it seemed things could not get any worse, the Supreme Court announced its decision in *United States* v. *Ju Toy.*

The Exclusion Acts, both the first and those that followed, it must be remembered, had never fully excluded the Chinese. Even the first act made exceptions for merchants, teachers, students, and their household staffs. So all through this period a limited number of Chinese were entering the country, some as permanent immigrants, others as American citizens who had left the country and were now returning. But in the *Toy* decision, the Supreme Court determined that Chinese immigrants denied entry to the United States, even if they alleged American citizenship, could no longer gain access to the courts to appeal the decision. Instead, it gave the secretary of commerce and labor, who oversaw immigration issues, jurisdiction on this matter. The decision of the secretary, the Court ruled, would be "final and conclusive even when the petitioner alleged U.S. citizenship."

The Supreme Court appeared untroubled by the contradiction between its previous ruling in *Wong Kim Ark* that U.S. citizenship could not be stripped from Americans of Chinese descent, and its new ruling denying due process to citizens by allowing immigration authorities to decide in effect who was and who wasn't a citizen without review by any court. According to a New York judge, immigration officials had so much power that if they wished "to order an alien drawn, quartered and chucked overboard, they could do so without interference."

Not surprisingly, after the Court endowed immigration officials with this power, Chinese admission rates started to plummet. From 1897 to 1899, 725 of 7,762 Chinese who had applied to enter the United States were rejected—about one in ten; then, between 1903 and 1905, the rejection rate rose to one in four.

Oddly enough, the most dramatic protest against America's discriminatory measures was undertaken in China, by a group of activists seeking a ban on American goods and businesses until the exclusion policy was repealed. On July 20, 1905, after the *Ju Toy* decision, the Chinese in Shanghai initiated a full-scale boycott. They quit working for American companies, moved their homes and businesses out of American-owned buildings, and pulled their children out of American schools. Some 90 percent of the businesses in the Chinese district of the city* displayed placards supporting the boycott. Chinese businessmen canceled contracts with American firms and refused to buy or sell American products; demonstrators prevented American ships from unloading their cargos; newspapers refused to run American advertisements.

The boycott spread first to other coastal cities in central and south China—with the Canton region, the homeland for most Chinese in North America, providing plenty of financial support—and then to the interior of the country and abroad. The movement fascinated Chinese from all walks of life; one American traveler, visiting a mountaintop monastery in China, reported that "even the old monks" wanted to talk about it. It also gained the support of overseas Chinese communities throughout Asia and attracted donations from the Chinese in the United States and Hawaii, where mass meetings and

---

*Shanghai was divided at the time into Chinese districts and international settlements, where Western foreigners enjoyed extraterritorial rights.

fund-raisers were held to sustain the boycott. This was one of the rare occasions when diverse groups of Chinese in the United States—the mercantile elite, the laborers, the journalists, Christians, even the tongs—put aside their differences and worked together toward a single goal.

So effective was the boycott that it devastated many American businesses in China and deprived the United States of some $30 million to $40 million worth of trade. It hurt textile mills in the American North and cotton plantations in the South. In Canton, Standard Oil's sales plummeted from about 90,000 cases of fuel monthly to 19,000. So low had American firms fallen in esteem that the British American Tobacco Company found it difficult to even give away free cigarettes to its agents in China.

A year after the boycott began, the U.S. government stepped in, pressuring the Manchu government to put it down. The royal family, still reeling from its humiliation in the Boxer Rebellion, acceded to U.S. pressure, no doubt fearing retaliation if it did not act and act quickly. It is likely that the government was inclined to move against the boycotters for another reason as well. At the time, the boycott was directed solely against foreigners, but the possibility was real that it could quickly turn into a domestic revolution that might topple the throne. The Manchus issued an imperial edict to crush the boycott.

Nonetheless, the embargo had made its point, not just in China but in the United States as well, which did not end the policy of exclusion, but did ameliorate its worst abuses. President Theodore Roosevelt issued an executive order to immigration officials to stop abusive treatment of Chinese merchants and other legitimate visitors, along with a warning that any official caught mistreating Chinese who had the proper paperwork would be dismissed. The U.S. government shortened delays in processing arrivals, discarded a proposal for a new round of Chinese registrations, and scrapped the humiliating Bertillon system of identification, instituted in 1903, which required detailed measurements of the nude body. The results were immediately apparent. In 1905, immigration authorities had rejected 29 percent of the certificates approved by American consuls in China; in 1906, after the boycott, they rejected only 6 percent.

But even more important, Roosevelt used his bully pulpit to set a new tone for the treatment of the Chinese in America. Speaking before Congress, the president noted, "Much trouble has come during the past summer from the organized boycott against American goods," and warned, "We must treat the Chinese student, trader and businessman in a spirit of broadest justice and courtesy if we expect similar treatment to be accorded to our own people of similar rank who go to China."

The cumulative effect of the restrictive immigration laws sharply decreased the number of new immigrants. In 1883, one year after the passage of the Exclusion Act, 8,031 Chinese managed to enter the United States. We do not know how many of these were immigrants returning from visits to China and how many were first-time arrivals. In 1884, the number dropped to 279; in 1885, 22. In 1887, a total of ten Chinese arrived in the United States. The new immigrants were virtually all from privileged classes—scholars, merchants, professionals, and diplomats. At the same time, the Chinese in America began an exodus out of the country to avoid persecution and massacre. Between 1890 and 1900, the number of male Chinese in the United States (at that time 95 percent of the Chinese population) dropped from 103,620 to 85,341.

An unknown number of Chinese tried to circumvent the exclusion laws, risking their savings, even their lives, in order to enter the United States. For no matter how bad things were in the United States, the opportunity to earn more money outweighed the risks. Some migrated first to Canada, Mexico, or the Caribbean, and then tried to smuggle their way into the United States by train or boat. Many of them did not make it. The files of border patrols from that era include stories of capsized boats and Chinese nearly drowning, of Chinese hiding in rice bins on steamers bound for America. "They would stab through the rice and you might be killed in the process," one immigrant recalled. "Sometimes you had to hide in a coffin, and

Afong Moy, the first recorded Chinese woman in the United States, appeared as a museum exhibit in New York during 1834 and 1835. Some of the first Chinese in America came as performers for theaters and circuses.
(Museum of the City of New York)

Chang and Eng Bunker, two of the earliest Chinese American celebrities. After years of touring the globe as the famous "Siamese Twins," they acquired U.S. citizenship, married white women, and retired as southern plantation owners. Two of their sons fought in the Confederate army during the Civil War.
(Hulton Archive)

Chinese passengers on board the Pacific Mail steamship *Alaska*. This 1876 engraving captures a glimpse of the first wave of Chinese emigration to America.
(California History Room, California State Library, Sacramento)

The Burlingame delegation in 1868. Anson Burlingame (*center*) was the U.S. minister to China whose diplomacy led to a treaty to promote free emigration between the two countries. (*Corbis Bettmann*)

Chinese workers on a Louisiana sugar plantation. After the Civil War, white southern plantation owners toyed with the possibility of replacing black slavery with Chinese labor. The plan backfired when the Chinese used translators to negotiate their work contracts and sued employers who violated them. (*The Historic New Orleans Collection*)

Chinese miners panning for gold in California. During the gold rush,
thousands of first-wave Chinese immigrants arrived to seek their
fortune in *Gum Shan*, or "Gold Mountain."
(Hulton Archive)

Occasionally, feuds between Chinese immigrants broke out during the gold rush. On
July 15, 1865, two rival tongs went to war in Weaverville, California.
(Hutchings' California Magazine, California History Room, California State Library, Sacramento)

Chinese transcontinental railroad workers in the Sierra Nevada. During the construction of the Central Pacific Railroad, the Chinese received the least pay for the riskiest work, and used nitroglycerin to blast a path along granite cliffs. By the time the railroad was finished, almost one in ten Chinese laborers had died from the effort.
(California State Railroad Museum)

A Chinese laundry in Delamar, Idaho, during the 1870s. In the male-dominated frontier of the American West, first-wave Chinese immigrants found a profitable economic niche by offering domestic services to other pioneers. Here, a laundryman relaxes by playing a Chinese guitar in front of his shack.
(Idaho State Historical Society)

In the Pacific Northwest, fish canneries employed Chinese workers until their labor was replaced by a machine dubbed the "Iron Chink."

(Manuscripts, Special Collections, University Archives, University of Washington Libraries, UW9422)

Chinese workers in a packing shed in the Sacramento delta of California. In western states, landowners exploited cheap Chinese migrant labor to develop agriculture. By 1886, almost nine out of ten farm workers in California were Chinese.
(Frank Cowsert)

A Chinese-owned store. Merchants endured low rank in China but enjoyed higher status in the United States.
(Arizona Historical Society, Tucson, AHS #78213)

The bachelor society of San Francisco Chinatown. Most of the nineteenth-century Chinese immigrants were men.
(Library of Congress, Arnold Genthe collection)

A prostitute in San Francisco Chinatown, circa 1896–1906. The split-family migration patterns of the early Chinese created a lopsided gender ratio in the United States. The shortage of Chinese women caused brothels to flourish.
(Library of Congress, Arnold Genthe collection)

A young Chinese American bride in Boise, Idaho. Although the picture was taken in 1927, the style of the wedding costume dates back to the previous century.
(Idaho Historical Society)

Typically, only the wealthiest Chinese men could afford to support families in the United States. In San Francisco Chinatown, Lew Kan, a labor manager and store owner, strolls with his two sons, resplendent in satin and velvet.

(Library of Congress, Arnold Genthe collection)

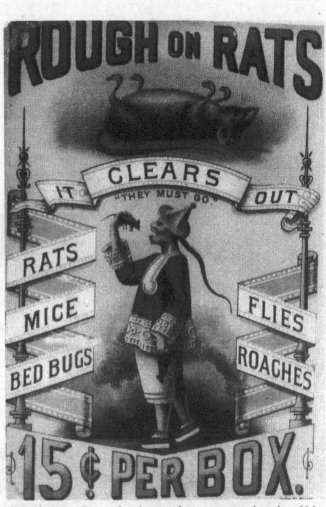

"Rough on Rats"—an advertisement for a pest-control product. Using the popular anti-Chinese slogan of the era ("They Must Go"), the ad suggests the Chinese not only ate vermin, but were themselves a form of vermin that deserved to be exterminated.

(Daniel K. E. Ching collection, Chinese Historical Society of America, San Francisco)

During the economic depression of the 1870s, white workers began to blame Chinese competition for the high rate of unemployment. As anti-Chinese feeling grew, the American media depicted Chinese immigrants as opium addicts and rat-eaters, crowded together on bunk beds to save money. In 1878, *Puck* magazine published this racist lithograph with the caption "A Picture for Employers. Why They can live on 40 cents a day, and They can't."

(Library of Congress)

As the depression deepened, anti-Chinese riots erupted in San Francisco. The Working-men's Party, led by demagogue Denis Kearney, held mass demonstrations on the "sand lots" of San Francisco.
(Hulton Archive)

In a period known as the "Driving Out," white workers assaulted, tortured, and murdered Chinese immigrants in settlements across the American West. One of the worst outbreaks of violence occurred in Rock Springs, Wyoming, when the Union Pacific hired Chinese labor to replace white strikers in the coal mines. A mob killed twenty-eight Chinese before federal troops arrived to restore order.

("*Massacre of the Chinese at Rock Springs*," Harper's Weekly, *September 26, 1885, California History Room, California State Library, Sacramento)*

The 1906 San Francisco earthquake reduced Chinatown to rubble, but opened the door to illegal Chinese immigration. The destruction of the city's birth records permitted some Chinese to emigrate during the exclusion era: they could buy false papers and assert they were children of U.S. citizens fathered during visits to China. Such immigrants, mostly men, were known as "paper sons."
(Library of Congress, Arnold Genthe collection)

The San Francisco immigration station in 1923. To detect "paper sons," authorities subjected Chinese newcomers to lengthy interrogations, quizzing them on the details of their family history. One wrong answer could result in deportation.
(National Archives)

you could suffocate to death." A few made it in, but not enough to reverse the decline of the Chinese American population.

Ironically, the event that opened a new immigration window for the Chinese in America was a historic natural catastrophe that changed the lives of Chinese and non-Chinese alike. At 5:13 A.M. on April 18, 1906, an earthquake struck San Francisco. "My cousin and I were asleep in the basement of the store on Washington Street," recalled Hugh Leung, a high school student at the time. "He woke me and I felt the trembling and saw pieces of plaster falling down like water. I thought I was on the ocean. I quickly dressed and ran into the street. The building across from our place collapsed." In panic, thousands of Chinese rushed into Portsmouth Square, a large open space in San Francisco Chinatown. A fire operator on the scene remembers, "It seemed not more than several minutes after the shock before the square was literally packed with hundreds of Chinese, of all ages, sexes and condition of apparel, jabbering and gesticulating in excited terror."

The *Chung Sai Yat Po* newspaper described the ordeal of the residents: "They carried their bundles, walking away but at the same time looking back as they did so, brooding or weeping softly." While the wealthier Chinese, terrified of white violence, fled the city, the poor stayed behind, for want of funds. Haunted by memories of persecution by whites, some were too frightened to seek food and shelter from city relief stations. Others were robbed by the soldiers brought in to maintain order in the city, and still others were ordered by these soldiers to perform physical labor. Uncertain about where to resettle the Chinese, city officials shuffled them from one camp to another, each move drawing howls of protest from whites who feared that the Chinese would stay in their neighborhoods permanently.

Finally the authorities ordered the Chinese to the far corner of the Presidio, and white looters had a field day. Thousands of men, women, and children descended on the charred remains of what was left of Chinatown, hauling away sacks of melted bronze, pitchers and teapots, artworks, and other valuable items. Looting was prevalent everywhere in the city, but because the Chinese were not permitted to return to protect their belongings, thieves rifled the vaults and safes of Chinese-owned banks, homes, and businesses. Army officials stood by with "shoot to kill" orders to prevent the wholesale pillage of the city, but they refused to enforce discipline in Chinatown, arguing they could not tell the difference between genuine thieves and innocent curiosity seekers, a patently ridiculous claim. Contemporaneous accounts suggest that the looters included some of the most prominent citizens in the Bay Area, and the *San Francisco Chronicle* reported that they included "high railroad officials," "society people in Oakland and San Francisco, and reputable businessmen." The plunderers also included members of the military. On April 21, the Chinese consul general in San Francisco protested to the governor that "the National Guard [is] stripping everything of value in Chinatown."

The fire destroyed much of the city, but most important for the Chinese, it destroyed city birth and citizenship records. The loss of these municipal files allowed many immigrants to claim that they were born in San Francisco, not China, thereby enabling them to establish U.S. citizenship. Because all foreign-born children of American citizens are entitled to U.S. citizenship, a Chinese immigrant who managed to convince the American government that he was a citizen could then return to his homeland and claim citizenship for children born in China.* Or he could tell American authorities that his wife in China had given birth to a son, when in reality no child had been born, and then sell the legal paperwork of this fictitious son to a young man eager to migrate to the United States. These so-called immigration slots were sold either through an individual's network of relatives and acquaintances or through emigration firms. Traditionally, these firms—known as Gold Mountain firms—were import/export com-

*Between 1855 and 1934, a child born abroad legally gained U.S. citizenship if his father was a U.S. citizen at the time of the birth, and had lived in the United States before the birth.

panies that also served as travel agencies, hotels, postal carriers, and banks for remittances. As crucial middlemen for Chinese émigrés, they were well placed to act as brokers in the illegal "paper sons" program.

The paper sons phenomenon naturally aroused the suspicions of the U.S. government. Authorities could not help but notice that the ratio of Chinese sons to daughters reported to be born during visits to the motherland was something like four hundred to one. They also commented on the high number of Chinese who alleged American citizenship. One federal judge noted that "if the stories told in the courts [are] true, every Chinese woman who was in the United States twenty-five years ago must have had at least five hundred children." To detect paper sons, the government detained the Chinese at immigration stations and subjected them to lengthy interrogations.

At first, San Francisco officials detained Chinese arrivals in "the Shed," a windowless two-story frame building at the edge of the Pacific Mail Steamship company's pier. The Shed was filthy; one observer reported that it was "overrun with vermin" and that "the odors of sewage and bilge are most offensive." After a period of detention at the Shed, one Chinese merchant declared the Americans "a race of pigs." Even Chinese immigrants in the classes exempt from the exclusion laws—merchants, professionals, intellectuals—faced humiliation upon arrival and then weeks of bureaucratic frustration.

In 1910, the government fenced off ten acres of Angel Island, in San Francisco Bay, as an immigration facility. This island had previously served as a military depot for recruits as well as a detention center for prisoners of the Spanish-American and Indian wars. Officials found its location advantageous for two reasons: as with nearby Alcatraz, the surrounding bay formed a natural barrier to escape; moreover, the physical isolation provided effective quarantine for the communicable diseases that American officials claimed were "prevalent among aliens from oriental countries."

Over the next thirty years, some 175,000 Chinese immigrants, along with arrivals from other countries, would pass through Angel

Island. Approximately 75 to 80 percent of the Chinese were detained until they could prove who they were, which usually required detailed investigations. Though modeled on Ellis Island near Manhattan, for decades the primary immigration gateway for the United States, Angel Island served a much different purpose. Ellis Island was a way station, with most immigrants processed and released within hours, whereas Angel Island was a long-term detention center, where many Chinese were imprisoned for months, even years. Looking back at how each was run, one might say that Ellis Island was operated to facilitate immigration and Angel Island to discourage it.

The Immigration Service used an elaborate process to inspect the Chinese. When a ship docked at San Francisco, the authorities went on board to examine the paperwork of the passengers. A few Chinese might be allowed to disembark, but most were ferried to Angel Island to await a more detailed review of their applications. At the station, government workers separated the men from the women, even if they were married, and then examined them for disease. "They are dumped together as so many animals," an observer wrote:

> There is no privacy whatsoever, and no means of comfort.
> Men and luggage are all thrown together as one . . . In one
> part of the room, in the men's quarters, was a group smoking
> and talking. Quite far away was another group of young boys
> and grown-up men gambling. Some of them were not prop-
> erly dressed and with hair uncombed and appearance not any
> too fresh and alert, the whole place has the appearance of a
> slum, such as I had never seen, even in our much talked of
> "Chinatown."

It was an unlucky immigrant who fell ill at Angel Island. Because hospitals in San Francisco still refused to accept Chinese patients, ailing Chinese were moved into a wooden building near the immigration station that one official called a "veritable firetrap." There were no separate rooms to segregate those with highly contagious diseases from those with milder, more manageable afflictions like trachoma or hookworm. When one Chinese man came down with cerebral spinal meningitis, the immigration authorities pitched a tent for him in a remote area on the island, where he was kept until he died.

Reports of mistreatment soon surfaced. In 1913, quarantine officers imprisoned a group of Chinese students at Angel Island for several days, for no other reason than their arrival in San Francisco by second-class passage. One Chinese man, L. D. Cio, was interrogated by authorities even though he had the requisite paperwork. Officials demanded to see evidence of the means of his financial support, forcing Cio to show them $300 in cash. Not until a telegram was received from the New York YMCA on his behalf (apparently one of his sponsors in America) was Cio considered free and permitted to travel eastward. Later, he described the Angel Island station as "a prison with scarcely any supply of air or light. Miserably crowded together and poorly fed, the unfortunate victims are treated by the jailers no better than beasts. The worst is that they are not allowed to carry on correspondence with the outside."

The Seattle immigration facility was no better. Chinese immigrants complained that inspectors treated them like "cattle," that they were "thrown into a big room with about 75 people," where they were forced to "pack ourselves like sardines" and "sleep on the floor beside an open toilet." "This," they wrote, "was our first impression of America."

And sometimes there wasn't enough to eat. At Angel Island, officials tried to justify scanty meals by claiming that it was customary for the Chinese to eat only twice a day. To protest these conditions, young immigrants held angry demonstrations in the dining room, prompting the Immigration Service to post a sign in Chinese warning inmates not to cause trouble or throw food on the floor. In 1919, the inmates rioted, forcing the government to suppress the disturbance by dispatching troops to Angel Island.

But the interrogations were the worst of all. The immigration process deteriorated into a mind game between inspector and immigrant, whereby American officials tried to identify paper sons or daughters through extensive questioning about their past history and home villages. Many questions were excessively detailed and had nothing to do with a person's right to enter the United States. When a Chinese arrived at the immigration station, paper son or not, he had to remember all the answers he gave to authorities, because he might be quizzed on them later if he left the United States and then tried to return. The transcripts of these conversations often ran for hundreds of pages, yet one wrong answer, no matter how trivial, could easily result in deportation. Even a correct answer might elicit suspicion, such as in the following exchange:

Q: Is your house one story or two stories?
A: There is an attic.
Q: Are there steps to the attic?
A: Yes.
Q: How many?
A: Twelve.
Q: How do you know?
A: I counted them, because I was told you would ask me questions like these.
Q: Then you were coached in the answers to be given? You rehearsed and memorized the information to make us think you are the son of Wong Hing?
A: No, no, no. I was not coached. I am the true son of Wong Hing, my father, who is now in San Francisco. He told me that you would ask me questions like these and that I was to be prepared to answer in the most minute detail.

In this environment, it was inevitable that some inmates cracked under the strain. Separated from their families, interrogated by hostile strangers, and haunted by the fear of deportation, a few lost all control of their senses. The most traumatized tended to be Chinese women separated from their children. "There are many cases at the

Immigration Station now where the Chinese wife of an American-born Chinese citizen is denied admission, while her little infant children are admitted," J. S. Look told interviewers for the 1924 Los Angeles Survey of Race Relations. To handle depression, panic, or hysteria, immigration authorities threw emotionally troubled émigrés into a special isolation room, a tiny windowless closet three feet square, where they were kept in solitary confinement, sometimes for weeks, until they were able to "calm down." These brutal immigration practices continued for decades, causing some Chinese women to attempt or commit suicide.*

Forbidden to communicate with the outside world, some educated inmates wrote or carved poetry on the walls of the immigration station, venting their sorrow, frustration, and rage, sometimes speaking of retribution. An immigrant who signed his work as "One from Taishan" wrote, "Wait till the day I become successful and fulfill my wish! I will not speak of love when I level the immigration station." Another penned the following lines: "Leaving behind my writing brush and removing my sword, I came to America. Who was to know two streams of tears would flow upon arriving here? If there comes a day when I will have attained my ambition and become successful I will certainly behead the barbarians and spare not a single blade of grass."†

---

*There was the infamous "chopsticks slaying case" involving Wong Shee, the wife of a New York merchant. In October 1941, she arrived at Angel Island, where immigration officials separated her from her nine-year-old son. After hearing rumors that she would be deported to China, Wong Shee killed herself by ramming a chopstick through her ear. A few years later, in 1948, thirty-two-year-old Leong Bick Ha hanged herself from a bathroom shower pipe after failing her examination. That same year, Wong Loy tried to leap from the fourteenth floor of an immigration building when told that she would be sent back to China.
†For years, the poetry remained unprotected from the elements. Some, written in pencil, could be easily smudged away, or disappear from flaking paint and water erosion. But a few scholars took the time to preserve the literature of Angel Island—to prevent this delicate legacy from crumbling away. In 1926, Yu-shan Han encountered the poems when he arrived in the United States to study at Boston University. Even though his trip was sponsored by a U.S. senator, immigration officials mistreated Han,

Immigration officials wrote poetry, too, although their verse contained different sentiments from those of the inmates. One inspector composed the following lines of mocking doggerel:

> *Now poor Wong Fong, he feels quite ill,*
> *As I am told by Ling,*
> *And won't eat any nice birds' nests*
> *Nor even will he sing.*
> *So just to make this poor Wong Fong*
> *Feel very good and nice,*
> *I've sent him back to China*
> *Where he can eat his mice.*

Release from Angel Island did not guarantee the Chinese freedom from further harassment by the Immigration Service, for exclusion-era policies gave immigration officials enormous discretion to seize and detain the Chinese as they wished. As the Chinese would soon learn, all it would take was one crime committed by one Chinese individual to tarnish the entire Chinese American community.

In 1909, a young white girl named Elsie Sigel was murdered in New York, her decomposing body found stuffed in a rusty trunk in her apartment. The chief suspect was William Leon, the owner of a chop suey restaurant in Manhattan who had courted Sigel but was believed to have become jealous when Sigel grew attached to another

---

calling him a "chink" and locking him away on Angel Island. While incarcerated, he read the poetry on the walls and, deeply moved, began to copy and translate them. Other efforts were made to record these verses. Detained in 1931, Smiley Jann copied ninety-two poems; the following year, Tet Yee, another inmate, recorded ninety-six poems. Some of these, and others, were later compiled by historians Him Mark Lai, Genny Lim, and Judy Yung in their book *Island: Poetry and History of Chinese Immigrants on Angel Island, 1910–1940.*

Chinese man. By the time Sigel's corpse was discovered, Leon had long vanished, no doubt having fled the city, if not the country. When the authorities threw a dragnet out for Leon, they suspended the constitutional rights of anyone who looked even remotely Chinese.

The memorable aspect of the Sigel case was not the tragedy of the murder itself but how the nation reacted to it, and its long-term consequences for the Chinese community. The New York City police ordered that no Chinese person could leave the city without permission, and those Chinese with railway and steamship tickets were turned away at the stations and docks. Every ship leaving New York harbor was searched, their Chinese crews interrogated. As the investigation rippled across the country and into Canada, officials rounded up Chinese men from Norfolk to Chicago, from Vancouver to Revelstoke, British Columbia, arresting some the moment they stepped off trains. Chinese businesses nationwide were placed under surveillance. In Providence, Rhode Island, the police commissioner even ordered all draperies to be removed from each room, stall, and booth of the city's Chinese restaurants so that the interiors could be viewed from the outside at all times. Japanese Americans were hauled off the streets and harassed by the police. In the end, countless Asians, entirely guiltless, bore the full brunt of suspicion, but the primary suspect, William Leon, was never caught. To the beleaguered Chinese, the Sigel case illustrated just how swiftly their rights could be stripped from them in times of mass hysteria and government-declared emergency.

Even without a sensational murder case in the background, all throughout the 1910s American immigration officials repeatedly raided homes and businesses, without warrants or just cause and at all hours, in searches for illegal aliens. Most of these unjustified searches were failures. In Cleveland, the Chinese complained that more than 90 percent of such raids produced no results—but this fact did not prevent authorities from arresting the Chinese in front of newspaper reporters and photographers, handcuffing them for the benefit of the cameras, and hauling them down to the immigration office, where they were fingerprinted, examined, and measured as if they were dangerous felons.

The public rarely saw the treatment of the Chinese once they were in government custody. Many Chinese later claimed that they were detained for hours, without food or water, sometimes in "solitary, dark confinement." Often they were not permitted access to counsel or even to learn the charges filed against them. The detainees also claimed that the interrogations were timed so that they would miss their meals, in hopes that hunger and exhaustion would disorient them and cause them to give ambiguous answers from which guilt could be inferred.

During raids, inspectors often demanded to see the residence certificates the Chinese needed to stay in the United States. In some cases, the inspectors confiscated them without providing receipts, causing the owners months of agony, knowing they could not prove their legitimate right to reside in the United States. If the Chinese could not produce their certificates, they were expected to explain how they had lost them, which was impossible for many to do. Some immigrants exhausted their entire life savings paying legal bills and hiring detectives to locate witnesses to testify on their behalf.

The deportation process was horrendous. According to a 1913 report compiled by the Chinese Chamber of Commerce and Chinese-American League of Justice of Los Angeles, the Chinese deportees were packed into railroad cars "unfit for the transportation of cattle," poorly fed, and then herded into the holds of ships, where they endured "real torture, especially in the summertime," when the ship sailed close to the equator. With the constant danger of such deportation hanging over their heads, the Chinese were vulnerable to legally sanctioned blackmail and could be fleeced mercilessly by officials and hoodlums alike. White racketeers would fabricate complaints about Chinese merchants and threaten to sue them unless they received payoffs. Many Chinese preferred the illegal payoff to the more expensive legal fees. But some of the worst extortionists were the immigration officials themselves, upon whose whim depended who was admitted or deported; with no restraint on their powers, many officials traded influence and authority for bribes.

Not all white Americans were callously anti-Chinese, and it must be noted that there were some who were seriously troubled by what was being done in their name. In 1916, when Washington could no longer ignore rumors of corruption at Angel Island, the federal government appointed John Densmore, a labor attorney, to head a special investigation. Densmore discovered a smuggling ring and system of graft within the Immigration Service that had been thriving since as early as 1896. "This business had been going on for a number of years and had mounted to colossal proportions in the number of Chinese illegally admitted and official records destroyed, and the amount of graft money involved in these transactions runs into hundreds of thousands," one report of the investigation asserted in 1917.

The graft business was a lucrative enterprise, with payoffs around the globe. Some American immigration authorities garnered as much as $100,000 a year by charging $1,400 to admit each illegal alien. The participants included not only high-ranking U.S. government officials but attorneys, notaries public, photographers, and Chinese merchants. The system entailed theft of documents, sale of biographical information, destruction or mutilation of data, creation of new records, substitution of photographs, and counterfeiting of official seals and stamps. So extensive was this Immigration Service racket that it even encompassed a special paper-son tutor school in Hong Kong, where prospective Chinese émigrés were coached on how to answer questions upon their arrival in San Francisco.

The Densmore investigation resulted in numerous arrests, as well as the discharge of some forty people from the Immigration Service. Transcripts of telephone conversations, secretly taped in 1917 by investigators, exposed the inner workings of collusion between Chinese smugglers and white officials. Here is a verbatim excerpt from one such transcript, of a phone call from a Chinese man to an official named McCall:

May 27 10:20 p.m. Chink called McCall.

McCall: Hello.

Chink: This Mr. McCall?

McCall: Yes.

Chink: This Yee Jim. How about Louie Ming?

McCall: The testimony is all wrong; I am afraid he will be rejected.

Chink: I will wait two days and then I send a different witness, I will send a good one this time.

McCall: All right.

Chink: You think then I have chance?

McCall: I am afraid I can't.

Chink: I will give you double price if you do.

McCall: I will see what I can do.

Chink: I send good witness over.

McCall: You had better see the attorney before you do that.

Under such a system, Chinese nationals who refused to pay off corrupt officials often faced trouble getting into the United States. According to an immigrant named Chen Ke, his troubles began when he refused to bribe the interpreter of the Boston customs office. In retaliation, the interpreter told the authorities that Chen Ke possessed fake documents and had him deported to China. Chen Ke later smuggled himself back into America, incurring a debt of $6,500, which took him twenty years to repay.

Such experiences left the Chinese American community with a profound sense of shame, terror, and insecurity. "Whenever my mother would mention it, she'd say 'Angel Island, shhh,'" recalled Paul Chow, a retired engineer who later led an effort to restore the immigration facility as a historical landmark. "I thought it was all one word 'Angelislandshhh.'" He later understood the reason for his family's embarrassment regarding the detention center: back in 1922, his father had bribed an immigration official to get into the country.

CHAPTER TEN

Work and Survival in the Early Twentieth Century

Through the decades immediately following the passage of the Exclusion Act, the Chinese in America continued to live suspended in a state of cultural limbo, not fully accepted by white American society, yet not able—or not willing—to return to China and sacrifice their American earnings. The strength of the U.S. dollar allowed some to support their families back in China in relative luxury. To the lowest-paid émigrés, the money sent home often assured the survival of family members. Now, with the exclusion laws in place, these men had to face the harsh reality of their strangely split lives. Even visiting their families would put them at the mercy of immigration officers, who could bar their reentry into the United States and cut them off from their treasured source of revenue forever.

There was another factor to consider. As hostile as the laws were in the United States, the political situation in China was far more chaotic and dangerous. By the end of the nineteenth century, Japan had bullied China into near submission. In 1895, the defeat of China in the First Sino-Japanese War forced the imperial government to sign the Treaty of Shimonoseki, which ceded to Japan part of Manchuria, four ports, Taiwan, and the Pescadores. But despite mounting pressure from Japan and other aggressors, the Qing government seemed oblivious to the need to build a strong military. The power behind the throne was the Empress Dowager Cixi, who appointed her nephew Guangxu as puppet emperor after her son died under mysterious circumstances. Legendary for her corruption, she used money desperately needed by the Chinese navy to build modern warships to finance instead a massive marble boat to decorate the lake at her summer palace.

As popular hatred against the Manchus swelled, a revolution appeared inevitable. In time, the Chinese émigrés would discover that even their marginal status in United States gave them a measure of political power and freedom unthinkable in China. They could organize against the hated Qing regime with less fear of retribution and provide much-needed financial support for political activists. These activists fell into two main groups: the reformers, who wanted to change the Qing from within, and the revolutionaries, who wanted to overthrow the regime entirely.

At the vanguard of the reform movement were two scholars, Kang Youwei and his protégé Liang Qichao. Their initial goal was to save the Qing dynasty through changes in policy. In 1898, Kang convinced the young emperor Guangxu to initiate a series of efforts to modernize Chinese education and national defense, a program known as the Hundred Days' Reform Movement. Kang also favored the idea of establishing a constitutional monarchy modeled after the government of Meiji Japan.

However, the Empress Dowager Cixi recognized that these reforms, crucial as they were to China's survival as a country, also gravely threatened her own position. A proven master at court intrigue, she staged a coup d'état that placed her nephew the emperor under house arrest and forced Kang Youwei and Liang Qichao to flee China in fear for their lives. In exile from their homeland, they organized in Canada the Protect the Emperor Society, also known as the Chinese Empire Reform Association or *Baohuanghui*, and gained a wide following among the Chinese in the United States. Chapters of their organization swiftly spread across the continent and to Hawaii. Their supporters began to train cadets in preparation for a military campaign in China. Homer Lea, an eccentric Caucasian strategist with grandiose fantasies about his role in China, founded a short-lived Western Military Academy in California for this purpose.

Before long, however, many Chinese immigrants grew so disgusted by the corruption within the Manchu regime that they lost interest in restoring the emperor to power. Instead, soon after the turn of the century, they threw their support behind a new movement, one intent on deposing the government entirely and establishing a new democratic republic in China. The leader and hero of this revolutionary movement was Sun Yat-sen, who, like Kang Youwei, had been born in Guangdong province, an anti-Manchu stronghold. But unlike Kang, an accomplished scholar from the gentry, Sun came from a peasant family with no vested interest in supporting the status quo. His early background, marked by ambition and a desire for upward mobility, resembled that of many other nineteenth-century Chinese who ultimately emigrated to America. Sun grew up in a rural coastal village near Canton, from which many of his relatives had gone to America to seek better opportunity; two of them died in California during the gold rush. Other family members had settled in Hawaii, and in the early 1880s Sun moved there as well, where he studied at a mission school, became a Christian, and learned the concepts and workings of Western democracy.

For years, Sun Yat-sen drifted in search of his place in society. He studied at a medical college in Hong Kong, but the British considered him unqualified to be a doctor and barred him from practicing medicine. At the same time, the Manchu government ignored Sun's eager offer to help them build up their national defense. In 1894, an angry and frustrated Sun created a secret organization in Hawaii called the Revive China Society, whose purpose was to oust the Manchu regime. The society worked closely with tong organizations, which, despite their illegal activities in China and the United States, were increasingly committed to the political goal of destroying the imperial government. Conspiring with other secret societies near Canton, Sun planned a poorly funded, ill-conceived military operation that was quickly discovered and crushed by local Qing officials. Many of the rebels were executed, but Sun managed to escape to Japan. Sun was now what Kang Youwei and Liang Qichao would soon become: an activist without a country, a fugitive from the law.

Then came an attempt on Sun's life that changed the course of China's history. In 1896 in London, he was abducted by Qing authorities, who intended to ship him back to China. Eloquent even in dire circumstances, Sun convinced a watchman to transmit a message to a friend, who helped free him. The botched kidnapping turned Sun into an instant hero. The Western media reported the sensational story of his capture and miraculous release, which gained world sympathy for his cause. Sun's new celebrity enabled him to relaunch his movement on a different level. In the United States, his public appearances drew thousands of eager supporters, and the Chinese American community raised enormous sums of money to help him overthrow the imperial government.

Sun's revolutionary alliance was eventually successful, and on October 10, 1911, a mutiny of army officers ended more than two and a half centuries of Manchu rule. The rebels declared the birth of a new government, the Republic of China, and elected Sun Yat-sen as provisional president. Adopting American democracy as their model, the revolutionaries called themselves the Kuomintang (National People's Party), also known as the KMT or the Nationalists. In the United States, the KMT began to establish local chapters in cities with great concentrations of ethnic Chinese, and the influence of American culture on Sun's new republic was plain from the beginning. His Three People's Principles—nationalism, democracy, and people's livelihood—was originally written in English, and was inspired by Abraham Lincoln's Gettysburg Address and its dedication to a government "of the people, by the people, for the people."

Sun's Republic of China, however, was doomed to an early demise. In 1912, to avoid civil war, Sun resigned in favor of Yuan Shikai, a powerful military leader from north China. However, although the Kuomintang was the dominant party in parliament,

Yuan quickly undermined the fledgling republic by arrogating dictatorial power, purging the Kuomintang, silencing the press, and liquidating thousands of his enemies. His dream of democracy for China in tatters, Sun was forced to flee the country. With Yuan's death in 1916, the central government splintered into many fiefdoms, leaving China in the control of feuding warlords.

While bloodshed and chaos reigned in China, thousands of Chinese immigrants fought their own quiet battles in the United States— namely, the daily struggle to make a living. During the early twentieth century, it was still unclear which career paths would lead to opportunity, and which to dead ends.

Many soon learned that it would be a hard road to travel if they remained in agriculture. In California, any Chinese who aspired to be landowning farmers found their dreams thwarted by a state law called the 1913 Alien Land Act, which barred aliens ineligible for citizenship from owning land, even if they could afford to buy it.* Without the right to purchase and own land, some Chinese were forced to become migrant farm laborers. In an oral history interview, émigré Suen Sum provides us a glimpse of this nomadic lifestyle. Arriving in the United

---

*The original purpose of the Alien Land Act act had been to discourage Japanese immigration into California. Like the Chinese, Japanese arrivals had endured anti-Asian racism and could not become naturalized citizens, but unlike the Chinese, they were not systematically excluded from the United States. To avoid the humiliation of having their people turned away from American shores, the Japanese government in 1907 signed the "Gentlemen's Agreement," in which Japan would voluntarily restrict and police contract-labor immigration to the United States. However, some of the Japanese émigrés began to buy and lease farmland in California, which so alarmed the state's politicians that they lobbied the federal government for legislation to stop Japanese immigration. When these efforts came to nothing, they decided to focus on state legislation. Believing that the Japanese would be reluctant to migrate to California if they could not acquire land, the California legislature passed the Alien Land Act, which, until its repeal in 1948, barred all Asians from owning real estate in California.

States as a paper son, he had settled in Locke, California, a rural community in the Sacramento–San Joaquin delta with an all-Chinese population. Drifting from farm to farm, he washed toilets, chopped wood, picked fruit, tended gardens. "The whites treated us Chinese like slaves," he recalled. Though he possessed some education—the ability to read and write in his native language, and a high school degree from China—he made barely enough money to live on: ten to twenty cents an hour, ten hours a day. At these wages, Suen Sum could not afford to marry, or do much of anything except work. There were days when he lacked money to buy food. "Every year it was the same. You work year after year, from youth to old age, and I still haven't saved any money."

Where landownership was allowed, a few notable Chinese prospered in agriculture, but they were generally the exception rather than the rule. On the Hawaiian islands, Lum Yip Kee, a Cantonese émigré, dominated the poi market with his plantations and processing factory, earning the title of "Taro King." Another Chinese immigrant to Hawaii, Chun Afong, became a millionaire thanks to his sugarcane holdings, his life inspiring the Jack London short story "Chun Ah Chun." In California, some Chinese profited by leasing land or by processing the harvests faster than their competitors. A few even managed to purchase land, in spite of the 1913 Alien Land Act. Thomas Foon Chew became known as the "Asparagus King" of San Francisco. In Alviso, California, he owned the Bayside Canning Company; the first cannery to preserve green asparagus. It grew into the third largest cannery in the world (after Del Monte and Libby's). Chin Lung, a near invalid in his Cantonese childhood, began his career by working in the reclamation of the tule lands in the Sacramento–San Joaquin delta, a job that left his hands and feet bloody and caused him to cry himself to sleep every night. He saved enough money to lease land across the delta, eventually emerging as the "Chinese Potato King" in the region.

For most Chinese immigrants, however, better opportunities could be found in small towns and cities, not in rural America. Over time, Chinese workers left the ranches altogether, their places taken by migrant Japanese, Filipino, and Mexican laborers. Many gravitated toward industries that had become virtual Chinese monopolies.

As always, restaurants remained a popular place to work. By 1920, roughly a quarter of all Chinese workers in the United States worked in restaurants. Most of these were tiny mom-and-pop enterprises, in which the owner worked as cook and dishwasher and his wife—if he had one—as the waitress and cashier. A few Chinese with sufficient capital rented their own buildings, installed expensive Asian décor, and hired battalions of chefs, waiters, and hostesses.

Regardless of the size of the operation, many Chinese sensed that profits could be made not by offering authentic cuisine from their homeland, but instead dishes that looked Chinese but appealed to the American palate. Chow mein ("fried noodles"), for example, was invented when a Chinese cook accidentally dropped a handful of Chinese pasta into a pot of simmering oil. When the crisp, golden-brown result delighted his customers, he added the item to his menu. It was an instant hit with his American patrons, and other Chinese restaurants quickly added the new concoction to their own offerings. David Jung, who opened a noodle company in Los Angeles in 1916, is credited with creating the fortune cookie. (Contrary to popular myth, the fortune cookie is not an ancient Chinese dessert, nor is it customary to insert messages in Chinese pastries. While it is true that during the Yuan Dynasty, rebels baked secret messages into Moon Festival cakes, outlining plans for an attack—the uprising overthrew the Mongolians and established the Ming Dynasty—the concept of slipping words of wisdom into fried cookies is completely American.) Chop suey, a fried hodgepodge of vegetables and meat, enjoyed an enormous following among Caucasians and became an icon of mainstream culture by the early twentieth century, when Sinclair Lewis mentioned it in his novel *Main Street* (1920). It varied greatly by region, as chefs tailored their food to suit local tastes. On the East Coast, some Chinese restaurants even offered chop suey sandwiches.

Some émigrés drew on their knowledge of traditional Chinese medicine to establish herbalist businesses. In the nineteenth and early twentieth centuries, California suffered from a severe lack of adequately trained Western doctors, prompting patients to try alternative medicine. After Western doctors pronounced them incurable, in desperation many Caucasians turned to Chinese healers. One herbalist, Tan Fuyuan, noted that "as a rule Caucasians have been unwilling to consult us until they had tried every other form of medical treatment within their reach. Therefore, it may be said that all of the cures which we have made have been cases given up by other doctors."

The ability of some Chinese herbalists to diagnose and cure their patients created a huge demand for their services. Though these herb doctors served people within their own community, most of their clientele were non-Chinese.* By the late nineteenth century, every Chinatown in the West had at least one herbalist business, some as many as three or four. In 1913, the *International Chinese Business Directory of the World* listed the names of twenty-eight Chinese herb doctors in Los Angeles (the real number may have been considerably higher), even though only two thousand Chinese lived in the city at that time.

Like other Chinese enterprises, Chinese herbal shops were typically family-run businesses. Historian Liu Haiming has portrayed the daily routine of Chang Yitang, who arrived in the United States in 1900. The family lived upstairs in Chang's house in Los Angeles, while the ground floor served as the doctor's office, pill factory, pharmacy, and teahouse. In his office, Chang would take the patient's pulse, then dole out advice and medicine. In the kitchen, his wife, Nellie, would steep herbs into tea, which his nephew, Yee Pai, would serve with crackers to patients in the waiting room. The family also

---

*As early as 1858, a San Francisco herbalist, Hu Yunxiao, used English-language business signs to bring in white customers, and, beginning in the 1870s, Chinese herbalists ran advertisements in English-language newspapers in California, some as large as half a page, with pictures of Chinese men taking the pulse of white patients.

made herbal pills from scratch, an exhausting job that required the efforts of several people. Using their feet or knees, they would grind the medicine into a fine powder beneath a heavy iron device they called a "rocking boat," as it resembled a boat with handles on the side. The powder was sifted through a sieve, mixed with honey, steamed, shaped into tiny balls, dried in the oven, and packed into bottles, to be sold later through the Chang family's thriving mail-order business.

Some herbalists owed their success more to marketing than medical knowledge. Tom Leung, who operated a booming herbal business in Los Angeles in the 1910s and 1920s, was particularly gifted at publicity. Though he claimed to be descended from a famous line of physicians in China and trained at the Imperial Medical College of Peking, his daughter, Louise Leung Larson, believes he invented those credentials. Leung advertised frequently in the Los Angeles newspapers, mailed Christmas cards to his patients, and gave away calendars and rulers with "T. Leung Herb Co." printed on them. Along with a prosperous local practice, he conducted a national mail-order business, sending clients herbs after they filled out questionnaires detailing their ailments. One of his most popular products was Thousand Wonders Oil, which Leung used for "countless" problems ranging from toothaches to insect bites, billing it as "one of the most valuable and inexpensive remedies in the world." As his reputation spread, Leung's practice flourished, and soon he was wealthy enough to afford a mansion, decorated with expensive Chinese art and staffed with maids, cooks, and private tutors for his children.

The American medical establishment, viewing practitioners like Leung as serious competition, conspired with authorities to drive them out of business. In the early decades of the twentieth century, Chinese herbalists were frequently fined or imprisoned for practicing medicine without a license. Tom Leung was arrested more than a hundred times, but he took the situation in stride; recognizing that his success required defiance of the law, he accepted trouble with the authorities as part of the cost of doing business and incorporated the arrests into his regular schedule, developing a system so that his secretary would call the bank to arrange bail the moment the police arrived. The raids actually provided a windfall benefit: free publicity. "The [more] he was arrested, the more business he got," his wife recalled.

A far less controversial Chinese business was retail trade. During the early twentieth century, the most famous Chinese department store owner was Joe Shoong, a former immigrant laborer. In 1903, he opened a tiny store in Vallejo, California, which he expanded into National Dollar Stores, a major chain recognized by 1920 as the largest Chinese business in the United States. Though the employees (and virtually all the customers) were white, the managers and stockholders were Chinese. Within a few decades, his empire, which provided Shoong with the second highest income in the state of California, included more than fifty stores in the western states, and prompted *Time* magazine to describe him as "the richest, best-known Chinese businessman in the U.S."

Of course, most Chinese-owned stores were very small. In the South, where the Chinese controlled much of the grocery industry, the typical store contained a large room in front for displaying merchandise and greeting customers, and a small room in back, where the owner ate and slept. Ray Joe, a Chinese émigré who arrived in the Mississippi Delta in the early 1920s, lived and worked in one such tiny store. During the day, he sold groceries, pies, cakes, and hot dogs, and at night, "I sleep on two trunks pulled together for bed. My brother pulled four stools together, he slept there—we tried as hard as we can to try to fight it out and make men of ourselves."

Opening a grocery store in the South posed distinct risks for a Chinese would-be merchant; his lack of English skills and local connections left him vulnerable to unscrupulous suppliers, complaining customers, and thieves. Nonetheless, the Chinese émigré also enjoyed certain advantages. His kinship ties and Guangdong background gave him immediate access to capital and business experience, as clans often pooled their resources to pay for a relative's emigration journey and to launch his overseas enterprise. Even more important, the southern Chinese grocer met virtually no competition. Apparently, his willingness to work long and hard hours for a thin return did not invite emulation by the locals.

One unexpected consequence of plantation slavery was that it left blacks and whites alike ill prepared to compete in a capitalist economy. As James W. Loewen, author of *The Mississippi Chinese*, points out, southern whites suffered from a precapitalist, almost feudal mindset. Many avoided service industries because they required waiting on customers, a practice the culture viewed as servile and demeaning, even when profitable. Meanwhile, most blacks were too intimidated by the white ruling class to open their own stores. Black business success in and of itself could be interpreted by whites as rebellious and "uppity," an act of defiance against the system.

Thus the caste system installed and rigidly enforced in the Jim Crow South left a void in the retail economy that the Chinese sought to fill. Because of the social stigma attached to trade, whites did not view the Chinese grocers as a threat. And black customers preferred to patronize Chinese-owned rather than white-owned businesses, where Chinese grocers would not harass, assault, or kill them if they forgot to call them "Mister" or "Sir." Chinese grocers also provided social services for blacks that often did not exist elsewhere. Serving in an informal banking role, the local Chinese grocery stores would often extend to black sharecroppers the credit and loans denied them by white institutions.

So severely had slavery weakened the entrepreneurial spirit in the South that even the lack of English skills did not hinder the Chinese grocers, who found nonverbal ways to conduct business. Most kept a stick in their stores for customers to use to point to the items they wanted. Chinese shopkeepers also saved the last one of each item that needed to be reordered so that they could show it to wholesale representatives. As a group, the Chinese grocers not only survived, but prospered even by white standards. In some areas, such as the Mississippi Delta region, they would eventually earn on average twice the white median income.

But the most popular business of all was the laundry, in many areas an almost exclusively Chinese enterprise since the gold rush days. According to the 1920 census, almost 30 percent of all employed Chinese worked in laundries: out of a total of 45,614 Chinese workers, 12,559 were laundry people. Opening a laundry appealed to many immigrants because it was a fast way to establish one's own business. It required almost no start-up capital—just a scrub board, soap, and an iron—and operating costs were low since the laundry owner usually saved rent by living in his shop. It also required no special training. "In the old days, some of those fellows were really ignorant though," one laundryman told historian Paul Siu.

They did not know even how to write down numbers. When a bundle of laundry was done, he had to put down the amount charged for the work. Being so illiterate, he could not write the numbers. He had a way though, and what a way! See, he would draw a circle as big as a half dollar coin to represent a half dollar, and a circle as big as a dime for a dime, and so on. When the customers came in to call for their laundry, they would catch on to the meaning of the circles and pay accordingly. It is indeed laughable.

The reality of the laundry business was harsh. Most Chinese washermen survived only because they lived frugally and charged at least 15 percent less for services than white laundries, leaving them with razor-thin profit margins. The work consumed almost every waking moment. Breathing steam and lint, the laundryman labored on a wet, slippery floor, washing and pressing, using an eight-pound iron heated over a coal stove, and then folding his customers' clothes by hand. The finishing work—the starching of detachable items, like collars, cuffs, and shirtfronts—required attention to detail and time. Collars had to be handled delicately lest wrinkles form. They were first pressed through a special mangle, then moistened with a tiny brush, and finally each was rolled by hand. Decades later, elder laundrymen would remember the ordeal of having to get up each morning to finish a thousand shirt collars.

In time, the laundry became a humid prison. The typical washerman not only worked in his laundry but slept there at night. He rarely left the premises because suppliers, sensing quick profits, came to him: salesmen called to peddle laundry supplies, wagon drivers delivered cooked meals. On some days, a laundryman might labor twenty hours continuously, without even stopping to eat. "My father used to joke [about] how flexible his stomach was—like rubber bands—he could skip meals for a couple of days," recalled a New York laundryman's son. "And once he ate, he had enough to last for quite a while! There was no time for meals." Another remembered, "I heard that some of them used a string to hang a piece of bread from the ceiling, in front of them, and had a bite when they had time to do so."

Most laundrymen did not have wives in America, but some managed to pass themselves off as "merchants" to secure permission for their wives to migrate. Arriving at their husbands' laundries was often a terrible shock. "In China in the old days women thought that people came over to pick gold," a veteran laundry wife recalled. "Ai! Really! They thought they were coming to Gold Mountain to pick gold. You think they knew that they were coming to work in the laundry?"

Those wives who did manage to get to America had to work alongside their husbands as well as care for the children and cook meals in the back of the laundry. With babies strapped to their backs, they bent over heaps of laundry until they developed swollen legs, strained neck muscles, and varicose veins. One recalled that her veins grew so monstrously big that they "became like balls and I wrapped them with cloth around my legs." Exhausted and overwhelmed by the volume of dirty linen, they, like their husbands, rarely stepped outdoors. One wife told an interviewer that in the thirty-eight years she worked in a laundry, she left it only three times—and then only to attend family celebrations in another city.

One reason for this slavish work ethic was the knowledge that they were giving their relatives in China a better life. "Some of these old-timers, they work almost sixteen hours a day," said Andy Eng, manager of the Wing Gong laundry in New York City. "They save a few dollars because they have no time to do anything else. The money they picked in their hands, they didn't spend it nowhere, except for their family back in China or in Hong Kong." And this money transformed entire regions in Guangdong. It paid for new technology, electric lights, paved roads, and new schools. Thanks to these remittances, by 1910, Toishan county, from which more than half of all the first-wave Chinese émigrés in the United States originated, enjoyed an astounding 90 percent literacy rate among its adult men.

But many people in Toishan had little appreciation of the hard life their relatives were living in the United States. The amount of money sent home was often huge by Chinese standards, which led them to picture their relatives as wealthy merchants in the American clothing industry, an image the émigrés encouraged. In their letters and during their rare visits home, proud laundrymen would refer ambiguously to their *yishanguan*, which in Chinese means either "clothing store" or a business related to clothing. That they did this was perfectly understandable. Why would they jeopardize their celebrity status in their home villages, the only bit of glory in their lives? Why would they want to jump off their pedestals to announce that they were not supermen or heroes, but only menial workers? For most laundrymen, the awe and admiration in the eyes of their children gave them the only bright moments in their lives.*

Sustaining this false image, however, carried a price. Believing that these laundrymen were moguls in the United States, relatives had no qualms about making financial demands upon them. The 1920s correspondence between Hsiao Teh Seng, a Chicago laundryman, and his

---

*By obscuring the truth, they promoted the myth of easy American success, and inspired others to emigrate. The myth persisted for decades. When researching *To Save China, to Save Ourselves*, his book on Chinese hand laundries in New York, author Renqiu Yu learned from his field interviews that as late as 1979 many descendants of laundrymen still had no inkling what these "clothing stores" had really meant.

family in China, revealed the endless pressures placed on the overseas Chinese by their kin. Letters he received from home all harped on one single theme: money. Bandits had kidnapped Hsiao's elder brother's concubine, and the family needed $20,000 to pay her ransom. A cousin asked for $200 to adopt a son. Younger clan members pleaded for money to purchase a house in Canton, because they had no suitable place to stay during their vacations ("We are indeed losing face . . . Please do not regard this as an unimportant thing"). After gangsters ransacked Hsiao's village, his family begged for funds to construct a wall ("The village's life and death is depending on you. Take note of this"). A nephew wanted financial assistance to cleanse himself from the "humiliation of an embezzling uncle." Even the embezzling uncle turned to Hsiao, seeking monetary relief from his own humiliation. Hsiao's daughter asked for a gold watch ("Big Uncle's daughters have gold watches, but we do not. My venerable one can use his own judgment whether jade should be inlaid or not"). His wife chastised him for his selfishness ("Month after month, I was longing for your money, but all you sent were plain letters"). His misplaced generosity, she wrote, had bankrupted her household ("I am so poor now, I have to pawn things in order to have money to buy food, while you go donating money, trying to wear your 'high hat' "). She resorted to threats ("I do not want to take care of your home anymore. Even though you are a slave to them, none of your brothers love you. Why should you have pity on your brothers?"). And finally she wrote, "There is a Lou-fal monastery near Canton; let me go there and become a nun, and let your brothers take care of the children. I am not your lifelong partner. Please think it over; when you are old in the future, are you going to depend on your children or depend on your brothers? I pray you send me $200 so that I can have money to spend in the monastery. Now, I do not care how hard you work in America; I have no pity on you." Hsiao never did learn on whom he could rely in his old age, because he died the following year.

Nonetheless, the Chinese laundrymen in America viewed their families back home with pride; for many, it was all that kept them going in their hard lives. Perhaps nothing better illustrates their enduring love and self-sacrifice than L. C. Tsung's novel *The Marginal Man*, in which the character Charles Lin walks into a laundry and sees a withered old Chinese man ironing under a bare light bulb, even though it is past ten o'clock at night. After a brief conversation, the laundryman tells Lin he has lived in the United States for forty years, working and sending money back to his family. He proudly shows Lin a photograph. "In the center sat a white-haired old woman, surrounded by some fifteen or twenty men, women and children, of various ages . . . The whole clan, with contented expressions on their faces, were the offspring of this emaciated old man, who supported not only himself but all of them by his two shaking, bony hands . . . Charles Lin realized that this picture was the old man's only comfort and relaxation. He had toiled like a beast of burden for forty years to support a large family which was his aim of existence, the sole meaning of his life. The picture to him was like a diploma, a summa cum laude to an honor student."

CHAPTER ELEVEN

A New Generation Is Born

It is ironic that so many Chinese émigrés, all part of a culture that cherished large families, would never enjoy the special satisfaction of raising their own children. True, many sent regular remittances back to their home villages in China to support wives, children, and other relatives, but this was hardly the same experience as watching one's own beloved sons and daughters mature into adulthood. Yet this was the price so many Chinese men paid for the extreme shortage of Chinese women in the United States; thousands of them were forced to live out their days either as bachelors, or in family arrangements split between two continents.

The numbers alone tell a discouraging tale. Back in 1880, on the eve of the Exclusion Act, the male-female ratio in the ethnic Chinese community was more than twenty to one—100,686 men and 4,779 women. By 1920, deaths and departures had reduced the male Chinese population, while a small number of births had increased the female population, but there were still seven Chinese men for every Chinese woman. One significant cause of this disproportion was that U.S. immigration policies prevented Chinese workingmen from bringing their wives into the country. The law automatically assigned to women the status of their husbands, so if their husbands were categorized as "laborers," their wives would be, too, making them ineligi-

173

ble for admission to the country. Only the wives of bona fide Chinese merchants were welcome.

So the arrival of any Chinese female in the United States was a rare event. From 1906 to 1924, only about one hundred fifty Chinese women secured legal permission to enter the United States. Then the Immigration Act of 1924 was enacted, prohibiting the entrance of any foreign-born Asian woman. Aimed primarily at ending the practice of Japanese mail-order brides, it hurt the Chinese American community as well: from 1924 to the end of the decade, not a single Chinese woman was admitted to the United States.

Despite the daunting numbers and the discriminatory laws, small communities of families gradually emerged. Because the typical Chinese immigrant could not afford to marry in the United States and was not permitted to bring his Chinese wife to his newly adopted country, those men with families by their side were almost always of the merchant or entrepreneur class, the petty bourgeois of Chinese American society. Consequently, the American-born Chinese children of these families (abbreviated as "ABCs") tended also to be part of an elevated socioeconomic stratum. Still, many of these families were hardly rich by American standards. And though their children had avoided the horrors of steerage and the struggle to adjust to a strange country, they faced their own unique challenges in the United States.

The first great challenge was the right to an education. Even more than many other immigrant groups, the Chinese, with their Confucius-infused culture, preached the importance of education to their American-born progeny. As they scrambled and grubbed for a living—washing other people's clothes, slaving away in sweatshops, stir-frying food in hot restaurant kitchens—they were driven by the all-consuming dream of all immigrants: that their children, particularly their sons, would lead a better life than they had. Education represented status, and some traditional Chinese parents, acutely sensitive to the stigma attached to merchants in China and the respect accorded scholars in Confucian society, venerated book learning as a worthy goal in itself, not simply as the path to skills that bring financial security or success. But the special place reserved for education was also based on its direct, practical outcomes. Immigrant parents especially favored careers such as medicine and engineering, not only because they were relatively lucrative, prestigious, and stable, but also because they did not require political connections, enormous outlays of capital, or advanced English-language skills. "My parents wanted us to become professionals," one American-born Chinese recalled of his childhood days. "If either of my brothers [had become] a doctor, my mother would have been thrilled."

Many parents also believed that if, for whatever reason, their American-educated children failed to establish themselves in the United States as doctors, engineers, or scientists, they could always go back to China and practice there the profession for which they had been trained in the West. Education was the one thing that could not be stripped from their children, and the parents frequently reminded them of this with adages like "You can make a million dollars, but a good education is better than a million dollars. You can lose everything but nobody can take away your good education."

But immigrant Chinese parents learned from painful experience that an American education—even public education—was not a right for their children, but a privilege that had to be fought for. As early as the mid-nineteenth century, state authorities tried to exclude Chinese American children from attending white public schools, over the protests and petitions of their parents.

In 1859, San Francisco school board members, making no secret of their contempt for the Chinese (referring to them even as "baboons" and "monkeys"), shut down a public school for Chinese children, even though their parents were required to pay school taxes along with other residents of the city. Under public pressure, authorities reopened the Chinese school but passed state laws in the 1860s to segregate Asians, American Indians, and blacks from the white public school system. Little more than a decade later, during Reconstruction, a new California state law granted separate public education for blacks and Indians, but not Asians, giving local school officials the legal right to close down even the segregated school they had established for Chinese American children.*

For fourteen years, from 1871 to 1885, Chinese children were the only racial group to be denied a state-funded education. Some Chinese parents home-schooled their children, sent them to private schools, or arranged for missionaries to tutor them individually, while others were too poor to exercise these options. The Chinese community made desperate appeals to the school board to admit their children into the public schools, but these were repeatedly ignored.

Finally, the Chinese turned to the courts. In 1884, Joseph Tape, an interpreter for the Chinese consulate, and his wife, Mary, a photographer and artist, sued the San Francisco Board of Education when their daughter Mamie was denied admission to a public white primary school. The school officials argued that "the association of Chinese and white children would be demoralizing mentally and morally to the latter" and tried to label Mamie as a child of "filthy or vicious habits suffering from contagious or infectious diseases." The Tape family submitted medical records that gave Mamie a clean bill of health, but the school board refused to budge from its position. *Joseph Tape* v. *Jennie Hurley* (the principal of the Spring Valley School) was argued at the height of violent anti-Chinese hostility in California, when the state superintendent of schools felt comfortable asserting that barring Chinese children from public schools was unconstitutional but necessary because they were "dangerous to the well-being of the state." One Board of Education member insisted that he would rather go to jail than permit a Chinese child to enroll in school.

In *Tape* v. *Hurley* at least, the courts served justice and not public passion. The Superior Court ruled in favor of the Tape family, and

---

*The School Law of 1870 specified that the education of black and Indian children would be provided in separate schools.

was upheld on appeal by the California Supreme Court. When the board adopted a resolution to fire teachers and principals who admitted "Mongolian" children to public schools, one judge warned that he would punish the board members with contempt citations if they attempted to enforce it.

After their defeat in court, the San Francisco school board lobbied for a separate educational system for Chinese children. A bill giving the board the authority to establish an Oriental Public School sailed through the California state legislature under a special "urgency provision." An outraged Mary Tape vented her feelings in an ungrammatical but passionate letter to the school board: "May you Mr. Moulder, never be persecuted like the way you have persecuted little Mamie Tape. is it a disgrace to be Born a Chinese? Didn't God make us all!!! What right! Have you to bar my children out of the school because she is a chinese Descend. Mamie Tape will never attend any of the Chinese schools of your making! Never!!! I will let the world see sir What justice there is When it is govern by the Race prejudice men!!!"

By the turn of the century, racially segregated schools were legal not just in California but nationwide. In the landmark case *Plessy* v. *Ferguson* (1896), the U.S. Supreme Court ratified racial segregation as constitutional by accepting the doctrine of "separate but equal," saying that states had the right to exclude nonwhites from public schools and other publicly supported services as long as equal facilities were created for them. Separate but equal remained the law of the land until the Supreme Court overturned *Plessy* in 1954 in another landmark decision, *Brown* v. *Board of Education*.

Despite *Plessy*, the Chinese continued to challenge segregation in several court cases, but with little success. One of the most notable was a suit filed in 1924 by Lum Gong, a grocer whose daughter Martha was rejected by the local white school in Rosedale, Mississippi. The case eventually went to the Supreme Court, which ruled that the state of Mississippi had the prerogative to reserve white schools for white children alone.

A few Chinese American children managed to find ways to attend

Caucasian schools. An unwritten rule was that they could enroll if the local community did not object—a situation that doubtless encouraged the ethnic Chinese students to be docile, respectful, and studious. This strategy could backfire, however, when high academic achievement inflamed white envy. In 1905, a group of white parents at Washington Grammar School in San Francisco insisted that four Chinese students, all academic superstars, were cheating by secretly exchanging answers in Chinese during tests. The students were separated during the next exam, but they still achieved the four top scores in the class. Undeterred, the white parents then complained to the Board of Education, which removed the four boys from the school altogether. In 1928, a white community in Mississippi decided to bar all Asians from attending the local white school after a Chinese boy graduated at the top of his class. The specter of segregation always lurked in the background, with the constitutionally protected right of school boards to expel Chinese students on any whim or pretext.

By the mid-1920s, it was becoming difficult to segregate Chinese students in California, largely because of the Chinese community's willingness to organize politically. An effort to create a segregated junior high school failed in the San Francisco Bay Area when Chinese activists and organizations made vociferous protests. It appears that these barriers gradually, informally dropped away, several decades before actual laws were codified to ban racial segregation. So as the years went by, more Chinese American children attended integrated schools, and their initial exposure to whites often threw them into a welter of confusion about their identity.

In most children, feelings oscillated between a fierce pride in their heritage and a near-total rejection of being Chinese. Some saw themselves as informal ambassadors of China, interpreting its culture for their white classmates while also serving as models of deportment for their white teachers, as if upon their words and actions hinged the reputation of an entire country. Others had so deeply absorbed the toxin of racism that they grew to loathe everything Chinese, even their own looks. To make themselves appear less Asian, some Chinese American teenage girls taped or glued their eyelids in order to create an extra fold, and while Chinese American boys were less likely to resort to such tactics, some must have been equally insecure about their self-image during the 1920s. Even late into the twentieth century, one man would recall, "I remember rushing home from school one afternoon—I was eleven or twelve years old—and desperately staring at the bathroom mirror and praying to God my face would miraculously turn Caucasian. Only fear of pain and death kept me from committing suicide."

A few American-born Chinese simply viewed themselves as white. Such individuals tended to live in rural areas, where the absence of an established ethnic Chinese community made them less threatening to whites and encouraged their participation in the mainstream. Bernice Leung, born in 1917 in the farming community of Fresno, California, remembered a period in her childhood in which she and her siblings did not believe they were Chinese at all. Asians, not Caucasians, looked strange to them, and they wondered why they themselves had not been born with blue eyes and blond hair. Noel Toy, who grew up in the only Chinese American family in a small northern California town, was astonished to meet another Asian woman in college. "I was brought up purely Caucasian, Western," she recalled. "When I went to junior college, I saw an Oriental woman. I said, 'an Oriental! My gosh, an Oriental woman!' I never thought myself one."

Somewhere in the middle were those torn between the demands and expectations of both cultures, Chinese and American. "There was endless discussion about what to do about the dilemma of being *caught in between*," remembered Victor Wong, an American-born Chinese who grew up in San Francisco.

Finding a comfort zone in a racially stratified society took time. For some ABCs it took decades. Confusion about identity was only one problem; another was overt and covert racism. Those who grew up in white areas often did not feel the full effect of racism until reaching puberty. "We have never lived in Chinatown but have always lived in an American neighborhood," Lillie Leung recalled in 1924.* "I mingled with all the children quite freely, but when I was about twelve years old they began to turn away from me. I felt this keenly. Up to that time, I never realized that I was any different, but then I began to think about it."

It was in the white or integrated public schools that many Chinese American children felt the sting of racism most sharply. Esther Wong of San Francisco remembers a French-language teacher who made no effort to hide her hatred of the Chinese. After asking Wong to read aloud in class, she remarked, "Well, you read all right, but I don't like you. You belong to a dirty race that spits at missionaries."

Racism also pervaded the curricula and textbooks, driving a wedge between Chinese Americans and their white classmates. "In grade school I was fairly successful in being admitted to the 'inner circles,' as it were," one ABC recalled of her childhood in the 1910s. "Children are not prone to think a great deal of their 'social selves' and since I spoke English as well as they, and played and dressed as they did, I was not regarded as an outsider." That is, until China was taught in geography and history class:

> When we came to the study of China, the other children would turn and stare at me as though I were Exhibit A of the lesson. I remember one particularly terrible ancient history lesson; it told in awful detail about "queer little Chinamen, with pigtails and slanting eyes" . . . and went on to describe the people as though they were inhuman, and at best, uncivilized. Even I, young as I was, resented these gross exaggera-

---

*During the early twentieth century, many ABCs used the terms "white" and "American" interchangeably, even though they were, like whites, American citizens. Such language only served to reinforce their sense of themselves as foreigners in the United States.

tions which were considered the gospel truth by other pupils.
I meditated on ways and means of absenting myself from class
that day; I would have welcomed a sudden and violent attack
of illness, or even sudden death, but since my health remained
disgustingly good, I was forced to sit through a very embarrassing hour.

Another kind of struggle was being waged after school, at home.
Many Chinese American children not only faced daily prejudice from
whites, but at home had to deal with rigid attitudes their parents had
imported from the old country. Fear and insecurity compelled many
Chinese parents to shield their children from the influence of the outside, alien world, especially their daughters. "Mother watched us like
a hawk," Alice Sue Fun recalled of her formative years in San
Francisco during the 1910s. "We couldn't move without telling her.
We were never allowed to go out unless accompanied by an older
brother, sister, or someone else."

In certain households, the girls were burdened with household
work while still very young. Many second-generation Chinese
women endured an unusually restrictive upbringing, with heavy
domestic responsibilities and orders to stay home, while their brothers were permitted to venture out into the streets to play. After coming home from Oriental Public School each day, Alice Sue Fun had to
do "a lot of housework for my mother—washed dishes, scrubbed the
children's clothes by hand, helped her sew." By the time she was eight
or nine years old, "I was cooking rice. If I burnt the rice, I would get
a *ling gok* [a knuckle-rap on the head]."

Boys also learned early to work hard, although, unlike their sisters, they were usually given more freedom to work outside the home.
The poverty of one ABC's family in California forced him to take
jobs after school—and sometimes before:

When we grew up, we just lived on a bare minimum. If there
was nothing to eat, we just ate plain rice and water. Whatever.

Just wash it down. I used to get up at 7:00 in the morning and go to work at a wholesale florist. And I worked there for an hour before I went to school. I'd take my bicycle and I'd ride from Fifth and Mission Street, all the way to Galileo High. After school, I'd go to an apartment to wash the kitchen or do housework for an hour. Then I'd go home and eat dinner. And we started Chinese school at 5:00. From 5:00 to 8:00, we had three hours Chinese school. After that, I'd go home and do the laundry, or clean up the house or whatever, and do some homework and then go to bed.

Some families forbade their children to speak English at home and insisted that they attend special Chinese-language schools after their public school classes, six days a week. Chinese-language schools represented the hopes and efforts of first-wave immigrant parents eager to maintain in their American-born children some vestige of their Chinese heritage. The earliest of these schools appear to have been informal arrangements between scholars and Chinese immigrant families. Known as *kuan,* and held in the private homes of their tutors, they consisted of classes of twenty to thirty children who learned the rudiments of Chinese language, calligraphy, philosophy, and classical literature. By the end of the 1920s, some fifty Chinese-language elementary schools and a half dozen Chinese-language high schools existed in the United States, mostly in the West.

The children's reaction to this additional education was mixed. Chinese lessons were "an ordeal that I grew to hate," Louise Leung Larson recalled of her childhood in the 1910s. "I didn't see why I had to learn Chinese when I was always going to live in America. The only way I could remember the characters was to write the American phonetic sound beside them." Rodney Chow had a Chinese-language teacher in Los Angeles with a "totalitarian attitude" toward the children: "It was just memorizing, writing, and reading, and it was very, very strict because he actually took the stick and hit us."

Even if the teacher was not abusive, it was difficult for some chil-

dren to concentrate on their studies. There was the problem of different dialects: one Chinese school made the mistake of employing a
Mandarin-speaking instructor for children of Cantonese-speaking
parents, which frustrated the students and led most of them to drop
out. And often the interest simply was not there. Pardee Lowe, an
ABC who grew up in San Francisco in the 1920s and graduated from
Stanford University and Harvard Law School, described his personal
struggle with Chinese school: "It was not that I was entirely unwilling
to learn, but simply that my brain was not ambidextrous. Whenever I
stood with my back to the teacher, my lips attempted to recite correctly in poetical prose Chinese history, geography or ethics, while
my inner spirit was wrestling victoriously with the details of the
Battle of Bunker Hill, Custer's Last Stand, or the tussle between the
Monitor and *Merrimac.*"

Yet immigrant parents believed these classes were necessary to
sustain continuity with the ancestral homeland and their identity. In
1924, a Los Angeles–born woman of Chinese parents recalled, "I had
to learn the Chinese language because father told me time and again
that I could never be an American because my skin was yellow and
only white people could be Americans."

But neither Chinese schools nor Chinese parents could shelter
children from the onslaught of American culture. Outside the narrow confines of Chinatown and family, a larger world beckoned.
Popular culture permeated even the most isolated ethnic ghettos,
shaping the desires of ethnic Chinese youths, exposing them to new
values, new ideas, beyond the reach of parental control. The children
listened to the radio for entertainment, read English-language newspapers, pored over comic books and pulp novels bought from
neighborhood drugstores, spent Saturday afternoons at the local
nickelodeons watching movies. Child-related activities of civic and
religious groups also encouraged the assimilation of the American-
born Chinese. Missionaries established Chinatown churches, and by
1920, almost all of the Chinese American children in San Francisco—
close to a thousand of them—were attending Sunday school. The

YMCA in San Francisco Chinatown organized athletic competitions in sports like soccer and basketball.* At the same time, Chinese American children took the initiative of starting their own clubs. In 1914, eight young Chinese American boys thumbed through a Boy Scout handbook in the playground of a Methodist church in San Francisco and decided to create their own Scout chapter. It became the very first Boy Scout troop in San Francisco, and probably the first ethnic Chinese Boy Scout troop in the world.

The urge to partake in American customs grew more intense as children got older. Chinese American adolescents craved what they saw on the silver screen, in glossy advertisements, and in the (mostly white) public schools. By the 1920s, one of the most prosperous decades in U.S. history, ABCs were increasingly torn between parental restraints and the seductive pull of American consumer culture. The urban enclaves of Chinese America of that decade were so profoundly transformed that their earliest settlers would have found them unrecognizable. "Take it all in all, the Chinatown of today is not the Chinatown of the bygone days," Dr. Ng Poon Chew, the founder of San Francisco's *Chung Sai Yat Po,* wrote in 1922. Chew and others noticed how American traditions supplanted Chinese ones—how Chinese costume and skullcap gave way to closely cropped hair and Western clothes, how Chinese women wore the latest fashions and styled their hair in pageboy bobs or marcelled waves, and how while older women tottered about in bound feet, younger women wore high heels.

But the most dramatic changes were the ones least visible to the casual observer: the shifts in thought, attitudes, and values. Chew noted that Chinese children spoke English and enjoyed American slang. Chinese American women, independent and assertive, dated whomever they pleased and selected their own husbands instead of leaving these decisions to their parents. And Chinese students—

---

*As more immigrant families possessed the financial means to let their children participate in leisure activities, softball, tennis, and golf became popular among the Chinese middle class.

ambitious and patriotic United States residents, Chew observed—
aspired to earn first-rate college degrees.

By the first few decades of the twentieth century, a substantial number of Chinese Americans, mostly children of small business owners,
had fulfilled their parents' dreams of becoming well educated and
were now enrolled at universities along the West Coast, especially in
California. But parents and children alike would soon learn that in
America, a university degree did not guarantee them respectability,
career success, or even employment.

Mainstream society thought of Chinese males as workers in service industries such as laundries, restaurants, and produce markets.
Those who aspired to break into the professions—that is, college
graduates with degrees in fields such as engineering, architecture, or
the sciences—faced difficulty in trying to secure positions at large,
Caucasian-controlled firms. In California, consonant with the state's
legacy of racial discrimination, many firms had specific regulations
against hiring Asians. "It is almost impossible to place a Chinese or
Japanese of either the first or second generation in any kind of position, engineering, manufacturing or business," the Stanford University Placement Service reported in 1928.

In a family memoir, *Father and Glorious Descendant*, Pardee Lowe
wrote about the discrimination he faced when seeking work, when
certain whites could not see beyond the stereotype of the Chinese as
houseboy or coolie. While a student at Stanford University, Lowe had
applied for a job as chauffeur for a banker's wife, who insisted upon
speaking to him in pidgin English. "You Chinee boy or Jap boy?" she
asked.

"Chinese, of course, but born in this country," an astonished
Lowe replied.

"Me no likee, me no wantee Chinee boy," she said.

Suppressing a "huge desire to laugh," Lowe responded, "Mrs.
Bittern, I understand perfectly."

Lowe saw with distressing clarity that it was his skin color and not some fault in his credentials that barred him from employment. Even his flawless, educated English could not overcome a prospective employer's prejudice about the Chinese. "Everywhere I was greeted with perturbation, amusement, pity or irritation—and always with identically the same answer," he wrote.

> "Sorry," they invariably said, "the position has just been filled." My jaunty self-confidence soon wilted. I sensed that something was radically, fundamentally wrong. It just didn't seem possible that overnight all of the positions could have been occupied, particularly not when everybody spoke of a labor shortage. Suspicion began to dawn. What had Father said? "American firms did not customarily employ Chinese." To verify his statement, I looked again in the newspaper that next morning and for the week after, and sure enough, just as I expected, the same ten ads were still in the newspapers.*

Chinese American college graduates were sometimes barred not only from professional positions but even from the lowliest jobs at white firms. During the exclusion era, even companies outside of California had strict policies against hiring Asians. "Recently two friends of mine wrote to no less than fifty firms throughout the country to apply for a position where they could get some experience along their own line and all they have got were negative answers," University

---

*This racism cooled Pardee Lowe's teenage ambition to be elected president of the United States, a fever he later called "Presidentitis," contracted when his teacher, Miss McIntyre, told the class: "every single one of you can be president of the United States someday!" As Lowe later recalled, "I broke down and wept. For the first time I admitted to myself the cruel truth. I didn't have a 'Chinaman's chance' of becoming president of the United States. In this crash of the lofty hopes which Miss McIntyre had raised, it did not occur to me to reflect that the chances of Francisco Trujillo, Yuri Matsuyama, or Penelope Lincoln [Pardee's classmates] were actually no better than mine."

of Washington graduate Fred Wong told an interviewer in the 1920s. "They went to the Oriental Admiral Line to apply for a job as common labor on the boat. The superintendent at first told them that it was not the policy of the firm to hire people other than Americans. The boys told him that they were American born and did not come into the excluding list. They talked with the supervisor for a while and finally he said, "I am sorry boys, I cannot employ you people."

Perceived as foreign, ethnic Chinese job seekers even endured linguistic standards that were not imposed on Caucasians. Some employers expected Chinese Americans to be fluent in both English and Chinese, hiring them to serve as the company's link between the white and Chinese communities. For instance, a Los Angeles bank hired a young second-generation Chinese man to serve its Chinese American customers. Although he spoke perfect English, his lack of proficiency in Chinese caused him to be fired, prompting his father to send him to China to study the language. Other employers expected ABCs to be verbally deficient in English and naturally gifted in Chinese. When a candidate for a teaching post answered questions using correct English diction, he was asked, "Don't you have an accent? You're Chinese."

Some Chinese Americans learned to ignore such racism, and forged ahead with little more than the energy of their own ambition. Frank Chuck, son of a Chinese schoolteacher in Hawaii, arrived at Stanford University with only twenty-five cents in his pocket. In desperate need of cash and housing, and knowing that Chinese students were not welcome in Stanford's dormitories (one Chinese boy, he recalled, was bodily "thrown out of Encina Hall"), Chuck worked his way through college by cooking for a Stanford professor in exchange for room and board, and earned a bachelor's degree in organic chemistry in 1922 and a Ph.D. in chemical engineering in 1925.

Chuck's education changed not only his life but America's eating habits as well. In 1927, after a stint teaching in China on a Rockefeller Fellowship, he became a research chemist for Western Condensing Company, the parent company of Carnation Milk. There he discovered the chemical actions responsible for milk dehydration and whey stabilization and in the process, invented powdered milk and instant cocoa. Later, Chuck would identify a way to prevent the parasitic disease coccidiosis from ravaging the poultry industry. He also developed livestock vitamins that profoundly benefited the American food industry.

Another American-born Chinese who pursued his career with relentless, single-minded determination was Chan Chung Wing. Born in Napa, California, he spent his early childhood in China, in the care of his grandfather, a merchant. When he returned to Napa at age nine, shortly before the turn of the century, he showed an early aptitude for learning, skipping from first to fourth grade within a single year. He continued his education in the San Francisco Bay Area, graduating from Lowell High School and Berkeley, where he studied engineering. His grandfather wanted Chan to be an engineer, but Chan opted instead for law. Upon graduation from the Saint Ignatius School of Law, he passed the bar exam with a score of 96 percent—one of the highest on record—and became the first Chinese lawyer to practice in California.

Friends warned Chan that as a lawyer he would starve to death. Indeed, he "found it very difficult to defend my clients, because there was a lot of discrimination against Chinese and many judges tried to throw me out of the courtroom," he recalled. "But I was very persistent and soon found out that playing golf with the judges and district attorneys afforded me the opportunity to discuss the problems of the Chinese community with them." Soon the Chinese community found Chan Chung Wing to be one of its greatest champions, a formidable defender of their civil rights. For instance, when Chan learned that the San Francisco police would habitually attack unemployed Chinese workers, striking them with their billy clubs and ordering them to leave town, he filed more than thirty lawsuits against the police, effectively ending the violence.

Second-generation Chinese American women also served as pioneers in their fields, but their struggle for acceptance was far more difficult than the men's. Before the turn of the century, the majority of working-class Chinese families could not afford to educate their daughters beyond primary school, but after World War I, the introduction of compulsory education in the United States permitted Chinese girls to attend and graduate from high school in numbers equal to Chinese boys. College, however, remained out of reach for most. These women were only a generation or two removed from an era when it was unthinkable for a respectable woman—white or Chinese—to appear alone in public. As was true of other immigrant groups, and the majority of native-born white Americans as well, many Chinese American families employed a double standard, urging their sons to go to college while expecting their daughters either to stay at home or to marry, preferably an educated man. Jade Snow Wong, author of *Fifth Chinese Daughter*, wrote poignantly of her San Francisco youth in the 1920s, and of how her father refused to finance her college education so he could send her brother to medical school instead.

Even if an ABC woman had financial support to pursue her degree and the encouragement of enlightened parents, she had few role models to inspire her. During the nineteenth century, the number of ethnic Chinese women—either American- or foreign-born—who had graduated from college could be counted on the fingers of one hand: between 1881 and 1892, a total of four Chinese female students, sponsored by missionaries, obtained medical degrees from American universities. They are believed to have been the very first Chinese women to study in the United States. Even at the secondary school level, it was difficult to find female mentors for Chinese girls. It was not until the 1920s that the San Francisco public school system began hiring female Chinese schoolteachers. Any Chinese American woman who wanted higher education needed extraordinary persistence and dedication to achieve her goal.

And education was only the first hurdle. The labor situation, dismal as it was for American-born Chinese men, could be even worse for their sisters, who occupied the lowest tier of a labor market stratified by race and sex. In the early twentieth century, most employed Chinese women, both native- and foreign-born, worked in low-wage, piece-rate industries. Home-based jobs, like sewing and shrimp peeling, gradually evolved into factory jobs that exploited cheap female labor. After World War I, Chinese immigrant women dominated the rank and file of the garment industry. Local Chinese businessmen, obtained contracts from white manufacturers and opened sweatshops with poor ventilation, dim lighting, and inadequate child care, where mothers worked with infants strapped to their backs or with children crawling across the factory floor. Some of the first memories of ABCs who grew up in the San Francisco or New York Chinatowns were of their mothers, mute and exhausted, hunched over sewing machines.

The American-born Chinese women, however, enjoyed better—slightly better—opportunities than their immigrant mothers. With education, fluency in English, and familiarity with American culture, they could move out of labor-intensive industries and into jobs that required specialized skills. By the 1920s, there was a detectable pattern of gradual upward mobility for talented female ABCs. Bilingual and high-school-educated women, overqualified for factory jobs, began working in gift shops and local businesses in Chinatown. Some became operators for the Chinatown Telephone Exchange in San Francisco, where they were required to speak fluent English, several Chinese dialects and subdialects, memorize 2,200 phone numbers, because the exchange handled an average of 13,000 calls a day.

Landing work outside Chinatown, however, remained a challenge. A few found employment in so-called pink-collar positions: as secretaries, clerks, or stock girls for large white corporations, largely because of the popular view that the Chinese were a hardworking and docile people. Sexism magnified the problems of race. White firms hired young Chinese women simply to capitalize on their physical appearance, outfitting Chinese department store salesladies, elevator girls, theater ushers, and restaurant hostesses in Asian costumes to provide an exotic atmosphere for white customers. But for every Chinese American woman hired, countless others met a wall of resistance—they could not obtain even the lowest-paid, most dead-end jobs; they were told flatly that the company didn't "hire Orientals."

Nevertheless, in the first few decades of the twentieth century a female Chinese American professional class began to emerge. Second-generation Chinese women entered arenas traditionally dominated by white middle-class women, such as teaching, nursing, and library science. When hired by the San Francisco public school system in 1926, Alice Fong Yu became one of the first Chinese American teachers in the country. Three sisters from a prosperous San Francisco family became pioneers in their chosen occupations: Martha Fong was the first Chinese American nursery school teacher, Mickey Fong the first Chinese American public health nurse, and Marian Fong the first Chinese American dental hygienist. College-educated ABC women also stepped into careers normally occupied by men. Faith So Leung is believed to have become the first Chinese American female dentist in 1905, and Dolly Gee the first Chinese American female bank manager in 1929.

Given the obstacles, it took women with exceptional willpower to rise to the top. Bessie Jeong, one of the nation's earliest Chinese American women physicians, was one such. Jeong saw what could happen to women who surrendered complete control of their lives to their husbands. In the 1910s, her sister Rose was told to choose between two marriage proposals from men she had never met—a man in his twenties and a fifty-year-old cook—with only their photographs and her family's advice to guide her. She decided to marry the older man: "Better to be an old man's darling than a young man's slave," her parents advised. But her husband turned out to be jealous, suspicious, and tyrannical—a "hard taskmaster," as Jeong described him. Sixteen-year-old Rose was far too Americanized and educated for his taste, even though she had had only two years of public schooling, and she found herself caught in a disastrous marriage, a life of poverty, a world of shrinking possibilities. In a poorly insulated log cabin in the lumber camp of Weed, California, Rose watched her husband fail in one business enterprise after another; he sold her wedding jewelry to recoup his losses. Finally, an exhausted Rose died at the age of twenty-six during a flu epidemic.

Bessie Jeong resolved not to share her sister's fate. When her father began to invite men to the house, and then asked her to return to China, she inferred it was her turn to be married off. "He was going to realize money out of it, or he was fulfilling his duty as a father," she speculated. "But I still would be on the auction block. Prized Jersey—the name 'Bessie' always made me think of some nice fat cow!" In 1915, at the age of fourteen, she fled her parents' home to live with Donaldina Cameron, the head of the Presbyterian Mission Home in San Francisco, which sheltered runaway Chinese prostitutes and battered Chinese wives. With Cameron's protection and financial support, Bessie enrolled first at the Lux Normal School for girls, then at Stanford (where in 1927 she became the first Chinese American woman graduate), and finally at the Women's Medical College of Pennsylvania. To help pay her way toward becoming a doctor, she performed a series of domestic tasks—cleaning and laundry, baby-sitting children, and serving dinners.

Like many successful people, Bessie Jeong approached life with a mixture of natural optimism and resilience. She harbored no bitter-ness toward her tradition-bound family and even reconciled with her father, who eventually came to terms with her refusal to return to China. (He visited her several times, but died before her graduation from Stanford and never saw her become a doctor.) She had a wide circle of friends, both Chinese and Caucasian, and claimed never to have experienced any racial prejudice in her entire lifetime. Jeong also proved adept at managing a career along with a family, balancing a happy marriage to an educated man of her choice—Wing Chan, the Chinese consul in San Francisco—with a private medical practice that flourished for almost forty years.

Women like Bessie Jeong, however, were rare. The majority of Chinese American women were still under enormous pressure to place family above their careers. But with the old traditions falling away, even aspiring young homemakers were uncertain about their roles in the arena of courtship and marriage.

Different expectations of courtship and marriage inevitably created misunderstandings between Chinese immigrant parents and their children. In the early twentieth century, the rituals of courtship fluctuated between old-country mores and American-style dating. Some ABCs submitted to arranged marriages brokered by their parents; others rebelled. "My parents wanted to hold onto the old idea of selecting a husband for me, but I would not accept their choices," Lillie Leung told an interviewer for the 1924 Los Angeles Survey of Race Relations:

> We younger Chinese make fun of the old Chinese idea according to which the parents made all the arrangements for the marriage of their children. Whenever a young Chinese goes back to China we tell him that he is going there to marry—that has come to be a standing joke, and even the older people join in with us.

As they entered the Western world of romance, many Chinese American youths invented their own rules as they went along. In the 1910s, teenagers in San Francisco Chinatown defied their parents by "spooning" along Dupont Street. Because single Chinese American women and men were not supposed to be seen together, the spectacle of youths openly kissing scandalized Chinatown.

A more acceptable form of social behavior was group dating: for instance, outings sponsored by respectable Western organizations like the YMCA. Such chaperoned activities—picnics, museum tours, church suppers—radiated a wholesome image and provided a setting where members of the opposite sex could meet. Many American-born Chinese youths got to know their future spouses at these events. One San Francisco ABC couple told historian Judy Yung that during the 1920s the two of them did not venture out alone on a date until they had known each other for four years.

A developing Chinese American subculture afforded young ABCs opportunities to select their own marriage partners. Excluded by white fraternities and sororities, Chinese American college students in California built their own Greek system. In 1928, six Chinese engineering students founded Pi Alpha Phi (nicknamed "Pineapple") at the University of California at Berkeley. Two years later, Chinese American women at San Francisco State Teachers' College created the first ethnic Chinese sorority in the country, Sigma Omicron Pi.

Cities with well-established Chinatowns, like Los Angeles and San Francisco, organized Chinese American social clubs at local high schools and colleges, where students could hold their own dances and parties. In 1929, a reporter in San Francisco observed large posters of a Chinese flapper dancing with a young Chinese man in formal wear; the caption read "Chinese Collegiate Shuffle!" "What would old John Chinaman think," the reporter wrote, "could he see one of these lively dancing parties of the Chinese students of the San Francisco district, jazz music, bright costumes, beautiful young women, gaiety on every hand. 'Everything but hip flasks,' someone said of the dance." In regions with smaller (or nonexistent) Chinese communities, such as the South, some ABCs were willing to travel long distances to socialize with other ABCs. Edward Wong recalled that "our parents always preached that you need to marry a Chinese. We used to have dances together. We used to drive from San Antonio all the way to New Orleans or Houston for a dance on Saturday night and go back home on the same night."

Some Chinese parents were apprehensive about this new freedom. Many immigrants who cherished the Confucian ideals of wifely obedience and filial piety believed that their sons would find the embodiment of these qualities only in native Chinese brides. They worried that American-born Chinese women were "spoiled," "too Americanized," and liable to be difficult daughters-in-law. One man recalled that the parents in his community would have been especially proud to have a daughter-in-law from China, because she represented "the real thing."

In addition, some immigrant parents wanted their daughters to marry native-born Chinese nationals, but often the legal and cultural barriers proved overwhelming. American-born Chinese women who married native Chinese men would lose their citizenship. The Expatriation Act of 1907, which forced all women to adopt their husband's nationality upon marriage, gave way to the 1922 Cable Act, which stipulated that any woman who married an alien ineligible for naturalization would relinquish her own U.S. citizenship.

While some foreign-born Chinese immigrants had Western educations and considered themselves modern men, they were not always prepared for the degree of female liberation in American society. In the 1920s, second-generation Chinese women enjoyed a level of freedom inconceivable to most families in China: they worked outside the home, volunteered for various social causes, married men of their own choice, and practiced birth control. Some native Chinese men were horrified by the casual displays of intimacy between Americans of the opposite sex. When Yu-shan Han arrived in the United States in 1926, he was greeted by a friend's girlfriend with a kiss. Appalled, he described the episode in an essay for a Chicago literary contest on the subject of "My Most Embarrassing Moment." He didn't win the contest, he later explained, because a kiss from a girl meant nothing in the United States.

"Chinese women who are born here are regular flappers," Mar Sui Haw, an upwardly mobile first-generation Chinese immigrant in Seattle, declared in 1924. He went to San Francisco to work for his uncle's store and newspaper, mastered English, and graduated from a business school. Though he viewed himself as modern and Americanized, he still yearned for a traditional Chinese wife:

> They [Chinese American women] do not have any virtues whatever. Chinese women who come over are so taken with them that they do not try to learn what they should. In China no women are immoral. Here they do not care. It is hard for me to pick up a mate here. I like to marry and have a family.

Before the new immigration law, I thought I would like to go back to China and get a wife, but now I cannot do this. It is hard. A class of Chinese girl here in this country who do not care. Shows, dancing all the time. I cannot stand that kind.

Other men shared these sentiments. "It is not right for Chinese man born in China to marry Chinese woman born in America," Andrew Kan asserted. "They will not be happy. They do not have the same training, the same feeling about the home the girls do in China." In the 1920s, when Wallace Lee, a Chinese immigrant in Buffalo, New York, was searching for a wife, his cousin warned, "Don't get married in the United States! Chinese girls talk about freedom, freedom, free, free, free too much! Too new, too fresh, couldn't make a good wife."

Still other taboos remained to be broken. Some American-born Chinese braved ridicule, gossip, and ostracism by entering into interracial marriages, which in many states were banned entirely by anti-miscegenation laws. For many immigrant parents, such marriages were unthinkable. Some could not tolerate their sons or daughters wedding outside the Chinese ethnic community, and a few Chinese Americans of that era recall being shunned by friends and relatives simply for marrying Japanese or Korean Americans. Within certain families, even marriage to a person of Chinese heritage was not enough to fulfill strict family requirements; Rodney Chow recalled that his grandparents did not want any of their offspring to marry outside their own dialect.

Yet interracial unions were more common than might be expected. Studies in some parts of the country found that as many as a quarter of all marriages involving Chinese partners were mixed marriages. In Los Angeles, Milton L. Barron surveyed 97 Chinese marriages contracted between 1924 and 1933 and found that 23.7 percent were interracial. For the same period, he examined 650 Chinese marriages in New York State (excluding New York City) and discovered that 150 were to non-Chinese partners. The interracial marriage rate for Chinese in the United States was much higher than that for Japanese, at 6.3 percent, or blacks, at only 1.1 percent.

In time, some of these marriages transcended the barriers of prejudice. When Tye Leung, a Chinese American interpreter at Angel Island, married Charles Schulze, a Caucasian immigration inspector, both were fired from their civil service jobs in San Francisco. Many Chinese snubbed them as well. At first, the residents of Chinatown referred to their mixed-race children as *fan gwai jai* ("foreign devil child"). But the Schulze family gradually gained acceptance, if only because Tye Leung devoted countless hours to volunteer service in the community. Later, she reminisced that her husband's mother and her own parents "disapprove very much" of their marriage, but as she observed, "when two people are in love, they don't think of the future."

While some parents fretted over the behavior of their children, others may have been even more concerned about the well-being of their families back in China. The 1920s were an era of prosperity for the United States, but in China the decade was a time of lawlessness, when the country was ruled by rapacious warlords. By the late 1920s, there were hopeful signs that the Republic of China would survive. A young Nationalist leader, Chiang Kai-shek, emerged to unify a fractured nation. The son of a merchant in the coastal province of Zhejiang, Chiang had gained his military training first in Japan and later, as a protégé of Sun Yat-sen, in the Soviet Union. Between 1926 and 1928 he led a campaign, known as the Northern Expedition, to defeat the warlords and consolidate control of China under the Nationalists. The following year, Chiang, now the supreme leader of the Nationalists, established the capital of the Republic of China in the city of Nanjing.

But it was still a troubled republic. The Northern Expedition had been supported by the Chinese Communist Party, but in 1927, shortly after the expedition began, Chiang purged his former allies from power. Enlisting his extensive contacts with organized crime syndicates, such as the notorious "Green Gang" in Shanghai, Chiang orchestrated the massacre of hundreds of left-wing labor activists. As the slaughter spread to other regions, the shattered remains of the Communist Party fled to the mountains. For the next few years, Chiang waged war against the Communist guerrillas, hoping to exterminate them altogether.

Chiang also faced relentless attacks from Japan, which viewed the chaos in China as a prime opportunity for military expansion. The first sign of trouble surfaced at the end of World War I. In the 1919 Versailles Treaty, Western powers decided not to return German concessions in Shandong province to China, but gave them to Japan instead. In a furor of national outrage known as the May Fourth movement, Chinese intellectuals held mass demonstrations in Beijing and across the country, but the Nationalist government was too weak to ward off Japanese encroachments. Less than a decade later, in 1928, Japan bombarded the city of Jinan in Shandong, killing or wounding more than seven thousand people. In 1931, Japan seized Manchuria, renamed it Manchukuo, and installed Henry Puyi, the last emperor of China, as puppet ruler. The following year, Japanese marines attacked Shanghai, but Chinese resistance forced them to retreat.

With heavy hearts, the Chinese American community followed these developments through ethnic newspapers and letters from relatives. Many immigrants wanted to help the new republic defend itself against Japanese assaults, but were uncertain how to do so beyond sending money home to their own families. But soon, even those remittances would be put in jeopardy, as their newly adopted country found itself mired in the deepest economic depression in its history.

CHAPTER TWELVE

Chinese America During
the Great Depression

The Great Depression struck most Americans without warning, ending one of the nation's most glittering decades. The 1920s, otherwise known as the Jazz Age or the Roaring Twenties, now evoke images of shocking new fashions and pleasures—of bootleggers in speakeasies, of flappers in short skirts dancing provocative new dances at wild parties flowing with gin. Everyone seemed to have money. The pervasive feeling of prosperity arose from off-the-chart economic growth in the twenties, a period when American business was given free rein by the government. New technological wonders that promised to liberate millions of Americans from drudgery—automobiles and radios, washing machines and vacuum cleaners—rolled off factory assembly lines and were snapped up by a boundlessly optimistic public, often on credit. The United States was now by far the wealthiest nation in the world, with a national income surpassing that of much of Europe and a dozen other countries combined. American corporations built skyscrapers as towering monuments to their ability to do so. Large numbers of people—not just moguls, but maids and shoeshine boys—eagerly played the stock market, hoping to amass a fortune, and most were doing well at it. It seemed that in this age of perpetual prosperity, with some companies starting to include workers in their stock plans, labor unions would soon become obsolete.

But after a decade of frenzied stock market speculation, the bubble burst. On October 24, 1929, "Black Thursday," came the first great crash on Wall Street, followed by a series of secondary shocks, and then a long, sickening slide toward a national depression.* The effect rippled away from New York deep into the hinterlands of the country, shutting down banks and putting companies out of business, until twenty million Americans found themselves unemployed, about 16 percent of the entire U.S. population.

The wheels of capitalism ground to a halt. Bankrupt executives flung themselves out of high-rises, hoping that their families could collect on their life insurance policies. Thousands of laid-off workers went hungry, as farmers, facing foreclosures, burned their crops because the new, lower prices for many farm products did not cover shipping costs. Young men and women lived as hobos, jumping freight trains and riding in boxcars, crisscrossing the country in their futile search for jobs. Growing numbers of homeless Americans slept in shanties made of newspapers and cardboard—"Hoovervilles," they were sarcastically named, referring to President Herbert Hoover's inability to revive the economy. Eventually, the depression spread across the globe. As pessimism deepened about the ability of capitalism to heal itself, youths began to read Communist literature and talk revolution.

California was spared the worst effects of the depression, largely because, unlike the industrialized East, its economy centered on agriculture. But the 1930s saw horrendous working conditions in the fields of California. The depression coincided with a severe drought in the Great Plains states, which baked the overworked soil into a giant "dust bowl." White farmers from those regions, especially Oklahoma, loaded their possessions into jalopies and fled to California, hoping to serve as migrant farm workers, crowding into

---

*Another date cited for the crash is October 29, the day on which the market took its worst beating.

squalid shacks in private labor camps where they were treated almost like slaves. Their plight was immortalized in John Steinbeck's novel *The Grapes of Wrath*, as impoverished whites, known as "Okies," the new serfs of California, took their place in the fields where the Chinese had worked decades earlier.

Most Chinese were able to avoid these upheavals in rural California. By the 1930s, they were largely concentrated in major cities, usually in their own racially segregated neighborhoods. The Great Depression did not affect the Chinatowns of 1930s as badly as the crisis of the 1870s, largely because of the self-sufficiency of these ethnic communities. The knowledge that they could not get easy access to white venture capital had long ago instilled in them certain protective habits, such as frugality, reliance on family connections, and avoidance of frivolous debt. Isolated from white mainstream America, deeply distrustful of white banks, most Chinese businesses had established their own informal credit systems. Aspiring entrepreneurs would borrow money from their own relatives, or partner with other Chinese immigrants to create a *hui*, a pool of capital into which they would make regular deposits and out of which loans would be made at mutually agreed rates of interest.

This is not to say, however, that they did not feel the impact of the depression. As growing numbers of white Americans were thrown out of work, there was less money to pay for services the Chinese provided, such as restaurant dining or laundry. As money grew tighter, Chinese families, like millions of white families, had to make do with less. "I remember wearing sneakers with holes in them," Lillian Louie said of her New York Chinatown childhood. She would patch the shoes with cardboard and not tell her parents. "We didn't want to bother them, you know, they had enough to do. They worked so hard."

As the decade progressed, the United States passed emergency legislation to combat the effects of the Great Depression. When Franklin D. Roosevelt entered the White House in 1933, he inaugurated, under an agenda known as the New Deal, a flurry of federal programs to regulate banks, initiate public projects, and put the unemployed back to work. Some programs benefited ethnic Chinese by giving them government jobs and financial assistance. By 1935, 2,300, or 18 percent, of the Chinese in San Francisco were receiving government aid, thanks to the Federal Emergency Relief Act. The number was lower than that for the general American population (22 percent), because many Chinese refused to participate in these programs, scorning them as charity. "During the Depression, I'd see these people taking canned goods [home] from school," recalled Mark Wong, an American-born Chinese in San Francisco. "And my dad refused. He told me simply, 'You're not going to bring back any canned goods back here, period.' I think the pride of the Chinese is very strong. We're not going to accept food from anybody even to feed ourselves, even when we're eating less."

Though loath to accept government handouts, many Chinese did not hesitate to fight when the interests of their community were threatened. During the Great Depression, Chinese laundry owners in New York City successfully battled white competitors trying to drive them out of business with restrictive municipal codes. In 1933, city aldermen proposed that U.S. citizenship be a requirement for operating a laundry, and set high license fees and security bonds that were far beyond the means of the majority of Chinese laundries, which for the most part were small operations. If it had passed, the ordinance would have damaged if not destroyed the entire Chinese laundry industry in New York.

The response was immediate. The Chinese washermen organized the Chinese Hand Laundry Alliance, which issued a public statement declaring that if they did not fight this ordinance immediately, "tens of thousands of Chinese laundry men would be stranded in this country, and our wives and children back home would be starved to death." Pooling their resources to hire a prominent white attorney, the CHLA succeeded in pressuring the city to reduce the license and bond fees substantially and exempt all "Orientals" from the U.S. citizenship requirement. CHLA continued to thrive for years, reaching its peak in 1934 with 3,200 members.

Smaller battles, less epic in scale but equally important, were also waged as individual Chinese tried to save their businesses during the depression. In some cases, they revealed remarkable reserves of strength within families. In her poignant autobiographical essay, "An Early Baltimore Chinese Family: Lee Yick You and Louie Yu Oy," Lillian Lee Kim described how she and her siblings survived double disasters before the onset of the depression: first the death of her father in 1928 from illness, then the physical collapse of her mother after battling her husband's first son from a previous marriage for control of the household savings. One evening, after vomiting a stream of blood, the mother was confined to bed, leaving her grade-school children completely responsible for the day-to-day operation of the laundry. Amazingly, they kept the business alive without adult supervision. Arranging for a wholesaler to wash the soiled laundry during the day, they rushed home from school each afternoon to sort, starch, and press clothes until bedtime, with the younger ones standing on stools to reach the ironing board. As they grew older, they found part-time jobs on weekends—doing housework, carrying groceries for shoppers, and helping vendors sell fruits and vegetables. Their valiant teamwork helped them rescue the laundry from bankruptcy and weather the Great Depression.

As Chinese family businesses worked harder during the depression, Chinese civic leaders joined together to discuss strategies for increasing their earnings. Tourism appeared to be a reliable source of cash. In San Francisco, immigrant Chinese merchants had sensed early the potential profits of this industry: after the 1906 earthquake and fire destroyed the old Chinatown, Chinese businessmen erected new structures that, according to the *San Francisco Chronicle,* were "thoroughly modern" yet projected an "Oriental charm and attractiveness." With a steady stream of articles, brochures, and advertisements, the local media, the San Francisco Chamber of Commerce, and the Chinese community itself all worked together to promote Chinatown as one of the city's visitor attractions. In 1915, San Francisco Chinatown staged its first beauty pageant to encourage white male tourism. Businessman H. K. Wong, founder of the contest, wanted to reward "the looks that made China's beauties so fascinating." Crown contenders sheathed their figures in skintight satin *chipao* gowns, the traditional costume for women in the Qing dynasty. These promotional efforts paid off. By the 1930s, Chinatown had captured almost one-fifth of the city's tourist trade.

During the Great Depression, the San Francisco Chinese, concerned about the business slowdown, redoubled their efforts to draw tourist revenue, no matter the means: "Make tourists WANT to come; and when they come, let us have something to SHOW them!" The result was a live fantasy version of the "wicked Orient," exploiting the most debased stereotypes of the Chinese. Tour guides spun tales of a secret, labyrinthine world under Chinatown, filled with narcotics, gambling halls, and brothels, where beautiful slave girls, both Chinese and white, were kept in bondage. They ushered gaping tourists into fake opium dens and fake leper colonies.

Other Chinatowns across the United States also played the tourist game. In Los Angeles, teenagers earned money after school by pulling rickshaws for white sightseers. In New York City, where tourism in Chinatown had already thrived for decades, guides warned visitors to hold hands for safety as they walked through the neighborhood's streets. They paid Chinese residents to stage elaborate street dramas, including knife fights between "opium-crazed" men over possession of a prostitute.

The reality of the 1930s was that Chinatown neighborhoods were actually becoming less violent. The tour guides, who entranced their white audiences with stories about hatchetmen and highbinders, were describing a bygone era that reflected poorly on the realities of modern organized crime within the Chinese community. By the early twentieth century, Chinese tongs had become more professional in their operations, less willing to risk scaring off white tourists with real bloodshed. If in previous years merchants and tong leaders had fought over money, they now colluded to increase profits. In fact, merchants themselves often joined tongs to expand their power base, and in some instances the line between respectable Chinese business-man and crime syndicate leader vanished altogether. Historian Adam McKeown has noted that in the 1930s, the minutes of the Hip Sing tong, historically a powerful criminal and extortionist association, resembled the meetings of "a joint stock company." Each branch voted for a "congressman" to represent local interests at the national meeting, the topics discussed including protection and extortion rates, deadlines for payment, and the distribution of revenue.

Although prostitution in Chinatowns also declined through this period, thanks largely to the efforts of missionaries and middle-class Chinese activists, the purveyors of the tourist trade continued to exploit flesh for profit. During the 1930s, Charlie Low opened the Forbidden City nightclub in San Francisco Chinatown, hiring hun-dreds of Chinese women (most of them middle-class and college-educated) to dance in his floor show. Like the famous Cotton Club in Harlem, Low's establishment featured ethnic minority talent per-forming before a largely Caucasian audience. When Low put nude acts on the stage, he scandalized all of Chinatown, which con-demned the dancers as whores. Outraged mothers forbade their daughters to work there or even to go near the place. But many young Chinese women continued to take the work. Sex appeal was lucrative, and the Forbidden City thrived, attracting more than one hundred thousand customers a year, among them senators, gover-nors, and at least one future president (Ronald Reagan, then a young actor, is reported to have been an eager patron). Toward the end of the decade, the World's Fair in San Francisco exposed the crass ambitions of certain Chinatown merchants eager to distort the image of Chinese women to entice white sensibilities. When the organizers of the fair committed $1.2 million to build an authentic Chinese village on Treasure Island, a few Chinese businessmen sug-gested having naked girls jump out of a cake to draw huge audi-ences. The proposal was dropped when critics strenuously objected, pointing out that the idea was not only trashy but hardly authenti-cally Chinese.

Many inhabitants of the nation's Chinatowns chafed whenever the tourists came around. For one thing, they hated being gawked at like zoo animals, and they had expressed their anger long before Chinese capitalists embraced tourism during the depression. "Every day and all year round there are special sightseeing motor cars decorated with Japanese paper lanterns bearing a huge signboard in front standing right in the midst of the business center of New York City and with a couple of people walking around shouting desperately, 'Chinatown, O, Chinatown, one dollar down to see Chinatown,'" S. J. Benjamin Cheng, a Columbia University student, wrote in a letter to the *New York Times*. "What do you think that a Chinese or any red-blooded human will feel when he passes by such a car and hears such shouting?"

They were also exasperated by myths that a subterranean community thrived under the city streets. "I never saw an underground tunnel," one Chinese man insisted. "Just mah-jongg rooms in the basements." In Los Angeles, residents denied the existence of tunnels, though they recalled that the Chinese district used to have alleys with ceilings so that chickens could be raised there. Some resentful Chinese threatened to beat up white tourists, and did occasionally resort to violence. "We hated them!" declared Lung Chin in New York Chinatown. "Because the sightseers, they would come around, they would always be talking bad stories about China." He seethed when he heard falsehoods about opium dens and slave girls; the Chinese, he said, were in the United States to "make a living, not to capture white girls for slavery." And he admitted, "We would have fights with them. How many times I go up there, I say, 'That's a lie!' and then I hit them."*

---

*Many whites believed the manufactured myths. "Last summer, on a day early in the afternoon, a big, husky, middle-aged American gentleman opened the [YMCA] door and asked in broken English for the location of the underground tunnels and opium dens," one observer in San Francisco noted. "On being told that no such places existed, he was quite disappointed and 'Chinatown' lost its glamour [for] him." White teenage girls, fed images of Chinese men as white slavers, seemed titillated by Chinatown's reputation. According to the *Chicago Tribune*, they searched for Chinese men in alleys on their way to mission schools and toured Chinatown in groups in New York.

Projecting a false image of their community to mainstream whites may have earned the Chinese a certain amount of money, but the prostitution of their heritage was an extravagant price to pay. The guides cultivated fear and suspicion among white tourists, whose brief glimpses of Chinatown may have been their only contact with Chinese Americans during the exclusion era. We will never know how many people walked away certain that the Chinese could never assimilate. Nor will we know how many Chinese Americans endured racial discrimination and a hostile job market in the United States as a direct consequence of the myths fostered by Chinatown tourism and spread through white communities by tourists who "saw it all firsthand." Worst of all, some of these negative images were perpetuated on the silver screen, where they reached a mass audience far beyond the numbers of tourists who actually came and spent money in Chinatown.

Stereotyping minorities was nothing new to Hollywood. Since the dawn of film, the movie industry had made them the butt of cruel jokes, and Chinese Americans had played their part. In an 1894 silent film, *Chinese Laundry Scene,* a Chinese character entertains white audiences by eluding an Irish cop. In *The Terrible Kids,* a 1906 film, a group of mischievous boys attack a Chinese man and yank his queue. But soon a different, more sinister image appeared. In 1908, D. W. Griffith released *The Fatal Hour,* in which the Chinese villain Pong Lee, aided by cleaver-wielding Chinese thugs, kidnaps and enslaves innocent white girls.

By the 1920s, as Chinatown tourism grew more popular, Fu Manchu made his debut in Saturday afternoon matinees. Writing under the pen name Sax Rohmer, Arthur Sarsfield Ward had introduced the diabolical Fu Manchu in a series of pulp fiction thrillers, describing the character as "the great and evil man who dreamed of Europe and America under Chinese rule . . . whose existence was a menace to the entire white race." The Fu Manchu created by Rohmer/Ward was not only a genius, but a beast: "The green eyes gleamed upon me vividly like those of a giant cat . . . a man whose brown body glistened unctuously, whose shaven head was apish low, whose bloodshot eyes were the eyes of a mad dog! His teeth, upper and lower, were bared; they glistened, they gnashed, and a froth was on his lips."

The Fu Manchu character had its female counterparts. Films depicted Chinese women either as victims, fragile China dolls, compliant and sexually available to white men, or villainesses, dragon ladies, cunning and dangerous seductresses. Anna May Wong, the first Chinese American—indeed, the first Asian American—movie star, built her entire career on such roles, playing a series of stock, one-dimensional characters, such as the evil daughter of Fu Manchu.

By the 1930s, during the heyday of Chinatown tourism, cinema had matured into America's most popular form of entertainment. The introduction of sound led to Hollywood's golden age, when people entered cavernous theaters to forget, if only temporarily, their depression-era woes, to lose themselves in the glamour of the screen. The images of the Chinese they saw on the screen did not reflect reality, but instead the taboo sexual desires or hidden anxieties of white audiences about a people they did not fully understand. The demonization, or oversexualization, of Chinese characters in films was akin to the presentation by lazy novelists and filmmakers of Italian Americans as preponderantly Mafia henchmen, personae created to resonate with the criminal stereotypes widely accepted by the general public even though the overwhelming majority of Italian Americans were and are law-abiding citizens.

During the depression, white audiences embraced Charlie Chan, a character who combined the contradictory stereotypes of Chinese mystic and Chinese buffoon. Between 1925 and 1932, six Charlie Chan detective novels, written by Earl Derr Biggers, appeared in the *Saturday Evening Post* in serial form and spawned forty-eight films. Chan was a brilliant, rotund Chinese detective who, while not evil, exuded, like Fu Manchu, an aura of Oriental inscrutability. As played by Caucasian actors, most famously Swedish-born Warner Oland, he had a face resembling an ancient Chinese mask, with half-closed eyes and a cryptic smile. He personified the wise old Confucian sage, dropping proverbs faster than his antagonists could drop clues. Yet his demeanor lent itself, inevitably, to ridicule. His words of wisdom sounded like fortune cookie messages, and his personality could be reduced to Chinese menu offerings: a white police sergeant in *Charlie Chan at the Opera* (1937) refers to Chan as "egg foo yung" and tells him, "You're all right. Just like chop suey. A mystery, but a swell dish."

Because the best dramatic roles went to whites, it was difficult for Chinese American actors to depict their people as genuine human beings. The whites' practice of adopting yellowface in Hollywood not only robbed ethnic performers of starring roles but also promoted Chinese caricatures. Smothered in heavy makeup and wearing prosthetic masks, many white actors—including top stars such as John Wayne and Katharine Hepburn—had no qualms about slanting their eyes and speaking with a fake accent. While some were delighted to assume exotic personae to expand their artistic range, it was often forgotten that Chinese American actors were being deprived of similar opportunities, and not just because no one would have seriously entertained the notion of a Chinese actor's donning whiteface to play a Caucasian.

At the pinnacle of her career, Anna May Wong failed to land the starring role of O'Lan in *The Good Earth,* a movie based on the novel by Pearl Buck, and one of few films that depicted China favorably to American audiences. The role went to Luise Rainer, who won an Oscar for her performance. When the studio offered Wong the part of Lotus, the wicked concubine, she protested: "You're asking me—with my Chinese blood—to do the only unsympathetic role in the picture, featuring an all-American cast portraying Chinese characters." Heartbroken by the snub, the Los Angeles–born Wong left Hollywood in 1936 to visit China, only to be criticized in her ancestral homeland. "Because I had been the villainess so often in pictures, it was thought that I had not been true to my people," she later told a reporter. "It took four hours one afternoon to convince the Chinese government this was not so. I couldn't give up my career, because I feel it is really drawing China nearer and making it better understood and liked."

If even Wong could not gain a major role in a film about China, then other Chinese actors faced even slimmer prospects. Only a few worked in the film industry, most of them as extras who rarely had speaking roles. The majority of them did little more than provide exotic background for films set in Asia. The work was sporadic; months, even years, could elapse between calls for jobs. Whenever a major film with a Chinese story line went before the cameras, some Chinese extras dared not venture far from the phone for fear of losing a rare chance at work.

A few enterprising individuals realized that they could make far more money in Hollywood as agents than as actors. As in other industries, entrepreneurial Chinese Americans assumed middleman roles in Hollywood, matching white capital with Chinese labor. Actress Bessie Loo started her own talent agency in Los Angeles. Tom Gubbins, the Eurasian owner of the Asiatic Costume Company, earned money both from the Chinese actors and the studios. As an agent, he placed extras in movies like *The Good Earth* (1937) and *The Bitter Tea of General Yen* (1933), charging the standard 10 percent commission on the actors' pay. He also made a fortune from the studios by renting out rickshaws, costumes, and props. And because he spoke both Cantonese and English fluently (he was born in Shanghai and reared in Hong Kong), Gubbins earned a third income as an interpreter, translating the director's instructions for the extras.

As these middlemen helped Hollywood package images of the Chinese for mass consumption, fiction replaced reality even for some Chinese Americans. A movie set was "the closest we would ever get to China," journalist Louise Leung observed in an article for the *Los Angeles Times* Sunday magazine in 1936. She described a typical day for a Chinese American extra, when "youngsters, Hollywood-stylish in gaucho shirts and berets, stood alongside Chinatown grandfathers who had never become reconciled to American shores." The extras walked through a replica of a south Chinese village: "The mingled odor of dried ducks, incense, preserved ginger, scented rolls of silk gave the marketplace a most authentic Chinese aura, the smell of Chinatown, the smell of China. The native Chinese looked at it all with a yearning nostalgia; even the young one with the movie eyelashes murmured, 'Gosh, this must be just like China.' "

To many American-born Chinese, the nation of China represented an ideal, a utopian world in which they would be fully accepted. According to Victor Wong, who spent his childhood in San Francisco Chinatown during the 1930s, "the older people, they were always talking about going back home. *All the time.* 'When we go back to China we'll have this and we'll have that; there won't be any more discrimination.' "

Even before the depression, some Chinese immigrant parents had encouraged their American-born children to straddle both countries: to obtain their education in the United States but build their careers in China. This was the message that Sam Chang, a southern California farm pioneer, passed down to his son in 1925. In the course of urging his brother—who held a medical degree from Georgetown University and a position at Beijing Union Hospital and was contemplating a return to the States—to stay in China, Chang wrote to his son, "If your uncle comes back to America, he might make a little money, but his reputation and social rank will be low; and his knowledge will be wasted. He will never become a respected man as America is the most racist society and very prejudiced against the Yellow race of people."

The Great Depression seemed to ratify those words. In the 1930s, the Oriental Division of the United States Employment Service in San Francisco reported that more than 90 percent of their placements were in the service sector, mainly the food industry. Some Chinese engineers and scientists were demoralized at finding themselves back in Chinatown working at menial jobs in laundries and restaurants. "Father used to tell me, 'Look at your boss,' " said James Low, an American-born Chinese, whose boss had been educated as a mining engineer, but ended up in a garment factory. " 'He was going to be an engineer, look what happened to him!' " One Chinese graduate of MIT became a waiter. Residents of Little Canton, a Chinese enclave in Cherrywood, California, remembered that several Chinese Americans with engineering degrees had no choice but to work in restaurants. "Oh, you couldn't get a job outside of the Chinese community because, you know, look [at] your face," one elderly bachelor said. "You're Chinese, you're not American. So what if you've got ten degrees?"

Perhaps China, then, was the better option for them. In 1933, the respected San Francisco Chinese-language newspaper *Chung Sai Yat Po* openly urged young Chinese Americans to seek employment in their ancestral homeland, where they would be less likely to encounter racism. The bleak job prospects during the Great Depression made it easier for some youths to vow allegiance to a motherland they had never seen. Rodney Chow remembered his Chinese American friends dreaming about going "back" to China, even though some had difficulty speaking the language and had never visited the country. In 1935, 75 percent of the attendees at the Chinese Young People's Summer Conference in Lake Tahoe announced that they wanted to serve China, many professing that it was their duty.

In 1936, the conflict over identity and loyalty was intensified in a national essay contest with the theme "Does My Future Lie in China or America?" The competition, sponsored by the Ging Hawk Club in New York, an organization founded by the International Institute of the YMCA, provoked a lively debate among second-generation Chinese Americans, and the *Chinese Digest* published the finalists' essays.

The winner was Robert Dunn, a student at Harvard. Dunn viewed himself as a human bridge between two cultures. He could achieve more in the United States, he wrote, by fostering understanding, goodwill, and business partnerships between the two countries. But he also noted that "ever since I can remember, I have been taught by my parents, by my Chinese friends, and by my teacher in Chinese school, that I must be patriotic to China." China had enjoyed a glorious four-thousand-year history and Robert owed his very existence to his Chinese ancestors, they told him, and he should recognize the humiliation endured by the Chinese in the United States. "Don't you realize that the Chinese are mocked at, trodden upon, disrespected, and even spit upon?" he quoted his parents as telling him. "Haven't you yourself been called degrading names? Have you no face, no sense of shame, no honor? How can you possibly think of staying in America to serve it?"

Yet Robert also felt that the United States was worth defending. "I owe much pride and gratitude to America for the principles of liberty and equality which it upholds, for the protection its government has given me, and for its schools and institutions in which I have partici-pated. Without them, I certainly would not be what I am now. I am cer-tainly as much indebted to America as I am to China." Employment opportunities were scarce in China, he wrote, and as an American he would have a hard time adjusting to life there. His future, he concluded, belonged to America.

The second-place winner, Kaye Hong of the University of Washington, had no feelings of ambivalence. His duty, "built on the mound of shame," lay in China. "The ridicule heaped upon the Chinese race has long fermented within my soul," he wrote. He believed that jobs for ABCs were more plentiful in China, where they were needed to build a greater, stronger nation. His advice to himself and others, ironically paraphrasing Horace Greeley, was, " 'Go Further West, Young Man.' Yes, across the Pacific and to China."*

A number of them did. In the 1930s, an estimated one in five ABCs migrated to work in China. Most were sojourners, living in their ancestral homeland for a few years and then returning to the United States. Those with professional training found employment as engi-

---

*Both winning essayists ended up doing precisely the opposite of their written inten-tions. After graduating with a degree in international law from Harvard, Robert Dunn worked in Nationalist China as secretary to a delegate to the United Nations. Kaye Hong stayed in America, where he became a successful businessman.

neers, scientists, doctors, professors, businessmen, social workers, and government bureaucrats. Foreign branches of American corporations, U.S. government agencies, educational institutions, and religious organizations like the YMCA needed the skills of college-educated Chinese Americans—preferably bilingual Chinese Americans, though individuals lacking fluency in Mandarin could still teach English. The Chinese Ministry of Industry sought engineers with experience in iron and steel, the Shanghai Aviation Association recruited pilots, and the Chinese government even invited ethnic Chinese farmers from the United States to migrate, promising them money, machinery, and property. Like the relatives of the first-wave immigrants, second-generation Chinese American expatriates (or true patriots, as some might define them) enjoyed a better standard of living than the typical Chinese native: many lived in prestigious residential areas populated almost entirely by other Chinese Americans, and hired teams of servants.

Interestingly enough, some fought fiercely to retain American customs in China, just as their parents had stubbornly retained Chinese customs in the United States. For instance, in 1932 Flora Belle Jan, the wife of a University of Chicago graduate, moved to Beijing when her husband accepted a position as a college professor there. Even though Jan, an ABC writer from Fresno, California, had always dreamt of living in her ancestral homeland, she could not establish an emotional bond with the natives because of her inability to read and write the language. She took a job at the U.S. Office of War Information in Beijing and befriended mainly English-speaking businessmen, diplomats, and students. She insisted that her Chinese-born children watch American films, wear Western clothes, and eat American food.

No matter what their personal feelings toward China, many American-born Chinese were forced to return to the United States for their own protection. For just when America was pulling itself out of the Great Depression, Nationalist China was facing a crisis so monumental it threatened to eclipse everything that had preceded it.

CHAPTER THIRTEEN

"The Most Important Historical Event of Our Times": World War II

hile the United States struggled in the 1930s to get through the depression, China faced a crisis the rest of the world would not face for the better part of a decade—the beginnings of war. By 1931, the Japanese had already seized Manchuria. There were further skirmishes in various places, including Shanghai, all marked by the brutality of the Japanese military against soldiers and civilians alike. Because the Chinese central government was weak and had failed to modernize its military, the Japanese were able to act with impunity. In the long term, their expulsion from China would require more than the efforts of the Nationalist government. It would require Japan's defeat by the West.

Alas, the first, and only, response to these incursions, which were clear violations of international law and were executed with total disregard for the loss of civilian life, came from the League of Nations, which censured Japan as an aggressor nation. Japan rejected the opprobrium and withdrew from the League, undermining that body's credibility just at a time when it needed it most; within a few years, Italy and Germany would pose bold new challenges to the weakened League's ability to act as a peacekeeper. So would Japan, which in 1935 moved into a region of China now known as Inner Mongolia.

215

Two years later, in July 1937, Japan's previous sporadic, but never haphazard, military thrusts into China reached the level of a full-scale invasion. The escalation began with a trivial incident—the mysterious disappearance of a Japanese soldier after military exercises at the Marco Polo Bridge near Beijing. A Japanese commander, claiming that the soldier had been abducted by the Chinese, led an assault on a nearby junction town. Hostilities continued even after the soldier reappeared on his own, clearly unmolested and unhurt; within a month the Japanese controlled the entire Beijing region.

The Japanese imperial government expanded operations by dispatching troops to northern and central China, as well as to the coastal city of Shanghai, China's largest metropolis. Chiang Kai-shek, the leader of the Nationalist government, invested his best forces in the defense of Shanghai, but they were no match for Japan's better trained and better equipped military. The Nationalist army suffered some 250,000 casualties in a vain attempt to save the city. Before the end of the year, Japanese forces had also conquered Nanjing (Nanking), the capital of the Republic of China. In one of the worst atrocities of the twentieth century, a bloodbath that came to be known as the Rape of Nanking, the Japanese imperial army raped and slaughtered hundreds of thousands of civilians, presaging a war that would last eight years and claim the lives of as many as 35 million Chinese.

Especially hard hit was the Toishan region, the point of origin for most of the Chinese immigrants in America. When the Japanese seized the region's crops to feed their own troops, many locals simply starved to death. Further, the Japanese capture of the port city of Hong Kong in 1941 closed off a major hub of communication between China and the United States. For generations, Hong Kong had served as the headquarters for major emigration firms, which safely and reliably delivered money from Chinese American men to their Toishanese families. The fall of Hong Kong ended this inflow of overseas money, turning the lives of many Gold Mountain families upside down almost overnight. Having settled in as members of the local leisure class, they were particularly vulnerable because they no longer had the skills required to provide for themselves and their families. To buy food, some pawned first their jewelry and furniture, then their homes, and finally themselves. In the most desperate cases, Gold Mountain wives entered into prostitution and sold their own children into slavery. Before the war's end in 1945, at least 150,000 Toishanese—about one in four—had either died or disappeared.

Galvanized by the plight of their families, and horrified by reports of Japanese atrocities, Chinese Americans rallied to promote public awareness of the Sino-Japanese War. Most Chinese immigrants had not been formally educated in the United States and were not fluent in English, but they did their best, however imperfectly, to make Americans aware of the situation in the Far East. The publicity campaign was waged both within and beyond the Chinese community. In general, the recent émigrés used Chinese newspapers, radio programs, and street demonstrations to disseminate within the Chinese communities news of the dire plight of China, while the American-educated Chinese used the English-language press and the lecture circuit to reach a broader segment of Americans. In New York City, the Chinese Hand Laundry Alliance distributed thousands of English-language flyers through their laundry shops, asking Americans to boycott Japanese goods.

The Chinese Americans not only talked, they acted. One practical contribution they could offer China was skilled manpower in aviation. During the early stages of the Pacific war, China's air force was so primitive that it posed virtually no threat to Japan's. At one point Nationalist China possessed fewer than ninety planes in safe working condition, compared to more than two thousand in the Japanese military. But in the United States, as early as the 1920s, Chinese Americans had founded a number of private aviation schools or clubs to train young pilots to defend their ancestral homeland should the need ever arise, which flourished in cities with large ethnic Chinese populations such as San Francisco, New York, Boston, Chicago, Portland, and

Pittsburgh.* Some of the graduates became war heroes in the United States military, like P-39 pilot Stanley Lau, who flew more than fifty missions over Europe, shot down seven Messerschmitts, and won the Distinguished Flying Cross. Others enlisted in the Chinese military, like Clifford Louie, who rose to the position of general in the Kuomintang air force.

Chinese Americans also organized to try to prevent the sale to Japan of American scrap metal, which was being turned into munitions used to kill Chinese. In January 1938, thirty-nine Chinese sailors in San Francisco refused to ship a cargo of scrap steel to Japan and were promptly dismissed from their jobs. Within months, Chinese American demonstrations broke out in New York and along the West Coast, effectively halting the shipment of raw war materials to Japan. One of the largest protests began in San Francisco in December 1938. When Japan's Mitsui Company leased the SS *Spyros,* a Greek freighter docked in the city, to transport steel to Japan, Chinese American groups and their allies threw up a picket line on the docks. A crowd of two hundred Chinese volunteers and three hundred Greeks, Jews, and other Caucasians demonstrated in front of the *Spyros.* Soon they were joined by more Chinese Americans, who had flocked in from nearby cities, until the picket line comprised eight thousand people. Drenched by rain, they made a pitiful spectacle: the red ink trickled from their posters, and their faces, in the words of one reporter, looked as if they were "spattered with blood and tears."

---

*Chinese American women took to the skies as well. One of the first female aviators of Chinese descent was Ouyang Ying, who resolved in the 1910s to help China build its military defense. Tragically, she died in a plane accident in 1920, at the age of twenty-five, before she could move to China. Another pioneer was Katherine Cheung; in 1931 she became the first Chinese woman in America to earn a pilot's license. Cheung became something of a celebrity, awing spectators with her aerial performances and earning headlines in San Francisco newspapers. A woman ahead of her time, she criticized the Chinese Nationalists for barring female students from their aviation schools. Cheung intended to start her own pilot training program in China but changed her mind after she survived a plane crash and her ailing father begged her never to fly again.

But pitiful sight or not, their demonstration won over the dock workers. Members of both the International Longshoremen (ILU) and the Warehousemen's Union (ILWU) passed resolutions of support, stating that they were "100 percent opposed to passing the picket line." Loading stopped for five days, and through negotiations between the union and the Chinese American leaders it was decided that the picketing would end if the ILWU hosted a conference to promote an embargo on all war matériel to Japan. In a rare moment of solidarity, organized labor actually joined forces with the Chinese War Relief Association, the American Friends of China, and the Church Federation to initiate a national embargo. Their efforts and those of others paid off when in early 1941 Congress authorized President Franklin D. Roosevelt to halt the sale of arms and certain raw materials outside the western hemisphere (except to Britain), angering the Japanese.

Simultaneous with the embargo drive were efforts to raise money and supplies for the Nationalists. Starting in 1938, San Francisco Chinatown organized "Rice Bowl" parties—massive street spectacles that drew hundreds of thousands of people. Cities with large Chinese populations, such as New York and Los Angeles, also hosted their versions of these parties. Like Mardi Gras celebrations, they were boisterous, noisy affairs, lavish in scale and lasting for days. Through confetti-filled streets, the Chinese orchestrated dragon dances, floats, fireworks, re-creations of "Old Chinatown," mock air raids, and sales of "humanity" buttons. Bystanders would pour money into rice bowls to support the Chinese war effort, or toss coins and dollar bills into a giant flag of the Chinese republic that was proudly paraded through the streets by Chinese women.

Fund-raising for the Pacific war united all levels of Chinese American society. Immigrants and American-born Chinese alike solicited money door to door and sold war bonds. Chinese physicians helped organize a blood bank in New York as well as the American Bureau for Medical Aid to China, to assist sick and wounded victims of the Japanese invasion. Chinese volunteers served the Red Cross, preparing shipments to China of bandages, drugs, and vaccines.

Middle-class women hosted bazaars, dances, and fashion shows for the cause, combining their social lives with social activism. Laundrymen placed relief-fund boxes on their counters and used the money collected to donate ambulances, cotton-padded clothing, and medicine to the Chinese military. In their scarce free time, garment workers sewed thousands of winter garments for wounded Nationalist soldiers. Even teenagers and young children pitched in, collecting tin cans, foil, and other scrap metal for the Nationalists.

In the end, some twenty cities collected about $20 million for the Chinese War Relief Association, and during the eight years of Japanese occupation, the Chinese American community donated a total of $25 million. These sums were not remarkable for their absolute dollar amount, but certainly so for the amount per individual. The ethnic Chinese community in the continental United States was minuscule during the Pacific war: about 75,000 at the start of the 1930s, a number that increased by only a few thousand as the decade progressed. The fund-raising efforts drew about $300 for every Chinese in the country, a substantial figure, particularly given the value of the dollar in the 1930s and the constricted budgets of most Chinatown residents, many of whom earned only five or six dollars a week; some gave almost every cent of their life savings to the cause.

However noble the intent, the effect of these fund-raising efforts on the outcome of the Sino-Japanese War is uncertain. Although some of the money bought clothes, gas masks, mosquito nets, and airplanes for the Nationalists, no one can determine if the funds collected, or provisions purchased with them, actually reached the Chinese soldiers. It is now clear that the Nationalist army was hardly a model of virtue or efficiency; during the war Chinese peasants were routinely kidnapped and conscripted into the army, given starvation-level food rations, and brutalized by their superiors. Montgomery Hom, the filmmaker of *We Served with Pride*, a documentary about Chinese American contributions to World War II, has expressed the belief that most of the money intended for the soldiers ended up in the pockets of corrupt Nationalist officials.

The heartfelt efforts did, however, give rise to a sense of political unity among the Chinese in the United States. Ironically, these fund-raisers drew on and in turn reinforced dormant feelings of loyalty to China during an era when ever-diminishing numbers of Chinese Americans had personal connections to their ancestral homeland. In 1940, for the first time, the percentage of U.S.-born Chinese Americans surpassed that of foreign-born immigrant Chinese. Thus, a majority of the Chinese in America had grown up in America, and most had never been to China. This left them with very little sense of personal identification with China, except through their parents. The war brought the entire community back together at just the time when a drift toward assimilation was gaining momentum.

By 1940, Japan had occupied nearly all of China's major cities, and the retreating Chiang Kai-shek was forced to establish a wartime cap-ital in Chongqing, in Sichuan province deep in the interior of China, but still subject to relentless Japanese air raids. With the coast firmly under Japanese control, the only route Chiang had available to obtain military supplies from the outside world was the Burma Road, a sin-gle treacherous ribbon of dirt highway twisting through the moun-tains between west China and Burma. Despite China's precarious condition, the country itself and its vast territories seemed uncon-querable. Japan found itself mired in Chinese guerrilla warfare, over-whelmed by the nation's size and enormous population.

Although foreign correspondents sent back grisly reports for U.S. newspapers, and short newsreels about the Japanese invasion were shown in theaters, the war in China meant little to most Americans. The United States, with its predominately European-descended pop-ulation, focused much more attention on the war in Europe, where one country after another was falling to the Nazi blitzkrieg. But so strong were the isolationist sentiments among Americans that even the rise of Hitler—and reports of atrocities by refugees who had seen firsthand the horrors committed by Third Reich—could not induce the country to enter another world war. Far-sighted American leaders made the case that if the United States did not enter the fray quickly it might well be too late to save itself. Even this dire warning could not engender support for action. Noninterventionist feelings remained so high that President Franklin Roosevelt made neutrality an important part of his 1940 reelection campaign. Addressing the mothers and fathers of America, he promised, "I have said this before and I shall say it again and again and again. Your boys are not going to be sent into any foreign wars."

On December 7, 1941, Japan solved the quandary for America's leaders, by launching a surprise attack on Pearl Harbor.

Earlier that year, Roosevelt had already ordered an embargo on war supplies to Japan—an embargo made politically feasible in part by the Chinese American rallies on the shipping docks. The Japanese high command, fearful that their plan for Asian conquest would be thwarted, recommended to Emperor Hirohito a short-sighted and, in retrospect, suicidal response—an aerial attack on the American Pacific Fleet in Hawaii. At dawn on December 7, carrier-based Japanese planes bombed the United States naval base at Pearl Harbor, sinking or badly damaging twenty-one naval vessels, destroying almost two hundred American aircraft on the ground, and killing or wounding approximately three thousand naval and military personnel.

From that moment forward, America no longer considered the Pacific war a remote Asian event. The next day, in his address before Congress, Roosevelt, referring to December 7, 1941, as "a date which will live in infamy," asked the legislature to declare that "since the unprovoked and dastardly attack by Japan on Sunday, December seventh, a state of war has existed between the United States and the Japanese Empire." Japan's allies—Nazi Germany and Italy—quickly declared war on the United States, thrusting the formerly isolationist country into a titanic global struggle on both sides of the world.

Almost overnight, the attack on Pearl Harbor transformed the American image of China and Japan—and redistributed stereotypes for both Chinese and Japanese Americans. Suddenly the media began depicting the Chinese as loyal, decent allies, and the Japanese as a race of evil spies and saboteurs. After the attack, a Gallup poll found that Americans saw the Chinese as "hardworking, honest, brave, religious, intelligent, and practical" and the Japanese as "treacherous, sly, cruel, and warlike"—each almost a perfect fit with one or the other of two popular stereotypes formerly promoted by Hollywood, in characters like Charlie Chan and Fu Manchu. The unspoken question for many Americans was how to tell the good guys from the bad guys. On December 22, 1941, *Time*, the premier newsweekly in the United States at the time, published an article entitled "How to Tell Your Friends from the Japs." According to *Time:*

> Virtually all Japanese are short . . . Japanese are likely to be stockier and broader-hipped than short Chinese. Japanese— except for wrestlers—are seldom fat; they often dry up and grow lean as they age. The Chinese often put on weight, particularly if they are prosperous (in China, with its frequent famines, being fat is esteemed as a sign of being a solid citizen). Chinese, not as hairy as Japanese, seldom grow an impressive mustache. Most Chinese avoid horn-rimmed spectacles. Although both have the typical epicanthic fold of the upper eyelid (which makes them look almond-eyed), Japanese eyes are usually set closer together. Those who know them best often rely on facial expression to tell them apart: the Chinese expression is likely to be more placid, kindly, open; the Japanese more positive, dogmatic, arrogant. . . . Japanese are hesitant, nervous in conversation, laugh loudly at the wrong time. Japanese walk stiffly erect, hard heeled. Chinese, more relaxed, have an easy gait, sometimes shuffle.

Time conceded, however, that there is "no infallible way of telling them apart, because the same racial strains are mixed in both. Even an anthropologist, with calipers and plenty of time to measure heads, noses, shoulders, hips, is sometimes stumped." The magazine noted that its Washington correspondent, Joseph Chiang, "made things much easier by pinning on his lapel a large badge reading 'Chinese Reporter—NOT Japanese—Please.' "

Pearl Harbor brought devastating consequences for the Japanese American community, even though as a group they had played no role in the attack. The U.S. Department of Justice rounded up a hundred thousand Japanese Americans along the Pacific coast and in Hawaii and interned them at remote concentration camps (in Wyoming, Utah, Idaho, and elsewhere), even though many were loyal American citizens who had lived in the United States for generations. Rodney Chow, who spent his boyhood in Los Angeles, remembers how Pearl Harbor changed the dynamics of playground politics in his neighborhood. A few Japanese American children, he recalled, used jujitsu to torment Chinese kids on the block. After December 7, these bullies were suddenly trying to convince their schoolmates that they were Chinese American, not Japanese. Then the Chinese in the neighborhood started to wear badges to distinguish themselves from the Japanese. Before long, the Japanese children disappeared altogether, and Chow did not see them again until the war was over, when they returned from the relocation camps.

A few progressive Chinese Americans, like the activist Hung Wai Ching in Hawaii, spoke out on behalf of Japanese American rights. But Hawaii had a fairly long tradition of Asian American activism, as well as better integrated Chinese and Japanese communities.* In the continental United States, however, the majority of Chinese Americans kept silent about the civil rights abuses against other Asian Americans while accepting the temporary, short-term gains they might enjoy as a preferred minority. Terrified of being mistaken for Japanese, some Chinese Americans even carried identification cards signed by a Chinese consul

---

*Despite the discrimination against their families by the United States government, Japanese Americans from Hawaii gave their lives in patriotic service to the United States. The Japanese American 442nd Regimental Combat Team from Hawaii became the most decorated U.S. military unit during World War II.

general, wore buttons announcing "I am Chinese," and placed similar signs in their shop windows to warn off potential vigilantes.

But ethnic profiling would hurt the entire Asian American community. Inevitably, some whites refused to distinguish between foreign Japanese nationals serving Japan's imperialist designs and Americans of Japanese and Chinese ancestry; it was easier to lump all Asians into a single despised group, "the Japs." Yu-shan Han became the target of anti-Japanese xenophobia when he was renting a house in Beverly Hills, California, during the war. Believing that Han was Japanese, the neighbors repeatedly reported him to the police, insisting that he was using a secret radio transmitter to communicate with enemy agents. Even Chinese Americans in the military were not immune to racist attacks. One Chinese American woman enlistee recalled how a white man spun her around in the middle of a street in Baltimore screaming, "You damn Jap, get out of that uniform!"

Some Chinese Americans saw a silver lining in this shift of racial antipathy and used the newly favorable Chinese image to bring about the repeal of the exclusion laws. After Pearl Harbor, several influential Americans, both ethnic Chinese and Caucasian, lobbied to overturn the ban on Chinese immigration that had been enacted back in 1882. In May 1942, more than 180 Caucasians founded the Citizens Committee to Repeal Chinese Exclusion, arguing that the United States should end exclusion for both moral and practical, war-related reasons.* The movement's leading activists included Ng Poon Chew, editor of *Chung Sai Yat Po,* Pearl Buck, the Nobel Prize–winning author of *The Good Earth* and daughter of Christian missionaries in China, and Buck's second husband, Richard Walsh, a New York publisher. But the woman who dealt exclusion the strongest blow was Meiling Soong, the wife of the Nationalist leader, Chiang Kai-shek.

---

*By fighting exclusion, the Citizens Committee unleashed some of the deepest fears of white Americans. One xenophobic letter called the Chinese the "enemies of the American people": "If you want a polyglot, mongrel race, then repeal the Chinese Exclusion Act, and amalgamate with the negroes and the Chinese."

Madame Chiang Kai-shek grew up in one of China's most powerful families. Her father, Charlie Soong, was a Shanghai mogul who earned his first fortune printing Bibles for Western missionaries. A former preacher who spent part of his youth in Boston and North Carolina, Soong used his Christian contacts to send his own children to the United States for their education. Meiling Soong first studied in Macon, Georgia, where she learned to speak fluent English with a slight southern drawl, then in 1913 enrolled at Wellesley College, where she majored in English literature. Upon her return to China, she and her American-educated siblings forged a dynasty within the new Nationalist regime. One sister, Chingling, married Sun Yat-sen, the first president of the Chinese republic; another sister, Ailing, wed the wealthy industrialist H. H. Kung; her Harvard-educated brother, T. V. Soong, helped Chiang Kai-shek finance his Northern Expedition to defeat the Chinese warlords, and was awarded the position of minister of finance in Chiang's government.

After America's entry into the war, President Roosevelt invited Meiling Soong to visit the United States. In November 1942, she arrived to rally support against Japan's campaign of aggression. The following spring, she embarked on a one-month cross-country tour, visiting New York, Wellesley, Boston, Chicago, San Francisco, and Los Angeles. The tour was a triumph. The articulate Soong attracted tens of thousands of supporters, captivating American audiences with her beauty, charisma, and elegance. The darling of the American media, her image graced every major magazine and newspaper. One of her most ardent fans was Henry Luce, publisher of *Time* and *Life*. The son of missionaries, Luce was delighted that the first family of China was Christian. He put Chiang Kai-shek and his wife on the cover of *Time* and called Chiang "the greatest man in the Far East."

Madame Chiang Kai-shek became the first Chinese woman and second woman ever invited to address a joint session of Congress, and she earned a standing ovation. One congressman was later heard to mutter, "Goddamnit, I never saw anything like it; Madame Chiang had me on the verge of tears." After her tour, Senator Warren

Magnuson (D-Wash.) introduced a bill repealing the Chinese Exclusion Act. Enjoying wide support and passed on December 17, 1943, the bill abolished exclusion, provided for an annual quota of 105 Chinese immigrants, and gave Chinese who had entered the country lawfully the right to naturalization. While the quota was extremely low, especially compared to admission rates for many European countries, the Magnuson Act was a landmark in Chinese American history: for the first time in six decades, foreign-born Chinese could become American citizens.

"To men of our generation, World War II was the most important historical event of our times," journalist Charlie Leong noted. "For the first time, we felt we could make it in American society." The war, he wrote, took them out of Chinatown ghettos, put them into American uniforms, and sent them overseas, where they became "part of the great patriotic United States war machine out to do battle with the enemy."

This was a theme heard frequently among Chinese Americans. The war, in which China and the United States had a common enemy, allowed them to contribute simultaneously to the survival of China and to victory for the United States. Some worked for the government as interpreters, code-breakers, and intelligence analysts. One notable example was Colonel Won-Loy Chan, a 1936 Stanford graduate who attended the Military Intelligence Service Language School after Pearl Harbor. As part of the U.S. Army's G2 intelligence and a member of General Joseph Stillwell's staff, Chan served in the China-Burma-India theater and later headed the Pacific Military Intelligence Research Section (PACMIRS) in Camp Ritchie, Maryland. Under his direction, a team of translators, some of them Chinese American, gathered and disseminated captured documents from the Pacific battlefront.

Chinese Americans also went to the front lines. Today, anyone envisioning men parading in World War II American military uniforms would see no Chinese faces, yet during the war, ethnic Chinese men gave their lives in numbers disproportionate to their presence in the country. An estimated 15,000 to 20,000 Chinese served in the military, representing about 20 percent of the Chinese population in the continental United States; the comparable figure for the general population was 8.6 percent. Almost 40 percent of the Chinese population in New York City was drafted, the highest rate among any of the city's ethnic groups. One reason for this high percentage, of course, was that most Chinese in the United States were male, single, and without dependents, the legacy of the Chinese exclusion laws, and the majority of the Chinese in New York were Chinese men living a bachelor existence in Chinatown. Nonetheless, it seems clear that if 40 percent were inducted, few tried to evade the draft when called. "New York's Chinatown cheered itself hoarse when the first draft numbers drawn were for Chinese Americans," the sociologist Rose Hum Lee wrote. "Some below-age boys tried to pass on their 'Chinese age,' which is often a year or two older than the American count. Since their birth certificates told a different tale, they had to be patient and wait."

Many joined the military voluntarily, even eagerly. "I remember Sunday, December 7th, vividly," wrote Dr. Richard Lee, the son of Clarence Lee, a graduate of the United States Naval Academy in Annapolis.* "We were raking leaves at our home in West Islip and my father upon hearing the news became very upset. I was terrified! He tried to enlist the next day but was told he was too old. He kept pestering the military selection process and was finally accepted into Army officer training despite his flat feet, poor vision and age." Clarence Lee would become the assistant chief of staff of the Army Air Force Bomber Training Command and retire in 1947 as a full colonel.

Some Chinese were enticed by government promises of U.S. citizenship in exchange for their service; others who were already citi-

---

*Clarence Lee was the Eurasian son of Yan Phou Lee, a member of the Chinese Educational Mission, a summa cum laude graduate of Yale in 1887, and author of the book *When I Was a Boy in China*, one of the first English-language autobiographies written by a Chinese American.

zens by being born on American soil signed up to eliminate doubts about their loyalty to the land of their birth. But many, perhaps most, enlisted for no other reason than patriotism. Sociologist Lee reported that all single Chinese American males of draft age in Butte, Montana, volunteered for service before they were called up. Chinese American David Gan spoke for countless others when he recalled, "I had never felt so happy and proud that I was an American, ready to fight for my country even if it meant that I must give up my life."

The Chinese in the U.S. military occupied a unique position, a "gray" area, as some would describe it, in which they were neither fully accepted, nor persecuted as outcasts. Unlike African Americans and Japanese Americans, whom all branches of the military segregated from whites, the Chinese were partially integrated into the U.S. armed services. Their experience reflected their ambiguous status in American society, and their treatment varied from region to region as they were sent throughout the country for training. In the Midwest, new Chinese American soldiers met people who had never seen an Asian before, and who asked if they were part of the Chinese army. Some recalled that in the South local whites eyed them suspiciously but accorded them more freedom than blacks, such as permission to sit wherever they wanted on buses.

For most young men in the military, World War II would be the first time in their lives they would be thrown together in close quarters with strangers from other parts of the country. Some had never before befriended men of a different race, much less slept and showered next to them. Although the new Chinese American troops wore their uniforms with pride, these uniforms did not always shield them from outright hostility. One Chinese American was labeled a "goddamn Chink" and assigned the dirty work in his unit; another had all his possessions thrown out the window by a GI who refused to sleep in the same room. "I was told that 'no Chinaman will ever fly in my outfit,'" William Der Bing recalled of his experience with the U.S. Navy. "I was told that by a doctor—a navy doctor. He gave me a physical. He said, 'I want you to know that I would do anything I can to fail you in your physical.' I looked at him and said, 'If you do, it would be the most dishonest thing that an officer in this United States Navy could ever do to another member of the United States Navy.'" True to his word, the navy doctor flunked him, but Bing managed to schedule another physical with another doctor, and passed.

Despite overt racism, for many the benefits of military service far outweighed the disadvantages. It empowered Chinese Americans, giving them a sophistication and worldly knowledge they never could have achieved in the insular world of America's Chinatowns. Their daily contact with white men made whites less threatening and mysterious. When Paul S. Wong taught an English-language class to illiterate white recruits, the myth of white superiority was forever demolished for him. "I was so damn surprised when they could not write their name [or] even add," he said.

The military also gave Chinese Americans the opportunity to be heroes. One such was Gordon P. Chung-Hoon, a Honolulu-born ABC and 1934 graduate of the U.S. Naval Academy in Annapolis. In the spring of 1945, Chung-Hoon served as commanding officer of the USS *Sigsbee*, which helped destroy twenty Japanese planes near the island of Kyushu. When a kamikaze pilot smashed into the *Sigsbee*, throwing the port engine and steering control out of commission, Chung-Hoon skillfully handled two crises simultaneously: he directed anti-aircraft battery fire against the enemy while overseeing damage control to allow the *Sigsbee* to reach port safely. He won the Navy Cross and Silver Star for conspicuous gallantry and extraordinary heroism, and in 2001 the Navy honored Rear Admiral Chung-Hoon posthumously by naming a guided missile destroyer after him.

Maybe most important, service in the U.S. military forced Chinese Americans to question their identity and every value taught them by their parents since childhood. For many ABCs, the war was the defining moment of their lives, the pivotal years that changed them, psychologically, from "Chinese" to "Americans of Chinese descent."

One military unit in China—the all–Chinese American 14th Air Service Group (part of the "Flying Tigers"), which had approximately 1,300 members—vividly illustrates this transformation. When Lawrence Chen was a boy, his parents told him, "China is your home." But after Chen joined the U.S. Army Air Force and entered the Pacific theater, China became more than a glorified abstract concept to be discussed over the dinner table; it was a daily reality. It soon became clear to Chen and other ABCs in the U.S. military that China was not, and never could be, "home." Their experience destroyed all their romantic illusions about China. They were shocked by the levels of KMT corruption—by the sight of Nationalist soldiers marching in straw sandals (or sometimes barefoot), of peasants being dragged out of their homes and forcibly impressed into the military. Their lives had been threatened not only by the Japanese but by hostile Nationalist troops. (One ABC, John Chuck, was accosted at gunpoint by a Nationalist guard demanding money, until others convinced him that Chuck was American.) They were disturbed by the level of poverty in some regions of China—the lack of flushable toilets, showers, or indoor running water, the construction of pebble roads by brute manpower, the throngs of starving refugees fleeing the Japanese invasion and ignored by Nationalist officials. China, in the words of these young ABCs, was "behind time—like cavemen," "primitive," and "scary." Wing Lai of the 555th Air Service Squadron described the people in China as "so poor. These beggars there—boy you feel sorry for them. You just had to give them something to eat, but how much can you feed so many people?"

These cultural barriers precluded true friendship between the ABCs and the native Chinese they met during their service overseas. Members of the 14th Air Service Group felt that the local villagers profoundly distrusted them, even though many ABCs could speak the local dialect fluently. Some natives called the Chinese American soldiers *yang guizi* ("foreign devils"). Others feigned friendship in an effort to use Chinese American soldiers as potential sponsors for emigration to the United States.

What the war did for the 14th Air Service Group was to forge a new Chinese American identity among its members. Not that there was a cookie-cutter similarity among them. They represented a cross-section of the ethnic Chinese population in the United States in terms of age, geography, and cultural background: the members ranged from teenagers to middle-aged men, from a guitar-playing Montana cowboy to college graduates from New York and San Francisco. Some spoke mainly Chinese; some did not understand Chinese; some were fluent in both languages. But their shared wartime experiences helped dissolve regional differences and create a new national Chinese American consciousness.

After the rollback of Japanese control of the eastern coastal area of China, Harry Lim and a few other Chinese American soldiers had an unsettling experience while walking along the Bund in Shanghai, one that reminded them of their own precarious status in the United States, and the fact that some white Americans would never accept them as equals. Coming upon a group of Japanese prisoners of war sweeping the road, the first time they had seen enemy soldiers up close, they suddenly realized that these prisoners looked just like them. "Except for the uniforms, those boys could have been us," Lim observed. "They were even about the same age. I was shocked. Incidents like these really made you think about the double standards in America and had you wondering how you would be treated when you went home."

The Chinese had suffered severe racism and a tight job market during the depression, but the war now gave them a better public image, as well as a booming American wartime economy that needed all the help it could get. As fighter planes rolled off assembly lines, as factories sought to fill the insatiable demand for new technology and new weapons, the Chinese easily found work in arenas previously closed to them. With so much work to be done, and with hundreds of thousands of young white men away in the armed services, the United States found itself facing what may well have been its greatest labor shortage in history. In 1944, California, home to an exploding defense industry, repealed a nineteenth-century law that forbade the state or public corporations from employing any Chinese.

The result was an era almost boundless in opportunity. Many educated Chinese landed positions as engineers, scientists, and technicians in the burgeoning high-tech industry. In the lower-echelon labor market, Chinese broke away from menial jobs to enter the industrial sector. Thousands of waiters and laundrymen found employment in shipyards and aircraft factories offering union wages and benefits. During this exodus from Chinatowns, as workers found more lucrative positions, small, family-run businesses suffered desperately from lack of manpower. During the war, Chinese restaurants operated with fewer waiters, while cities like Pittsburgh and Philadelphia borrowed help from larger Chinatowns in Chicago and New York.

Job opportunities multiplied for women as well. Many left Chinatown to secure new positions as secretaries, clerks, and assistants for government contractors. The U.S. government also recruited second-generation ethnic Chinese women to work for the Army Air Force as Air WACs (Women's Army Corps), whose duties included air traffic control and photograph interpretation. (In deference to the high esteem in which the first lady of China was held, these women in the Army Air Force were often referred to as the "Madame Chiang Kai-shek Air WACs.") Another valuable source of employment came from the U.S. Army Nurse Corps, which trained Chinese American women to become powerful leaders in the military. Helen Pon Onyett, who nursed wounded soldiers in the North African campaign, earned the Legion of Merit and other major citations during her thirty-five-year army career. She would later retire as a full colonel, one of the few American women ever to do so.

In August 1945, the war finally came to a close when the United States dropped atomic bombs on Hiroshima and Nagasaki, forcing Japan to surrender. After four years of combat in the Pacific, thousands of battle-scarred veterans returned home, anxious to put the war behind them, eager to start new lives and new families. The resulting baby boom comprised not only white births, but Chinese American ones as well.

Before the war, many Chinese men could not find wives because of the terrible shortage of Chinese women. In 1924, an immigration act prevented American citizens of Chinese heritage from importing alien Chinese brides, and as a result, no Chinese immigrant woman—not one—gained admission for the next six years. Then in 1930, the U.S. government decided Chinese wives could enter as long as the marriage had occurred before May 26, 1924, a specific time requirement that limited the number of women arrivals. During the next decade, only about sixty Chinese women a year joined their husbands in the United States, but more recent Chinese brides faced difficulty gaining admission.

After World War II, the U.S. government decided to overhaul this immigration policy to reward Chinese American veterans for their service. The 1945 War Brides Act permitted them to marry in China and bring their wives to the United States. Given the low number of ethnic Chinese women at home (the male-female ratio was three to one), many servicemen decided to wed foreign-born Chinese women. Before the act expired on December 30, 1949, almost six thousand Chinese American soldiers went to China and returned with brides. For many, there was no time for elaborate rituals or lengthy, romantic courtship. They faced not only the deadline of the act's expiration date but also the time constraints of their own furloughs. One soldier on leave flew to China, picked a bride, married, and then landed at San Francisco airport the night before his month's furlough expired. As a result of such hasty marriages, after the war about 80 percent of all new Chinese arrivals were female. In March 1948, the maternity ward of the Chinese Hospital in San Francisco recorded an average of two births a day. According to historian Him Mark Lai, so many pregnant women came into this hospital that many had to sleep in the hallways. In part because of these new arrivals and new births, during the 1940s the ethnic Chinese population in the United States soared from 77,000 to 117,000.

For thousands of Chinese American men and their wives, the end of World War II was a time of celebration—a time of new hope, new beginnings. But in China it would be a different story. The defeat of Japan would inaugurate a new era of bloodshed and tragedy. Few people could have foreseen that the horror of war—the eight agonizing years under Japanese occupation—would serve as only the prelude to more war, this time a civil war between the Nationalist government and rebel Communist forces.

CHAPTER FOURTEEN

"A Mass Inquisition": The Cold War, the Chinese Civil War, and McCarthyism

The postwar period opened with the Chinese in America enjoying a greater level of acceptance by fellow Americans than they had ever experienced. China and the United States had fought together to defeat an empire that had attacked both nations, and their wartime amity continued into the early postwar period. This new American perception regarding the Chinese led to a whole new direction in government policy, very much easing the lives of Chinese Americans.

But over the next decade, certain international events strained the wartime alliance, and Chinese Americans soon found themselves facing renewed hostility from their fellow Americans. The precipitating events were the start of the cold war, the Chinese civil war, in which the Chinese Communist Party under Chairman Mao Zedong replaced General Chiang Kai-shek's Kuomintang as the ruling party of China, and the Korean War, in which the new People's Republic of China (PRC) and the United States found themselves on opposite sides.

Of the three, the key event was the defeat of Chiang's forces in the Chinese civil war. Neither the cold war nor the Korean War—which began when the UN attempted to help South Korea repel an invasion by North Korea, and ended as a conflict between the mighty armies of China and the United States—would have strained Chinese-American relations without the Communist victory in China, which put the two nations in opposing cold war camps.

The fall of China to the Communists shocked many Americans. Only a decade earlier, Chiang Kai-shek had the insurgent Communists on the run. In the early 1930s, Mao Zedong established a Communist government in remote Jiangxi province, called the Jiangxi Soviet, and Chiang launched a campaign that appeared to destroy the movement. In 1934 the Communists were forced to retreat northward in an epic journey that came to be known as the Long March. For five thousand agonizing miles, the Communists fled on foot to Shaanxi, fording rivers and crossing mountains in an ordeal that fewer than one in four survived. The Chinese Communist Party as a national institution was surely dead: this exhausted, half-starved group of guerrilla fighters could hardly pose a threat to the central government of China yet again.

But Japan's invasion of China in 1937 resuscitated Mao's group. First, it demonstrated conclusively the inability of the Nationalist government to protect the Chinese people against a foreign invader. Second, it gave the Communists an opportunity to win the loyalty of the peasants in north China. As the war exacerbated poverty in the countryside, the Communists won widespread support by embracing land reform and organizing rural forces to fight the enemy. When the Japanese military imposed its ruthless "three all" policy—"kill all, burn all, destroy all"—it bred deep hatred against the invaders and compelled many Chinese to join underground Communist guerrilla forces.

The first priority of Mao's guerrilla force was to defeat the Japanese military, and in the early years of the war it waged a hit-and-run campaign of harassment against the Japanese.* But it also adopted

---

*During the early 1940s, the Chinese Communists had to contend not only with a Nationalist economic blockade but also the lack of foreign military aid. The Russians signed a Soviet-Japan neutrality pact in 1941 and later devoted their resources to fight against a German invasion.

a longer view, working to organize the peasants. Communists held meetings, called "struggle sessions," that resembled religious revivals in their fervor, in which peasants were encouraged to share with others their stories of exploitation by powerful landlords. These emotional, cathartic sessions inspired a cult following among the poor in rural areas, and by the time the Japanese were expelled from China in 1945 the Communists were not only firmly entrenched in the northern countryside, but had also matured as a political and military force, with a trained and dedicated cadre in place. It was now much better prepared to launch a serious challenge to the KMT.

At the February 1945 summit meeting at Yalta, Franklin Roosevelt, Winston Churchill, and Joseph Stalin seemed to give Chiang's Nationalist government their imprimatur as the legitimate government of China. The Communist Soviet Union, the only one of the three powers in close proximity to China, expressed "its readiness to conclude with the National Government of China a pact of friendship and alliance between the U.S.S.R. and China in order to render assistance to China with its armed forces for the purpose of liberating China from the Japanese yoke."

But in international diplomacy every syllable of every word is important, and the Western Allies failed to note or question the Soviet Union's assertion that it was pledging its readiness for friendship and alliance not with the "Nationalist" government of China, but with the "National" government of China, a term that could be construed to describe whatever government exercised effective control over China.

As the Pacific war ground down through early 1945, and the ultimate defeat of Japan drew closer, the Chinese Communists mounted powerful attacks against the Japanese from their strongholds in northern China, liberating great expanses of Chinese territory and seizing immense stores of Japanese weapons. After the United States dropped an atomic bomb on Hiroshima on August 6, the situation turned further to the advantage of Mao's forces when the Soviet Union declared war on Japan and advanced into Manchuria.

As the postwar political map of China was being drawn, both

Mao and Chiang scrambled to expand the areas over which they had effective control. Mao's forces moved quickly to accept the surrender of Japanese military units in the north and replace them as the governing group. Fearful of China establishing a second enormous Communist state, the U.S. tried to contain the area of Communist control by airlifting Chiang's troops to key cities in northern China, where they could accept and claim credit for Japanese surrenders. The stage was now set for a showdown between the CCP under Mao and the KMT under Chiang.

In an attempt to avert civil war, the U.S. government tried to negotiate peace between the two sides. U.S. ambassador Patrick Hurley arranged talks between Mao and Chiang, but after the talks failed, Hurley resigned his post in disgust. President Harry Truman then dispatched as his special representative to China General George C. Marshall, America's World War II army chief of staff, future secretary of state, and author of the Marshall Plan, which many would later credit for saving much of Europe from communism. In China Marshall managed to negotiate a temporary cease-fire, but even as both sides discussed the terms of implementation, they were busy preparing for further war. The cease-fire ended in the summer of 1946, after the Soviets withdrew from Manchuria and Chinese Communist troops moved in.

Even at this late date, the Kuomintang, the de jure governing party of China because of its control of China's major cities, seemed to be the stronger contender for national power. Poor leadership, however, had eroded the people's trust in the Republic. When the Nationalists reclaimed the capital of Nanjing from the Japanese, they failed to punish officials known to have collaborated with the occupiers. Many Chinese believed that the collaborators escaped justice because of their influence within the Nationalist regime. There were also charges that the Nationalists had retained property expropriated by the Japanese instead of returning it to the original owners.

In addition, the Nationalists behaved despotically when Japan was obligated to return Taiwan, an offshore island originally named

Formosa by the Portugese, that the Qing dynasty had ceded to Japan in 1895. Under the pretext of confiscating Japanese holdings, the Nationalists indiscriminately seized native homes and businesses. "When a Chinese with some influence wanted a particular property, he had only to accuse a Formosan of being a collaborationist during the past fifty years of Japanese sovereignty," one Taiwanese observed. When news organizations began to publish such grumblings of discontent, the KMT, rather than address the problems provoking the discontent, chose to arrest a number of local news reporters, editors, and publishers who had brought the issue to light. Many Taiwanese natives now complained, in private, that the "dogs" (the Japanese) had left, but the "pigs" (the Nationalists) had replaced them. On February 28, 1947, simmering hatred of the Nationalists exploded into a serious uprising on the island. KMT reinforcements dispatched from the mainland brutally crushed the rebellion, in the process slaughtering thousands of Taiwanese.

Political unrest in Taiwan and elsewhere was only a fraction of Nationalist China's concerns. The country was teetering on the brink of economic collapse. During the war, as inflation spiraled out of control, the government had inflicted heavy taxes on farmers and forced them to sell grain at fixed prices. In the immediate postwar years, many Chinese lost what was left of their fortunes when the Nationalist government, attempting to impose strict control over the nation's money supply, asked its citizens to exchange their gold and foreign currency for government certificates. The result was hyperinflation. In 1947, the government issued at least 10,000 billion Chinese dollars in bank notes. Within one six-month period in 1948 prices soared by a factor of 85,000. A sack of rice priced at 12 yuan in 1937 cost 63 million yuan by August 1948. Shoppers pushed heaps of paper currency in wheelbarrows just to buy a few groceries. When a Guangdong paper mill recycled "eight hundred cases of notes ranging from one hundred to two-thousand-dollar bills which it used as raw material in the manufacture of paper," it was reasonable to conclude that KMT currency was literally worth less than the paper it was printed on.

During the exclusion era, Chinese immigrant families opened groceries in the southern states. Most were mom-and-pop operations, with the shopkeepers and their families living in the back of the store.
(Herbert and Diana Kai)

中華民國十五年

映攝日六月六

國民學校開紀念

Main Street, 1926, the opening of the Locke Chinese School. Locke is the last surviving all-Chinese rural town in America. *(Sacramento River Delta Historical Society)*

Thousands jam the streets of New York Chinatown in 1938 to support a World War II fund-raising drive on behalf of the victims of Japan's invasion of China. These huge spectacles, held in major cities such as New York, San Francisco, and Los Angeles, were known as "Rice Bowl" parties.
(AP/Wide World Photos)

Holding a Chinese Nationalist flag, volunteers in Los Angeles collect donations for the war effort.
(Chinese American Museum, Los Angeles)

Chinese American activists rallied against shipments of scrap metal to Japan and succeeded in winning public support for an embargo. This picket line in Astoria, Oregon, halted loading for a day in February 1939.
(Oregon Historical Society)

Anna May Wong, the first Chinese American and Asian American movie star.
(Hulton Archive)

In 1959, Hawaiian-born Hiram Fong became the first Chinese American and Asian American U.S. senator.
(AP/Wide World Photos)

An Wang achieved Horatio Alger–style success after building a computer empire from an initial investment of $600.

M. C. Chang, co-inventor of the birth control pill. *(Patrick O'Connor)*

Chinese American architect Ieoh Ming (I. M.) Pei in front of his pyramid design at the Palais du Louvre in Paris.
(Luc Novovitch for Reuters, Getty Images)

The world-renowned cellist Yo-Yo Ma performing at a National Endowment for the Arts ceremony in which he was awarded a National Medal of Arts.
(Getty Images)

During the late 1960s, Chinese American students united with other racial groups to demand multicultural academic programs at universities. In 1968, the Third World Liberation Front (TWLF), a coalition of students of Asian, African, Latin, and Native American heritage, organized a four-month strike at San Francisco State College, the longest college strike in U.S. history, resulting in the first ethnic studies program in the country and inspiring similar protests at other schools. This image, taken on January 28, 1969, captures the TWLF strike at the University of California at Berkeley, which later created an ethnic studies department in response to student demands.

(Douglas Wachter)

Normalized relations between the United States and the People's Republic of China launched furious protests and demonstrations from supporters of the Nationalist government. Here, a pro-Taiwan group called Friends of Free China burn a banner during a New Year's rally in San Francisco. The end of the cold war with mainland China, however, would open the door to a new wave of emigration to American shores. *(AP/Wide World Photos)*

The brutal murder of Vincent Chin by two unemployed Detroit autoworkers galvanized the Chinese American community. The tragedy goaded some American-born Chinese to devote their lives to political activism.
(Corky Lee)

During the 1990s, Chinese American groups, such as the Global Alliance for Preserving the History of World War II in Asia, organized to seek full disclosure and justice for the victims of the "Pacific Holocaust," Japan's wartime campaign of atrocity and genocide. *(Iris Chang, September 8, 2001, San Francisco, during the 50th anniversary of the signing of the San Francisco Peace Treaty)*

In New York, Chinese Americans protest a 1997 cover of the *National Review* after it ran caricatures reminiscent of the pre-exclusion era.
(Corky Lee)

Illegal immigration from China to the United States increased after the early 1980s, when rapid economic changes in China drove thousands abroad in search of better employment. When the *Golden Venture*, a cargo ship, ran aground near New York in 1993, hundreds of Chinese stowaways tried to swim for shore. Most were rescued, but some drowned in the icy water.

(AP/Wide World Photos)

When the one-child policy in China created a surplus of unwanted baby girls, thousands of Americans traveled to the PRC for their adoption needs. By the 1990s, mainland China had become the single largest source of international adoptions for the United States. *(Stephen Wunrow)*

The American Dream. In Flushing, New York, all three sons of the Wu family ranked first in their class at Harvard. The second wave of Chinese immigrants—many of them intellectuals and professionals from Taiwan—reared American-born children who entered, in record numbers, the nation's most prestigious universities.
(*Magnum Photos*)

Among those who saw their wealth evaporate were many Chinese Americans. After the happy resolution of World War II, thousands of ethnic Chinese, both American- and foreign-born, left the United States to visit relatives in China. Some brought their entire life savings, eager to launch new companies or to retire, only to watch their nest eggs disappear within months. In 1947, for instance, a Houston businessman of Chinese heritage returned to Canton to open a travel agency and rice company. Rampant inflation ravaged his savings, leaving him bankrupt and forcing him to return to Houston to start over again. Another Chinese American deposited $6,000 into the Bank of China, in mainland China, in 1948. A year later his funds were worth scarcely enough to buy a postage stamp.

As the Nationalists were forfeiting the confidence of the people, the Communists were rapidly gaining stature in north China. When Soviet forces withdrew in the summer of 1947, the Communists began to consolidate control over Manchuria, employing well-honed skills in educating those under their control to look at the incipient civil war as a class struggle. As committed recruits expanded the Communists' numbers, Chiang's forces were being depleted by a growing discontent within the military that reflected the discontent within the general population. During both World War II and then the Chinese civil war, the KMT exempted young men of privilege from the draft while conscripting sons of peasant families. Ill fed, ill equipped, ill paid, and physically abused by their superiors, many of these Nationalist soldiers deserted at the earliest opportunity, often switching sides to join the Communists. By 1948, the Communists had 1.5 million troops—and each new victory brought more men and arms over to them.

During this period, some upper-class Chinese, alarmed by the successes of the Communists, began to leave the country. But most, even among the wealthy, did not emigrate immediately. For it is a reality universally acknowledged that to leave one's community, to abandon one's business or profession, to discard whatever wealth and status has been achieved over a lifetime and start all over again in a new country requires uncommon courage and resolve. For the majority of upper-class Chinese, it seemed better to sit tight and hope what they were witnessing was a transient political aberration, nothing more, and that everything would soon settle back to normal.

As 1948 slid into 1949, the Communists destroyed KMT forces in the north and then turned south into central China. One by one, major regions fell under Communist control: Shenyang, Manchuria, Tianjin, Beijing. In April 1949, the Communists seized Nanjing, the Nationalist capital, and in May, Shanghai, the country's most populous city. There was no longer any doubt which side would be the victor.

Much of what remained of the establishment—bureaucrats, businessmen, intellectuals—now left in great haste. Abandoning businesses, homes, and real estate, they sewed gold bullion and jewelry into belts and seams of clothes, even shoes, and shoved their way onto trains so mobbed that people clung to the tops and sides of the railway cars in order to get away. During later stages of their journey, many left trunks and suitcases filled with cherished family possessions at the side of the road.

As a group, these new émigrés had more education, status, and wealth than the earlier waves of Chinese to the United States, but they also had a less coherent plan. Given the confusion of the last few months of the civil war, some Chinese were not sure, initially, whether to leave the mainland or to simply move to another region farther from the conflict. Many exhausted their savings to book passage to Hong Kong or Taiwan, leaving China with little more than the clothes on their backs. The impulse behind their migration was not, like the first wave of Chinese gold rushers in America, to provide a better living for themselves and their families, but to escape persecution and possible death at the hands of the Communists.

On October 1, 1949, in Beijing, Mao Zedong declared the birth of the People's Republic of China. In December, Chiang Kai-shek abandoned mainland China and fled to Taiwan with the remainder of his troops and the bulk of the nation's gold supply. The Qing dynasty had lasted almost three centuries; the first Republic of China had lasted fewer than four decades on mainland soil.

In the United States, the Communist revolution shook the halls of academe, leaving about five thousand foreign Chinese intellectuals marooned. While some were skilled professionals and scholars, most—4,675 of them—were students at colleges and universities scattered throughout the country. With few exceptions, these students came from the privileged upper strata of society, precisely the group that had the most to lose from Mao's victory.* Their original plan had been to return to China with the pedigree of a Western education and to establish their careers there. A foreign diploma offered an inside track to the best positions in Nationalist China; an examination of the 1925 edition of *Who's Who in China* shows that most entrants—about 57 percent—had studied abroad. "We joked about getting gold-plated," recalls Linda Tsao Yang, a former student at Columbia University who became the U.S. executive director on the board of directors for the Asian Development Bank in Manila. "That means you go abroad, you study, you get a fancy degree, and then you can go back and say, 'I've been to the United States and I graduated from a leading university.' " Now Chinese students at American universi-

*The 1924 Immigration Act required foreign Chinese graduate students wishing to study in the U.S. first to complete a college education, gain acceptance by an American university, possess English-language skills, and prove they had the financial means to support themselves and pay for their journey back to China. Of course, these criteria entirely favored students from wealthy elite families. In *Chinese Intellectuals and the West,* Yichu Wang found that the fathers of most Chinese nationals who studied abroad before 1949 had four major occupations: landowner, professional, businessman, or government official. Most of the students had spent their formative years in large coastal cities, one-third from only two metropolitan areas, Shanghai and Canton, and many had graduated from universities established by missionaries, with Western-style curricula, such as the University of Nanjing, Yanjing University in Beijing, and St. John's University in Shanghai. A few academic superstars—the intellectual cream of the crop—received Boxer Rebellion scholarships, under a program funded by Chinese indemnities to the United States after the failed uprising of 1900, but most students paid their own way, with the backing of their families.

ties faced the unimaginable prospect that upon graduation there would be no country to go home to.

As the society they had known crumbled away under Communist reorganization, many students stared into an uncertain and frightening future. Even before Chiang's final rout, they had received letters from home about the rampant inflation, the impending Communist victory, and the frantic family conferences about what course of action to take. Some parents urged their children to return immediately, so that the family, for better or for worse, would at least be together. Others counseled their children to stay in the United States, telling them they had decided to abandon all business and property in order to move to either Hong Kong or Taiwan. "We came to a fork in our lives, not knowing whether to take branch A or branch B and what the final destination would be," Linda Tsao Yang remembered. "And there was no one who could give you advice because we were all in the same boat."

Now those who decided to stay in the United States had to fight for survival, unable to rely on parents or even the Nationalist government to pay their tuition or mail them scholarship checks. The ugly sequence of skyrocketing inflation, followed by a Communist revolution that was social, political, and economic, had depleted the fortunes of entire families, many of whom were now themselves refugees. With their private funding cut off, these students desperately needed money. By 1949, the entire foreign Chinese student community was in crisis—not only had these students lost their country, most could no longer even meet their basic living expenses. *Time* magazine estimated that more than 2,500 Chinese students lacked basic funds for rent and tuition.

Some American colleges and universities helped out by waiving tuition payments and giving the Chinese part-time jobs and loans, but the scope of the problem required federal intervention. After 1949, the United States allocated emergency funds for Chinese foreign students, whether or not they intended to return to mainland China. In total, between 1949 and 1955, the government appropriated slightly more than $8 million to help the stranded students complete their degrees in the United States.

During this time, many of these stranded scholars resolved to build new lives for themselves in the United States. Some decided to work for their doctorates, if only to remain full-time students and avoid cancellation of their visas. Those who already held a Ph.D. took research positions as visiting scholars at various institutions. As it turned out, their timing was fortunate: they had obtained their credentials just before American universities began a rapid expansion. The arms race between the United States and the Soviet Union brought massive U.S. government investment in science and technology, which led to new academic departments in those fields at many universities. At the same time, World War II veterans, eager to get their degrees on the GI Bill, were filling college classrooms, necessitating the hiring of new professors. With universities scrambling to find qualified faculty, and with a shortage of existing Ph.D.s in the United States, foreign Chinese intellectuals soon became hot commodities in the academic market.

When the government of the world's most populous country is ousted and replaced by a radically different form of government, the reverberations are felt around the world. As China became a second Communist world power, few groups were more sensitive to the aftershocks than the ethnic Chinese in the United States.

A loyalty schism opened within the Chinatowns of America, with KMT agents and pro-PRC supporters jousting for influence within and control over the Chinese American community. In October 1949, the liberal China Workers Mutual Aid Assocation hosted an event in San Francisco Chinatown to mark the inauguration of the People's Republic of China. Suddenly, a "Guomingdang-hired goon squad," as one Chinese-language newspaper put it, burst into the auditorium, vandalizing property, stealing a PRC flag, and spraying blue dye over the crowd. Bystanders were assaulted and some needed to be hospitalized. The pro-KMT Chinese-language press, however, blamed the incident on "Communist bandits."

The revolution also sent tremors through the small community of diplomats and government bureaucrats stationed in Washington, D.C., and in consular offices across the United States. Appointed by the Nationalist government, they now faced an uncertain future. Although its area of effective control was now restricted to the island of Taiwan, the Nationalist Republic of China would for many years continue to claim, with the support and concurrence of United States, to be the legitimate government of China, but its prospects for a victorious return to the mainland were dim.

As the foreign-born Chinese desperately sought to build new lives, the American-born Chinese began to rethink their own futures. Many had grown up believing that if they failed to establish themselves professionally in the United States, they could always find careers in China. That option was now foreclosed, and assimilation became a much more attractive possibility. In 1949, the participants of the Chinese Young People's Summer Conference in Lake Tahoe urged youths not only to leave Chinatowns, but to discard Chinese traditions altogether—the best way, they believed, to advance "understanding" between the races.

Racial harmony, however, was difficult to realize as world events led Americans to see themselves as the last bulwark against a giant worldwide Communist conspiracy. The end of World War II had inaugurated the cold war, a quiet but intense struggle between the two great superpowers of the twentieth century, the United States and the Soviet Union. After the defeat of Nazi Germany, the United States watched with growing alarm as one Eastern European country after another became a Soviet satellite and disappeared behind the "Iron Curtain." Viewing communism as operating like a contagious disease, the United States tried to contain the spread of Soviet power in 1949 by establishing the North Atlantic Treaty Organization (NATO), an alliance whose members—the U.S. and democratic Western European countries—pledged to unite if any one of them were attacked. Later that year, the Soviets exploded their first atomic bomb, ending the American monopoly on nuclear weapons.

This Soviet triumph sent the United States into hysteria. Many Truman administration experts had thought the Soviets incapable of developing an atomic bomb for at least fifteen years; some, such as Harry Truman himself, believed that, left to their own devices, they might never be able to build one at all. To them, the clear explanation was that the Soviets had gotten help from the outside. Thus the Soviet atomic bomb triggered not only a U.S.-Soviet arms race, in which scientific secrets on both sides would be jealously guarded, but a witch hunt for those suspected of loyalty to the other side. In January 1950, the American public's deepest fears were confirmed when Dr. Klaus Fuchs, a British atomic scientist who had worked on the Manhattan Project in Los Alamos, was arrested for passing secrets to the Soviets. The Chinese Communist revolution and the developing Sino-Soviet alliance subjected the Chinese American community to the same suspicions of disloyalty.

The following month, February, Senator Joseph McCarthy capitalized on the national mood by proclaiming he had a list of 105 card-carrying Communists in the State Department—a claim he never substantiated, but which provoked a frenzy of finger-pointing. McCarthy's accusations fueled suspicions in Washington that the government was infested with subversives who had assisted China's fall to communism. Supporters of Chiang Kai-shek demanded to learn who "lost" China, and Republicans in Congress called for a wholesale purge of the State Department, accusing the Far East experts of "sabotage," treason, and conspiracy to oust the Nationalists from the mainland. The inquisition destroyed the careers of several prominent China specialists in the State Department, who were scapegoated for international events far beyond their control.

National paranoia permitted almost limitless excesses, as long as their ultimate goal was defending America against communism. In what is now known as the McCarthy era, anti-Communist investigations in the U.S. Senate and House ravaged Hollywood, the media, academe, and government. The Communist Party was outlawed, loyalty tests were established, mail-opening and wire-tapping operations were conducted by the CIA and FBI. During this period of national hysteria Chinese were particularly vulnerable, because they *looked* foreign and were presumably linked to a country that had chosen communism over freedom.

In Chinatowns, U.S. government surveillance of left-wing organizations began as soon as the People's Republic was founded. Federal authorities bugged the headquarters of the Chinese Hand Laundry Alliance and kept close watch over liberal Chinese American organizations, like the China Youth Club and the *China Daily News*. If during World War II China was America's great friend, the cold war thrust it into the role of Communist ally of the Soviet Union—and potential enemy.

Surely many Chinese Americans hoped that U.S. anxiety would subside over time, that diplomacy would bring greater acceptance of the new government in China. But with the outbreak of the Korean War, matters went from bad to worse to worst.

On June 25, 1950, Communist North Korea, under the leadership of Kim Il Sung, invaded South Korea, and within days seized 90 percent of the peninsula. Believing that Moscow had masterminded the invasion, President Harry Truman immediately called on the United Nations to join an American military effort to assist South Korea. UN troops, predominantly American and under the command of General Douglas MacArthur, swiftly drove the North Korean forces back. Through diplomatic channels the People's Republic of China warned it would attack if the United States crossed the 38th parallel, the preinvasion border. UN forces sped far into North Korea, and on November 24, 1950, as they neared the Yalu River, the border between Korea and China, the PRC held good to its promise and threw more than a quarter of a million troops into the conflict.

The Korean War was the salvation of the Nationalist regime in Taiwan. Before the Korean conflict, the CIA had predicted that the Communists would invade Taiwan before the end of 1950, and the

State Department was prepared to recognize the People's Republic of China as the official government of China. But as American soldiers died in the Communist Chinese onslaught, the United States decided to protect Taiwan and cultivate the island as a Pacific base from which to combat communism in Asia.

For Americans of Chinese descent, the Korean War meant something else entirely. As the American public heard reports of white soldiers being slaughtered, imprisoned, and tortured in POW camps, they were baffled that their government did not drop nuclear bombs on China, as General MacArthur had suggested before Truman relieved him of his command. Chinese Americans, meanwhile, endured an atmosphere of hostility reminiscent of what Japanese Americans had experienced during World War II. A white mob tore apart a Chinatown restaurant in San Francisco to avenge American deaths in Korea. Reports began to appear of ethnic Chinese being physically attacked, their property vandalized.

As the shadow of the cold war fell over their communities, Americans of Chinese heritage found their finances scrutinized. The Korean War led to a U.S. trade embargo of the PRC, which not only prohibited Chinese imports but also prevented American money from entering China. On December 17, 1950, the United States Treasury Department used the Foreign Assets Control Regulation to ban all remittances to mainland China, shutting down the flow of capital from the Chinese American community to relatives across the Pacific. Even Hong Kong, then a British colony, fell under this regulation, preventing Chinese Americans from using the city to funnel money to their families in China. The regulation had teeth. Violators could be fined up to $10,000, and imprisoned for up to a decade. In counties such as Toishan, this created tremendous hardship for those who depended on American money for their very existence.

The regulation did more than choke off the pipeline of funds between the United States and China. On at least one occasion, it helped silence pro-Communist voices in Chinatown. In 1951, in a crackdown that ruined careers, the Treasury Department subpoenaed several staff members of the *China Daily News,* the largest Chinese American newspaper sympathetic to recognizing the PRC as the government of China. The following year, the Justice Department charged that Eugene Moy, the managing editor, and four others had violated the Foreign Assets Control Regulation, the only time anyone had been prosecuted under this law since its passage in 1917. Sentenced to two years in prison, Moy died shortly after his release.

To undermine leftist newspapers, the U.S. government launched a campaign to intimidate subscribers. Throughout the country, FBI agents visited Chinese Americans, warning them to drop their subscriptions to the *China Daily News.* In New York, the FBI interrogated Tan Yumin, the English-language secretary of the left-wing Chinese Hand Laundry Alliance, asking him the same question over and over: why did he read the *China Daily News*? The distraught Tan later jumped off—or was pushed from—the Brooklyn Bridge, his body buried under river mud for days before it finally surfaced.

As they found their mail opened, their phone lines tapped, their movements shadowed in the streets, some Chinatown residents felt trapped in a police state. American authorities even probed the lives of U.S. World War II veterans of Chinese heritage, and interrogated children in Chinatown playgrounds. One Chinese man had a public shouting match with an agent who was following him: "The FBI guy shouted back—'You are a Communist!' I stepped forward and pointed my finger at his nose—'You are a Communist!' He got frustrated. He did not have any evidence to prove that I was a Communist. So I called him a Communist without evidence—in his own way."

Even the end of the Korean War in 1953, and the cessation of open hostilities between China and the United States, brought no respite. Indeed, the darkest moment may have come in December 1955, when Everett F. Drumwright, the U.S. consul in Hong Kong, released a report in his Foreign Service dispatch that accused the community of, among other things, orchestrating "a fantastic system of passport and visa fraud." Drumwright insisted that almost all Chinese in America had entered the United States illegally, all the way back to those who

mined for gold and built the transcontinental railroad in the nineteenth century. Drumwright not only leveled a host of broad-brush
charges (trafficking in narcotics, using fake passports, counterfeiting
American currency, and illegally collecting Social Security and veteran's benefits), but also suggested that a network of Chinese spies
had exploited the paper sons system to infiltrate the country. All the
PRC had to do, according to the report, was to dispatch agents to the
port of Hong Kong to buy fake American citizenship papers. Steps
had to be taken "to destroy that system once and for all," before
"Communist China is able to bend that system to the service of her
purpose alone."*

After Drumwright's report was released, virtually the entire
Chinese community fell under federal scrutiny. No one was immune
from investigation: if you were Chinese it was likely that you would
soon receive that knock on the door and be subjected to a long series
of questions about every aspect of your life. "Only once before in
modern times, has an entire race been charged with 'a criminal
conspiracy,' " wrote Dai-ming Lee, editor of the *China World*. In
1956, U.S. Attorney Lloyd Burke subpoenaed forty major Chinese
American associations, demanding that they produce all records and
photographs of their membership and a full account of their income
within twenty-four hours. "Chinatown was hit like an A-bomb fell,"

---

*During the cold war, J. Edgar Hoover, head of the FBI, also believed the Chinese
American community was riddled with spies. Testifying before the Senate, Hoover
warned that "Red China has been flooding the country with its propaganda and
there are over 300,000 Chinese in the United States, some of whom could be suscep-
tible to recruitment either through ethnic ties or hostage situations because of relatives in Communist China." He added, "Chinese communists carry out their
intelligence activities through representatives in third countries and contacts with
sympathetic Chinese Americans. The large number of Chinese entering this country
as immigrants provides Red China with a channel to dispatch to the United States
undercover agents on intelligence assignments." Hoover's words suggest that he saw
little if any distinction between Chinese foreign nationals and American citizens of
Chinese heritage, and that he viewed the latter as untrustworthy merely because of
their race and ethnicity.

one observer wrote. Another called it "the worst incident since the 1882 Chinese Exclusion Act."

Chinatown leaders fought back by appealing to politicians for help and by posing legal challenges to the constitutionality of the Justice Department investigations. Fortunately, in March 1956 a federal judge threw out the subpoena attack, calling it a "mass inquisition." But by then, much damage had been done. Business activity dropped when investigators raided Chinatowns on both coasts; Chinese merchants in New York City lost $100,000 a week in sales. American authorities also leaked the Drumwright report to the press, which ran stories accusing the Chinese community of immigration fraud.

In 1956, three years after the end of the Korean War, the U.S. government initiated a "confession program" to encourage the Chinese who had immigrated illegally to voluntarily confess their true status. Each confession, however, could implicate dozens of Chinese relatives, who in turn would be compelled to cooperate with authorities to protect themselves. In San Francisco, some ten thousand Chinese confessed, and 99 percent of them were permitted to stay in the country. A few, however, were deported as a direct result of their political activities. In psychological terms, the impact was far greater than the number of actual deportations. Long after the Drumwright-inspired inquisition was over, its shadow remained over Chinatown, instilling in the Chinese American community a terror of government authority and a legacy of silence.

Another group vulnerable to accusations of espionage were Chinese intellectuals at the universities who were capable of designing technology vital to national security. As Communist China developed into a world power and technologically competent cold war opponent, many American officials failed to distinguish between Chinese Americans and foreign Chinese nationals, nor did they overcome the suspicion that members of both groups were passing secrets to the PRC. With new State Department regulations, the Immigration and

Nationality Act of 1952, and President Harry Truman's proclamation of 1953, the American government assumed the power to stop the departure of foreigners whose knowledge might jeopardize national security. As a result, some 120 Chinese intellectuals were detained and not permitted to leave for years.

One of these was Dr. Tsien Hsue-shen, a top Chinese aerodynamicist who helped pioneer the American space program before becoming involved in one of the strangest episodes of cold war history. His story illustrates not only the capriciousness of the American government during the McCarthy era, but also the disastrous consequences for U.S. defense brought about by the frenzied witch hunts of the time.

Though much of Tsien's later life is hidden in shadow, the story of his early days is relatively straightforward. In 1935, Tsien arrived in the United States on a Boxer Rebellion scholarship to study at MIT, and then later at Cal Tech. He rapidly ascended to the very top of his profession, making substantial contributions to both American science and national defense. He revolutionized the fields of fluid dynamics, the buckling of structures, rocketry, and engineering cybernetics, all of which helped the U.S. enter into the space age early. While still a graduate student at Cal Tech, he helped found the Jet Propulsion Laboratory in Pasadena, where he was intimately involved in designing some of America's earliest missiles. Because his contributions during World War II were so valuable, the U.S. government repeatedly granted Tsien clearance to work on classified government projects, despite his legal status as a Chinese national. By the end of the war, Tsien had received numerous commendations and praise from the American military establishment.

In 1949, the year China fell to the Communists, Tsien must have decided that his future no longer lay with his homeland, but with the United States. He applied for U.S. citizenship and accepted a professorship at and directorship of the Jet Propulsion Laboratory of the California Institute of Technology. What he had not counted on, however, was America's entrance into cold war hysteria. In 1950, the

FBI accused him of being a former member of the American Communist Party, on the grounds that during the 1930s he had befriended a number of pro-Communist Cal Tech students.

Although Tsien fervently denied being a Communist, the U.S. government revoked his security clearance, something Tsien considered an unforgivable insult, especially after his record of substantial contribution to the U.S. war effort. A proud man, he impulsively decided to return to China. After informing Cal Tech that he was taking an indefinite leave of absence, he booked passage for himself and his family to mainland China. His real troubles began when a U.S. customs agent found thousands of pounds of scientific papers in his luggage. Believing he had nabbed a spy red-handed, the agent held a press conference to announce that he discovered secret "code books" in Tsien's possession.

The Los Angeles media went wild, printing articles with headlines such as "SECRET DATA SEIZED IN CHINA SHIPMENT." The putative codebooks in Tsien's luggage turned out to be logarithmic tables, and a subsequent government investigation disclosed that nothing at all in the shipment had been classified. But the newspapers did not run a retraction or even a follow-up story, leaving many readers believing that Tsien was indeed an agent for the PRC.

Within days of the seizure of his baggage, Tsien was arrested and locked in a cell in San Pedro for more than two weeks. Confused if not panicked, he lost twenty pounds. The renowned physicist Robert Oppenheimer offered his help, suggesting that Tsien move to Princeton University. That turned out not to be an option for Tsien. Upon his release, the Immigration and Naturalization Service, to the surprise of everyone, started deportation hearings against him, proceeding on the grounds that Tsien, a foreign national Communist, was an undesirable alien deportable by law.

The government kept Tsien in a state of limbo while trying to decide what to do with him. One faction—mainly defense officials—fought to keep him in the United States, arguing that his technical knowledge was too valuable to let fall into the hands of Communist

China, while another—primarily immigration authorities—believed he should be packed off. Meanwhile, the government would not let Tsien leave the boundaries of Los Angeles until his case was resolved. For five years, from 1950 to 1955, he lived under constant FBI surveillance, with his phone bugged, his mail opened and read, his family followed in the streets. Finally, on September 17, 1955, the U.S. government deported Tsien and his family to mainland China.

Whether Tsien was a Communist in the United States cannot be determined, but the evidence suggests that he was not. His wife was the daughter of a top military strategist for Chiang Kai-shek, and survivors of the Cal Tech Communist cell to which Tsien had allegedly belonged insist he was not a member. After a five-year investigation, the INS failed to turn up any documentary proof of Tsien's Communist involvement. As it later turned out, however, his political leanings had no bearing whatsoever on the final decision to deport him. Decades later, declassified State Department documents revealed that the United States and the PRC had negotiated a secret prisoner swap: Tsien Hsue-shen for a group of American POWs captured during the Korean War.

In the end, the case against Tsien hurt rather than helped U.S. national defense. By deporting him, the nation lost a first-class scientist who almost certainly would have been a valued adviser to the American lunar and missile programs. As early as 1949, Tsien had predicted that a trip to the moon would be possible within thirty years and that the journey could be accomplished in a week. Meanwhile, with Tsien's return the PRC gained a man who helped launch a technological revolution in his homeland. As the director of the Fifth Academy of National Defense, China's first missile institute, Tsien oversaw the development of China's first generation of nuclear missiles, the Dongfeng "East Wind" series. He also proposed and guided the development of the first artificial Chinese satellite, a tracking and control telemetry network for ICBMs.

Perhaps Tsien's attorney, Grant B. Cooper, best summed up the repercussions to the United States of its irrational persecution of

Tsien: "That this government permitted this genius, this scientific genius, to be sent to Communist China to pick his brains is one of the tragedies of this century."

As the cold war escalated, American society turned inward, as if cocooning itself against the risk of nuclear destruction. It was an age of burgeoning suburbs, when American men embraced the security of a safe income in a large corporation, while women were encouraged to forgo careers and devote themselves to motherhood. Glossy advertisements projected images of the ideal American marriage: the company man cruising in his long-finned car to his job in the city, the blissful housewife surrounded by gleaming new gadgets in her suburban kitchen. TV dinners—packaged food with disposable utensils and trays—enabled families to eat at home, often right in front of the television, under the hypnotic power of mass media. It was a time of affluence, consumerism, and anesthetizing conformity. Yet underneath it all was a persistent anxiety, arising out of fear that some national leader would miscalculate and the Bomb would annihilate them all.

Despite this anxiety, or because of it, the postwar baby boom produced a culture centered almost exclusively on the needs of children. Couples married earlier and had more children, until birth rates exceeded even those of India. People who had survived the Great Depression and World War II were determined that their own children would want for nothing, and soon the rhythm of American society was governed by the scheduling of Brownie and Boy Scout meetings, birthday parties, and PTA meetings.

Chinese American culture, with its own explosion of births, became even more family-oriented as well. In San Francisco Chinatown, Cameron House, formerly a rescue mission for prostitutes, became a community center that hosted recreational activities for Chinese American children. Youths enjoyed slumber parties there, sleeping in a room painted like a log cabin so they could pretend to be campers in the wilderness. Historian Judy Yung, who spent her youth in 1950s San Francisco, recalled that "many of my peers strove to be all-American, participating in integrated high school club activities and competing to be cheerleaders, student body officers, and prom queens. Others of us chose to become socially active in the Chinese YMCA, Cameron House, Protestant churches, or Chinese language school."

The 1950s were also a period of decline for Chinatowns. Quietly, the "old-timers" of Chinatown—the elderly Chinese men who had led a bachelor existence as they supported families overseas—were aging, losing affluence, and dying. The passing of these men coincided with both the government surveillance of Chinatowns, which decreased business revenue, and the conservative political climate of the 1950s, which devastated Chinese casinos and nightclubs. In 1954, the federal government passed an anti-gambling law that crushed Chinese lotteries across the country, thereby destroying a significant source of business revenue for Chinatown neighborhoods and causing residents to move out and seek new business opportunities elsewhere.

Simultaneously, upwardly mobile young families were reluctant to rear their children in old Chinatown tenements, most of which required significant retrofitting. In 1950, a New York State Housing Survey of New York City Chinatown dwellings found that almost a third did not have flush toilets, almost half lacked showers and bathtubs, and almost three-fourths had no central heating. To escape these privations, many of the children or grandchildren of the nineteenth-century Chinese immigrants or exclusion-era "paper sons" left their ethnic neighbor-hoods and headed for the suburbs, to join their fellow Americans.

Even those who had grown up with a certain degree of prosperity were anxious to move on. One such individual was William Chew, whose family had achieved upper-middle-class status in two genera-tions. His grandfather labored on the transcontinental railroad, worked in mines, and sold vegetables for a living. His father served with distinction during World War I, became one of the first Chinese American Masonic Lodge masters in the United States, and rose to the position of superintendent at the Bayside Cannery in Isleton, California. William, who earned a master's degree in engineering, would later design an experiment for the space shuttle and watch his two sons become a dentist and a professional sports photographer. But when his boys were young, Chew faced a difficult decision: "whether to [remain in] the Chinese community where I grew up, or to move away to rear my family in a medium-income community with more opportunities and a better lifestyle." He chose the latter. Although he knew moving into a white neighborhood would "eventually dilute my family's cultural identity," the enticements were too strong to resist: "I longed to mow a green lawn and wax my car on weekends; to take my children to Sunday school and have backyard bar-b-ques with our neighbors and friends."

Many Chinese now had the means to buy into this life. During the 1950s, increasing numbers of ethnic Chinese—among them college-educated children of the immigrant Chinese merchant class, and the World War II veterans who earned university degrees on the GI Bill—rapidly assumed white-collar or professional positions as engineers, doctors, accountants, lawyers, and businessmen. Some were achieving national prominence, and by the end of the decade the new Chinese American luminaries included mogul Chinn Ho, whom *Time* magazine dubbed the "Chinese Rockefeller of Hawaii," his high school classmate Hiram Leong Fong, the first American of Chinese as well as Asian ancestry to win a seat on the U.S. Senate, Delbert Wong,* the first Chinese American (and Asian American) judge in the United States, and James Wong Howe, one of the best cinematographers in the world, whose mastery of the camera would win him two Oscars.

Through this period, the Chinese American community achieved material wealth far above national averages. In 1959, for instance, they had a median family income of $6,207, while the comparable figure

---

*Delbert Wong's life was transformed by military service and federally subsized education. A third-generation Chinese American born in California, Wong served in the Army Air Force during World War II, flying thirty bombing missions over Europe and winning the Distinguished Flying Cross. The government supported his education at Harvard Business School, and after the war he also studied law at Stanford, which launched his forty-year judicial career.

for all Americans was $5,660. Flush with disposable income, the Chinese American middle class could now afford mortgages in upscale white suburbs, if the legal obstacles to their purchasing such homes could be eliminated.

For generations, racist laws, mostly in California, had barred the Chinese from living in white neighborhoods or attending white schools, though some Chinese were informally integrated into white society. After World War II, these laws, both state and federal, were rapidly disappearing from the books. In 1948, the Supreme Court ruled unconstitutional the real estate covenants that barred home-owners in certain areas from selling to Chinese or other minorities, giving the Chinese the legal right to purchase housing or land any-where in the country. Legislators in California also struck down laws in the education code mandating racial segregation.

The absence of these laws did not mean, however, that new Chinese suburbanites were welcomed with open arms. Many white homeowners feared that minority families in their neighborhoods would lower property values, and many local realtors catered to those fears, refusing to show homes to Chinese buyers. To circumvent these exclusionary tactics, some Chinese purchased homes directly from progressive-minded whites, or worked out secret arrangements with white friends, who bought the property first and then immediately resold it to them. To avoid possible confrontation with angry white neighbors, many of these new Chinese homeowners moved in furtively, in the middle of the night.

In extreme cases, a few whites resorted to harassment, vandalism, and even violence in hopes of driving out the Chinese newcomers. It was not uncommon for Chinese American families in prestigious sub-urbs to find unpleasant notes tacked on their doors, or garbage thrown into their yards. "The first night, they broke my windows, but I ignored them," recalled Lancing F. Lee, who bought a house in a white neighborhood in Los Angeles. "Then they brought dogs over to cause trouble. If you crossed the street, they would bully you."

Underneath the placid surface of suburbia, some Chinese American families would soon learn, lay a dormant xenophobia. In an era when homeowners erected fallout shelters in anticipation of nuclear war, when children practiced "duck and cover" exercises in schools in the event of a nuclear missile attack, fear was often an instinctive if irrational reaction to anyone who did not look true-blue American.

Alice Young, a Harvard-educated attorney, remembers growing up in "the only Asian family in what was then essentially Pentagon-CIA land": the lily-white, conservative Washington suburb of McLean, Virginia. One day, her third-grade teacher showed a social studies film on the Communist threat, in which all the Communists depicted happened to be Chinese. "At the end of the film they said if you notice anyone suspicious, please call your local CIA or FBI," she recalled. "There I sat in the third-grade class and when the lights came on all of my classmates had moved their chairs further back."

Yet the exodus out of the Chinatowns into America's suburbia continued. Not only did the Chinatowns shrink in size, but some vanished altogether. In 1940, a nationwide study recorded twenty-eight American cities with Chinatowns; by 1955, that number had fallen to sixteen. Some predicted that the Chinatowns of America would soon become ghost towns.

They were wrong. By the next decade, the People's Republic of China would undergo cataclysmic political changes so severe that American Chinatown neighborhoods were soon filled with new immigrants.

CHAPTER FIFTEEN

New Arrivals, New Lives: The Chaotic 1960s

I n the 1960s, the Chinese in America may have looked to outsiders like one people with a shared culture, shared traditions,
and a shared immigration experience. But this was not the case,
nor was it for most other immigrant groups. As discrimination against
each immigrant group abates over generations, and the enticement of
assimilation increases, ethnic ties are rarely strong enough to bind
people of different aspirations and talents to a monolithic group identity. This is especially true when immigration is a continuing process,
and later arrivals tend to push earlier arrivals out of the ghettos.

In the 1960s, anti-Chinese discrimination remained strong, but
the ethnic Chinese were also no longer bottled up in Chinatowns, as
they once were, dependent upon community organizations to protect
their rights, their livelihood, and at times their lives. Indeed, some
newer arrivals—the intellectuals and those members of the educational and social elite of China who had managed to find their way,
however circuitously, to the United States—had not even passed
through America's Chinatowns. They had moved directly into university towns and cities, aided by their English-language skills. They
also benefited from the fact that America, whose Declaration of
Independence held as self-evident that "all men are created equal,"
was about to confront the fearful reality of its own racism.

Of this group of Chinese in America, the intellectuals, mostly graduate students stranded in the United States by the 1949 revolution in China, were likely to socialize and associate with other intellectuals of Chinese descent. But intellectual communities were already becoming the first outposts of multiculturalism, and Chinese scholars were able to participate in university town life without being self-conscious about their non-Caucasian appearance and speech patterns. As I look back on my own youth as the daughter of two academics, growing up in the community organized around the University of Illinois at Urbana-Champaign, I remember driving to Chicago Chinatown with my family, but only for the same reason Americans of other ethnicities went there—for a particularly good Chinese meal, not to strengthen any connection to my roots.

In addition, as previously noted, by the 1960s quite a few Chinese Americans had been born in the United States. If others saw them as Chinese, not American, that was their problem. Many of these Chinese Americans saw themselves first as Americans, albeit of Chinese descent, and their only real knowledge of the "old country" came through stories they heard from their parents and grandparents. This lack of personal connection was particularly true of the children of the earliest immigrant waves, especially those I refer to as the "long dispersed" immigrants, whose ancestors had left the American Chinatowns long ago. Many now lived and worked in suburban areas throughout the country, and their children had relatively few contacts with other people of their own race. The children's lives were in many ways indistinguishable from those of the children of other immigrant groups.

But for Chinese who did not feel secure enough to move out of Chinatown, having strong local community groups to turn to in times of trouble was still important. Their comfort was eroded when, in the 1960s, a large wave of new immigrants, mostly refugees from Communist mainland China, came to the United States. Their arrival in America's Chinatowns resulted in a clash of cultures between those who were getting ready to move on but had not yet left and those who had just arrived.

In 1957, in what has come to be known as the "anti-Rightist" movement, Mao Zedong encouraged open criticism of the Communist Party by proclaiming, "Let a hundred flowers bloom, a hundred schools of thought contend." Those who took Mao at his word, however, and actually voiced criticisms of any aspect of the Communist system suffered serious reprisals. Labeled "counterrevolutionaries," thousands of intellectuals who had foolishly suggested reforms landed in prison or reeducation camps. Many others kept silent and quietly applied for exit visas.

A year later, in 1958, the Chinese Communist government began an obsessive national effort to increase industrial output under a plan named the "Great Leap Forward." Seven hundred million people were placed in agricultural communes and ordered to build "backyard steel furnaces." Forced to abandon the fields to tend cauldrons of molten steel, peasants melted down their metallic possessions—from pots and pans to bedsprings—for gains that had only symbolic value. Livestock and crops perished from neglect, and soon the country found itself in the throes of the worst famine in Chinese history, possibly the worst in human history. Food was tightly rationed, but millions of Chinese died of starvation. Eventually the Great Leap Forward was abandoned, and even Mao admitted it had been a mistake, announcing, "The chaos caused was on a grand scale, and I take responsibility."

To ease the pressure of widespread hunger, the Communist leadership suddenly allowed thousands of Chinese to emigrate. Within a twenty-five-day period in 1962, seventy thousand people, mostly residents of Guangdong province, were permitted to leave. At that time, it was easier to emigrate to Hong Kong than to the United States, so most went there, hoping to move on to America at a later date. But those who attempted this two-step migration to the United States faced numerous frustrations.

Even though they were now residents of a British territory, and

U.S. emigration policy still heavily favored northern Europeans while restricting immigration from other parts of the world, most of these Chinese émigrés were still denied entry. According to the McCarran-Walter Act, the statute on immigration, U.S. nation-of-origin requirements separated applicants not by country of residence, but by country of birth.* Thus, the Chinese trying to get to America from the British territory of Hong Kong were treated not as British applicants, but as Chinese. The established quotas permitted only a token 105 Chinese to be admitted annually. Beyond the quota, some Chinese, thanks to special legislation, could enter either as political refugees or on the strength of their individual talents, but their numbers were small.

Many did not even make it to Hong Kong. With so many Chinese streaming across the border, conditions in the city became so overcrowded that British authorities threw up barbed wire to prevent more from entering and rounded up as many refugees as they could to ship them back to China. Hong Kong's problems were exacerbated by the callousness of the British to the plight of these homeless Chinese as well as restrictive U.S. immigration practices. These issues prompted President John F. Kennedy to sign a presidential directive on May 23, 1962, admitting refugees who were in Hong Kong but had been born in mainland China. By 1965, some fifteen thousand Chinese refugees had arrived in the United States.

---

*The United States reserved 70 percent of its admission slots for only three countries—the United Kingdom, Ireland, and Germany—slots that largely went unused. Countries in southern and eastern Europe or Asia had tiny quotas and long wait lists: Italy had an annual quota of only 5,666, Greece 308, and Yugoslavia 942. For the Chinese, the number was even smaller—105. Furthermore, according to the U.S. government, a Chinese alien was not simply someone who originated from China, but any foreigner with at least 50 percent Chinese ancestry, no matter where he or she lived in the world. Thus, immigrants of Chinese heritage born in Europe, or even people of half Chinese, half white ancestry in Europe, were categorized not as European but as Chinese, and were barred from using European quotas.

Even more were able to come after the U.S. revised its immigration law. In 1963, President Kennedy attacked the nation-of-origin provision as having "no basis in either logic or reason," arguing that "it neither satisfies a national need nor accomplishes an international purpose. In an age of interdependence among nations, such a system is an anachronism, for it discriminates among applicants for admission into the United States on the basis of the accident of birth." Two years later, on October 3, 1965, President Lyndon Johnson signed a new Immigration and Nationality Act, also known as the Hart-Celler Act, abolishing racial discrimination in immigration law.* Under the new act, each independent nation beyond the western hemisphere had a yearly quota of twenty thousand, while the spouses, parents, and unmarried minor children of American citizens could enter as nonquota immigrants. This legislation would have a dramatic impact on the size of the Chinese community in America. Before the passage of the Hart-Celler Act, the 1960 census counted only 236,084 ethnic Chinese in the United States—about one-tenth of one percent of the general population. After the act, the ethnic Chinese population in the United States would almost double in size every decade.

The newest Chinese arrivals moved directly into Chinatown neighborhoods. They were by no means the poorest or least educated

---

*Supporters of the bill assured their opponents that the purpose was to fight racial discrimination, not swamp the country with newcomers from Third World countries. Senator Edward Kennedy (D-Mass.) predicted that "the ethnic mix of this country will not be upset" and that the bill would not "inundate America with immigrants from any one country or area, or the most populated and deprived nations of Africa and Asia." Hiram Fong (R-Hawaii) echoed these sentiments, pointing out that "Asians represent six-tenths of one percent of the population of the United States" and that "the people from that part of the world will never reach one percent of the population . . . Our cultural pattern will never be changed as far as America is concerned." President Johnson added, "This bill we signed today is not a revolutionary bill. It does not affect the lives of millions. It will not restructure the shape of our daily lives." These claims, however, were wrong—the act profoundly changed the history of modern immigration and affected millions of lives.

in Guangdong province, but most came without savings, having sold almost everything they owned to pay for transport to the United States. Worse, most could speak no English, which restricted their job searches to Chinese-owned businesses.

At the end of the 1960s, Lillian Sing, then associate director of the Chinese Newcomers Service Center, conducted a small survey of the occupational changes of several Chinese men who had left Hong Kong for new lives in the United States. Their downward mobility was apparent.

In Hong Kong	In San Francisco
Chinese doctor	Laundryman
Sweater-weaver	Cook
Seaman, first mate	Kitchen helper
Factory owner	Janitor
Accountant	Busboy
Chinese doctor	Errand boy
Social worker	Student
Teacher	Busboy
Newspaper reporter	Busboy

These new arrivals weakened the negotiating position of the ethnic Chinese who were already living in Chinatown but still working as laborers. The original inhabitants were also insufficiently fluent in English to take other jobs or to start their own businesses. With a fresh pool of labor available, local Chinese businessmen understood that they could slash salaries and stretch work hours at will. Workers who fell ill could easily be replaced, those who complained, blackballed. With this imbalance in power, employers had no incentive to improve working conditions. Chinatown factories became so hazardous that conditions there prompted several government investigations. One, by the 1969 San Francisco Human Rights Commission, discovered that ethnic Chinese women garment laborers were receiving no overtime pay, no vacation time, no sick leave or health benefits. "It's really amazing how the Chinese exploit themselves," one worker noted.*

For some families, even minimum wage was an unattainable American dream,† and some émigrés made desperate, almost pathetic attempts to learn English, to help them break out of a ruthless job market. In San Francisco and New York, they enrolled in federally funded adult education courses to study English, but their age and physical exhaustion from sixty-hour work weeks made it difficult to concentrate. More significant, their isolation from native-speaking Americans prevented them from practicing English on a daily basis.

Trying to make do on very little, many immigrants crowded into unfurnished single-room apartments, with no furniture or heat. "We each slept on a small piece of plywood which we put on top of two oil cans or chairs right before bedtime," one recalled. "That's how we all learned to sleep perfectly still." Her family bathed just once a week because they had no hot water or bathtub, only a galvanized iron tub that they also used to wash clothes. After she rented a room of her own, she admitted, "I have been showering twice a day! Just to make up for the past."

---

*According to the documentary *Sewing Woman*, seamstress Dong Zem spent almost every waking moment hunched over a sewing machine after she migrated to the United States: "I can still recall the times when I had one foot on the pedal and another one on an improvised rocker, rocking one son to sleep while the other was tied to my back. Many times I would accidentally sew my finger instead of the fabric because one child screamed or because I was falling asleep on the job."

†In her memoir *Paper Daughter*, M. Elaine Mar describes how her family emigrated from Hong Kong to Denver in 1972, when she was five. Her father, employed by a Chinese restaurant managed by one of his relatives, was too poor to buy a ten-dollar T-shirt with her grade school logo printed on it. "Your father has to work a long time, many hours, to make ten dollars," her mother explained. "How much money do you think we have? We're not like the Americans, with their English and their four-dollar-an-hour McDonald's jobs! Don't you think your father would work at McDonald's if he could speak English?"

Neglect and exhaustion soon bred disease and despair. Immediately after the influx of the refugees, San Francisco Chinatown suffered the greatest tuberculosis rate in the country, six to seven times higher than the national rate at the time. The most despairing resorted to drugs, alcohol, and even suicide. San Francisco Chinatown recorded the highest suicide rate in the country: between 1952 and 1969, Chinese men took their own lives at the mean rate of 27.9 per 100,000, almost triple the national figure.

Immigrant children suffered as well. During the 1960s, teachers in San Francisco Chinatown observed students dozing off behind their desks in class. When confronted, some youths confessed that after school they had to labor in sweatshops for at least eight to ten hours a day. Edward Redford, then assistant superintendent for secondary education, explained why: "They work half the night in laundries or sewing shops, apparently because they owe money to someone who brought them here."

Sleep deprivation was not the only problem. Another was that classes were conducted in English, and that most of these children had minimal English-language skills. Even though some had spent their childhoods in the British colony of Hong Kong, the public schools there had offered woefully substandard English-language instruction.

Fights broke out frequently between the ABCs—the American-born Chinese—and the FOBs, the "fresh off the boat" foreign-born Chinese from Hong Kong. In his memoir *Chinese Playground,* Bill Lee, a native of San Francisco Chinatown, remembered the taunts as the first Hong Kong families moved into his neighborhood in the early 1960s:

It began with the newcomers getting hassled.
"Fresh-off-the-Boat!"
"Fuckin' China Bugs!"
"Ching Chongs!"
"Look at them clothes, dude!"
"No speaka' English?"

In turn, the FOBs called the ABCs "Tow Gee" (privileged and spoiled landowners) and "Juk Sing" (empty and hollow bamboo). Soon, some of the immigrant teenagers banded into a gang of their own called the Wah Ching, or "China Youth." According to Lee, they terrorized the ABCs:

> It was payback time and their retaliation was fierce. This was now a different ball game. ABCs were getting jumped left and right and the beatings were severe. After school, if you made it out of the grounds, they'd find you at the bus stop or cable car turn-table. It wasn't just a one-time payback. The assaults were repeated over and over. Make fun of any foreign-born kid in class or bump one of their brothers or cousins in the hall and you'd pay dearly for it. These guys grew up in the rough streets of Hong Kong and Macao where gangs were hardcore. Many had spent a good part of their youths in brutal prisons.

Unable to learn English quickly enough to succeed in school, many children of the newest arrivals dropped out and hit the streets. Dressed in black from head to toe, wearing bouffant hairstyles and high-heeled boots, they strutted through Chinatown, followed by little boys who idolized them and helped carry their guns. Skirmishes broke out between rival factions, and within a few years, juvenile violence had escalated into full-fledged battles. Journalist Ben Fong-Torres recalled that era: "delinquency was too clinical a word for what was going on in Chinatown. People were being killed in the streets, merchants were being extorted; gangs were at war not only with each other but with community leaders and cops."

Beneath the violence came open pleas for help. At a Human Rights Commission hearing in San Francisco in 1968, the Wah Ching gang asked for a community clubhouse and a two-year training program so they could gain vocational skills and high school diplomas. In response, the Human Rights Commission turned for assistance to the Chinese Consolidated Benevolent Association (CCBA), an umbrella organization that grew out of the historic Six Companies in Chinatown, but the CCBA responded coldly: "They have not shown that they are sorry or that they will change their ways. They have threatened the community. If you give in to this group, you are only going to have another hundred immigrants come in and have a whole new series of threats and demands."

Other Chinese Americans, however, eager to defuse a situation they recognized as a ticking time bomb, expressed far greater sympathy. "Some of these kids are talking about getting guns and rioting," one observer noted. "And I'm not threatening, the situation already exists." Socially progressive Chinese Americans—in particular, college students and young professionals in the San Francisco Bay Area—began returning to their old Chinatown neighborhoods to volunteer as mentors to foreign-born Chinese youths. At San Francisco State College, students organized the Inter-Collegiate Chinese for Social Action, a group that worked with immigrant youths in the Bay Area and tutored them in English. In 1968, the Concerned Chinese for Action and Change, founded by American university students and professionals, picketed Grant Avenue, one of the busiest streets for tourists in San Francisco Chinatown, to draw attention to the social problems in their community, in hopes of embarrassing the Chinese elite into making much-needed reforms.

Some American-born Chinese felt a special obligation toward these émigrés as a result of early parental influence. In his memoir *The Rice Room*, Ben Fong-Torres describes belonging to two separate worlds during the 1960s: one as a pioneer rock radio deejay and the first Chinese American writer and editor at *Rolling Stone*, the second as the "number two son" of immigrant restaurant owners in Oakland Chinatown. In the evenings, his mother took piecework home from local garment factories and talked as her children held skeins of yarn for her. "I knew to expect stories about China," Fong-Torres recalled, "and what the Communists were doing to our family in the village, and how important it was for us to do well, so that we could help provide for them."

The Communists were never out of the minds of certain Chinese American families. Although they could never visit mainland China, because of either finances or the lack of legal permission, they received occasional, tissue-thin air mail letters from relatives, their last fragile link to China during the cold war. "I was nine years old when the letters made my parents, who are rocks, cry," wrote Maxine Hong Kingston,* daughter of Chinese immigrant laundry owners in Stockton, California, and author of *The Woman Warrior: Memoirs of a Girlhood among Ghosts.* The letters described how the new Communist regime forced her uncles to kneel on broken glass and confess to being landlords. They told of relatives who had been sent to rural communes, of others who had been executed, and of still others who had simply disappeared. A few resurfaced in Hong Kong and asked her parents for help. "The aunts in Hong Kong said to send money quickly; their children were begging on the sidewalks, and mean people put dirt in their bowls."

The crusading spirit of the 1960s prompted some American-born children of Chinese immigrants to respond to Chinese calls for help. Two forces in particular stoked the fires of activism. One was the civil rights movement led by the Reverend Martin Luther King, Jr., which began as a grassroots effort among southern blacks in the 1950s to end Jim Crow but spread rapidly across the country through the following decade, when television cameras brought into middle-class homes the ugly spectacle of southern sheriffs turning hoses and police dogs on blacks engaging in peaceful protests. Sympathy for the plight of African Americans in the American South soon expanded to include a more general interest in human rights, particularly for people of color living in white-controlled societies.

The second force was the Vietnam War, in the background of which was the largest college enrollment at any time in American history. As the nation debated why we were in Vietnam, students on

---

*Maxine Hong Kingston, winner of the National Book Award and National Critics Circle Award, is the most widely taught living author in the United States.

campus after campus organized marches to protest the war. Once again, television played a critical role, first in dramatizing the horrors of war in a way never before possible, and second by sensitizing white Americans to the fate of nonwhites in developing countries across Asia.

Few regions in the country were more politically active than the San Francisco Bay Area. Campuses like the University of California at Berkeley and San Francisco State College became centers of protest, not only over the war but also about a wide spectrum of social ills in American society. Relatively large numbers of ethnic Chinese students attended these schools, and, inevitably, many of them, inflamed by the passion of the times, carried that passion back to their Chinatown neighborhoods, determined to address the discrimination, against American-born Chinese as well as new immigrants.

The results of their activism were mixed. For one thing, reentering Chinatown put some of these ABC crusaders at tremendous risk. Not only were they at loggerheads with the powerful capitalists who exploited new immigrants, but they also came into close daily contact with dangerous youth gangs. Volunteers were often threatened and harassed, and one social worker was murdered. Barry Fong-Torres, the idealistiq, Berkeley-educated twenty-nine-year-old brother of journalist Ben Fong-Torres, had taken a one-year leave of absence from his job as a probation officer to become director of the Youth Service and Coordinating Center in San Francisco Chinatown. Despite his genuine efforts to reach out to troubled immigrant teenagers, the local gangs feared he was an undercover agent and resented his talking to leaders of rival groups. Eventually, Barry Fong-Torres was gunned down in his apartment, with a misspelled note left near his body: "PIG INFOMERS DIE YONG."

One unexpected and controversial legacy of ABC activism in Chinatown was the growth of the bilingual education system in the United States. During the 1960s, Chinese immigrant parents in San Francisco had complained that their children were unable to follow classroom instruction in English. The Chinese for Affirmative Action, founded in 1969 to fight racial discrimination against Chinese and other Asian Americans, helped ethnic Chinese students file a class action lawsuit against education officials to get them to address their language needs in the public schools. The case eventually reached the Supreme Court, which in 1974, in *Lau* v. *Nichols*, overruled a lower court decision, not on constitutional grounds but instead by finding, "It seems obvious that the Chinese-speaking minority receive fewer benefits than the English-speaking majority from respondents' school system, which denies them a meaningful opportunity to participate in the educational program—all earmarks of the discrimination banned by [H.E.W.] Regulations. In 1970 H.E.W. issued clarifying guidelines which include the following: 'Where inability to speak and understand the English language excludes national origin–minority group children from effective participation in the educational program offered by a school district, the district must take affirmative steps to rectify the language deficiency in order to open its instructional program to these students.' " The Supreme Court concluded that it was a "mockery of public education" to demand that all children possess basic skills in English before availing themselves of a public education. This decision paved the way for historic language reforms within the American education system.

At San Francisco State College, ethnic Chinese students joined the Third World Liberation Front, which called for solidarity among Americans of Asian, African, Latin, and Native American descent. In 1968, demonstrators at San Francisco State refused to attend class and demanded an ethnic studies program that would include not only black studies but also Asian American studies. The strike lasted more than four months, the longest college strike in American history, leading not only to the establishment of the first ethnic studies program in the country but also to the beginnings of the Asian American political movement. Other strikes quickly followed at Berkeley and UCLA, which instituted similar departments.

While many activists were educated and middle-class, some came from the margins of Chinatown society. They too seized the opportunity to demand more, and the end of the 1960s bore witness to the rise of militant groups calling for actual revolution. In 1969, in the San Francisco Bay Area, American-born Chinese youths, many of them former street gang members, founded the Red Guard Party, in honor of the state-sanctioned vigilantes of Mao Zedong's Cultural Revolution. (Three years earlier, as Mao struggled with other Communist leaders for power, he had asked millions of Chinese adolescents to continue his revolution as "Red Guards," to destroy the last vestiges of feudal, bourgeois tradition in China.) As youths on the mainland studied *The Quotations of Chairman Mao* (also known as the "little red book"), so did ABC members of the American Red Guard Party wave copies of Mao's book in the streets of Chinatown. Unlike their counterparts in China, however, the Red Guards in America remained a small fringe group. Forging alliances with the Black Panther Party in Oakland and the Third World Liberation Front at San Francisco State, the Red Guard Party went underground for weapons training and later disappeared.

Chinese American radicals who adopted socialism as their platform were often long on rhetoric and short on results. A few, however, did achieve tangible gains for the working-class community in Chinatown. In 1969, Chinese American youths in New York partnered with other Asian Americans to start the I Wor Kuen, named after the secret society that terrorized Westerners in China during the 1900 Boxer Rebellion. I Wor Kuen provided free health services to the poor, administered tuberculosis tests in Chinatown on weekends, served meals to the elderly, and fought for the right to low-income housing. Their causes included joining forces with the "We Won't Move" committee that prevented the Bell Telephone company from evicting thousands of tenants to construct a switching station, a cause that temporarily united ethnic Chinese and Italian residents in the area.

Much of America, however, did not associate the ethnic Chinese with radical activism. The images burned into the national consciousness were starkly black and white—the throngs of African American demonstrators, linking arms, singing "We Shall Overcome," followed by Black Power advocates and white hippies in tie-dye and dreadlocks laying siege to university administrators. Even less visible were the quiet upheavals shuddering through another group of Chinese Americans—those who had spent their youth in suburbs and small towns, far from the Chinatowns of major cities. During the 1960s, the emphasis would shift away from simply fitting in, and more toward openly questioning their place in society.

In her autobiographical novel *Mona in the Promised Land* (1997), Gish Jen opened a window onto Chinese American life in a privileged white suburb during the 1960s. Describing a prosperous Chinese American family, owners of a pancake house, who live in the fictional Scarshill, an affluent Jewish community, Jen shares memories of her hometown of Scarsdale, New York. It is 1968: "the blushing dawn of ethnic awareness has yet to pink up their inky suburban night," and there are hardly any other Chinese in town, but in another ten years "there'll be so many Orientals they will turn into Asians; a Japanese grocery will buy out that one deli too many."

Jen's work describes a world of contradictions, where youths talk about subverting society while also preparing to take their places within the East Coast establishment. When not obsessing over SATs, college admissions, and scholarships, Mona and her classmates experiment with ethnicity, acquiring or discarding new cultures like designer suits. Mona decides to be Jewish, her Jewish boyfriend decides to be black, an African American friend decides to be Buddhist. But her parents cannot shed their heritage as quickly as Mona can—and Mona's private thoughts betray her impatience with them:

"You know, the Chinese revolution was a long time ago; you can get over it now. Okay, you had to hide in the garden and listen to bombs fall out of the sky, also you lost everything you had. And it's true you don't even know what happened to your sisters and brothers and parents, and only wish you could send them some money. But didn't you make it? Aren't you here in America, watching the sale ads, collecting your rain checks? You know what you are now?" she wants to say. "Now you're smart shoppers"... But in another way she understands it's like asking Jews to get over the Holocaust, or like asking the blacks to get over slavery. Once you've lost your house and your family and your country, your devil-may-care is pretty much gone too.

In the midst of this suburban soul-searching, a few Chinese Americans would discover black culture, borrowing liberally from it to create new personae of rebellion. In the 1960s, composer Fred Ho found that jazz could voice his alienation from white society, his rejection of Chinese American bourgeois values, his kinship with the oppressed and downtrodden. The son of a professor of Chinese politics, Ho grew up in the wealthy white communities of Palo Alto, California, and Amherst, Massachusetts, where, unable to win acceptance from his Caucasian classmates, he turned to the Black Power movement instead, becoming an avid reader of Malcolm X and Martin Luther King. Fusing his fascination with both Chinese and African American cultures, Ho applied ancient Chinese instruments to jazz, thereby inventing a new strain of music. His works include *Bound Feet*, to expose the ancient abuse of Chinese women; *Chi Lai!* (literally, the Chinese term for "rise up!"), to celebrate the struggle of early Chinese laborers in the United States; *Journey Beyond the West*, a ballet based on the myth of the Chinese monkey king; and *Chinaman's Chance*, a Chinese American opera documenting the epic story of the Chinese immigrant experience, the first to be written in jazz.

Grace Lee Boggs was another Chinese American who drew spiritual and political sustenance from the black community. Born in Providence, Rhode Island, the daughter of Chinese immigrants, Boggs, a highly educated, middle-class intellectual, refused to become a token member of the white elite. After earning a bachelor's degree from Barnard and a doctorate in philosophy from Bryn Mawr, she turned to radical politics as a protégée of C. L. R. James, a renowned

West Indian Marxist scholar. The first president of Ghana proposed marriage to her, but she decided instead to wed James Boggs, an African American automobile assembly-line worker and Black Power activist. Through the 1960s—and for decades afterwards—she and her husband served as tireless civil rights leaders in Detroit, organizing unions and reviving the inner-city black community. The FBI labeled her an "Afro-Chinese Marxist," but Boggs resisted easy categorization: "Through sheer will, without waiting for social conditions to come around and without waiting to explore her identity, she turned her back on who she was and barged into new territories," Louis Tsen wrote of Boggs. "She was a woman who barged into men's territory; she was a Chinese who barged into black territory; she was an intellectual who barged into workers' territory."

Indeed, Boggs was an exceptional activist, even in an age filled with self-proclaimed rebels. Many Chinese Americans paid lip service to fighting the system in the 1960s, but few had the courage to dedicate their whole life to such a cause. Instead, like the majority of Americans, most preferred to accommodate to the status quo, to not challenge it, or, still better, to quietly distance themselves from social problems.

Perhaps nowhere did Chinese Americans tread more carefully than in the South, where a small population of ethnic Chinese had long kept low and quiet, avoiding open conflict with the white community. Not until the civil rights movement erupted in the 1950s were southern Chinese forced, at last, to confront the racial codes by which they had lived their lives.

By the 1960s, Chinese Americans in the South, primarily a community of grocers and merchants, had already made the remarkable transition from "colored" to "white," leaping over the chasm of race and class to win acceptance as honorary Caucasians. Their social rise was made possible by both their financial status and their racially ambiguous position. Although the Chinese worked closely with black customers, they also gained entrance to white institutions, such as churches, schools, barbershops, and theaters. Their children excelled in white classrooms and mimicked white customs. Incredibly, the Chinese community had achieved integration in white society not by dint of federal intervention or organized protest, but through quiet networking with white friends and behind-the-scenes negotiations with local white leaders.

All this required a delicate balancing act, especially since blacks formed most of the customer base for Chinese stores. For decades, the Chinese community had survived in the South by appearing to be friendly to both black and white interests. However, as the 1960s went on, this façade was difficult if not impossible to maintain, as Chinese grocers found themselves caught in the crossfire of a race war. Black civil rights leaders asked Chinese grocers for financial donations and for display space for political signs in shop windows. Meanwhile, white supremacist groups, in a supreme stroke of irony, insisted that the Chinese join their White Citizens' Councils, to help them counter black activism. Aware of their precarious status in the South, the Chinese, as a group, made every attempt to remain politically neutral. Some tried to hedge their bets by hiding their White Citizens' Council memberships from black customers, and their civil rights contributions from the white business elite. This was not an entirely successful strategy, and their unwillingness to take a stand finally angered the black community. After the assassination of Martin Luther King in 1968, Chinese stores in Memphis were singled out for violence during black riots.

"If you sided with the whites, the blacks would be all over you, but if you sided with the blacks, the whites could crucify you," said Sam Chu Lin, a California radio and television broadcaster who grew up in Mississippi. No Chinese American, he recalled, dared to become a civil rights activist in his region: "I saw none on the picket lines— they would been either killed or socially ostracized." The Chinese in the South, he said, were "skating on thin ice," anxious to survive in a society where even the smallest transgression of the racial code could be met with violent retaliation. Once, while he was working as a radio disc jockey in Mississippi during the 1960s, two young white women came into the station looking for him, completely unaware that the voice they admired was not the voice of a white man. "They were groupies who wanted to make moon-eyes at the deejay," Lin remembered. "And I told them, 'I'm just cleaning up the station—the guy's busy right now.' The Chinese knew what happened to blacks who dated white girls. And Sam Chu Lin wasn't going to take any chances."

An undertone of bitterness can be detected in many interviews of American-born Chinese who grew up in the South during this era. Like the Jewish community in the region, the Chinese had successfully adopted white culture, yet they could not earn full acceptance by the white elite, not even as honorary Caucasians. Nor did they feel entirely comfortable among their own people, especially the gossipy, tight-knit social network of their parents. "I didn't go to the Chinese dances," one American-born Chinese woman told sociologist James Loewen. "My parents tried to push us to go, and we resented it. I always tore up the invitations before Dad saw them." In addition, they expressed disgust for the Jim Crow laws that humiliated the black community. When they came of age, many ABCs protested not with their mouths, but with their feet. Gradually, the South witnessed an exodus of the American-born Chinese, who left the small towns of their childhood for the cities of the North and West.

Such was the decision of Sam Sue, son of an immigrant Chinese grocer in Clarksdale, Mississippi. His father had worked seven days a week, every night until ten o'clock, providing blacks with essential social services. His store was not only a warehouse and a home but also an informal bank and accounting firm. Speaking broken English in a black dialect, his father would extend black sharecroppers the credit denied them by white institutions. The conditions under which local black farmers labored for whites landowners resembled the Dark Ages, and the primitive cabins they rented from whites had no running water or electricity. The blacks bought from Sue's father kerosene for lamps and Clorox to purify drinking water. Sam Sue, who grew up in the store, did not recognize his own poverty until years later. "It was tenement-like conditions, though we didn't know it at the time. I didn't even know how poor we were until I left. Everyone slept in one big room. There was a kitchen in the back. We used to use the place to store goods too, so there would be boxes all around. If you went into the living room, you'd be sitting on a box of laundry detergent."

Worst of all was the vague sense of being a second-class citizen, yet having an unspoken, tentative membership in the first class. "As a kid, I remember going to the theatre and not really knowing where I was supposed to sit," Sam Sue told an interviewer. "Blacks were segregated then. Colored people had to sit upstairs, and white people sat downstairs. I didn't know where I was supposed to sit, so I sat in the white section, and nobody said anything. So I always had to confront those problems growing up. So these experiences were very painful."

Sam Sue eventually became a lawyer in New York City, but his father remained in Mississippi after retiring, despite efforts by the family to get him to leave. "It is all he knows," Sue said. His father was "attached to the area—not that he has affection for it, only that he is used to it—he feels it is home."

One group remained relatively untouched by the chaotic 1960s— the community of scholars who had migrated to the United States to study, teach, or conduct research. While American-born Chinese youths talked revolution, these foreign-born immigrants had already witnessed one, or escaped its effects. Ensconced at universities, research laboratories, or corporations, often high tech, they had a mindset different from the rest of Chinese America. As creative artists and intellectuals, they defined themselves more by ideas than ethnicity or region, belonging to international communities that recognized no borders. Many, especially those who came from lives of education and privilege, believed they could adapt to life anywhere, as long as they had their work to sustain them.

Their interviews fairly glow with confidence. I. M. Pei, the world-famous architect and son of a Shanghai banking magnate, recalled a childhood filled with servants, summer vacations in Suzhou, and private schools. "I had the impression that anything I wanted, I could get," he said. An Wang, a self-made computer mogul and son of a teacher in China, felt optimistic about his future prospects when he arrived in America at the age of twenty-five to study at Harvard. "I had heard that there was discrimination against Chinese in the United States, but I came here with no insecurities about what I might try to do." For a young man who had spent his formative years in the international city of Shanghai, the United States did not seem at all like a foreign country: "Frankly the United States seemed a lot like China to me." Perhaps most importantly, as a doctoral student in applied physics, he understood the lingua franca of his field: "Science is the same the world over—a language I could speak."

What this group had lost in China they quickly found—or rebuilt—in the United States. Success came rapidly for them, and some would emerge as world celebrities by the 1960s. I. M. Pei designed many of the most important structures of the twentieth century. An Wang, who started Wang Laboratories in 1951 with $600, took his company public in 1967 in one of the largest initial public offerings in history, turning him into a billionaire and one of the richest men in the world. Chin Yang Lee, born in Hunan, China, and educated at Yale, wrote *The Flower Drum Song*, which achieved instant best-seller status upon its publication in 1957, was turned into a Broadway musical in 1958 by Rodgers and Hammerstein, and then into a film musical in 1961. In 1957 Tsung-Dao Lee and Chen-ning Yang became the first Chinese American Nobel laureates* after their

---

*Lee and Yang first met as students at National Southwest United University, when the Japanese invasion forced them to flee to the city of Kunming in Yunnan. After World War II, they won doctoral scholarships to study physics under Enrico Fermi at the University of Chicago, beginning a scientific collaboration that continued even after Yang moved to Princeton University and Lee to Columbia. When they received the Nobel, Yang was only thirty-four years old, and Lee barely thirty-one, the second youngest scholar ever to win this honor.

research on the decay of the subatomic K-meson shattered a universally accepted "inviolate" law of physics, the principle of the conservation of parity.*

Other stranded scholars were not household names, but their colleagues revered them as giants. In mathematics, Shing-Shen Chern developed differential geometry theories that would later earn him the National Medal of Science, and Chia-Chiao Lin, a theoretical astrophysicist, created a famous density wave theory to explain the spiral structure of galaxies. In engineering, Tung-Yen Lin, a professor at Berkeley and the founder of T. Y. Lin International, became one of the greatest authorities on bridges and pre-stressed concrete.† In medicine, Min-Chueh Chang, a Cambridge-educated scientist at the Worcester Foundation for Experimental Biology, co-invented the birth control pill and successfully performed in-vitro fertilization with rabbit ova, a process that later helped make possible the first "test tube babies."

These pioneers would serve as the academic role models for a new wave of Chinese intellectuals who began arriving in the United States in the 1960s and 1970s. They too would come from upper-echelon families, seeking graduate degrees and fortunes in America. But unlike the generation of scholars who preceded them, they would not come directly from mainland China. Instead they would migrate from the island of Taiwan—the last hope and refuge of the exiled Nationalist regime.

---

*Chien-Shiung Wu (also known as Jian Xiong Wu), a Chinese woman physicist at Columbia, confirmed their theory experimentally. Though many felt that Wu, then the world's leading female physicist, also deserved to be honored by the Nobel committee, she ended up winning honorary doctorates from twelve universities, including Harvard and Yale, and earned the title of the "Queen of Nuclear Physics."
†T. Y. Lin International later built some of the most daring structures in history, such as the giant arches of the Moscone Center in San Francisco, which support, without columns, the biggest underground room in the world.

CHAPTER SIXTEEN

The Taiwanese Americans

J ust a step ahead of Mao's advancing forces, thousands of Chinese who had supported Chiang's Nationalist government made hurried plans to leave mainland China. Their children would later recall their panicked, even hysterical parents attempting to coordinate last-minute departures of family and close relatives. Suddenly yanked out of lives of luxury and crammed into trains and ships, swept along by a mass exodus characterized by fear and chaos, these former children of privilege would never forget being torn away from the security of their previous lives.

From November 1948 through early 1949, more than five thousand refugees, many former rank-and-file bureaucrats in Chiang's government, arrived in Taiwan from the mainland each day.* Eventually, between one million and two million refugees would reach the island. To get a sense of the size and character of the dislocation, one would have to imagine the United States government suddenly moving virtually its entire bureaucracy to the island of Puerto Rico.

---

*The natives later claimed that Taiwan was the "number three" choice for mainland refugees: the most powerful went to the "number one" destination, the United States, and those with money went to the "number two" location of Hong Kong. Everyone else, they said, headed for Taiwan.

It was easier for children, because of their youth and inexperience, to adapt to their new surroundings. Many saw Taiwan as a tropical paradise, a welcome change in their lives. In the sixteenth century, the Portuguese had named the island Ilha Formosa ("Beautiful Island"), and its natural splendor was not lost on the young arrivals. Years later, they would remember fondly the joy of netting exotic butterflies, of playing in rice paddies on the outskirts of town, of savoring all the juicy mangos, papayas, and pineapples they could eat. They were far better off than the mainland refugees who entered the United States directly from China during the early 1960s, who had suffered the extreme hardship of the famine years under Mao's rule. Still, the relocation to Taiwan was not entirely positive for these children. They grew up under a different set of oppressive conditions, under a regime-in-exile determined to install and sustain on Taiwan the same strongly authoritarian and oligarchic system of governance with which it had ruled China.

The adult émigrés had a difficult time on all fronts. Accustomed to sophisticated urban life, most were ill-prepared for the humid climate and slow pace of the island. People who had lived in mansions now found themselves in bamboo houses, with rooms separated only by paper screens and with open-air windows that insects and lizards crawled through at will. In many areas there was no electricity or natural gas, so housewives were forced to cook with *maige*, cakes of mud mixed with coal. Some had to sleep on bare reed mats, under mosquito tents, breathing air as oppressively hot and moist as steam.

Yet these primitive conditions were hardly the most pressing problems on their minds. The migration had been so swift and so immense that the natives of the island were stunned. Every day the émigrés had to contend with the smoldering hostility of the indigenous Taiwanese, who deeply resented KMT confiscation of their property and the brutal reprisals to their 1947 rebellion.* Worst of all, the

---

*The natives viewed them as the latest arrivals in a long parade of conquerors. During the seventeenth century, the island fell under the domination of the Dutch,

Nationalist newcomers lived in constant fear that the Communists would attack from the mainland.

During their early years on Taiwan, some mainlanders refused to accept the island as a permanent home and set their sights over the horizon. My own mother's family, like many other mainland refugees, believed an invasion of Taiwan was imminent. In late 1949 and early 1950, my maternal grandfather, who had been a poet, scholar, and journalist in mainland China, anxiously pored over stacks of books, researching the culture and geography of other countries in which the family might settle. America was out of the question, because my grandfather believed only rich, well-connected Nationalists could go there, but the Philippines or perhaps Brazil might lie within their reach. A year after arriving in Taiwan, the family moved to Hong Kong, intending to proceed to another country, either in Asia or Latin America. Courageously—or perhaps naively—my grandfather attempted to support himself, his wife, and their five children in Hong Kong as a freelance writer. As Chinese American Anna Chennault would later write in her memoirs, Hong Kong in the 1950s was a "desolate place both in literary and in cultural terms. Writers could seldom practice their craft and make ends meet, and even well-known columnists could rarely hope to make more than ten dollars an article." My mother's entire family squeezed into a single room without a kitchen, and prepared meals over a charcoal burner in the hallway. They later moved to another boarding house where water for cooking or cleaning had to be fetched from a faucet in the street. While my grandfather diligently wrote editorials and political commentary for a local newspaper, my grandmother looked into the possibility of earn-

---

the Spanish, and then the Manchus. In 1895, after its humiliating defeat in the First Sino-Japanese War, the Qing dynasty ceded Taiwan to Japan. Half a century later, when Japan lost World War II, they returned Taiwan to Nationalist China. Originally, many Chinese natives on the island, ecstatic at Japan's surrender, looked forward to reunification, but their excitement soon turned to rage and disappointment. In 1947, KMT malfeasance and corruption ignited a local revolt, which the Nationalists swiftly and brutally crushed.

ing extra money by frying beans for vendors or mending clothes. Decades later, my mother says her family was just one step away from being homeless.

Many, even some of those who stayed through the 1960s, saw Taiwan as only a temporary resting ground, a refugee way station en route to their next destination. By the time the first generation of Taiwanese Chinese children came of age, it was clear that starting a career on this island, just a few miles across a narrow strait from Communist-controlled China, could not promise a glowing future. With the encouragement of their parents, the best and brightest of them actively worked to leave Taiwan and start new lives abroad. The most popular destination turned out to be the United States, the former patron of the Nationalist government. By the late 1960s and early 1970s, about two thousand students were leaving Taiwan each year to pursue graduate degrees in America.

Those like my grandfather who were certain that mainland China was about to invade and annex the island were not simply pessimistic prophets of doom. The PRC had fully intended to deliver the coup de grâce with a military assault on Taiwan, when the Korean War unexpectedly intervened, turning the PRC and the U.S. into deadly enemies. The American government, an ally of South Korea, threw its protection to Taiwan and used the island as a forward Pacific base. Most important, the United States continued to recognize the Nationalists as the sole legitimate government not only of Taiwan but of all of China. Only when it was clear that Taiwan had the unwavering support of the United States did my maternal grandfather have the confidence to leave Hong Kong in 1950 and move back to Taipei, the capital of Taiwan, where he soon became a regular newspaper columnist and a professor.

Since United States backing was key to Taiwan's survival, the KMT devoted tremendous resources to maintaining good relations with Washington. At the vanguard of what would become known as Taiwan's "China Lobby" in the United States were two of Chiang Kai-shek's brothers-in-law: T. V. Soong, the finance minister of the

Republic of China, and H. H. Kung.* In 1954, in part because of the influence of the China Lobby and its supporters, the United States pledged to safeguard Taiwan by signing a mutual defense treaty. For the next three decades the United States recognized the Nationalist regime as the official government of China. Indeed, until 1971, more than twenty years after the Nationalists were driven from the mainland, U.S. power in the United Nations enabled a government that exerted effective control over only one small island of less than 20 million people to hold one of the five permanent seats on the Security Council, while the People's Republic of China, the de facto government of a billion people, was not even a UN member. So powerful was the China Lobby in American politics that *U.S. News and World Report* later ranked its influence as an international lobby in Washington second only to that of the state of Israel.

But while the Nationalists gained powerful friends in Washington, they were much less concerned about winning the hearts of those at home. Within a few years, Chiang's island regime rivaled its former mainland regime in cronyism and corruption. The new administration threw thousands of native bureaucrats out of work and suspended all national-level elections on the island on the pretext that Communist occupation of the mainland prevented a fair vote on Taiwan. In their view, the civil war was far from over, entitling all elected Nationalist politicians to keep their positions until the Communists were driven from the mainland and new elections could be held. On March 1, 1950, Chiang Kai-shek became, once again, the president of the Republic of China. In 1960, the government revised the constitution to eliminate the two-term limit on the presidency during "the period of Communist rebellion," so that Chiang could parlay his position into a lifelong dictatorship.

---

*Soong had exploited his position to exchange worthless Chinese currency into U.S. dollars, which he used to profit through black market speculation, and before the entire Nationalist monetary system collapsed, Soong had converted his wealth into gold and moved to New York City.

The period of the 1950s was known as the reign of "White Terror," during which Chiang's National Security Bureau harassed thousands of people suspected of being pro-Communist, often solely on hearsay and circumstantial evidence. The government silenced, jailed, and in some cases executed or assassinated members of the intellectual landowning elite, and laws were applied retroactively to punish innocuous activities committed long before the Nationalists had even arrived on the island.* The Nationalist crackdown bred a deep hatred of the KMT on the island and fostered the growth of secret organizations of natives for Taiwanese independence.

To ensure their control into the future, the KMT went about indoctrinating a mindset of unquestioning loyalty in the youth on the island. "By grade school, they had already started to brainwash you," recalled Dick Ling, a Taiwanese American engineer now at Lawrence Livermore National Laboratory. He remembered the school assemblies and the Chinese Boy Scout meetings designed to instill in him a sense of Sun Yat-sen as an almost mythic hero and of the Three People's Principles of the Nationalist Party as beyond challenge. In junior high, he endured interminable flag-raising ceremonies, in which the school principal and his assistant addressed motivational speeches to their captive audience: how they all must "work hard, study hard, be loyal to the country, and help Chiang Kai-shek, the savior of China, recover the mainland to rescue the people from Mao Zedong." As in many cult-based dictatorships, pictures of Chiang appeared everywhere—in classrooms, hallways, the streets. On October 10, National Day, Ling said, students would wave flags in front of the presidential palace and sing, "Long live Chiang Kai-shek! May he live more than ten thousand years!"

Censorship was strictly enforced, as intelligence officials freely steamed open and read the public's letters. Not only did the citizens

---

*For instance, one journalist who had read Marxist literature before migrating to Taiwan found himself sentenced to several years of hard penal labor after authorities discovered evidence of his literary tastes by reading his friend's diary.

lose their right to privacy, but also their right to free speech and unfettered access to information. Foreign publications were sanitized as they came through the mail: bureaucrats, rifling through American magazines like *Time* and *Life*, stamped on each photograph of Mao Zedong the Chinese character *Fei*—"bandit"—for the benefit of unenlightened readers. Creative works, no matter how small, were scrutinized for hidden political messages. For example, when Dick Ling was moonlighting as a freelance cartoonist during his college years, he was warned by a Taiwanese newspaper editor never to draw "bald old men with little moustaches," because they might be perceived as caricatures of Chiang Kai-shek.

People were punished simply for careless, offhand remarks. Carl Hsu remembered that during his military service in Taiwan, the authorities ordered the entire boot camp to join in a group denunciation of Communist and Marxist philosophy. One boy asked how he could do this since he was not legally allowed to read books on the subject. "That student got into deep, *deep* trouble," Hsu recalled. "Even though we were very young, we were trained to be very careful about what we said."

The government even discouraged its citizens from building their own shortwave radios, for fear of their listening to broadcasts from the People's Republic of China, an activity outlawed by the Nationalist government. Shortwave radios were also associated with espionage, because they could enable secret communication with the mainland. "You couldn't even buy vacuum tubes then," remembered Ching Peng, a Chinese American engineer from Taiwan. "The KMT was paranoid about people using the tubes to build shortwave radios." Caught with such a radio, one of his relatives ended up with a three-year jail term, even though there was no evidence whatsoever that he had tuned in to any Communist propaganda.

As the years went by, a schism opened between parents and children in many Nationalist families. Some parents could not free themselves from the past, and for the rest of their lives they would obsess, bitterly, on lost fortunes and ruined careers. Some could talk of nothing but their glory days in China—their mansions, their servants, their titles—and how it had all vanished overnight in the 1949 Communist revolution. Some clung to a dream—which grew more remote with each passing year—that one day the Nationalists would somehow expel the Communists, reclaim their rightful role as leaders of China, and restore the émigrés to their former, proper status in Chinese life.

Their children took a more realistic view. While many would fondly recall the beautiful island where they had come of age, most came to detest the pinched xenophobia of the Nationalist government, which reduced the culture to a near-monolithic society controlled by an oligarchy of aging politicians. This generation had little interest in returning to mainland China, now a Communist society even more constraining than Taiwan. Once these young people accepted that their future did not lie here, two questions arose: where would they go to build their futures, and how would they get there?

Science and technology provided the means to get them out of Taiwan. Within a few years, the island would undergo an industrial revolution so breathtakingly rapid it would be heralded worldwide as an economic miracle.

One of the most formidable tasks the KMT faced in the 1950s was building a modern economy almost from scratch. Like many tropical economies based on the ready availability of at least a subsistence diet, Taiwan had little concern about foreign-trade balances, and consequently no interest in developing foreign export. Aid from the United States paid much of the cost of sustaining the huge government bureaucracy, but the Nationalist leadership understood that Taiwan could not long survive in the changing global arena without the ability to generate its own income.

Before the arrival of the KMT, Taiwan had been largely an agrarian society, with many families drawing little more than a subsistence income directly from the land. Those who remember that era describe a poor world, yet one infused with a slow-paced, simple beauty. Sayling Wen, co-author of *Taiwan Experience,* wrote that few people owned chairs or tables in his childhood village: families ate sweet-potato porridge as they stood or squatted around a wooden bench; when meals were cleared away, the bench might be moved under a tree and used as a place to nap. Children walked to school barefoot, and did not receive their first pair of shoes until their middle school years. At night, with no electricity, adults lit oil lamps while children captured fireflies and kept them in jars.

But this life would soon vanish forever. Within a few decades, the sleepy agricultural society of Taiwan would morph into a global high-tech superpower, one of the wealthiest regions per capita on the planet.

During the 1950s and 1960s American aid provided about 40 percent of Taiwan's income. Between 1951 and 1964, Washington gave the Nationalists $100 million in funding every year, as well as free supplies in certain industries. But government officials recognized that if the United States had been unable to keep the Nationalists in power on the mainland, it might one day be unable or unwilling to do so on Taiwan. Taiwan would have to become self-reliant, and, thanks to aggressive economic planning, it succeeded.

First the Nationalist government introduced land reform and redistribution, coercing the native aristocracy to sell much of their property at low prices to tenant farmers. By monopolizing the rice and fertilizer markets, and through price controls that encouraged farmers to produce ever more crops, the Nationalists created a "developmental squeeze," producing a surplus of capital which they funneled into nonagricultural industries.

Next they cultivated light industries for export. Investment and entrepreneurship were encouraged in labor-intensive fields, such as canned foods, household appliances, textiles, rubber, and plastic goods. "Turn your living room into a factory," proclaimed Shieh Tung-ming, then the provincial governor and later the vice president of Taiwan. "Don't cry about not having a production factory," he advised the people. "The living room can be your factory." This policy transformed typical households in Taiwan into warehouses stuffed with plastic, which the family would assemble for eventual export to other countries in exchange for hard currency.*

Soon, the island's success in exports resulted in huge trade surpluses. By 1965, when the United States cut off aid to Taiwan to husband its resources for the Vietnam War, the island had become financially, though not militarily, self-reliant. In fact, Taiwan had outstripped all other countries in its rate of growth, expanding faster than any other economy in the world. In the 1970s, the Nationalist government began investing in petrochemicals and steel, shifting the island's attention from light to heavy industries. During that decade, Taiwanese companies also began manufacturing calculators and electronic games, which set the stage for Taiwan's later entry into, and dominance of, certain sectors of the fast-growing computer industry.

The island's economic boom propelled thousands of young Chinese to seek an education in preparation for a career in technology. This was a new trend, for under Japanese occupation the native Taiwanese had not been encouraged to study the physical sciences or engineering, perhaps out of concern that such expertise could be exploited to build weapons that would be used against their colonizers. Most sons of the elite had majored in non-defense-related fields, such as medicine and education. But now the hot fields on the island were physics and engineering—skills desperately sought by burgeoning high-tech industries both in Taiwan and abroad.†

*One Chinese American, who asked to remain anonymous, remembered that his childhood home in Taiwan became a miniature factory. Between 1948 and 1979, his father purchased tons of milk powder stored in metal buckets, as well as hundreds of food cans with rusted surfaces. "We children had to use sandpaper to scrub away the rust to make the can like new for resale," he recalled.

†The KMT needed scientific expertise to fill the ranks of a new government technocracy, and in 1979 the government created the Hsin-chu Science-Based Industrial Park to recruit talent from the United States.

Before long, Taiwan's most valuable export would be its own youth. By the 1960s, both the Soviets and the PRC had developed atomic and missile technology, stripping the United States of its old confidence in the protective buffer of its two oceans. Terrified of losing the cold war to the Communist powers, the United States invested billions of dollars in science and technology, expanding research and development not only in defense facilities but at universities as well. As American funding for graduate programs increased, thousands of Taiwanese students began to realize their dream of studying abroad.

"In schools, teachers taught us about the task of recovering mainland China," Sayling Wen recalled. "Students, however, only cared about advanced study in the United States." That was where the future lay, and soon peer attitudes gave study abroad, especially in the United States, an enhanced social cachet. Wen remembered that soon people were pretending that they were going abroad to study, even if no plans had been settled. "Otherwise, no girl would date a guy with no plans to study in America."

The reality was that to reach the United States, students had to endure years of ruthless competition. They had to pass a succession of stiff entrance examinations before enrolling in junior high, high school, or college. To prepare for these tests, some children studied under private tutors, or took weekend group preparatory classes, or even pushed themselves through intense, all-night cram sessions. They fought to enter the most prestigious secondary schools that served as pipelines to the best universities on the island, such as National Taiwan University, where success might earn them a fellowship in an American graduate program. They also had to master English, which was not only key to their success in American doctoral programs, but was also required to obtain official permission to leave Taiwan and enter the United States. Before receiving the necessary exit and entry permits, college students had to prove their proficiency in the language in written and oral exams administered by both the Nationalist government and the U.S. embassy in Taiwan.

All these stipulations created an emigration cohort consisting almost exclusively of the brightest and most ambitious. It seems evident that through this period most alumni of the famous National Taiwan University—and virtually all in certain departments, such as physics and engineering—pursued advanced degrees in the United States, funded by teaching or research assistantships. Even graduates from less prestigious undergraduate programs in Taiwan found ways to migrate to the United States. Some applied to dozens, even hundreds of universities in America, until they found one willing to pay their way. Others, having gained admission but not a fellowship, sought alternative means of support, such as loans from friends and relatives, or the sponsorship of American churches and Christian organizations. This created a special community of immigrants in the United States. While all immigrant groups are to a certain extent self-selected for courage, ambition, and pure adventurousness, members of this subgroup of the Chinese in America were also selected, by the institutions that had the power to advance or frustrate their dreams, for educational achievement.

Many students from Taiwan arrived just as the United States was undergoing one of the most radical cultural transformations in its history. The 1960s were a time of rebellious challenge by young Americans; in the 1970s American institutions were forced to reinvent themselves in response to these challenges. The social upheaval bewildered even America's native-born citizens, but for those who had spent their formative years in a repressive island culture, seeing America in such open and often successful rebellion against authority must have been astounding. It was a strident age, a time of growing militancy among all sectors of the population. Women demanded their rights and pushed for an Equal Rights Amendment. One-third of the college-age population in America viewed marriage as obsolete. The assassination of Martin Luther King destroyed the idealism of the civil rights movement, hastening the rise of new black leaders, many

of whom clamored for revolution and the violent overthrow of the
U.S. government.

It was a time of mass disillusionment, of eroding trust in govern-
ment. American students felt betrayed when President Richard
Nixon, who had pledged to end the Vietnam War, sent troops into
Cambodia to interrupt the flow of arms from North Vietnam to the
Vietcong guerrillas in the south. This decision ignited riots at
American universities, and led to the deaths of four students at Kent
State in Ohio. Gasoline prices soared when Arab nations, angered by
American support of Israel in the Yom Kippur war of 1973, drastically increased the price of oil exported to the United States, which
the major oil companies exploited to raise prices even further. In this
decade Germany and Japan, America's former wartime adversaries,
emerged as serious economic competitors, and for the first time in the
twentieth century the United States began to import more than it
exported. The value of the dollar plummeted, while inflation skyrock-
eted into double digits. Money dropped in value faster than pay raises,
shaking the American middle-class dream of prosperity.

Disgusted by the Vietnam War, government corruption, and the
country's economic problems, many American youths simply refused
to participate in the system. Tens of thousands decided to challenge
the establishment by rejecting consumerism, spurning corporate
America, and seeking spiritual enlightenment. They flocked to communes and lived off the land. They embraced, spontaneously and voluntarily, a national uniform that erased distinctions of class: denim
blue jeans. Discarding traditional bourgeois values, they experi-
mented with alternative lifestyles: cohabitation without marriage,
homosexual and lesbian relationships, discos and drugs. While many
found these changes liberating, others despaired at what they considered mindless hedonism and the collapse of American civilization.

The newcomers from Taiwan had no frame of reference with
which to assess these upheavals. Upon arrival, many were simply trying to distinguish one Caucasian face from another. "White people all
looked alike to me in the beginning," my mother recalled of her first

year at Harvard. "Pale skin, big noses—that was all I could notice in the beginning." Despite the profusion of different shades of eye and hair color, all she could take in about the Caucasian population were those racial features that would not be seen on a Chinese person.

American food repulsed them. Many Taiwanese Americans remember being half starved through their first term in graduate school because they could not stomach the meals. They described the horrors of barbecues, college cafeterias, and inauthentic Chinese restaurants in the United States. Wrote Cai Nengying, the wife of a graduate student, "The sight of a hot dog dripping with red tomato sauce and yellow mustard is enough to take your appetite away . . . hamburgers are even worse: semi-raw beef with a slice of raw onion and a slice of raw tomato." And to add insult to injury, good manners required that the "terrible tasting food must be praised to the skies." Once she almost threw up when served a dessert of cored apples stuffed with plum jam and coated in sugar, yet knew she was obligated to say, "Delicious! Delicious!"

And inevitably, the newcomers struggled with the language. At first most could not grasp the freewheeling American vernacular. Their studies back in Taiwan had not prepared them for the slang terms and many idiomatic expressions in which words had meanings they had never learned. There were also hand and facial gestures that seemed like coded signals. Jokes had incomprehensible punch lines. It was often difficult to follow the lectures of professors, to decipher certain passages in textbooks and academic papers, and to make oneself intelligible during classroom discussions.

The first semester was a frightening time for many. They saw themselves competing with American-born graduate students who had spent their entire lives immersed in English. If writing a clear and cogent paper was daunting for native-born Americans, it was far more difficult for students still groping for fluency in a new language. If their grades slipped, they could lose their scholarships and stipends. Most did not come from wealthy families and could not afford to continue their studies without some sort of financial help. A few, in fact, were in debt, having borrowed money from relatives in America. To quit would mean returning to Taiwan a disappointment to family and relatives, a failure.

Even with help, many had to be ruthlessly focused and frugal. My uncle, Dr. Cheng-Cheng Chang, remembered that when he first arrived for graduate studies in electrical engineering at the University of Oklahoma in the 1960s, his first priority was to earn the top grades that would allow him to transfer to the doctoral program at the University of California at Berkeley. He also resolved to slash his expenses and save a nest egg to support his education in the United States. His budget was so tight that he dared not spend even a few cents for any nonessentials, however trivial. One of his most poignant memories was pacing around a Coke machine one hot, dusty afternoon, trying to decide whether to part with a single coin to quench his thirst.

As a result of disciplined saving, many Chinese students were not only able to maintain themselves on their American stipends, but to help their families back in Taiwan as well. Like the Chinese immigrants who had preceded them, the Taiwanese students placed great emphasis on family, and their loyalty to kin created a pattern of chain migration. Because exchange rates inflated the value of American currency on the island—often by a factor of ten—their small remittances home seemed a small fortune to the recipients in Taiwan. The most frugal students were able to sponsor the migration of spouses, siblings, and parents to the United States. The funds also gave younger students in Taiwan a glimpse of American opportunity, inspiring them to excel at their studies so they themselves could apply to U.S. doctoral programs.

After an initial period of adjustment, many students found life in the United States both exhilarating and liberating. "As I grew up in Taiwan under a fairly controlled society, I was blown away by the freedom and [the fact that] everyone can do what they want," remembered Albert Yu, head of Intel's microprocessor division. "I felt that I was set free."

This freedom, however, was overshadowed by one sobering fact. Even though they were thousands of miles from home, the Nationalist government kept careful tabs on its students in the United States. During the 1960s, when thousands of young Chinese began to leave the island to pursue advanced degrees, the Nationalists, ever sensitive to their image in the United States, cultivated an extensive network of spies to watch over them at American universities.

As some would learn the hard way, potential troublemakers were arrested and imprisoned during their visits back to the home island. In 1966 authorities apprehended Huang Qiming, a doctoral student at the University of Wisconsin, during a visit to Taipei, slapping him with a five-year prison term for allegedly attending Taiwanese independence meetings in the United States. In 1967, the Nationalists accused Chen Yuxi of reading Communist literature in the library of the East-West Center in Hawaii and participating in Vietnam War protests. Within weeks of Chen's acceptance by Hosei University in Tokyo, Japanese immigration officials handed him over to KMT agents, who transported him back to Taiwan. The KMT sentenced him to death on charges of sedition, then reduced the sentence to seven years after activists in the United States and Japan lobbied furiously to save his life. Eventually, in 1971, the uproar from the human rights activists resulted in Chen's release from Taiwan.

Because of the risks associated with activism, many Taiwanese Americans decided to focus on their careers instead of politics. As the years flew by and their lives were established, they had to make the difficult decision that all of America's immigrants eventually face: should they apply for U.S. citizenship and commit to living in the United States?

After earning their degrees, only one in four students returned to Taiwan to settle down permanently. The majority remained in the United States, accepting positions at universities, government laboratories, and corporations, swiftly moving into upper-middle-class

American society. Whereas previous generations of Chinese were forced by law or social custom to live in segregated Chinatowns, only to watch their descendants leave for the suburbs, most Taiwanese Americans never had any contact with Chinatown other than to eat meals there. Instead, their lives followed the pattern of a more privileged class of Chinese Americans. In 1970, Chia-ling Kuo provided a glimpse of this world in his study of Chinese émigrés living in Long Island, New York. Many of these people had grown up in upper-class families in coastal cities like Shanghai, attended Christian schools in China, and gained early exposure to Western culture. Now they were highly paid professionals, such as executives and bankers, with lives almost indistinguishable from their white neighbors. Owning expensive homes, they hosted dances and parties and led active lives in the community. Most attended church regularly and belonged to white country clubs, where they played tennis and golf. Their children often felt more comfortable among whites than among other American-born Chinese, because most of their friends and schoolmates were white.

Most interesting, many Chinese Long Islanders exuded confidence in the face of prejudice. Contempt, rather than fear or hurt, was the most frequent response to racist white Americans: "I would not let those ignorant people bother me," one immigrant told Kuo. "After all, we have had four thousand years of civilization. You just can't reason with fools and little people, as Confucius once said."

Such attitudes caused some Americans to conclude that anti-Asian prejudice had all but disappeared. In 1970, the *New York Times* announced that bias against Chinese Americans had dropped significantly: "The great majority of Chinese- and Japanese-Americans, whose humble parents had to iron the laundry and garden the lawns of white Americans, no longer find any artificial barriers to becoming doctors, lawyers, architects and professors." The article went on to report that many Asian Americans under the age of thirty could not remember a single personal instance of racial discrimination. "If you have ability and can adapt to the American way of speaking, dressing, and doing things, then it doesn't matter anymore if you are Chinese," the article quoted Mr. J. Chuan Chu, vice president of Honeywell Information Systems, as saying.

Individual success stories seemed to validate this position. Indeed, a number of Taiwanese Americans would soon reach the pinnacle of their professions within a single generation. In 1976, Sam Ting, a physics professor at MIT and head of a research team at Brookhaven National Laboratory, won a Nobel Prize for the discovery of the J/psi particle, which contained a new kind of quark and its anti-particle.* The following decade, another prominent Taiwanese American scientist, Yuan Tseh Lee, a professor at Berkeley, would win a Nobel Prize in chemistry for his research in the collision of molecular beams.

One Taiwanese American professor, Chang-Lin Tien, became the first Chinese American, as well as the first Asian American, to head a major research university in the United States. His career was propelled by personal determination and a fierce reverence for education—a reverence to which his family had introduced him by example.

Tien was born in Wuhan, the son of a wealthy banker. His father had earned a degree in physics from Beijing University, the most prestigious university in China. ("A degree in anything and you were automatically Mandarin; it was a ticket anywhere," Tien explained years later.) The pedigree enabled his father to become a financial commissioner in the Nationalist government, but no one foresaw that events would crumble the very foundations of their society. The Japanese invasion of China stripped the Tiens of everything—their home, their servants, their luxurious lifestyle. Fleeing the Japanese forces, the family uprooted themselves from Wuhan and moved into the French concession of Shanghai.

---

*Born in Ann Arbor in 1936, the son of a Chinese engineering student at the University of Michigan, Ting moved to mainland China at the age of two months. The Communist revolution forced the family to migrate to Taiwan, where his father taught at National Taiwan University, and Ting later returned to the United States to study at the University of Michigan in the 1950s.

With extraordinary resolve, Tien's father rebuilt his life as well as his fortune, eventually becoming the CEO of a major bank and Shanghai commissioner of commerce. Their world became lavish once again, complete with servants and chauffeured cars: "We lived like the Rockefellers!" But then, once again, it all disappeared: the 1949 revolution wiped out their charmed existence, and the family, once again refugees, escaped from Shanghai to Taiwan with little more than the clothes on their backs.

"My father couldn't cope with the loss," Tien later told a *San Francisco Focus* reporter. "It was the second time he had lost everything." When Tien first arrived in Taiwan at age fourteen, his entire family—twelve people—had to squeeze into one tiny room. "There wasn't even room for all of us to sleep at the same time," he recalled. "We had to take turns."

One evening, Tien awoke to find his father sitting in the room, staring into the darkness. "Go to sleep," Chang-Lin told him. "Don't worry about us. We'll find jobs." Bitterly, his father retorted, "I don't care whether my children even have nothing to eat. What I worry about is I cannot send my children to get an education." Young Tien never forgot those words.

Shattered and depressed by the memories of his ruined career, Tien's father later died of a heart attack, at the relatively young age of fifty-four. To help support the family, Chang-Lin worked odd jobs in high school and college. After graduating from National Taiwan University, he left nothing to chance and applied to 240 schools in the United States. The University of Louisville in Kentucky granted him a full scholarship, and in 1956 he borrowed money to pay for an inexpensive plane ticket to Seattle, then boarded a Greyhound bus for the seventy-two-hour ride to Louisville.

In the American South, Tien caught his first whiff of America's obsession with race. The moment he stepped off the bus, he saw signs marking bathroom doors and water fountains "Whites Only" or "Colored." He felt uncertain about his category, but local whites told him to use the white facilities, explaining that he was a guest of the

United States. Tien was privately repulsed by the system and agonized over its injustice. Observing that all local buses were segregated by race, with whites sitting in front and blacks in back, he chose to walk whenever possible instead of taking public transportation.

Later he found that racism permeated not just street life, but academia as well. At the University of Louisville, one of his professors repeatedly called him "Chinaman" (at first, Tien recalls, "I was so ignorant, I thought it was a term of endearment"). Eventually he decided to put an end to these insults. "For two nights I could not sleep, staying awake and thinking about what I should do . . . As a refugee, I had insecure status; I owed my livelihood to his employment. He could end my position and I might have to go back to Taiwan. I was very afraid." Finally Tien worked up the nerve to tell the professor never to call him "Chinaman" again. The confrontation was a partial success—while the professor reacted defensively, saying it would be difficult to remember Tien's "foreign" name, he never again used the derogatory term of "Chinaman." However, he looked for other ways to humiliate Tien, leaving him uneasy and insecure. On one occasion, this professor ordered him to climb a ladder and shut off a steam valve. He slipped and broke his fall by seizing a 400-degree Fahrenheit pipe, but he dared not complain about his severely burned and bleeding hand for fear of being ridiculed.

A less resolute man might have abandoned academic life, but Tien forged ahead with laser-like focus. In 1957, only one year after his arrival, he earned his master's degree at the University of Louisville. Two years later, he got his doctorate at Princeton and immediately joined the mechanical engineering department at the University of California at Berkeley. He would spend the next four decades at Berkeley, rising swiftly through the ranks, becoming a full professor, chairman of the department, vice chancellor of research, and finally chancellor of the university. On top of his administrative duties, he would also work on the design of the Saturn booster rocket, correct a heat-shield problem in the U.S. space shuttle, and conduct breakthrough research on superinsulation that would be used to construct high-speed levitation trains in Japan.

The energy and ambition that Taiwanese immigrants applied to academia also helped build the American high-tech industry. David Lee, a computer pioneer, became one of the first Chinese success stories in Silicon Valley. His resilience in the fast, ruthless world of technology can be traced to his childhood. Born in Beijing in 1937, David—then called Sen Lin Lee—grew up amidst war and revolution, where abrupt change was part of his daily existence.

To escape the Japanese invaders, and later the Communists, his family moved thirteen times during the first twelve years of Lee's life, each time leaving more wealth behind. In 1949, the family fled the civil war for Taiwan. The twelve-year-old Lee left China with nothing more than the clothes he was wearing and two silver dollars hidden in his shoes. Fearful of a Communist invasion of the island, the family moved again in 1952, this time to Argentina. They settled in Belgrano, a suburb of Buenos Aires, where the family had no business contacts, no knowledge of English or Spanish, and no idea about how they would survive.

Relying on ingenuity fueled by desperation, they opened a Chinese restaurant in the living room of their apartment. Lee's parents hired a Chinese man bilingual in Mandarin and Spanish to serve as the host in front, while the family labored in the back of their home to cook the meals. The restaurant thrived (soon expanding into the bedrooms), and the following year the Lee family used their restaurant earnings to launch an eventually successful import/export business. David, then a teenager, swiftly became fluent in Spanish and served as his father's translator. As he negotiated with vendors by translating his father's exact words, he learned invaluable lessons in business, lessons he later believed equivalent to earning an MBA.

His father wanted David to have the formal education that had eluded him during the war years, specifically, to study toward an engineering degree at an American university. In 1956, David enrolled at Montana State University in Bozeman, where he worked two hundred hours a month to pay his way through college. "I worked every job in the dorm," he later told a reporter, "cleaning rooms, making beds, counselor, dietitian, washing dishes—you name it, I did it." It was hard, but overall his experience at Montana State was positive. In 1960, he graduated with a bachelor's degree in mechanical engineering, then earned a master's in the same field from North Dakota State University.

At first, David took the conventional path of working as an engineer at established companies. In 1962, he started at NCR in Dayton, Ohio, then moved to Frieden in San Leandro, California, then the largest mechanical calculator company in the United States. There he designed the keyboard for the first electronic calculator, as well as the first electronic calculator printer. But in 1969, several employees at Frieden left to form their own company, Diablo, and Lee decided to join them.

It was a radical move at the time, for the majority of Taiwanese arrivals in the early 1960s aspired to become professors, a career deemed both prestigious and secure. Those who did not plunge into academia tended to work as scientists or engineers at large commercial companies, like IBM or Bell Laboratories. In David's memory, there were perhaps no more than a thousand Chinese American engineers in Silicon Valley—and most of them were wage-earning professionals, not capitalists. Very few dared to create their own companies.

At the Diablo start-up, Lee developed the first daisywheel printer for mass production. In 1972, the Xerox Corporation, avidly seeking a product to compete with IBM ball-type printers, bought Diablo for $28 million, turning David into a multimillionaire. Xerox retained him as head of its printer department, but appointed someone else as his boss—a white man whom Lee asserts knew nothing about daisy-wheel printers. "During that time, Chinese Americans were not viewed as capable managers," he remembered. "Many companies didn't want to promote the Chinese—they just wanted to use them." Knowing that he had hit the glass ceiling at Xerox, Lee trained his new boss and resigned in 1973.

The same year Lee left Xerox, he co-founded Qume Corporation, a manufacturer of computer peripheral equipment, with the primary goal of creating a new daisywheel printer to compete with the one purchased by Xerox. In 1978, ITT bought Qume for $164 million and asked David to stay at the company to manage its growth. He rose to become the president of Qume, then a vice president of ITT and chairman of its business information systems group.

Under his leadership, Qume grew into the largest printer company in the world as well as the largest manufacturer of floppy drives in the United States. By contracting with Chinese manufacturers, Lee also helped foster the growth of the personal computer industry in Taiwan. Three Taiwanese companies that built products for Qume—Acer and Mitac for personal computers, and Jing Bao (also known as Cal-Comp Electronics) for terminals—became giants in the industry, transforming the island into a major export leader in PCs and computer peripherals.

Looking back on his life, Lee observed that many of his fellow émigrés followed safe trajectories and shunned entrepreneurialism, while he was inclined—eager, even—to take risks. "To this day I believe that if you have a Ph.D., you can always get a regular job if your company fails," he said. "My father—who could not speak Spanish and who had no advanced degrees—faced far worse odds when he launched his own business in Argentina."

Not everyone, however, shared Lee's optimism. During the 1970s, Chinese American professionals began voicing complaints of racial discrimination, and of exploitation by white employers. Some felt they were treated like honorary whites rather than as fully equal fellow Americans, and believed their advancement in academia, government, and corporate America had been arrested by an artificial barrier, what some called a "bamboo ceiling."

Many claimed they had to work harder just to win second-level status in their companies. "Orientals are inordinately industrious, reliable, and smart in school but like Avis Rent-A-Car, 'being only number two,' Chinese must try harder to prove their middle class Americanization," James W. Chin wrote in the *East/West* newspaper in 1970.

On the surface, the statistics seem to refute charges of racism. In the 1970s, studies found that on average, the Chinese in America possessed more education than whites and earned more money per household. But these studies neglected three important factors: the regional concentration of the Chinese American population, the number of wage earners per family, and the professional and financial returns on their academic degrees. Most Chinese resided in urban centers with higher costs of living, so any somewhat higher earnings were spent on significantly higher rent and taxes.* Also, while the average household income of Chinese Americans exceeded that of whites, more Chinese women worked full-time than white American women, and more children held part-time jobs.

The one dimension in which many new Chinese immigrants managed to compete successfully was education. In 1970, one in four Chinese American men sixteen years or older had college degrees, compared to 13 percent of the white male population. In advanced degrees, they were even further ahead of the mainstream. But the true measure of a minority's success is not just the number of advanced degrees attained, but the career gains achieved as a result of those degrees, and here comparisons do not favor the group. In the Bay Area at that time, for instance, the median income of Chinese men was only 55 percent that of white men.

In 1970, the California State Fair Employment Practice Commission (FEPC) held hearings to investigate charges of job discrimination against Chinese and other Asian Americans, the first such hearing of its kind. That year, five Asian American health inspectors

---

*In 1960, almost half of all Chinese people in the continental United States—43 percent—lived in either the New York or San Francisco Bay areas, two of the most expensive regions in the country.

claimed to be victims of racial discrimination at the San Francisco department of public health. During the hearings, the Chinese American community learned that all five Asian inspectors had graduated from the School of Public Health at Berkeley, but several Caucasians promoted over them had earned nothing more than high school diplomas. One of the five Asian Americans had received the highest score on a written test but was assigned to work at the lowest level because "he presumably lacked the ability to deal with the public."

The complaining inspectors asserted that the oral examinations were subjective and racist, and later, tape recordings of the oral exams proved that some questions indeed drew on negative stereotypes of the Chinese. When Chong D. Koo mentioned that he occasionally vacationed in Reno, A. Henry Bliss, the examiner, responded, "I suppose you like to play the lotteries like all good Chinamen."

The Fair Employment Practice Commission also uncovered prejudice against Chinese American women. According to the 1970 hearings, many employers believed that "Oriental women had been trained to be subservient to the man at home, and therefore would make good secretaries." That year, $10,000 was considered a top earnings bracket, but only 2.5 percent of Chinese women made that much. Overall, their median income was only 27 percent of white male income.

Judy Yung, author of *Unbound Feet*, wrote that female clerical workers of Chinese descent of that era, seen as docile "office wives," received low returns on their education compared to whites. A Chinese American woman had to work twice as hard to be judged the equal of a Caucasian. "In fact, the better educated we became, the further our income fell behind relative to white men, white women, and Chinese American men with the same educational background," she observed.

Though Chinese Americans soon earned a reputation for being talented, diligent workers, they were viewed as shunning power, uninterested in management. Many considered this perception about

Chinese Americans more of an impediment to career advancement than outright anti-Chinese racism, and they resolved first to document it and then to address its inequitable consequences.

In the 1970s, a group of Chinese Americans and other minorities conducted an in-house study at Bell Labs that concluded that Asian American employees were grossly underrepresented in management. And the few Asian American managers working at Bell Labs tended to occupy the lower rungs of the corporate ladder. As a consequence, the group organized Asian Americans for Affirmative Action, also known as "4-A," to try to improve their representation within the company's highest ranks.

When the study's results were released, some white managers expressed genuine surprise that Chinese and Asian American employees wanted executive positions. According to Carl Hsu, one of the founders of 4-A and now a vice president at Lucent, many white managers had simply assumed that Asian Americans were content to perform technical work and harbored no aspirations whatsoever to rise within the organization.

Many Taiwanese believe this stereotype arose in part from their own deep-seated but well-founded anxieties about challenging authority, which were somehow visible to white colleagues. "Most of us had very deep fears about retribution by management," Hsu recalled. Even though these particular fears were unjustified, some members of 4-A worried about what management would "do" to them—a Pavlovian response, they believe, to their childhood under the 1950s "White Terror" in Taiwan when critics of the KMT were dealt with summarily. Suspected subversives, Hsu said, would simply disappear in the middle of the night, never to be heard of again, without benefit of a regular trial or even a court-martial. And even though these former Taiwanese were now working in corporate America, thousands of miles from Taiwan and years after the White Terror, many could not shake their early conditioning to the expectation that one wrong word or act, or even a posture of defiance, could lead to severe punishment, even death.

In the early 1970s, the Nationalists running Taiwan faced dangerous currents in the political wind. The People's Republic of China had won a certain grudging respect from the international community when it joined the nuclear club in the 1960s. Soon its size and threat as a military power could not be ignored, and, one by one, governments around the world began to recognize the PRC not as usurpers but as the legitimate government of China.

In 1971, President Richard Nixon suggested in his State of the World address that the United Nations give the People's Republic a seat, but recognize Taiwan as well. Predictably, supporters of Taiwan in the United States reacted with howls of outrage. Anna Chennault, a vocal leader within the pro-Nationalist lobby, called this move "worse than the betrayal of a loyal ally, it is, simply, wrong-headed." Shocked by Nixon's overtures to the PRC, Chennault scolded, "Mr. President, if you decide to abandon Taiwan, it will be tantamount to the United States telling the Free World that it can no longer depend on it for support."

But these protests could not hold back the river of history. The UN decided not only to grant membership and China's seat in the Security Council to the PRC but also to expel the Nationalists altogether. In February 1972, Nixon became the first American president to visit the People's Republic of China, bestowing additional legitimacy upon the Communist government. During his highly publicized tour, Chinese and American diplomats announced in Shanghai a "joint communiqué," in which the United States acknowledged "there is but one China and that Taiwan is part of China." Further, the United States promised to withdraw military forces from Taiwan, cultivate trade with the People's Republic, and normalize U.S. relations with Beijing.

It is difficult for outsiders today to imagine the terror this declaration of U.S.-PRC friendship provoked in Taiwan. The Nationalists considered American recognition crucial to the island's independence—indeed, the only force capable of preventing military conquest by the mainland. Withdrawal of staunch, public U.S. support, they believed, would jerk the trip wire to a PRC attack.

Shortly after Nixon's landmark visit to China, his political star plummeted with the Watergate scandal. Tapes of his White House conversations provided "smoking gun" evidence that he had personally obstructed justice, and in 1974, before the House could impeach him, Nixon resigned from office. Even though Nixon's visit to the People's Republic had provoked much hatred and criticism in Taiwan, his decision to abdicate from power baffled many there. "During Watergate, we didn't understand why Nixon had to resign, why Americans made such a big fuss over a president trying to cover up something: That's just what they do," said Academy Award–winning director Ang Lee, who had grown up in Taiwan during the 1970s. "But America's different, because it's such a young country, it's still so innocent."

Nixon's China diplomacy was not the only event of the 1970s that made Taiwan's future insecure. The United States was now rethinking its cold war policies in Asia. The Vietnam War had become an embarrassment for the United States. For a decade, the world's most powerful nation had dumped billions of dollars in technology and manpower into its war against a Third World country of peasant guerrilla fighters—and the Third World country had won. In January 1973, shortly after Nixon's landslide presidential victory in November 1972, the United States signed the Treaty of Paris with North Vietnam, whereby South Vietnam was to remain a separate state and American military forces were to exit all of Vietnam. After Watergate, however, the North Vietnamese sensed that America would no longer enforce the treaty, and in April 1975 they overran the south and captured the capital city of Saigon. Television pictures showed American helicopters evacuating the American embassy with panicked South Vietnamese clinging to their landing skids. Many on Taiwan feared their island would be the next place to be abandoned by the United States.

In 1979, the worst fears of the Taiwanese were realized. President Jimmy Carter officially broke off diplomatic relations with Taiwan and formally recognized the People's Republic of China with its capital in Beijing. Outraged Taiwanese mobs torched Carter in effigy and stomped on peanuts to dramatize their hatred of the American president, a former peanut farmer from Georgia. While the PRC gleefully established their embassy in Washington, the Nationalists were relegated to a merely informal presence in America with a pseudo-embassy. As reports filtered home of Taiwanese officials being snubbed or barred entirely from diplomatic functions in Washington, a pall of despair fell over the island.

Fearful middle-aged and elderly KMT bureaucrats began to leave Taiwan to join their children in the United States. But they were not the only Chinese affected by world events. In the following decade, the 1980s, the thaw in Sino-American relations would lead to open exchanges between the United States and mainland China, shattering the Bamboo Curtain and opening the way to a new era of emigration.

CHAPTER SEVENTEEN

The Bamboo Curtain Rises:
Mainlanders and Model Minorities

In 1976, Chairman Mao Zedong suffered a massive heart attack and lay paralyzed for months. His death on September 9, 1976, ended a life of almost mythic proportions. Born a humble peasant, he rose to stratospheric heights as the unchallenged leader of the most populous nation on earth. And while the nation he led depicted itself as a classless society, Mao reigned over China like a modern emperor.

Mao's state funeral, organized by the Communist Party leadership, was a lavish affair befitting an emperor. Eight full days were devoted to public mourning, and more than a million people paid their respects to Mao's body, enshrined in a crystal sarcophagus in Beijing's Tiananmen Square, where he was laid to rest in a giant mausoleum under the Gate of Heavenly Peace.

Publicly, the nation expressed profound grief, but privately many Chinese felt a deep sense of relief. In her memoir *Wild Swans*, Jung Chang wrote that the moment she learned of Mao's death, "the news filled me with such euphoria that for an instant I was numb. My ingrained self-censorship immediately started working: I registered the fact that there was an orgy of weeping going on around me, and that I had to come up with some suitable performance."

Although Mao had been virtually deified as a savior of the

Chinese people, the reality was that under his leadership China had experienced one of its worst eras, characterized by starvation and repression. Millions died during the famine caused by the failure of the Great Leap Forward, Mao's 1958 program for the forced, rapid industrialization of China. Then, during the Cultural Revolution, between 1966 and 1976, Mao promised to free China from the "four olds": old habits, old customs, old ideas, and old creeds. Instead, the Red Guards, his juvenile shock troops, destroyed much of China's priceless heritage, ransacking libraries and museums, desecrating Buddhist temples, burning irreplaceable books, archives, and historical relics. The Cultural Revolution was in essence a form of cultural genocide. By the time Mao passed away, Chinese agriculture, industry, and intellectual life were in shambles. Perhaps even more culturally destructive, an entire generation had been cheated of a serious education during a time when technical training was the basis of much society-building throughout the world. China's first census, conducted in 1982, reported a sobering finding: half its people were either partly or completely illiterate.

Mao's death offered his successor, Deng Xiaoping, the opportunity to reverse the damage. During the 1980s, under Deng, China began to develop a nonideological, capitalist economy. Deng abolished the people's communes in the countryside and permitted farmers to keep their profits after state taxes. A practical man, Deng valued expertise over ideology: "I don't care whether the cat is black or white so long as it catches mice," he once said. Entrepreneurial activity began to flourish, providing a much-needed spur to industry; the per capita gross domestic product doubled every decade. Waste and inefficiency in rural China soon gave way to increased productivity, and then to a broader-based prosperity than China had ever known. Many, including farmers, grew wealthy enough to build mansions, complete with satellite dishes. Some even bought their own airplanes. The nation's readiness for a new economic path was illustrated by its enthusiastic embrace of one of Deng's most popular slogans: "To get rich is glorious."

Deng also opened China to the rest of the world. In 1979, the PRC reestablished diplomatic ties with the United States, inaugurating an era of amity between the two countries. The following year, a new American president, Ronald Reagan, seen by many as an aggressive cold warrior, was swept into office with a landslide victory; to the surprise of his critics, his administration worked to thaw relations between America and its two cold war rivals, the Soviet Union and China.

As the decade progressed, the Reagan and Deng administrations signed historic agreements to promote scientific, technological, and cultural exchanges between the two countries. Mainland Chinese students responded eagerly, knowing that an American education meant greater opportunity in the future not just in the West, but in China itself. A "study-abroad fever" soon convulsed the PRC. Chinese students began taking the Test of English as a Foreign Language (TOEFL) and actively sought contact with foreign scholars visiting their institutions.*

In the cold war years before 1979, most foreign Chinese students in the United States had come from Taiwan. The 1965 Immigration Act had established a quota of 20,000 for the Chinese, and the vast majority of those slots went to Taiwanese Chinese. After resuming diplomatic relations with the PRC, the American government doubled the immigration slots for the Chinese, giving both mainland China and Taiwan their own quotas of 20,000 each. Meanwhile, a separate quota of 600 was reserved for Hong Kong, which the U.S. government increased to 5,000 in 1987. These revisions meant that every year, more than 40,000 Chinese immigrants could establish permanent residency in the United States.

In addition, no limit was placed on the number of Chinese traveling to the United States as non-quota immigrants, such as those on student, diplomatic, or tourist visas. After settling in the United

---

*TOEFL is an English-language proficiency exam for international students aspiring to study in North America or other regions with English-language curricula.

States, many of these non-quota émigrés adjusted their status, first becoming permanent residents, and later U.S. citizens. By the end of the 1980s, more than 80,000 PRC intellectuals had arrived in the United States—the largest immigrant wave of Chinese scholars in American history.

The Deng-Reagan pact ended three decades of isolation under the Mao regime. But as diplomacy lifted the Bamboo Curtain, the initial exchanges were shocking to visitors from both sides of the Pacific.

Before Deng, few Chinese Americans knew what was really happening in their ancestral homeland. The occasional rare visitor saw only a sanitized picture of China through tours carefully arranged by the government. During the 1970s, when a few prominent Chinese Americans were allowed to visit the mainland, PRC authorities quickly released many scholars from rehabilitation camps and prisons in order to project a more favorable image of China to the West. Often, all it took was a single appearance from a Chinese American to transform overnight the status of an individual or an entire family. In 1971, for instance, PRC officials immediately freed Deng Jiaxian, developer of the Chinese atomic and hydrogen bombs, from a "study camp" when Nobel laureate Yang Chen-ning asked to see his old friend. Furthermore, in 1973, when Yuan Jialiu, a physicist at Brookhaven National Laboratory, decided to tour the mainland, Chinese authorities frantically attempted to undo some of the Red Guard offenses against his family.*

---

*Yuan was the grandson of Yuan Shikai, a military commander who had served briefly as emperor after the 1911 Republic revolution, and his family had suffered heavy persecution during the Cultural Revolution. But Yuan Jialiu's sudden appearance from America changed everything. Acting under orders from Premier Zhou Enlai, local officials hastily returned confiscated houses to Yuan's relatives and even gave them job promotions. (They were not, however, able to repair in time Emperor Yuan Shikai's tomb, which the Red Guards had tried to demolish with explosives.)

But gradually, as the number of exchanges increased, uncensored stories of life under Mao emerged. Some former "stranded scholars" in the United States—the Chinese intellectuals who chose to remain in America after the 1949 revolution—had an opportunity to learn what had become of former classmates who had chosen to return to China during the civil war. Computer mogul An Wang remembered that roughly half the Chinese foreign students in Cambridge, Massachusetts, had decided to move back to mainland China in the late 1940s. Decades later, he found that some had obtained powerful positions in the Communist hierarchy, while others had perished during the Cultural Revolution.

Linda Yang, another stranded scholar, met a few of her former American-trained classmates at her fortieth college reunion at St. John's University in Shanghai. Some told her, with downcast eyes, about the persecution their families had endured, and how their children were deprived of the opportunity to attend school. She would never forget the "regret in their eyes," the searing knowledge that, by returning to China during the Mao years, they had "not only sabotaged their own future, but the future of their children and grandchildren."

While many Chinese Americans were reeling from the shock of these revelations, new immigrants from the PRC would be equally astounded by what they found in the United States. Some had incorrectly assumed that America was a vast utopia. During the 1930s, Let Keung Mui's family in south China had gone hungry during the Japanese invasion: "All we ate was wild plants and grass roots." Things were not much better under the Communists. People fought each other for food, and his favorite daughter committed suicide by taking poison. He was thrilled when, in 1979, a brother in New York secured permission for him to migrate to America. "The U.S. was a place I had dreamt of for a long time," he recalled. "People had said, 'America is a place with gold floors, diamond windows, tall buildings, and seven-foot-tall whites with red moustaches.'"

The reality was very different. When Let Keung Mui and his family flew to New York, what he found was hardly an American nirvana: "I felt that everything that my people said about how good the U.S. was, was not true. I felt like I had gone to the wrong place." His brother found him housing in Chinatown, a dilapidated apartment with a crumbling ceiling and only three windows. Living there was a cold and alienating experience. Every resident shoveled his own snow, and he felt "like a stranger" when his neighbors locked their doors at night.

His nephew gave him a job in his garment factory, and there Let Keung Mui labored long hours, past 9 P.M. most nights and often as late as midnight, six days a week. The work was difficult, the pay low, and he received no preferential treatment from his nephew or brother merely because he was family. "I was so mad that I started not to rely on them and started looking for jobs on my own," he said later. Soon he landed a position as a restaurant chef at a much higher salary, then served as a machine operator in a noodle factory. After toiling in the factory for five years, six days a week, twelve hours a day, he saved enough money to purchase a house in Queens, New York. But his disappointment persisted. He later told an interviewer that he hoped his children would not lead lives like his, or endure what he had suffered in his life.

Other Chinese saw a much different side to America. In 1980, when Liu Zongren traveled to Illinois to study at the Medill School of Journalism at Northwestern University—one of a handful of visiting scholars sponsored by the PRC Ministry of Education to study abroad for two years, at government expense—he was spared the need to work for a living. Still, he was perturbed by the excessive waste and extravagant materialism in the United States. Upset to find six lights in his guest room in Evanston ("Why would one person need so many lights?" he wondered), he asked his host to be more vigilant about conserving electricity. Also, the sight of an American using a metal detector along the shores of Lake Michigan astounded him. Upon learning that the detector cost $100, he exclaimed, "A hundred dollars to buy a machine to look for pennies! How strange these Americans are."

Despite or because of the abundance in his host country, Liu did not feel he could ever become an American. In 1982, shortly before returning to the PRC, Liu saw *E.T.*, Steven Spielberg's blockbuster film about an extraterrestrial who befriends a little boy while trapped on earth. "I liked *E.T.* for a reason that most American kids might not think of: E.T. wanted to go home," he later wrote. Many of his friends in the United States were like E.T.'s friends: "They had helped me in every way they could to understand American life. But few of them really understood me or knew why I couldn't feel comfortable among Americans, why I preferred to live a poorer or simpler life in China."

The great disparity in experiences among newcomers from the People's Republic of China owed much to a growing American social inequality. During the 1980s, steep cuts in the income tax rates paid by the highest earners increased the gap between the haves and have-nots. It was a decade of intense class envy in America, with extremes in wealth and poverty not seen since the Gilded Age and the Roaring Twenties. It was also a time when a culture of greed ruled Wall Street. Moguls such as Michael Milken and Ivan Boesky made billions of dollars by acquiring some companies and merging others, often relying on illegal tactics and insider trading, with little regard for the general public or the consequences to workers who would lose their jobs as a result of their activities. During the Reagan years, the wealthiest one percent of Americans almost doubled their share of the national income, and the four hundred richest Americans almost tripled their financial worth. The decade also saw the rise of a new class of young urban professionals, known as "yuppies," their lifestyles marked by the conspicuous and competitive consumption of luxuries, usually purchased on credit.

Simultaneously, a host of new problems began to plague the inner cities and small towns of America, exacerbated by deep cuts in federal spending on social programs. As financiers reaped huge profits by manipulating paper rather than building industries, thousands of middle-class Americans were thrown out of work. Decaying urban neighborhoods became fertile ground for a highly addictive narcotic—crack cocaine. Cutbacks in spending for public health may have seriously delayed the recognition of a deadly new epidemic, AIDS.* This decade of economic expansion, now remembered as an era of high living, saw increases in the size of the homeless population, and new despair within the minority underclass.

The 1980s were also a time when the national debt soared, turning America from the world's greatest creditor into the world's greatest borrower. Much of the country's wealth flowed to foreign investors in Germany and Japan. During the previous decade, the oil crisis had boosted the Japanese automobile industry, which, unlike American manufacturers, offered small, fuel-efficient, reliable cars. The American automobile industry had used its monopoly and its influence with the government to resist changes in the safety, performance, and durability of its products. As American consumers recognized that Japanese-made cars were safer, more serviceable, and more fuel-efficient, the American auto industry went into recession, widening the country's trade deficit with Japan.

Even as Sino-American relations thawed, anti-Asian hostility smoldered in certain regions of the United States, for reasons that had nothing to do with China. The Japanese—or Asians in general—were widely perceived to be the source of America's troubles, foreign competitors who stole American jobs by working cheaply. "Many of Detroit's corporate heads, politicians, and leaders are blaming the

---

*At the forefront of the battle against AIDS is Taiwanese American scientist David Ho. Born in Taiwan in 1952, Ho migrated with his parents to Los Angeles at the age of twelve, and after graduating from the California Institute of Technology with a degree in physics and earning an M.D. from Harvard, he decided to devote his career to finding a cure for the HIV virus. As the world-famous director of the Aaron Diamond AIDS Research Center in New York, Ho has created a potent blend of three antiviral drugs to suppress HIV in his patients, giving them fresh hope after the failure of traditional AZT treatments. To reward Ho's revolutionary findings, *Time* magazine placed him on the cover and named him its 1996 Man of the Year.

Japanese for America's economic woes," said Helen Zia, a Princeton-educated Chinese American writer who had been working in auto factories to build Asian American political consciousness on a grass-roots level. "In Detroit, the bumper stickers say it all," she observed. "Honda, Toyota, Pearl Harbor" was one. "Unemployment—Made in Japan" was another. The reality, of course, was that the rejection of American-made cars was related to management failures in planning and design, not to cheap Asian labor. It was not that Japanese workers worked for less, but that Japanese cars worked better.

In June 1982 in Detroit, Vincent Chin, the adopted son of a Chinese laundry owner, was beaten to death with a baseball bat by two disgruntled auto workers who mistook him for Japanese. Chin, a twenty-seven-year-old Chinese American engineering student about to be married, had gone to a topless bar with three friends to enjoy that quintessential American prenuptial activity, the bachelor party. At the bar, two Caucasian auto workers—Ronald Ebens and his step-son Michael Nitz, who had been laid off from his job—began to taunt them. They called Chin a "Jap" and yelled, "It's because of you moth-erfuckers that we're out of work!" Insults soon led to blows, and when the manager threw them out, Ebens and Nitz grabbed a baseball bat from the trunk of their car and chased Chin through the streets. Twenty minutes later, they seized him in front of a McDonald's restaurant. Nitz held back Chin's arms while Ebens shattered his skull. Expecting to attend his wedding, Chin's friends and relatives came to his funeral instead.

Charged with second-degree murder, Ebens and Nitz entered into a plea bargain and pled guilty to manslaughter. Charles Kaufman, a Wayne County circuit judge, apparently unwilling to confront the xenophobia in that part of the country, placed the pair on probation for three years and fined them $3,750 each. Neither spent a single night in jail. "What kind of law is this? What kind of justice?" cried Lily Chin, mother of the victim. "This happened because my son is Chinese. If two Chinese killed a white person, they must go to jail, maybe for their whole lives . . . something is wrong with this country." Others echoed her outrage: "Three thousand dollars can't even buy a good used car these days," one Chinese American protested, "and this was the price of a life."

Infuriated Chinese American activists organized the Justice for Vincent Chin Committee, which prompted an investigation by the U.S. Commission on Civil Rights. The federal government indicted Ebens on charges of committing a racially motivated crime. In a new trial, he was found guilty and sentenced to twenty-five years in prison, but an appellate court overturned the conviction. Lily Chin, Vincent's mother, felt betrayed by the justice system. "I don't understand how this could happen in America," she cried. "My husband fought for this country. We always paid our taxes and worked hard . . . Before I really loved America, but now this has made me very angry." Disillusioned, she moved back to China to live there permanently.

The only positive outcome was that this tragedy reminded the Chinese American community—immigrant and ABC alike—of the need to organize politically. Suddenly people realized that as long as they looked Asian, they could all be vulnerable to assault. The murder of Vincent Chin galvanized the ethnic Chinese community. "My blood boiled when I first learned that Vincent Chin was deliberately attacked and murdered as an act of racial hatred," said Harold Fong of the Chinese American Citizens Alliance at a rally in San Francisco. George Wong pointed out, "The killing of Vincent Chin happened in 1982, not 1882, the year of the Chinese Exclusion Act!" The Chin murder spawned demonstrations, films, and a new generation of Chinese American political activists. It launched the careers of several prominent human rights leaders in the Chinese American community, among them Helen Zia, author of *Asian American Dreams,* and Stewart Kwoh, executive director of the Asian Pacific American Legal Center in Los Angeles.

The tremendous publicity generated by the Vincent Chin murder did not mean that the United States had actually become more dangerous for Chinese Americans. A century earlier, when the Exclusion

Act precipitated anti-Chinese riots, dozens were murdered with virtually no media scrutiny whatsoever, the victims presented more as clumps of statistics than as individuals whose lives were snuffed out. But by the 1980s, the Chinese American community had come to expect more from the United States, and had learned to broadly disseminate information about injustices suffered by their people. Seven years after the death of Vincent Chin, activists drew on the political lessons learned from his tragedy when another Chinese person became a fatal victim of a hate crime.

Jim Loo (also known as Ming-Hai Loo) was a twenty-four-year-old immigrant from China, working in a restaurant to save enough money for college. In 1989, Loo and several Vietnamese friends were playing pool in a Raleigh, North Carolina, billiards hall when two whites started to push them around. Robert Piche and his brother Lloyd Piche called them "chinks" and "gooks," and even blamed them for American deaths in Vietnam. "I don't like you because you're Vietnamese," Lloyd Piche told them. "Our brothers went over to Vietnam, and they never came back." He also threatened, "I'm gonna finish you tonight." The manager ordered the two brothers to leave the premises, but they waited outside, ambushing Loo and the others as they walked out. Robert Piche struck Loo in the back of the head with a gun, causing him to collapse onto a broken beer bottle. The glass forced a bone fragment through his brain, killing him.

Initially, Lloyd Piche was found guilty of only two misdemeanors—simple assault and disorderly conduct—and his brother Robert was sentenced to thirty-seven years in prison by a state court for second-degree murder and assault with a deadly weapon. But the Chinese American community, observing the parallels between the Jim Loo and Vincent Chin cases, lobbied for federal intervention. After the U.S. government stepped in with a federal trial, Lloyd Piche was sentenced to four years in prison and ordered to pay $28,000 in reparations to Loo's family.

Not all the murders of Chinese Americans during the 1980s were committed by whites. As diplomatic relations between the U.S. and the PRC steadily improved, the KMT appeared obsessed with the idea of controlling Taiwanese intellectuals in the United States. There was, for instance, the mysterious death of a Carnegie Mellon professor, Chen Wencheng, when he returned to his native Taiwan in 1981. Shortly after being interrogated by authorities about attending certain political meetings during his student days in the United States, Chen fell to his death from the window of his Taiwan hotel room. Though exactly what occurred will probably never be determined, many Chinese Americans believe the KMT gave Chen some help through the window.

Three years later, another death shook the Taiwanese community in America. In 1984, Wang Xiling, head of KMT military intelligence, dispatched members of the island's criminal "Bamboo" gang to Daly City, California, where they assassinated Henry Liu in his home. Liu had written an unauthorized biography of Chiang Ching-kuo, the son of Chiang Kai-shek and at that time president of the Chinese Nationalist government on Taiwan. Though the story of Liu's activities before his murder was far more complicated than it appeared on the surface (he was apparently a triple agent between the United States, Taiwan, and the People's Republic of China), the fact that the KMT could operate with such impunity in the United States sent a chill through both the Chinese American community and the intelligentsia in Taiwan.

Knowing that even American borders might not protect them from retaliation caused many Chinese to focus their energies on economic achievement rather than politics. Most grew up in families that had fled mainland China to either Hong Kong, Taiwan, or the United States, and had witnessed firsthand the risks of being caught on the losing side of a political struggle. Many of their parents had urged them since childhood to seek their fortune in a lucrative field that required neither English-language skills nor personal connections in a foreign country. One obvious career path ran through the newly developing high-tech industries.

The 1980s spawned a revolution in personal computers, and the

Chinese in the United States would play their part right from the beginning. In 1980, David Lam, a Hong Kong immigrant with a doctorate from MIT, founded Lam Research, which produced the first completely automated plasma etcher for chip wafer processing. The firm later grew into a global giant in the semiconductor field. In 1987, David Wang, a Taiwanese immigrant with a Berkeley Ph.D. in material sciences, co-invented the Precision 5000 multiple chamber single-wafer system, which combined two of the most complex steps in chip-making into a single process, thereby transforming the manufacture of integrated circuits.

Taiwanese immigrants John Tu and David Sun became billionaires with memory modules, Pehong Chen with software. In the 1980s, Charles Wang, son of a supreme court justice from Shanghai, kept a small company, Computer Associates International, alive by juggling credit cards and bartering computer services in Manhattan. Within two decades, his company grew into the second largest independent software maker in the world, an empire that spans two dozen countries on five continents.

The 1980s would bear witness to the growth of a nouveau riche class of Chinese immigrants. As the People's Republic gained political support from the United States, many better-situated residents of Taiwan and Hong Kong, fearing that the PRC might soon take over Taiwan and Hong Kong, quietly searched for new sanctuaries. Taiwanese and Hong Kong capital began to flow to American cities. While many Chinese businessmen moved their families into exclusive white neighborhoods in the United States, others created their own communities, mostly in California. As they invested in real estate, banks, restaurants, malls, and Chinese-language newspapers, they formed wealthy new ethnic enclaves that some would later call "suburban Chinatowns." These communities, populated by people of diverse backgrounds, such as émigrés from mainland China, Taiwan, Hong Kong, and Southeast Asia, are called "ethnoburbs" by sociologist Wei Li. Within these enclaves, many relied on their Chinese heritage to broker symbiotic business deals, such as matching Taiwanese or Hong Kong money with ethnic Chinese manpower from Southeast Asia. "Say I am Chinese, I come from Vietnam," a journalist explained. "You are Chinese and you come from Taiwan or maybe Singapore, or maybe Hong Kong. I need money—I need you to support my business . . . you have the money, but you don't know how to run [this] business. So you check my credit and ask the other people . . . Maybe you are partner or maybe I give you interest in six months. It works because we [are] all Chinese."

One affluent enclave was Monterey Park, near Los Angeles, nicknamed the "Chinese Beverly Hills." Toward the end of the twentieth century, Chinese constituted more than one-third of Monterey Park's population and more than one-quarter in the nearby communities of Alhambra and San Marino. Before long this region of southern California, known as the San Gabriel Valley, would contain the largest suburban concentration of ethnic Chinese in the United States, surpassing the populations in the long-established Chinatowns of many major American cities.

So great were the number of new Chinese arrivals that some whites came to view them as part of a massive foreign invasion. "I feel like I'm in another country," a white resident of Monterey Park complained to Timothy Fong, author of *The First Suburban Chinatown: The Remaking of Monterey Park, California.* "I don't feel at home anymore." "I feel like a stranger in my own town," another said. Cars flashed bumper stickers with messages like "Will the Last American to Leave Monterey Park Please Bring the Flag?" In 1986, a gas station in town posed the same question, along with a picture of two slanted eyes.

Anti-Chinese jokes began to surface: about senior citizens wearing pajamas in the streets, about reckless driving habits. "I Survived the Drive through Monterey Park," one bumper sticker boasted. Monterey Park was dubbed the "Traffic Collision Capital of the World" and Atlantic Boulevard was "Suicide Boulevard," causing residents to remark it should be illegal to be "DWC"—Driving While Chinese. But simmering below the taunts and snickers was hatred that often reflected envy of the openly displayed success of the new arrivals. When the local newspaper, the *Monterey Park Progress,* announced it would print a section in the Chinese language, vandals attacked Chinese-owned movie theaters, smashing windows and throwing paint on the marquees.

Hostility toward the newcomers in Monterey Park came not only from Caucasian residents but from many local Chinese Americans as well. Previously, up to the early 1970s, the Chinese in Monterey Park were mainly young professionals, usually salaried engineers, respectable, upper-middle-class Chinese Americans with quiet, conservative lifestyles. Like their white neighbors, they were scarcely prepared for the arrival of fast-talking, aggressive businessmen from Hong Kong and Taiwan, who turned the streets of the city into a crass showcase for their expensive jewelry, designer suits, and custom-made mansions. The newcomers grated on the nerves of those who could not afford such ostentation, or who believed that flaunting wealth was unspeakably vulgar. "First it was the real estate people, and then trading companies, heavy investors, people who came with hundreds of thousands of dollars in cash," Wesley Ru recalled. "Their first stop would be the Mercedes dealer, and the second stop would be the real estate broker."

Another way the nouveau riche Chinese disturbed their neighbors was their children's success in school classrooms. In an increasingly class-conscious America, Chinese academic ability would create another source of anxiety.

By the 1980s, ethnic Chinese children no longer had to struggle for educational opportunities. Generations of civil rights activists had ended the system of segregated schools, and federally funded public schools and public libraries made education more accessible to even the most impoverished Chinese immigrant families. At the same time, America saw the rise of a Chinese professional class, who comprised not only the descendants of earlier Chinese Americans but also new émigrés with education and status. The children of these groups grew up in privileged settings such as white suburbs or university towns.

Their parents were professors, scientists, engineers, or doctors, not laundry or restaurant workers who needed their children to help out with the family business. These parents spared no expense in sending them to the best schools, where they could devote their full energy to academic achievement.

Large numbers of Chinese American students were now attending elite private preparatory schools, such as Phillips Exeter, Groton, and Deerfield, or top academic programs in competitive public programs, like the Bronx High School of Science and Stuyvesant High School in New York, or Lowell High School in San Francisco—all of which served as fast-track conduits to the best universities in America. Many spent their summers in gifted children's programs run by universities like Stanford and Johns Hopkins. By the 1980s, they were routinely entering prestigious Ivy League schools and winning national competitions, like the Westinghouse Science Talent Search (now called the Intel Science Talent Search), in disproportionate numbers.

The Chinese immigrant community soon considered excellence in school not as a lofty standard, but as a minimum expectation. Franklin Ng, a professor of anthropology at California State University, revealed the intensity of parental ambition for their children when he published an inside joke circulating in the Taiwanese American immigrant community:

HOW TO BE A PERFECT TAIWANESE KID
(from the first generational perspective)

Score 1600 on the SAT.
Play the violin or piano on the level of a concert
    performer.
Apply to and be accepted by 27 colleges.
Have three hobbies: studying, studying, and studying.
Go to a prestigious Ivy League university and win
    enough scholarships to pay for it.
Love classical music and detest talking on the phone.

Become a Westinghouse, Presidential, and eventually
   Rhodes scholar.
Aspire to be a brain surgeon.
Marry a Taiwanese-American doctor and have perfect,
   successful children (grandkids for *ahma* and *ahba*!)
Love to hear stories about your parents' childhood . . .
   especially the one about walking seven miles to school
   without shoes.

HOW TO BE A PERFECT TAIWANESE PARENT
(from the second generational perspective)

Don't "ai-yoh" loudly at your kid's dress habits.
Don't blatantly hint about the merits of Hah-phoo
   (Harvard), Yale-uh (Yale), Stan-phoo (Stanford), and
   Emeh-I-tee (MIT).
Don't reveal all the intimate details of your kid's life to
   the entire Taiwanese community . . .
Don't give your child a bowl haircut or your daughter
   two acres of bangs . . .

By the 1980s, the media began to report the educational triumphs of ABCs, profiling those who won National Merit Scholarships and the Westinghouse Science Talent Search. In 1982, *Newsweek* ran a favorable article under the headline "Model Minority." Sociologist William Peterson had invented the term in 1966 to describe Japanese Americans, but the media soon borrowed the phrase to describe other Asian Americans, including the Chinese. Other stories soon appeared in the popular press to celebrate Chinese achievement. In 1986, both the *MacNeil/Lehrer NewsHour* and the *NBC Nightly News* praised the academic prominence of the Chinese and Asian American community. "Why are Asian Americans doing so exceptionally well?" Mike Wallace of CBS's *60 Minutes* asked in 1987. "They must be doing something right. Let's bottle it."

Chinese American enrollment at top universities soared. MIT soon gained the nickname of "Made in Taiwan," UCLA of "University of Caucasians Lost in Asians," UCI (the University of California at Irvine) of "University of Chinese Immigrants." In certain academic departments where ethnic Chinese students were concentrated (such as math, science, and engineering), the elevators were called the "Orient Express." Engineering became synonymous with Chinese. At Stanford, when a professor scolded a Caucasian engineering student for not scoring higher on his tests, the student responded, "What do you think I am, Chinese?" Rumor had it that certain white engineering majors at Berkeley would drop a class if they counted too many heads of glossy black hair in the auditorium. Some ABCs even started wearing buttons on campus announcing, "I am NOT a Chinese American electrical engineer."

Even the ABCs themselves were intimidated, and often overwhelmed, by the large numbers of Chinese American students on college campuses. Phoebe Eng, the daughter of a Taiwanese American and an American-born Chinese of Cantonese heritage, grew up in Westbury, a suburb near New York. When she attended college in California, she was shocked: "I had never been around so many Asian faces, so much black hair," she wrote in her book *Warrior Lessons*. "Berkeley seemed like China to me. It took me a full year to learn how to distinguish one Asian face from another."

If Chinese achievement provoked awe in some quarters, it incited fear in others. Anti-Chinese hate graffiti suddenly appeared on college campuses: "Stop the Yellow Hordes"; "Stop the Chinese before they flunk you out"; "Chink, Chink, Cheating Chink!" And by the 1980s, some ABCs began to feel victimized by their own success. Some complained of institutional racism, insisting that the harder they studied, the higher the bar was raised to block their admission to top universities. Many alleged that university officials at elite schools, concerned by the growing presence of Asian Americans on campus, intentionally sought to reduce their numbers through racial discrimination.

In 1983, the East Coast Asian Student Union, a coalition of Asian American student organizations at schools like Harvard, Princeton, and Yale, analyzed the admissions data at twenty-five universities and concluded that an "alarming barrier" had been erected to prevent ethnic Asian students from "seeking higher education and better lives." This inspired other studies, and from 1983 through the rest of the decade, students and administrators alike would search for evidence of racial bias. At Princeton, it was found, the admission rate for Asian Americans was only 14 percent, compared to 17 percent for white applicants and 48 percent for children of alumni. At Brown, research revealed that the admit rate for Asians had plummeted from 44 percent in 1979 to 14 percent in 1987. At Stanford, Asians had filled out as many as one-third of the applications, but secured less than one-tenth of the enrollment. At Harvard, critics asserted that Asian Americans had the lowest rate of admissions for any racial group, even though the number of Asian applicants kept rising, and the applicants were "actually more qualified than anybody else." After scrutinizing Harvard's 1982 statistics, an outside team even concluded that, "in order to be offered admission, Asian Americans had to score an average of 112 points higher on the SAT than the Caucasians who were admitted."

Even the state schools were turning away qualified Chinese American applicants. Traditionally, the best students in California had viewed Berkeley and other UC schools as safety nets in case they were rejected by more prestigious universities such as Stanford, Cal Tech, MIT, and the Ivy League schools. For years, the only requirement for admission to Berkeley or UCLA was graduation within the top 12.5 percent of one's high school class. Given the high concentration of Chinese and other Asian Americans on the West Coast, their numbers soared within the University of California system. Between 1966 and 1980, for example, the percentage of Asian American undergraduates at Berkeley had quadrupled from about 5 percent to 20 percent of the students. According to the *New York Times* in 1981, Berkeley officials fully expected 40 percent of the entering freshman class to be Asian American by 1990. But suddenly, in the mid-1980s, the pattern reversed and the numbers abruptly dropped.

In 1984, Ling-chi Wang, an ethnic studies professor at Berkeley and veteran activist, noticed that the number of Asian American enrollments fell 21 percent within a single year. Something, he believed, was terribly wrong. "As soon as the percentages of Asian students began reaching double digits at some universities, suddenly a red light went on," he told the *Los Angeles Times*. "I don't want to say there's a conspiracy but university officials see the prevalence of Asians as a problem, and they have begun to look for ways to slow down the Asian American admissions. Are they scared of Berkeley's becoming an Asian university? They're shaking in their socks."

A volunteer task force in the San Francisco Bay Area—including activists, judges, and professors of Chinese descent—quickly formed in 1984 to investigate the situation. They were shocked to discover that Berkeley had turned away students with perfect GPAs while admitting others who had not even submitted their grades or test scores. Reporting on the Berkeley controversy, the media began to draw parallels between the declining admission rates for Asian Americans and the stringent racial quotas that Jewish students had faced at Harvard, Princeton, and Yale between the 1920s and 1940s.

The media started to interview Chinese Americans who believed they had been unfairly treated by Berkeley. In 1987, Berkeley rejected Yat-Pang Au, the son of Hong Kong émigrés and a star student at Gunderson High School in San Jose, California. A straight-A student, Au had been the valedictorian of his class, won prizes for ten extracurricular activities, earned letters in cross-country and track, served as a justice on the school's Supreme Court, and even operated a Junior Achievement company. When Au received the rejection letter in the mail, he read it over and over, "because I thought maybe I had misunderstood or that it wasn't addressed to me," he told the *Los Angeles Times*. "I had my mind and heart set on Berkeley. I'd thought about Berkeley for years; I'd worked hard in high school to get into Berkeley. I couldn't believe I'd been turned down."

Stunned to learn that ten other students with lower grades and test scores had been admitted, Au went to the press and publicly complained about the situation. When the Bay Area media reported the story, the Au family's house was vandalized, and Au's terrified mother ended up buying a gun and taking shooting lessons. For two years, Au attended De Anza, a local community college, before finally enrolling at Berkeley.

In 1989, *NBC Nightly News* interviewed Hong Kim, an A student of Taiwanese heritage. He had been rejected by Berkeley, while two of his black friends with lower grades were accepted. "I don't hold it against them, they're my friends," he told NBC. "I want to tell them I still love them, but . . . I think I'm more qualified."

The public furor in the Chinese American community triggered federal investigations and policy changes. In the wake of the controversy, the Justice and Education departments began to probe allegations that Chinese and other Asian American applicants were victims of racism. Federal officials eventually exonerated Harvard and Berkeley but found UCLA guilty of bias.*

The discrimination even extended to the high school level. In 1983, prestigious Lowell High School in San Francisco adopted different admissions standards for different ethnic groups, with the harshest ones reserved for Chinese Americans. To settle a lawsuit filed by the National Association for the Advancement of Colored People (NAACP), the San Francisco school district agreed to increase the number of black and Hispanic students in the city's top public schools. The settlement mandated that at least four ethnic groups had to be represented at each school and that no more than 40 to 45 percent of the enrollment could be dominated by one single ethnicity. To enforce this racial cap, Lowell required Chinese American applicants to outperform Caucasians and all other ethnic groups in order to be

---

*In 1995, the University of California regents decided to remove race and gender from consideration during admissions, hiring, and promotion; the following year, Californians voted to pass Proposition 209, which outlawed racial quotas in the state.

accepted. The minimum test score for admission to Lowell was 62 (originally 66) for ethnic Chinese applicants, 59 for Caucasians, 58 for other Asian Americans, and 56 for Hispanics and African Americans.*

Some activists depicted the fight over racial quota systems as a struggle for limited slots between Asian Americans and other minority groups, such as blacks, Latinos, and Native Americans. But in reality, asserted Henry Der, head of Chinese for Affirmative Action, "Asian applicants are competing with white applicants." The "legacy" programs for children of Ivy League alumni, the "old-boy networks" that maintained places in elite universities for the children of the East Coast establishment, Der said, were a form of affirmative action for Caucasians. Noting that two-thirds of all Asian Americans opposed the system of affirmative action, Der told *A* magazine, "Most Asian immigrant families would ask for meritocratic standards. These families don't understand that selection has never been based on meritocratic standards."

_____

*After several ABCs were rejected, Chinese American families in 1994 sued the school district, the state of California, and the NAACP, alleging that unfair racial quotas were unconstitutional. Six years later, the school board resolved the suit by abandoning its plans for affirmative action and upholding a racially neutral admissions policy. Immediately, the number of black and Latino acceptances plummeted while that of Chinese Americans and whites soared; severe racial imbalances emerged within a year.

CHAPTER EIGHTEEN

Decade of Fear: The 1990s

As the 1980s drew to a close, the leadership of the People's Republic of China faced the greatest threat to its power since its defeat of Chiang's Nationalists. Their public embrace of a new openness during the Reagan-Deng years had encouraged long-suppressed but deep-seated dissatisfaction with the Communist Party to bubble to the surface. Now they would have to deal with it.

The trouble began small. In 1986, Fang Lizhi, an astrophysicist and vice president at the University of Science and Technology in Hefei and a Party member, emboldened others by openly criticizing the government. Soon afterward, a student movement protested PRC corruption, charging that elections to the people's congresses had been fixed. When demonstrations spread to other cities, including Beijing and Shanghai, Fang Lizhi was fired from his position and dismissed from the Communist Party. But serious damage had already been done. The secretary-general of the Chinese Communist Party, Hu Yaobang, an outspoken advocate of both democracy and immediate government reform, was made a scapegoat for the protests and forced to resign.

In April 1989, Hu Yaobang died of a heart attack, provoking another mass gathering in Beijing. His death coincided with a year of anniversaries within China—the tenth anniversary of U.S. recognition of the People's Republic of China, the fortieth anniversary of the birth of the PRC, and the seventieth anniversary of the May Fourth movement, an early intellectual and literary revolution based on Western concepts of freedom. To bolster their demands for political change, Beijing students held street parades in homage to May Fourth and staged a broad-based hunger strike in Tiananmen Square. The state visit of Soviet premier Mikhail Gorbachev that month added fuel to the fire, for under his leadership the Soviet Union was instituting serious reforms, such as *perestroika* (restructuring), which edged his people in the direction of capitalism, and *glasnost* (openness), a policy offering greater access to information on government policies and a new freedom to comment on them.

By late May 1989, the Beijing students had erected in Tiananmen Square a Chinese "Goddess of Democracy" statue, inspired by the American Statue of Liberty. More than a million people came out to support the students, and outside the capital similar rallies erupted. It was the largest pro-democracy movement in the history of China, and possibly, considering the number of participants, the largest anywhere in the world. It seemed to many in both China and the United States that China might be on the threshold of its first democratic society. According to high-level documents leaked out of China, later published anonymously as *The Tiananmen Papers*, such optimism was not entirely unrealistic. Many top officials initially wanted to negotiate with the student activists and reach some sort of compromise with them. But eventually they deferred to an elite group of party elders, including Deng Xiaoping, who decided that the best course was to declare martial law and crush the movement.

In the pre-dawn hours of June 3 and 4, 1989, fully armed Chinese troops, accompanied by tanks, stormed into Tiananmen Square and opened fire, killing hundreds of people and wounding many more. While some of the most visible pro-democracy leaders were rounded up and arrested, others fled the country and sought asylum in the United States. Fang Lizhi and his wife fled for their lives to the U.S.

embassy, which, to the great indignation of the PRC leadership, secured their safe passage out of China.

The massacre, widely reported by the international media, left a lasting scar on Sino-American relations. Footage of the bloody corpses was smuggled out of the country and shown on Western television, creating enormous sympathy for the Chinese students. Over the next few days, Chinese television ran pictures of some of the better-known protestors who had been captured, all appearing much the worse for their few days in custody. Overnight, the warm Western stereotype of China—a country of lotus flowers, pavilions, and pandas—was replaced by violent images of a brutal Soviet-like totalitarian regime.

On June 5, 1989, President George H. W. Bush signed an executive order allowing all Chinese nationals to remain in the United States. On April 11, 1990, he issued another order giving Chinese immigrants who could prove they were in the country before that date the right to stay. Bush also combined domestic with international politics when he made clear that "individuals from any country who express fear of persecution . . . related to their country's policy of forced abortion or coerced sterilization" would be welcome to stay in the United States.

Many students felt little interest in returning to China. One law student from Beijing told an interviewer that it would be "political suicide" to go back: "It is a waste of life." A Berkeley engineering student said the PRC would "make Chinese intellectuals as scapegoats, just like what they have always been doing in every political movement in the last forty years." A few expressed interest in returning only after the ruling-class elite had passed away. Observed a Stanford doctoral candidate, "China will definitely change because it just cannot get worse. Political changes might come faster after the death of some old guys." In 1992, in response to the plight of these pro-democracy student activists, the U.S. government passed the Chinese Student Protection Act, permitting more than fifty thousand students and scholars to gain permanent residence status in the United States.

The Tiananmen Square massacre of 1989 had other consequences as well. It provoked fears of political instability across Asia, encouraging ethnic Chinese capitalists to establish second homes in North America. Perhaps no group was more concerned about its future than the people of Hong Kong, which by treaty the British were obligated to return to the People's Republic of China on July 1, 1997. Could the freewheeling capitalist culture of Hong Kong survive under the Communist old guard? No one knew. To allay fears, the mainland Chinese government promised not to change the city's social conditions for the next fifty years, but many Hong Kong residents did not fully trust them. "No sane person should have faith in the promises," announced one Hong Kong skeptic. "Mao made the same pledge to Shanghai in 1949, but it lasted for just three months. My parents escaped to Hong Kong, giving up everything." He pointed to the tragedy of the 1989 Tiananmen massacre. "Shouldn't we leave before it is too late?"

Many felt they could not afford to wait to find out. Not surprisingly, those who most wanted to leave were the ones with the most to lose under Communist rule—the capitalist and professional elite of Hong Kong. Late-1980s surveys found that 70 percent of Hong Kong's government doctors, 60 percent of its lawyers, and 40 percent of its civil engineers intended to move out before 1997. According to a review of visa applications, between 1987 and 1991 some 15 to 19 percent of Hong Kong émigrés held college degrees, compared to only 4 percent of the general population. A 1989 telephone poll of 605 Hong Kong residents found that the wealthier the household, the stronger the desire to leave. Many émigrés were, in fact, millionaires. In the 1990s, the typical household of a Hong Kong émigré investor in Canada was worth an estimated 1.5 million Canadian dollars, equivalent to about $1.2 million U.S.

Like the 1949 refugees from Hong Kong, most of those trying to leave in the 1990s found the logical destination—England—closed to them. Although Great Britain traditionally issued British passports to all those born on its territory, it refused to do so with the Chinese born on Hong Kong while it had been British. These passports would have ensured entry to England for those who chose that path. Many Hong Kong residents felt profoundly betrayed, convinced that Great Britain had shirked its responsibilities to avoid ruffling the feathers of the PRC. Even though the British had enjoyed a century of colonial rule in Hong Kong, benefiting from the wealth created by the colony, it appeared they were unconcerned about the fate of their former subjects.

Fortunately, other countries had friendlier policies. Canada, for instance, had lenient immigration laws, especially for political refugees. Thus Canada became the most popular destination for the Hong Kong émigrés, followed by Australia and the United States. No doubt many former residents of Hong Kong were attracted to these countries not only because of their liberal admissions policies, but also because English was their primary language. As people left in droves for those regions, the annual rate of migration from the city of Hong Kong soared from twenty thousand in the early 1980s to over sixty thousand after 1990.

But the road out of Hong Kong was anything but smooth, even for those who had money. First, their desperation made them easy victims for con artists, as some Hong Kong families handed over outrageous fees—often in excess of $30,000—to immigration "consultants" who promised to handle the paperwork for them. Second, after settling into their new homes, some found it impossible to replicate their earlier business success. Unlike Hong Kong, a city of unbridled capitalism, the United States had far greater government regulation, higher taxes, and more stringent labor laws, all multitiered, with complex local, state, and federal mandates to be met. Some entrepreneurs lost hundreds of thousands of dollars of their life savings when they launched enterprises doomed to early failure. Yet many were surprisingly free of bitterness. They simply wrote off the losses as the price of establishing themselves in America, obtaining U.S. citizenship, and assuring themselves of American political protection.

Over time, many found it easier to conduct business in Hong Kong than in America and hedged their bets by maintaining ties in both regions. They moved their families and transferred wealth to the United States, while continuing to operate their businesses out of Asia. Soon, they came to be known as "astronauts": international commuters who spent many hours flying back and forth between Hong Kong and North America.

Coincidentally, the Chinese term for "astronaut"—*tai kong ren*—sounds like the Chinese words for "empty wife" or "home without a husband," an appropriate description for women who, like the nineteenth-century "Gold Mountain widows," rarely saw their husbands on a regular basis. And to a certain degree, the lives of these Hong Kong astronauts mirrored the lives of the early Chinese immigrants in America, but with a high-tech twist. During the nineteenth and early twentieth centuries, the Chinese in America lived an odd paradox: their American income was too low to sustain families in the United States, yet high enough to elevate their families to the status of gentry in China. A split-family arrangement emerged, in which wives reared children in Guangdong villages while the breadwinner worked on the other side of the ocean and mailed money back. During the 1990s, the split-family tradition reappeared as the astronaut phenomenon, but the direction of cash flow had reversed: wives and children resided in North America, while the husbands earned money in Asia to support their families in fine style in America.

The number of these Hong Kong astronauts ran in the thousands, and they ranged from moderately successful executives to celebrity moguls. The most prominent ones included Jimmy Lai, a newspaper and magazine publisher and founder of the Giordano clothing empire; Ronnie Chan, a billionaire real estate developer and chairman of the Hang Lung Group, a property development corporation; Frank Tsao, a real estate and shipping magnate; and Tung Chee-hwa, another shipping tycoon. All of them regularly commuted between Hong Kong and their homes in California.

Instead of cramped quarters in Hong Kong, some astronaut families moved into larger homes in North America, such as gigantic mansions in the Los Angeles area (which locals dubbed "monster houses"), or in Canadian cities like Toronto and Vancouver (which natives there nicknamed "Hongcouver"). But not every family was happy with the new arrangement. In Hong Kong, where labor was cheap, many wives had servants at their disposal. Now they had to adapt to a society in which even upper-middle-class American house-wives were expected to cook, clean, and chauffeur their children around. Also, in Hong Kong, most had enjoyed an adrenaline-charged social schedule, a whirlwind ritual of dim sum luncheons, karaoke parties, banquets, and nightly receptions. In the United States, some found it difficult to adjust to the slower pace of social activities, to the physical isolation and cool privacy of suburban living.

Inevitably, the loneliness caused by the prolonged absence of a spouse would lead many to adultery. According to psychologist Alex Leung, some astronauts experienced "a second bachelorhood" when they returned to Asia. "Hong Kong is a place which is famous for its materialistic glamour and night life," he wrote. "It is very easy for these 'single' men to indulge themselves in these 'niceties'—while writing off the excesses as 'Business Entertainment.'" Meanwhile, there were reports of bored, frustrated Chinese housewives develop-ing friendships with local men in their lives, platonic business rela-tionships that may at times have evolved into something else. Extramarital sex—real or imagined—destroyed many astronaut mar-riages. The wife of a Hong Kong bank executive and mother of three children aroused her husband's jealousy when she became close friends with an unmarried male neighbor in San Francisco. Her hus-band accused her of having an affair, while she confronted him with rumors of cavorting with strange women in Hong Kong nightclubs. Upon these words, he immediately left for Hong Kong and asked for a divorce a week later.

Of course, many if not most astronaut marriages withstood these tensions and survived, but the special pressures of split-home arrange-ments caused other fissures in family relationships. To allay their guilt over their extended absences, some Chinese fathers tried to express their love through expensive gifts—trendy toys, luxury cars, enormous allowances. But no matter how much money they spent, they learned that a father's obligation to his children could not be satisfied solely in terms of dollars. Some sons and daughters came to view their fathers more as money machines than as loving advisers and reliable role models, and over time many fathers found themselves psychologically and emotionally estranged from their families. Alex Leung described a Mr. Lee whose children preferred to converse in English, not Chinese; when he insisted they speak to him in his native tongue, they often found it easier not to talk to him at all. In another home, a Mr. Wong, when staying with his wife and children, obsessively checked his stock quotes on the other side of the planet through fax and cell phone, often in the middle of the night, North American time. When they grew annoyed and asked him to stop, he warned he would never visit them again if they continued to complain about his behavior.

Without a strong father presence, troubled behavior among young people increased. One daughter of a Hong Kong astronaut confided to an interviewer that she was deeply worried about her brother: "He starts gambling and smoking, being involved with the gangs in Chinatown, having sex with a lot of bad girls. He has been caught once for breaking and entering. I try to cover for him as much as possible. My parents do not know yet and I am sure they will be devastated."

But surely the ones who paid the greatest price for the astronaut lifestyle were the astronauts themselves, suffering the cumulative health risk of long flights, daily restaurant meals, and sleep deprivation caused by jet lag. A typical day for them might consist of meetings in a city far from home, sending e-mails from the airport, eating and sleeping onboard a red-eye flight to the next destination. Some astronauts trained themselves to work continuously for several days in a row before collapsing in deep slumber during the flight across the Pacific. In the long run, as Alex Leung noted, the astronaut risked losing all that was important to him: "his marriage, his children, and even his legal immigration status in the host country as a result of his long and frequent absence."

Hong Kong was not the only place in Asia troubled by the renewed hard-line posture of the People's Republic. During the 1990s, the Taiwanese felt new pressure to move themselves and their capital to the safety of the United States. The brutal crackdown at Tiananmen Square raised concerns that the gains achieved during the Deng years might be suddenly reversed. Then, in 1996, the island's first direct presidential elections challenged the four-decade reign of the Kuomintang. Fearing that pro-Taiwan independence groups would declare the island a separate nation, not an integral part of China, the PRC resorted to a show of saber-rattling. Conducting a series of military exercises near the coast of Taiwan that included the firing of several missiles, it sent a message that it was prepared to act militarily if Taiwan tried to present it with a fait accompli on the issue of independence. The Taiwan stock market plunged, and many residents fled to the United States. But no formal steps to establish independence were taken, and eventually the crisis passed. Economic investment returned to Taiwan, and diplomatic relations between the island and mainland China reverted to their previous status. Nonetheless, many Taiwanese families were shaken, and some found it prudent to keep bank accounts, homes, and even relatives in the United States, in case a quick move became necessary.

Largely because of these fears, Taiwan, like Hong Kong, suffered its share of fractured families in the 1990s. In Taiwan, the most common split-family lifestyle was the "parachute children" phenomenon. Unlike youths who were plunked down in the suburbs with their mothers while their "astronaut" fathers lived in Hong Kong, the parachute children lived in the United States without supervision from either parent. The motivating force behind this choice was not solely concern over the island's political future, but also the wish to spare children the cutthroat academic competition in Taiwan.

The pressure to be admitted to a good college in Taiwan started as early as grade school. To increase their chances of getting into the island's most prestigious middle schools, students enrolled in special preparatory programs and private cram courses. At the secondary school level, the competition for college admission became even more fierce. "You may be the best in your class but many still flunk the entrance exams for college," one parachute child told an interviewer. "In Taiwan, people almost have to kill themselves to survive annual comprehensive entrance examinations for high school and college."

The rigidity of the system ensured that some capable students would fall through the cracks, never to climb out again. Many working-class families in Taiwan, unable to afford tutors and the extra coaching required, gave up hope of having all their children attain university degrees. And without those degrees, opportunities on the island were limited. Barred from applying to graduate school, they had few chances to travel abroad. Worse still was the prospect of leaving school without a high school diploma. Typically, dropouts entered low-skilled, labor-intensive industries, such as assembly work in home-based factories. Knowing the odds, some Taiwanese families threw all of their resources behind only one or two children, in hopes that they might achieve the success that was sure to elude their siblings.

Other Taiwanese families shrewdly decided to avoid the exam system entirely by sending their children to the United States. They viewed the American education system as a shortcut to success, offering a dual advantage: less-competitive high schools, and more prestigious universities. But unlike the émigrés who owned their own international businesses, the fathers in these families could not leave their careers and start over in the United States. And with the rising number of two-career families on the island, many mothers could not abandon their jobs to accompany their children to America. So they sent them alone, either to live with caretakers or relatives, or to remain completely unsupervised. Amazingly enough, such parents would typically visit their children in the United States only a couple of times a year.

According to a 1990 study conducted by Helena Hwang and Terri Watanabe, some thirty thousand to forty thousand Taiwanese students between the ages of eight and eighteen were living as unaccompanied minors in the United States. The majority were boys, because

Taiwanese parents wanted to protect their sons from mandatory military service. (In Taiwan, all males over the age of twenty were required to serve in the military for two years, a tour of duty that could be postponed if they enrolled in college.) While these parachute kids could be found in urban areas across the country, approximately ten thousand of them lived on the West Coast, mostly in affluent neighborhoods in either Los Angeles or the San Francisco Bay Area.

In those neighborhoods, some lived in what seemed like a teenager's paradise: no parents, no curfew, unlimited expense accounts. The wealthiest enjoyed the services of maids and housekeepers, received allowances of $4,000 or more a month, and cruised the streets in their BMWs and Mercedes-Benzes. But even with these luxuries, many were desperately unhappy.* Some youths told investigators that they missed their parents, feared their new surroundings, and wept often. A 1994 study of 162 Taiwanese adolescents in southern California found that parachute children suffered from higher levels of anxiety, distress, oversensitivity, depression, and paranoia than American-born Chinese youths who lived with their parents. One girl who had lived with relatives in California since the age of twelve told the *Los Angeles Times*, "It looks happy on the outside, but inside the kids are hurting. I wish people wouldn't do this to their kids." She admitted that "in my heart there was a dark place." Occasionally, her fourteen-year-old brother came to her room, sobbing, "Patty, I want Mommy." She did her best to comfort him: "Sometimes we hug each other and we cry; it's all we can do."

The behavior of these parachute children followed a typical pattern: first, hysterical phone calls home, weeping and begging their parents to join them in the United States (many ran up thousands of dollars in phone bills during the first few months away from home);

---

*Research has shown that adolescence is already one of the most traumatic stages of human life, and moving from one culture to another during this period only makes the experience worse. For those who arrived without the protective support of their parents, the experience could be devastating.

then, signs of resignation and numbness; and finally, emotional alienation. Some parents recalled a chill creeping into conversations with
their children—long pauses over the telephone, robotic "yes" and
"no" replies to questions—as if strangers had taken their place.

Many parents believed that this sacrifice of intimacy was necessary in order to give their children better futures. Nonetheless, most
remained guilt-ridden by the separation and, like the Hong Kong
astronaut fathers, used money to compensate for their absence.
During the 1990s, the average expense account for a Taiwanese parachute child was about $15,000 a year, and when the cost of domestic
services was tallied, the total was much greater. In 1993, the *Los
Angeles Times* estimated the total annual cost to support a single parachute child in the United States at about $40,000. Accustomed to a
regular cash flow, some youths became adept at manipulating parental
guilt for larger allowances, especially when resentment gave way to a
sense of entitlement. "If they're going to dump me here and not take
care of me, they owe me something," one parachute kid told an interviewer. "That's my right."

With an ocean separating parent from child, discipline was difficult to enforce. One boy said his parents counseled him to "work
hard, to focus, no drugs, no smoking, no dating, and no this, no that.
That kind of phone call got boring after a while. Now I call home
only because I am expected to. I really don't have much to say on the
phone with them." To tighten their control, some parents demanded
that their children fax them copies of report cards and homework,
punishing low marks with cuts in their allowance. Many youths
admitted that so long as they earned high grades, they could do just
about anything they wanted. And so, in some families, the parent-
child relationship mimicked that of employer and telecommuter, in
which attentiveness to the demands of the job was controlled through
bonuses or wage reductions.

In a sink-or-swim environment, some parachute children excelled
academically, while others, unable to cope with the situation, ended
up dropping out of school. By the early 1990s, both the mainstream

and Chinese ethnic media exposed serious problems among the Taiwanese parachute population. There were reports of juvenile delinquency, gang warfare, and suicides—all of which did much to erode the "model minority" image of Chinese Americans. In the most extreme cases, parachute kids turned to violence. In 1995, a sixteen-year-old Taiwanese girl was arrested for attempted murder after she detonated a homemade bomb in her host family's residence. The following year, another sixteen-year-old parachute student who had lived in Los Angeles for two years was charged with arms smuggling and apprehended in Taipei. Alarmed by the level of truancy among its Taiwanese student population, in 1991 the officials of the San Marino school district in the Los Angeles area adopted a policy mandating that all students live either with legal guardians, such as court-appointed foster families, or with relatives no more distant than first cousins. Offenders would be expelled or reported to immigration authorities.

As the decade progressed, Taiwanese parents had to face yet another danger in their parachute children's lives: kidnappers who preyed on youths with rich parents. In December 1998, abductors seized seventeen-year-old Kuan Nan "Johnny" Chen from the driveway of his home in San Marino, California. Chen was a parachute child whose parents commuted between Los Angeles and their native Taiwan, and after a secretary in his father's office revealed to the kidnappers the extent of the family's wealth, they monitored Chen for more than a month before striking. Gagged and shoved into a waiting car, Chen spent two terrifying weeks in the clutches of his assailants, his limbs chained and shackled, his eyes and mouth sealed with duct tape. Immediately after his abduction, Chen tried to escape, but the kidnappers caught and tortured him by striking his head with a hammer. They demanded a $1.5 million ransom from his father, a fee that was negotiated down to $500,000. Before the money was delivered, however, the FBI, local police, and authorities in both the PRC and Taiwan all joined forces to rescue the teenager. The Los Angeles County Sheriff's Department later asserted that a shocking two out of three abductions like Chen's in the Chinese community—some said it was more like nine out of ten—were never reported to the police.

About 80 percent of parachute children were Taiwanese, yet there was also a largely unreported flow of parachute children from the very country that had precipitated the phenomenon in the first place: the People's Republic of China. Ironically, even some of the most powerful officials in the PRC saw the United States as a safe haven for their children, a form of protection against the vagaries of Chinese politics.

In 1999, American immigration authorities discovered what appeared to be a conspiracy to smuggle mainland Chinese youths into the United States. A group of prestigious, elite families from Shanghai, including Communist Party leaders, bankers, and executives, had paid $19,000 each to send their children to Los Angeles for English-language studies. The original plan, it appears, was to have these youths enter legitimate academic programs, obtain student visas, then remain in the United States for years. As long as the students stayed enrolled in school, the visa could be extended almost indefinitely, permitting the families to work on achieving naturalization for their children through the sponsorship of friends, relatives, or American companies. No doubt for some of these Chinese nationals, this was the easiest way to obtain U.S. citizenship.

On the day they were scheduled to fly back to Shanghai, the teenagers disappeared from the Los Angeles airport. Fearing abduction and a possible international crisis, American authorities launched an investigation, only to discover that the youths had been spirited away to private homes, to be enrolled in a different English-language program. The situation created terrible press for the Shanghai families and inspired proposals within the PRC to bar all high school teenagers from studying overseas. When interviewed later, a few parents said they had wanted to give their children better opportunities by having them live in the United States. "In China, we can have only one child," said one father, with tears in his eyes. "These are our princes and princesses. We will do anything for them."

CHAPTER NINETEEN

High Tech vs. Low Tech

For the United States, unanticipated success in the international sphere during the 1980s paved the way for unbridled prosperity at home in the 1990s. A forty-year nuclear standoff with the Soviet Union had ended in 1989 not with a bang but with a series of cheers across Eastern Europe as the Berlin Wall was demolished by people using nothing more than sledgehammers and bare hands. When one satellite state after another broke away from the Soviet bloc, and when in 1990 and 1991 the republics of the Soviet Union declared themselves to be independent nations, the United States found itself the winner of the cold war by default. Miraculously, the long-dreaded and seemingly inevitable nuclear apocalypse had never materialized. The disintegration of America's former antagonist brought to Americans a new era of confidence born of the fact that the United States was now the world's number one economic and military power.

Supporters of Ronald Reagan like to say that he ended the cold war not by backing off from the arms race but by accelerating it. According to this scenario, he engaged the Soviet Union in a high-stakes, no-rules poker game that threatened to bankrupt both countries, but a game in which the poorer of the two would have to cry uncle first. This last-stage arms race left the United States two legacies. The first was an enormous national debt, by far the largest ever. But the huge expenditures were not solely for weaponry, but also to develop and support new technologies, especially in computers and information processing. Once unleashed, these technologies placed enormous pressure on the American industrial economy, triggering a business revolution that would have broad social consequences.

In the new economy, power flowed to those who could create or master new technology faster than their competitors. It should be no surprise that the richest man in the world, Bill Gates, would make his fortune in computers, as the co-founder and leader of Microsoft. By the end of the decade, his net worth was estimated at $85 billion, greater than that of entire countries, as well as the one hundred million poorest Americans combined. The wealthiest one percent of America emerged from the 1990s with 40 percent of the country's assets, twice as much as they had held only two decades earlier.

Meanwhile, the poor—indeed, all those without the skills demanded by this new economy—grew poorer. According to economist Edward N. Wolff, between 1983 and 1995, poor, working-class, and lower-middle-class families—the bottom 40 percent of American society—lost 80 percent of their net worth; when adjusted for inflation for 1995 dollars, their holdings shrank from $4,000 to $900. One reason for the disappearance of their wealth was that highly paid manufacturing jobs, which had once afforded working- and middle-class Americans a certain measure of prosperity, gradually disappeared as corporations farmed labor-intensive work to Third World countries.

The growing divide between American haves and have-nots was felt keenly not only among whites and blacks, but within the ethnic Chinese population as well. The decade of the 1990s would witness the development of a two-tiered society among new Chinese arrivals: the rise of an elite group of highly visible, educated people, and the disappearance of thousands of illegal aliens into servile positions in an underground economy, where they were forced to endure dismal working conditions. But whether they were "high-tech" or "low-tech" immigrants, both groups would face a series of crises during the 1990s related to their Chinese ethnicity.

For "high-tech" Chinese, the 1990s resembled the gold rush days, except that the 1990 fortune seekers were mining for nuggets in a new form of sand—silicon. The modern gold rush, like the 1849 gold rush, occurred in northern California, but this time south of San Francisco, in a region dubbed Silicon Valley. The area had already witnessed the birth of the personal computer revolution in the 1970s, when two young men, Steve Jobs and Steve Wozniak, started the Apple corporation, selling desktop computers they had built in their garage. Proximity to Stanford University in Palo Alto, the University of California at Berkeley, and San Francisco as a major port for trade with Asia, helped transform the area into a world center of the high-tech industry.* But an even bigger revolution erupted in the 1990s—the Internet revolution.

The roots of the Internet stretch back to the 1960s, when academic and government experts envisioned building a global computer network that could function even in the event of nuclear war. Preliminary research at MIT led to a government contract with the Advanced Research Projects Agency (ARPA), which linked together a few computers at major universities through telephone lines. For the next two decades, a small community of academics—mostly computer scientists, engineers, and librarians—would exchange information with colleagues by posting messages on this cyberspace bulletin board, a government-funded system of electronic mail (or "e-mail").

In the early 1990s, this network crashed into public awareness when companies such as America Online, CompuServe, and Prod-

---

*A symbiotic relationship evolved between the Bay Area and Asia. For instance, while new companies in Silicon Valley produced cutting-edge hardware and software, the island of Taiwan served as a manufacturing center, supplying the industry with computer components and peripherals.

igy began offering the general public unlimited access to this new form of communication for a monthly fee. The unprecedented growth of what came to be called the Internet spawned a rash of new Silicon Valley startups. Known as "dotcoms," these companies were typically run by young men and women fresh out of school. To attract employees with the special computer talents needed, most of these cash-poor start-ups offered employees stock options in lieu of high pay. When the companies were able to offer their stock to the general public, a rush to get in on the ground floor of a brand-new industry that seemed to have an unbounded future led to over-subscribed initial public offerings (IPOs). The outstanding stock was then bid up to astronomical levels, despite the fact that most of these companies had not yet shown a profit (and many never would). Before the dotcom bubble burst, many young Americans of Chinese heritage, both founders and those who had received stock options, joined the ranks of twenty-somethings with million-dollar portfolios, with many expecting to accumulate their first billion before age thirty. This kind of wealth, noted Stanford historian Gordon Chang, transformed the image of the young Asian American male from "son of a laborer or laundryman" to "future Internet millionaire."

One icon of the dotcom world was Jerry Yang, the billionaire founder of Yahoo!, an Internet search engine and Web service. Born in Taiwan in 1967, Yang moved with his family to San Jose, California, while he was still a teenager. His company grew out of a simple idea: to create a directory of his favorite sites on the international network of information now referred to as the World Wide Web. By the early 1990s, any location on the Web could be accessed by typing the location's Web address into an address box. Yang helped develop the first popular search tool for the Web, so that users could type names or relevant phrases into a search box, and have the search engine find all documents with a string of characters matching those in the search box. In a tiny office trailer at Stanford University, Yang, then a twenty-six-year-old doctoral student in electrical engineering, and his classmate, David Filo, sorted hyperlinks by subject and posted them on the Web. Their directory grew so popular that its level of traffic crashed the computer servers at Stanford, forcing the company to move off campus. Yang and Filo took Yahoo! public and watched its worth increase exponentially as the Internet market exploded. By March 2000, the market capitalization of Yahoo! had exceeded $100 billion.*

Of course, not all Chinese moguls of the information age made their wealth through dotcom firms. Some, like Morris Chang, earned their fortunes by enabling high-tech companies to outsource their manufacturing to Taiwan. Revered as the "godfather of high technology" in Taiwan, Chang, an electrical engineer educated at Harvard, MIT, and Stanford, pioneered the integrated circuit foundry industry as the founder and chairman of Taiwan Semiconductor Manufacturing Corporation (TSMC). Recognizing that fabricating chips required enormous startup capital (a semiconductor factory could cost literally billions of dollars), Chang's company, largely funded by the government of the Republic of China in Taiwan, permitted small American chip companies to contract their fabrication work in Taiwan. Taiwan Semiconductor provided independent chip designers, who could not compete on their own against giants like Intel, Motorola, and NEC, access to affordable manufacturing services, freeing them to focus on creative design work. Thus Chang's insight accelerated the pace of computer innovation worldwide. Thousands of entrepreneurs were now able to compete by offering their own innovations, instead of leaving the industry's development to just a

*During those heady years of the Internet boom, there were other success stories, though less well known. Tony Hsieh founded a startup called LinkExchange with a fellow Harvard classmate and immediately sold it to Microsoft for a reported $250 million. (The terms of the agreement prevented him from disclosing the actual figure.) Initially, his parents—both scientific professionals with doctorates—had been distressed by Tony's decision to become an entrepreneur. "At first my parents were a bit surprised and not happy that I was leaving a steady job at Oracle to start this company," Hsieh said. "Actually, they weren't even happy that I went to Oracle in the first place, because they wanted me to get my Ph.D." It didn't matter whether the Ph.D. was in computer science or not: "They just wanted the letters after my name."

few corporate players. By the end of the twentieth century, even colossal semiconductor companies began cutting costs by farming out their fabrication work to Taiwan.

Any gold rush has a few celebrity winners and many exhausted losers. Some Chinese immigrants found themselves in a quandary when Congress passed the Immigration Act of 1990, introducing the H1-B visa program for highly educated and skilled immigrant workers, but restricting the time such visa holders could work in the United States to a maximum of six years. The act abruptly reversed previous immigration policy, which had eagerly welcomed foreign immigrants with advanced education or professional occupations. After 1965, the government had imposed virtually no limits on the admission of Chinese foreign nationals with specialized training. In 1989, the foreign Chinese students who happened to be in the United States during the Tiananmen Square massacre were allowed to obtain green cards immediately. But for those who came after the 1990 act, it was a different story.

High-tech employers viewed the H1-B program as an attractive solution to their labor needs because it gave them a fresh crop of minds to exploit every six years. The policy was perceived as giving domestic industry the opportunity to harness the brainpower of foreign immigrants, but without granting these contributors the full rights and privileges of American citizenship. At first, Congress capped the program at 65,000 visas per year, but the 1990s high-tech boom created a massive shortage of computer programmers, engineers, and systems analysts, which companies hoped to rectify by recruiting from abroad. After intense lobbying from corporations like Microsoft, the U.S. government raised the cap on H1-B visas to 115,000 in 1998, then to 195,000 two years later. India provided the greatest number of skilled foreign workers in the program, followed by the People's Republic of China.*

---

*Most of the Chinese H1-B visa holders came from the People's Republic of China, not Taiwan. During the late 1980s and 1990s, Taiwan experienced a reverse brain drain in relation to the United States. Unlike the Taiwanese who chose to stay in the

Critics soon denounced the H1-B visa program as "white-collar indentured servitude." Middlemen recruiters took as much as half the salary of the workers they procured for companies, and visa holders were beholden to their employers, whom they needed as sponsors for permanent immigration status. If an H1-B visa holder wanted to switch companies, the potential new employer had to petition the Immigration and Naturalization Service, a process that could take several months. Those with H1-B visas had to wait years for a coveted green card, knowing that their visas might expire before they obtained one. Severe backlogs for green card applications developed because applicants from any one country could not make up more than 7 percent of the total number of green cards issued each year.

By the end of the decade, a few Chinese H1-B visa holders had begun to organize. In 1998, for example, Swallow Yan, a green card applicant from the PRC, helped create the Immigration Council of the Chinese Professionals and Entrepreneurs Association, a grassroots effort that lobbies politicians on behalf of H1-B visa holders. But in general, most H1-B visa holders were too terrified to voice their complaints to the press or lawmakers. While researching this book, I interviewed several Chinese on H1-B visas who spoke to me only on condition of anonymity.

One woman, whom I will call Sally Chung, asserted that the H1-B visa program had turned her into "a high-tech slave." An immigrant from mainland China, she came to the United States in 1992 to obtain a bachelor's degree in engineering. After graduation, she accepted a position as a software designer at a local company, where she was expected to work at least ten hours a day, including weekends, without raises or compensation for overtime. Though Chung was unhappy with her situation, she could not afford to leave—her appli-

---

United States after graduating from American universities during the 1960s and 1970s, more Taiwanese students are now returning to the island after obtaining their degrees, to take advantage of better employment opportunities there. High-tech workers from the PRC, however, are more eager to stay in the United States.

cation for a green card depended on being employed by this particular company. Quitting her job meant starting the paperwork all over again as well as forfeiting the $10,000 she had invested in legal fees for the green card. A backlog at INS caused the wait to stretch from months to several agonizing years. When she complained that she earned even less than entry-level workers in her field, her boss demoted her title from software engineer to librarian in order to justify her low wages. At the same time, however, he expected her to serve as a software engineer by programming a computer database for the company. "My boss enjoys calling me into his office, shutting the door, and then screaming at me," she said. "He tells me I have to speak perfect English without an accent before I can get a raise. He says that if he lived in China for only one month, he would be able to speak perfect Chinese. My boss warned me that if I ask him for a raise one more time he will fire me." Now, she says, "I'm scared to death I'll lose my job."

In addition to the H1-B visa system, another development worked against the interests of the "high-tech" Chinese. The sudden demise of the Soviet Union left a vacuum in the arena of international politics, helping China emerge from the cold war as the second greatest military power in the world after the United States. While the economies of Russia and the former Soviet republics were still paying the price for the arms race the Soviet Union could not afford, the economy of the People's Republic of China was growing almost exponentially. After Mao's death, the Chinese gross national product had almost tripled by the 1990s, giving rise to American fears of future competition. During the 1990s, economic experts and historians predicted that the next century would belong to mainland China.

One irony of the 1990s was that the United States would come to view China both as its great business partner and its most powerful rival. While the decade saw an explosion of Sino-American corporate partnerships, it also witnessed the dawn of a new era of suspicion regarding the People's Republic. The *Washington Post* reported the emergence of an anti-PRC "Blue Team" in Washington, D.C., "a loose alliance of members of Congress, congressional staff, think tank fellows, Republican political operatives, conservative journalists, lobbyists for Taiwan, former intelligence officers and a handful of academics, all united in the view that a rising China poses great risks to America's vital interests." A spate of books published in the late 1990s or shortly afterward by members of this Blue Team—*The Coming Conflict with China*, by Richard Bernstein and Ross Munro; *Hegemon: China's Plan to Dominate Asia and the World*, by Steven W. Mosher; *The China Threat: How the People's Republic Targets America*, by Bill Gertz; *Year of the Rat* and *Red Dragon Rising: Communist China's Military Threat to America*, by Edward Timperlak and William Triplett—suggested that a future showdown between the United States and the PRC was inevitable, echoing earlier cold war themes with only the name of the enemy changed.*

In 1999, Representative Christopher Cox (R-Calif.) released a seven-hundred-page report accusing mainland China of stealing classified data on American nuclear weapons. Although the report was later denounced by American scientists and missile experts as grossly distorted and erroneous, it received enormous media attention upon its release. In an initial response, *Time* magazine published a cover story about the possibility of the United States entering a new cold war, this time with China.

With this atmosphere of suspicion came greater scrutiny of ethnic Chinese scientists and engineers, greater fears that they might be potential spies. Historically, the fate of the Chinese American community has always been linked to the health of Sino-American relations, and the 1990s were no exception. Like Tsien Hsue-shen and other Chinese victims of the McCarthy era of the 1950s, Chinese intellectuals who worked in national defense in the 1990s found them-

---

*Some of these books asserted, on the basis of scant evidence, that President Bill Clinton had sold out American security for PRC bribes, that mainland China had stolen military secrets from the United States, and that the Communist Chinese leadership was targeting the United States with nuclear weapons.

selves suspected of espionage because of their racial heritage and their great number within the high-tech industry.

In 1992, the NASA Ames Research Center fired Raymond Luh, an aerospace engineer and immigrant from Taiwan, for possessing "a paper with Chinese writing on it." The following year, a court order confined Andrew Wang, a computer scientist, to his Denver home for almost a year after he e-mailed computer code to a friend in town. Wang's employer had accused him of stealing the code to start a business with alleged Chinese financing. The FBI wanted to pursue the matter as an interstate crime—because Wang's e-mail had been routed through the Internet by a switching system outside of Colorado—but the authorities later dropped the charges when they learned that Wang's boss had given him permission to copy the information and that none of it was particularly important. David Lane, Wang's attorney, attributed the entire matter to a "yellow high-tech peril" kind of fear, adding that his client's life had been "virtually ruined" for more than a year.

Émigrés, even those reared and educated in Nationalist-controlled Taiwan, were soon being accused of passing information to Communist China. The new climate of suspicion prompted people to come out of the closet and speak frankly about their past treatment by the U.S. government. In 1982, Dr. Chih-Ming Hu had received an unexpected visit from an FBI agent. At the time, Hu, a graduate of National Taiwan University with a doctorate from the University of Maryland, was working on a nonclassified flight simulation project at Computer Sciences Corporation, a contractor for NASA Ames in Mountain View, California. The FBI agent asked Hu if he had ever given classified secrets and his doctoral dissertation to a friend in mainland China. No, Hu said, adding that he had no access to classified data and that his dissertation was already in the public domain, having been published in the *Journal of Chemical Physics*. A few days later, the agent reappeared, this time accusing Hu of lying and threatening to have him fired by NASA. Vehemently, Hu insisted he was telling the truth and even offered to take a polygraph test. The agent, who did not take up his offer, warned Hu that he suspected him of hiding something. A week later, NASA fired Hu for security reasons, even though he was never officially charged with anything.

Sadly enough, his initial impulse was to do nothing. "It happened so fast, and I was so shocked and scared that I did not know what to do," Chih-Ming Hu later wrote. He feared that the United States government would retaliate if he fought back: "Most people from Taiwan still remember that during the 1950s to 1970s Taiwan was under Nationalist Party's dictatorship. During that 'White Horror' period, [officials] there could arrest any citizen without court order and put that person in jail or make him/her disappear. So after NASA fired me, I worried so much about what the FBI would do to me next."

Stigmatized by NASA's treatment of him, Hu acted like a rape victim, withdrawing from society to hide the shame that had been inflicted upon him. Because he failed to take the natural next step, which many Americans would have done without hesitation—hiring a top lawyer on a contingency basis to sue NASA, Computer Sciences Corporation, and the FBI—his inaction was perceived as a concession of guilt. His peers began to believe that perhaps Hu had committed some sinister, though unspecified, crime. And so they kept their distance from him. During this period, which Hu describes as "a nightmare," he remained unemployed for eight months. ("When I went to high-tech company job interviews no one dared to make me an offer after they heard my story," he later told a reporter. "Who dare hire a spy?") His friends shunned him, and his wife demanded a divorce. Desperate for money, Hu tried to sell real estate, then insurance, but few people wanted to be associated with him in any way. Finally, he secured a job in his field, but only after deciding not to disclose his previous contract with NASA.

The scars remained, however. When he finally broke his silence in the late 1990s, Hu had bitter regrets about not speaking out at the time. "I was scared," he later told a reporter. "I should have fought back." The memories still haunted and infuriated him: "I was 100 percent innocent! This was purely due to the FBI agent's rudeness and power abuse! This kind of thing happened a lot in China during the Cultural Revolution. Who would expect this would happen in the U.S.?"

The most notorious case of unjustified treatment involved Dr. Wen Ho Lee, a Taiwanese American scientist at the Los Alamos National Laboratory in New Mexico. In March 1999, a *New York Times* article claimed that Los Alamos was the source of the W-88 nuclear warhead technology that the People's Republic of China was believed to have obtained through espionage. Lee was abruptly fired without a hearing, and that December, authorities indicted him for allegedly transferring nuclear secrets from a classified computer network onto an insecure computer, and then onto ten portable tapes, seven of which were missing. FBI agents immediately arrested Lee and charged him with fifty-nine counts of mishandling sensitive information and secrecy violations of the Atomic Energy Act.

After a comprehensive three-year investigation involving more than 260 agents and a thousand interviews, during which time Lee was held in custody, under especially dreadful conditions, the United States Justice Department conceded it had no evidence that Lee had committed espionage. The U.S. government also admitted the embarrassing fact that they either knew, or should have learned early in the investigation, that the secret information in the design of the W-88 warhead in Beijing's possession could not have come from Los Alamos. What China had was based not on the early-stage design used in Los Alamos, but a later-stage version distributed to at least 548 addresses within the U.S. government, available to hundreds if not thousands of people across America.

While many details of the Wen Ho Lee case remain classified, what has emerged is a pattern of government incompetence and outright misconduct. During an interrogation conducted on March 7, 1999, federal agents tried to coerce Dr. Lee to confess to espionage, resorting even to death threats. The FBI told him that he had failed his polygraph, when in fact he had passed it with flying colors. They hinted at the power of the government to manipulate the media by leaking information, and the power of the subsequent coverage to destroy his career and ruin his life, even if he were completely innocent.* Agents even warned Lee that he could be executed if he did not cop to a lesser plea and confess. "Do you know who the Rosenbergs are?" FBI agent Carol Covert asked Lee. "The Rosenbergs are the only people that never cooperated with the federal government in an espionage case. You know what happened to them? They electrocuted them, Wen Ho."

When the Justice Department could find no evidence that Lee had spied for Beijing, they changed focus, seizing upon the fact that he had improperly handled data within Los Alamos National Laboratory. Lee later admitted that he had moved nuclear codes from a secure computer system to an insecure computer within the laboratory, but claimed he did it only as backup, to protect his files in the event of a system failure.

Most people who have lost important data due to a power-failure crash will understand how such a breach of regulations could occur. In his autobiography, *My Country Versus Me,* Lee described losing several important files in 1993 after the computers at Los Alamos were converted from one operating system to another. Determined not to experience such a loss again, he decided to make several backup files. Since he lacked his own tape drive, he borrowed one from a friend who worked in the insecure, unclassified region within the laboratory. After making the backups, Lee claimed he left the information on the open system as an extra precaution against future loss, protecting it with three levels of passwords. Later, he acknowledged that this was a mistake and a breach of security, but stressed he did it only "for my convenience, not for any espionage purposes."

---

*"Do you think the press prints everything that's true?" one FBI agent told Lee. "Do you think that everything in this article is true? . . . The press doesn't care . . . Do you know what bothers me? You're going to have this kind of reputation! . . . You know what's going to happen, Wen Ho? People are going to read this stuff, and they're gonna think you're not a loyal American."

According to Lee's colleagues, such security lapses were common, and the data Lee had downloaded fell in a gray area of classification: "protect as restricted data," or PARD. This meant the data had to be handled with care, as it might contain sensitive information, but did not merit the same kind of security precautions as "secret" or even "confidential" data. Scientists could leave PARD on their desks overnight, and a former weapons designer at Los Alamos admitted to the *Times* that he had committed his own blunder with PARD when the wind blew a sheaf of documents out a window. But after Lee's arrest, the U.S. government reclassified the downloaded PARD files to a much higher level—as "secret restricted data"—a decision critics described as politically motivated, an attempt to justify what had already been done to Lee.

To put Lee's actions into context, his supporters pointed to the contrasting treatment of John Deutch, a former director of the CIA, who had committed gross security violations. Wen Ho Lee had transferred PARD information from one computer to another within the laboratory, but Deutch had actually removed top-secret files from the CIA and carried them home in a briefcase. In December 1996, the CIA discovered that Deutch's unprotected home computer contained seventeen thousand pages of documents that included ultrasecret "black programs," presidentially approved covert operations, and even a twenty-six-volume personal diary of his tenure at the CIA and the Pentagon. An "alien resident" housekeeper had full access to the room with this computer whenever Deutch and his family were away from home. The computer was routinely used to access the Internet (including porn sites) through America Online, and neither encryption nor a secure phone line had shielded the computer from access by hackers. The CIA also learned that Deutch would leave important memory cards lying around in his car and kept extremely sensitive files on his laptop computer, which could have been easily copied or stolen.

When Deutch learned about the investigation, he immediately began deleting more than a thousand files from his personal computer, and he refused to give interviews to CIA agents on the subject. Given Deutch's lack of cooperation, the CIA shelved the investigation, even though officials believed the former director had broken three major laws. Security investigators at the CIA wanted to alert the Justice Department about "three crimes we knew were sure-fire violations with clear evidence, but the [current] chief said 'no,' " according to one CIA official, who spoke to the media only under condition of anonymity. These crimes included the unauthorized removal of classified information (punishable by up to one year in prison), the concealment or attempt to remove or destroy government documents (punishable by up to three years in prison), and working on personal projects with a financial interest involved.

The disparity between the Justice Department's handling of the two cases was stunning. While Wen Ho Lee—a man never formally charged with espionage—was imprisoned and denied bail, Deutch, who had committed far graver offenses against national security, never spent a single night in jail. The only penalty he suffered was the removal of his security clearance, two and a half years after his security breach was discovered. Meanwhile, his life and career went on as usual. When Deutch failed in his efforts to become secretary of defense, he went back to teaching chemistry at the Massachusetts Institute of Technology. More significantly, Deutch may have abused his power as former director of the CIA to obstruct justice. He recommended Nora Slatkin, a CIA official overseeing the internal investigation of Deutch's security lapses, for a top executive position at Citibank. After Deutch resigned as director in 1996, he joined the board of Citibank, and in 1997, Slatkin became a vice president there.

The double standard in the Lee and Deutch cases infuriated people both inside and outside the Chinese American community. "Deutch can get away with anything because his racial and class background enables him to behave like he owns the country and even if he has done anything illegal, he retains his privilege," Ling-chi Wang, head of the Berkeley ethnic studies department, wrote in a public e-mail. Indeed, Deutch's violations caused no great public outcry, no public debate about whether he, like Lee, might have been guilty of espionage. Robert Scheer, a columnist for the *Los Angeles Times*, wondered if this was because "Deutch is a leading member of the old-boy intelligence establishment, and Lee is not." Others wondered how much of the case was driven by racism. Robert Vrooman, former head of counterintelligence at Los Alamos National Laboratory, told the *Washington Post* he believed that the federal government had targeted Lee because he was ethnic Chinese, and that the entire investigation was "built on thin air."

Critics began to compare the handling of the Lee case with the conduct of foreign dictatorships during the cold war. In a New Mexico jail, Lee had endured conditions that few convicted felons face: for more than two hundred days, he lived in solitary confinement and was shackled in chains whenever he stepped out of his cell, which was one hour a day for exercise, and one hour a week to see his family. "While Deutch has been coddled," Robert Scheer wrote for the *Los Angeles Times*, "Lee sits in a solitary jail cell after having been lied to by the FBI, which, acting like goons from some totalitarian country, told him he had failed the lie detector test that they knew he had easily passed." Many people believed Lee was imprisoned without bail so he would plead guilty under pressure. "This case stinks and the resolution doesn't make it smell any better," said Harvard law professor Alan Dershowitz. "If he pleaded innocent, he had to remain in jail, but if he pleads guilty, he gets out of jail—it is so Soviet. It is un-American." Fang Lizhi, the renowned scientist and human rights activist who had escaped from the PRC after the Tiananmen Square massacre, compared Lee's experience in jail with human rights abuses in mainland China. The extraordinarily brutal conditions of Lee's incarceration led even Plato Cacheris—the attorney for Aldrich Ames, the convicted spy for Moscow—to comment that Wen Ho Lee was treated far worse than his own client.

In the fall of 2000, to salvage a rapidly eroding case against Lee, the Justice Department worked out a plea bargain with his attorneys, dropping all but one of the fifty-nine counts in exchange for his agreement to cooperate with federal authorities. The judge later apologized to Lee, asserting that he had been "terribly wronged" and admitting that federal prosecutors had "embarrassed our entire nation." It was later discovered that several government leaks to the media were not only lies but also violations of U.S. law. The following year, declassified portions of an eight-hundred-page report commissioned by Attorney General Janet Reno concluded that "the FBI has been investigating a crime which was never established to have occurred."

The incident left a lasting wound on the psyche of the Chinese American community. They would remember not only the unbounded arrogance of the Justice Department but also the role of an irresponsible press that fanned flames of racist paranoia across America. During the Lee investigation, the media exploited cruel caricatures of the Chinese, reminding historians of the racist cartoons that led to the exclusion era of the nineteenth century.

A big part of Lee's problems must be laid at the feet of the well-respected *New York Times,* whose reporters and editors too gullibly did the government's bidding by running unsubstantiated government leaks on its front page. Within days, the Lee story degenerated into an orgy of yellow journalism across the nation. Talk-radio and television hosts lumped together all ethnic Chinese—Chinese Americans and foreign Chinese nationals alike—as potential spies.* Major newspapers drew fantasies of millions of Chinese united by a nefarious master scheme to commit espionage. "China's spying, they say, more typically involves cajoling morsels of information out of visiting foreign experts and tasking thousands of Chinese abroad to bring secrets home one at a time like ants carrying grains of sand," the *Washington Post* wrote. "The Chinese have been assembling such grains of sand since at least the fourth century B.C., when the military

---

*"Bill Press, a prominent Democrat and co-host of CNN's *Crossfire* program, was the guest host of the Ron Owens show this morning," wrote one listener, Eddie Liu. "Within just five minutes of my listening, Press twice referred to Lee as a 'spy,' with no qualifying adjectives such as 'alleged.'"

philosopher Sun Tzu noted the value of espionage in his classic work, 'The Art of War.'"

Eventually the *New York Times* faced criticism, both within the organization and by outsiders, for its careless reporting of the Wen Ho Lee case. In the series of articles that started it all, the *Times* reported a mysterious $700 withdrawal that Lee had made from an American Express office in Hong Kong, and speculated that he used it to buy an airplane ticket to Shanghai. It was later discovered, however, that the money had in fact been used by his daughter on a sightseeing tour outside Hong Kong. No detail was too small to be interpreted as possible evidence of Lee's guilt. When Lee was warmly greeted by a PRC nuclear expert at a public function in Los Alamos, as scientists greet foreign colleagues whenever and wherever they meet, the *Times* wrote that the Chinese scientist hugged Lee "in a manner that seemed suspiciously congratulatory."

The Chinese American community would also remember offhand comments made by certain politicians during the Wen Ho Lee affair that revealed the depth of their anti-Chinese feelings. In March 1999, Senator Richard Shelby (R-Ala.), chairman of the Select Committee on Intelligence, told the NBC program *Meet the Press*, "We've got to remember the Chinese are everywhere as far as our weapons systems, not only in our labs that make our nuclear weapons and development, but also in the technology to deliver them. We've seen some of that. They're real. They're here. And probably in some ways, very crafty people." Though a spokesperson from his office later explained that Shelby meant Chinese spies, not Chinese Americans in general, his remarks infuriated the Asian American community. "He doesn't distinguish between Chinese foreign nationals, Chinese graduate students, and Chinese Americans, some of whom are fifth-generation Californians," Frank Wu, a Howard University law professor, told the *San Francisco Examiner*. "He sees them everywhere. That should be troubling."

Equally disturbing was the fact that Robert Smith, a Republican congressman from New Hampshire, mixed up Wen Ho Lee with Bill

Lann Lee, the assistant attorney general for civil rights. "The problem is guilt by racial association," said Wu. "This gives Asian Americans insight into African-American complaints about racial profiling."

After the press coverage of the Wen Ho Lee affair, a cloud of suspicion descended over all ethnic Chinese scientists at the national laboratories. The U.S. government began to investigate Chinese Americans for the most innocuous activities. According to Brian Sun, the attorney for Wen Ho Lee, one Chinese American in Los Angeles was interrogated merely because he sent his laptop computer out to be repaired. As one of several authors of a memo distributed at Lawrence Livermore National Laboratory, one Chinese American employee felt she was considered guilty just because of her race: "The Lab treated me as a suspect when it denied my access to the computers in my office until my computers proved that I was innocent . . . I love my job. Please don't squeeze me out."

During the Wen Ho Lee affair, the U.S. government shocked the Chinese American community by openly acknowledging that it would use racial profiling as a tactic to investigate possible PRC espionage. Paul Moore, former head of FBI Chinese counterintelligence, said the FBI would focus their efforts on Chinese American scientists as long as PRC agents were "interested obsessively in people of Chinese American ancestry to the exclusion of people from other groups."

The Wen Ho Lee case served as a wake-up call for the Chinese at the national laboratories. The case and its aftermath forced many Chinese American scientists—particularly those in the second wave—to rethink their priorities. Why devote their energies to supporting institutions that regarded them as untrustworthy? Would their talents not be better served in a more respectful environment? If the U.S. government did not reward their effort, or withheld promotions on the basis of skin color and ethnicity, then why did it deserve the best years of their lives? They began to complain of an environment rife with nepotism, incompetence, and racial prejudice, all of which deprived Chinese Americans of recognition. Joel Wong, an immigrant engineer at Lawrence Livermore National Laboratory in California, spoke for thousands of other Chinese Americans in *Science* magazine: "The term going around now among us is that we're high-tech coolies—if we work hard, we're given more work." He and other Asian Americans, several of them Taiwanese American, charged that a glass ceiling kept them from the ranks of upper management. They called the performance evaluations "subjective, arbitrary and capricious" because they were conducted in secret, were hard to contest, and were influenced by the "old-boys network."

According to their analysis of lab salaries, the average Asian American physics Ph.D. earned as much as $12,000 less than other employees with similar credentials. In fact, Asian American compensation was often lower than white compensation by as much as 15 to 20 percent. Pointing out that racial discrimination violated federal law, the group voiced their desire for management to use "the same appropriate yardsticks for everyone, instead of the current rubber yardsticks."

Some believed the problem arose from different values: the military culture of the administration at the national laboratories, and the academic culture of the ethnic Chinese who worked not as policymakers or analysts, but as rank-and-file scientists. At Lawrence Livermore National Laboratory, the highest echelons of management tend to be retired naval officers. Several Chinese Americans who worked under these officers believed their bosses were deeply suspicious of all Asians because of the legacy of three wars fought in Asia: World War II, the Korean War, and the Vietnam War. Many ethnic Chinese scientists asserted that this racism existed at such a deep, visceral level that the perpetrators themselves were often unaware of it. "Subconsciously, you become the enemy," said one Taiwanese American employee at the lab. "The moment they hear your accent, they distrust you."

Many Chinese immigrant scientists had originally entered the labs because they appeared to offer not only an intellectual environment, but also the secure haven that had eluded their early years. As immigrants who had fled war and revolution since childhood, many longed for a certain measure of peace and stability. Now they began to wonder about their decision. "In hindsight, there are some things I might have done differently," Wen Ho Lee later wrote. "I might have made different career decisions, maybe going to work in private industry, or teaching at a university, rather than devoting more than twenty years to the national laboratories."

In response to Lee's experience, many have urged scientists of Chinese heritage not to work in the field of government defense. "Boycott Los Alamos, Lawrence Livermore, and other national labs run by the Energy Department," read one Web page that supported Wen Ho Lee. "Don't apply for jobs there. You'll just be a high-tech coolie, a glass ceiling will prevent you from advancing, and they'll do to you what they did to Wen Ho Lee." The unofficial boycott was a success. In February 2000, not one single Chinese graduate student from universities in the PRC, Taiwan, or the United States applied for the top postdoctoral fellowships at Los Alamos National Laboratory. Before the Lee affair, about half of the ten finalists would have been ethnic Chinese.

The boycott led to protracted negotiations between officials at the national laboratories and Chinese American activists, which, as this book went to press, had not yet been resolved. And the boycott was soon followed by litigation. In March 2002, a class action lawsuit was filed on behalf of hundreds of Asian American employees at Lawrence Livermore who alleged they were victims of discrimination.

Only time will tell if the racial profiling tactics and obsessive security measures of the late 1990s have jeopardized U.S. national security more than protecting it. According to Michael May, a Stanford University physicist, the United States evolved as the world's leader in technology because for more than a century it had embraced the talent of foreign immigrants in academia, industry, and government. The nation's entire scientific system—its universities, companies, and defense institutes—had been fueled by a brain tap from other countries, European as well as Asian. In the first half of the twentieth century, men like Albert Einstein, Enrico Fermi, and Edward Teller enriched the American scientific community and assisted, either directly or indirectly, the nation's national defense. In the second half through to the twenty-first century, Asian immigrants have also been making important contributions.

The degree to which the United States academic community has benefited from the Chinese is borne out by statistics. By the end of the twentieth century, Chinese immigrants constituted the largest group of foreign students in the United States, mostly concentrated in science and engineering. In 1997, about half of all foreign scientists with doctorates in the U.S. came from either the PRC or Taiwan. If the scientists of Chinese heritage from other regions were included, the numbers would be even higher.

Officials at Los Alamos had to confront their need for foreign brainpower when in 1999 they advertised a postdoctoral position in nuclear materials—and not one of the twenty-four applicants was American. They also learned that the fallout from the Wen Ho Lee case had cost them several world-class Chinese scientists. One was Feng Gai, an expert on the proteins that might unlock the secrets of Alzheimer's and Parkinson's disease. When the Department of Energy fired Wen Ho Lee, it ordered Feng Gai to stay home from work while Los Alamos erected a new screening system for foreigners. At this point, the lab lost him to the University of Pennsylvania, which gave him a professorship in chemistry as well as a new $400,000 laboratory. In a *Newsweek* "My Turn" column, David Pines, a senior scientist at Los Alamos, wrote that he had discouraged a brilliant young scientist from the PRC from accepting a postdoc at the lab, because he "felt his every move would be monitored." Pines wondered "whether we've lost a chance to attract to America a major contributor to science—and a potential Nobel laureate."

For Chinese American intellectuals not interested in working for the government, the 1990s were a time of extremes. Some "high-tech"

Chinese made fortunes, while others were badly fleeced. The media depicted them as moguls and geniuses, crooks and spies. But no matter how great the economic and political pressures against them, these could not compare to the experiences of another population, mostly hidden from view. This group of Chinese immigrants—the "low-tech" Chinese—came from the poorest echelons of society, and their fates differed widely, depending on a random throw of life's dice.

One group of new émigrés was Chinese baby girls, abandoned by their biological parents in China and adopted by American families. Perhaps it was inevitable that China, an overpopulated nation filled with parents who could not afford to feed their children, would provide the answer to thousands of desperate couples in the United States, a country with soaring infertility rates and a diminished supply of infants available for adoption.

This emigration pattern grew out of a Chinese experiment in social engineering. The Chinese population had exploded under the leadership of Mao, who had long considered birth control a form of genocide. In 1979, to reverse the trend, the Deng administration created the "one-child family" policy: couples who gave birth to only one child received better government benefits, while those who had more than one could be penalized with heavy fines. The goal was to shrink the population to 700 million people by the year 2030.

But centuries-old traditions die hard. In China, a woman's value historically hinged on her ability to give birth to sons to preserve the family name. Restricted to one child, families in some regions came to consider female life so worthless that they did not even bother to name daughters; in those same areas, many couples were willing to risk everything, even government persecution, to try to have a male heir.

After the 1982 Chinese census revealed the population had surpassed one billion people, the one-child policy was enforced rigorously, even ruthlessly. To circumvent the law, Chinese couples who longed for sons hid their daughters with relatives, or, in extreme cases, even resorted to infanticide or abandonment. Female Chinese babies began to turn up in public areas such as parks, bus stations, on the doorsteps of orphanages, and even at the side of the road. Occasionally, handwritten notes were tucked into her clothes. "Owing to the current political situation and heavy pressures that are too difficult to explain, we, who were her parents for these first days, cannot continue taking care of her," one note read. "We can only hope that in this world there is a kind-hearted person who will care for her. Thank you. In regret and shame, your father and mother."

The sheer number of homeless girls overwhelmed Chinese orphanages, and underfunding and understaffing soon led to monstrous conditions. Eyewitnesses described babies who had starved or choked to death because they were tied to beds during feedings. Without shoes or socks, barely covered with thin cotton clothes, even in freezing weather, these children were often kept strapped to chairs, cribs, or toilets for days. In 1995, a journalist from the German magazine *Der Spiegel* described the Shanghai Children's Welfare Institute as a "children's gulag":

> In a dim room, as big as a dance hall, babies and small children are lying—no, they are not lying, they are laid out, in cribs: handicapped small bodies, some just skin and bones. Kicking and thrashing, they doze in their own urine, some naked, some dressed in a dirty little jacket. The older children have wrapped the [corpse of a baby] in a couple of dirty cloths, which serve as a shroud. Then they shoved the dead baby under the bed, where it stays until the staff gets around to removing the corpse. On weekends that can take two or three days.

Possibly to relieve the orphanages of their workload, in 1992 mainland China began encouraging large-scale international adoption. That year, about two hundred children from China joined American families. Payment for services often occurred under mysterious circumstances (some American parents were asked to donate $3,000 in $100 bills to an orphanage), causing the U.S. media to hint at a profit motive. In 1993, the *New York Times* Sunday magazine ran a cover story about adoptions from China under the headline "China's Market in Orphan Girls," calling the babies "the Newest Chinese Export." In response, the PRC temporarily shut down its adoption program, but resumed it shortly afterward—no doubt because the American demand for Chinese children was simply too great for the program to end permanently.

Because of a trend among American women to delay marriage and childbearing in favor of their careers, there were, by the end of the twentieth century, greater numbers of affluent, childless couples eager to adopt. But they also had to compete for fewer available children, because growing social acceptance of single mothers in the United States meant more of these mothers were keeping babies born out of wedlock. Moreover, the United States adoption system had become a bureaucratic nightmare, and other countries enforced strict rules regarding international adoptions, which favored younger, traditional, and heterosexual couples. For many Americans, adopting a baby girl from China was their only opportunity to start a family, and between 1985 and 2002, Americans adopted more than thirty-three thousand infants from the PRC—the largest source of American adoptions from abroad.*

The typical couple adopting a Chinese immigrant baby was educated, older, and upper-middle-class. According to one study, their median age was 42.7 years, and about 65 percent of them had completed postgraduate studies. Because most Americans could not afford the cost of adopting a baby from China (from $15,000 to $20,000), the median household income of those adopting in the 1990s was high, in the $70,000-to-$90,000 range. The process was not only expensive but tedious and laborious, requiring background checks by the FBI, a visit from a social worker, fingerprinting by the police, and filing papers with the Immigration and Naturalization

*Mainland China received so many adoption applications from the United States that in 2002 the government decided to impose a yearly quota.

Service. Typically, the adopting parents had to wait a year and a half just to have the paperwork completed.

The wait period was excruciating for many couples, especially as some formed psychological bonds with their future children even before meeting them in China. For instance, one Massachusetts woman had already received a photograph of the Chinese baby she would be adopting when the PRC abruptly closed its adoption program after the negative *New York Times* Sunday magazine article. "She spent eight months in purgatory, looking at that picture and thinking about how her baby was faring in a very distant country and orphanage," wrote Christine Kukka in the anthology *A Passage to the Heart: Writings from Families with Children from China.* Shanti Fry remembered writing a new will: "I thought that if I got a child, Jeff and I could be traveling back with her from China and the plane would crash and somehow I would die and Jeff and the baby would survive—in the middle of the Pacific Ocean!"

For the lucky, the long-anticipated date would eventually arrive. The adoptive parents would fly to China, meet with orphanage officials, and receive their babies in hotel rooms and lobbies. After the realities of parenthood sank in—the diapers, the squalls, the constant feedings—some agonized over the best way to handle the ethnicity of their new children. Should they be reared as Americans or as Chinese? Would the child be culturally deprived after leaving her homeland? Jean H. Seeley remembered fighting back tears when she boarded the airplane with her new daughter. "Say good-bye to China, I don't know when you will be back again," she told her infant. Then she wondered, "Was it the right thing to take her to grow up in a country where she would be a minority?"

That their children would one day grow up and suffer racism was evident from remarks uttered from strangers. "Why are you kissing that child?" demanded a Los Angeles police officer when he saw a Caucasian mother nuzzling her toddler from China. After the expense and time required to adopt a baby, it did not occur to many parents that they might be viewed as kidnappers or pedophiles. They were shocked by the crudeness and insensitivity of other Americans. Some heard their children called "a chink baby" and suffered offhand jokes, like "Couldn't get a white one, huh?" Others received hostile stares from men who had served in the Vietnam War. One outraged parent even met a Vietnam War veteran who told her baby that he had "killed a lot of your cousins."

They knew their children would one day question their own identity, and the mystery surrounding their birth and first months. Some infants were found with gifts from the birth parents—sometimes a bracelet, a pendant, a sack of rice—while others bore tiny scars or birthmarks on their skin. Were these clues that might be used one day to trace their children to their original families? The children themselves, especially the precocious ones, were tormented by the enigma. Several Chinese daughters demanded to know why they were orphaned at birth, venting their confusion during temper tantrums: "You're mean," one daughter screamed. *"I want my other Mommy in China!"*

To handle these challenges, many parents did their best to teach their children about their heritage. They delved into ancient Chinese mythology, Confucian philosophy, and the novels of Pearl Buck. Although this education was not really Chinese, but rather an American interpretation of Chinese culture, the effort, nonetheless, was genuine. One proud parent announced that "we shop at Asian markets, we go to festivals." Her daughters loved pandas, could identify China on a map, and could recite all the Chinese spoken in *Big Bird Goes to China*. The parents also networked with each other, exchanging information and child-rearing tips through Internet organizations such as Families with Children from China.

The adoption process sensitized thousands of parents to subtle racism in America. Suddenly they noticed the often cruel stereotypes of the Chinese in the media, even in children's television programs like *Sesame Street*, which featured a female worm-puppet named "Lo Mein." They became more attentive to the treatment of foreign aliens by the Immigration and Naturalization Service, and aggressively lobbied for citizenship rights for their children. Annoyed by the red tape required to naturalize their Chinese babies, adoptive parents have demanded legislation to allow citizenship immediately and retroactively for all adopted foreign-born children. As a consequence, these children are serving as bridges between the Caucasian and ethnic Chinese communities in the United States. "I began to see children and their 'differences' in a new light," one mother explained. "Suddenly the nonwhite kids weren't 'nonwhite,' they were 'like my daughter.' "

It is ironic that some infants who had been discarded like garbage in the PRC ended up in some of the most affluent households in the United States, while thousands of adult Chinese worked for years to earn their passage to America. These nonstudent, nonprofessional adult immigrants were the group least visible to the white community, a group largely made up of illegal menial laborers hidden in the nation's Chinatowns.

Some started as part of a "floating" migrant population of peasant workers in China, a population estimated to be as high as 200 million to 250 million people for the year 2000. Drifting from the countryside into the cities, they serviced the needs of the urban Chinese nouveau riche, and, treated like second-class citizens, many yearned to migrate abroad, in order to secure better wages and a better future for their children. Others came from the small business or entrepreneur class in China, frustrated by a system that favored those with political clout and by the incessant need to bribe the powerful in order to survive. A factory owner from Fuzhou claimed that when he refused to pay extortion money to local officials, they accused him of a crime he had not committed. "That's why I left in a hurry," he later said. "I made up my mind in a few days." Others echoed similar dissatisfaction. According to Xiao Chen, formerly an illegal alien from Fuzhou, "In China today, unless you are the child of an official, or know how to open back doors, it's hopeless."

For many ambitious Chinese, only three choices seemed open: to resign oneself to one's station in life; to master the game of politics; or to leave. The globalized Western media made the third alternative the most enticing. During the Deng era, the glamorous lives of Hollywood celebrities reached the Chinese masses through satellite dishes and VCRs.* By the early 1990s, the prospect of unlimited wealth in America had infected the Fuzhou region with immigration fever. One cause for the perceived differences in national wealth was the exaggerations of movie and television dramas, but the greatest reason could be found in hard numbers. In 1991, the per capita income in the United States was $22,204, compared to a figure that ranged between $370 and $1,450 in China, leading many Chinese to become obsessed with the prospect of making a quick fortune in America. "Everyone went crazy," the *Sing Tao Daily* reported. "The area was in a frenzy. Farmers put down their tools, students discarded their books, workers quit their jobs, and everyone was talking about nothing but going to America . . . If people found out someone had just successfully arrived in the United States, his or her home will be crowded with people, both acquaintances and strangers, to come to collect information about going to America."

Even though the United States granted an annual quota of twenty thousand immigration slots to the PRC, these usually went to the Chinese with education, official connections, or relatives in the United States. Consequently, many of the poorer or less-educated Chinese had to emigrate illegally, turning to the underworld for help, to achieve their Western dream. No one knows how many resorted to

---

*Many believed that America was synonymous with wealth, and viewed their relatives in the United States as "Gold Mountain uncles" and tycoons. When visiting ancestral villages during the 1980s, Chinese Americans reported excessive demands for money and gifts, a culture consumed by greed. "Those friends and relatives would all want money from you," one Chinese American remembered. He was appalled to find that his PRC relatives scorned certain gifts, such as a black-and-white television set, because they had expected something more expensive. "They were all dissatisfied, they'd wanted a color model. We don't even have one ourselves."

such methods, for it is not the nature of illegal operations to maintain records. Estimates range from ten thousand to one hundred thousand people a year, but an exact figure is impossible: "It's like trying to pin jello to a wall," said one FBI agent in New York.

These arrivals bore a striking resemblance to the first wave of Chinese who arrived during the nineteenth century. Both émigré waves consisted largely of young, able-bodied adult men with wives and families remaining in their native land. According to a survey conducted by Ko-lin Chin, a professor in the School of Criminal Justice at Rutgers University, most illegal Chinese immigrants in New York City were married men between the ages of twenty and forty, former laborers with an elementary or junior high education. But instead of originating from Canton like the early waves, they came mostly from Fuzhou, a commercial and fishing city of five million in Fujian province in the south of China.

Like Canton, Fuzhou enjoyed a tradition of citizens migrating abroad and establishing overseas communities in other countries. Close-knit family relationships provided émigrés with international capital and extensive business networks. Fujian province, like Guangdong, was also renowned for its independence and entrepreneurial spirit. Historically, it had been a frontier country overrun by outlaws and adventurers, something like the Wild West in the United States. The Chinese stereotyped the Fujianese as ruthless and ambitious, obsessed with making their fortunes. It is notable that among the forty billionaires of Chinese heritage in Asia, over half either came from Fujian or were descended from Fujianese people.

The story of illegal Fujianese immigration to the United States was not new. Some of the first Fujianese arrivals were sailors who served as staff on ships of the American armed forces during World War II. Many jumped ship, then settled secretly in New York City or other areas along the East Coast. Almost six thousand Chinese crewmen, many of them Fujianese, deserted and entered the United States between 1944 and 1960. As a result, the first links—kinship ties—so helpful in establishing immigration patterns, were forged between the

United States and the Fujian region, especially the city of Fuzhou. By the end of the twentieth century, some PRC officials estimated that the vast majority of illegal Chinese aliens in the United States were natives of Fuzhou.

Clearly, some had left to escape political repression. Rutgers professor Ko-lin Chin, who surveyed dozens of illegal Fujian aliens, published some of their reasons for leaving. "During the Cultural Revolution, I was wrongfully labeled as a 'counterrevolutionary' and tortured," one said. "I was victimized under the one-child policy, and I am disgusted with the Communist regime," reported another. "When my wife was pregnant with our second child, she was forced to have an abortion five days before she was to give birth."

But the most popular reason for emigration was not political but economic. According to Ko-lin Chin, 61 percent of the people in his study cited one dominant reason: money. Dreams of riches abound in the responses collected in his survey. "I heard that everything was so nice in America, you can even find gold in the streets." "Before I came, I thought America was a very prosperous country, that it was a heaven filled with gold." "When overseas Chinese came back, they spent money like water . . . That's why I envied the American lifestyle before I came here." "When I was in China, I considered going to America as going to heaven." "For us, it doesn't mean freedom," a Chinese villager told a reporter when describing the Statue of Liberty. "It means opportunity."

To fill an insatiable demand for illegal immigration, organized crime figures—known as "snakeheads" for their stealth and speed—ran elaborate smuggling enterprises. By the end of the 1990s, the industry had become highly lucrative, earning up to $8 billion a year. Indeed, some international gangs came to favor human smuggling over narcotics, because the former was low-risk but highly profitable.

Smuggling was largely a game of cat-and-mouse played between the smugglers and the authorities. The first stage was routine. The snakehead would negotiate a fee for bringing the client to the United States (in the year 2000, the going rate was about $60,000 to $70,000).

After receiving part of the fee as a deposit, the smuggler would secure a list of telephone numbers and addresses of relatives in both Fujian province and the United States who could provide down payments for the journey.

The second stage—preparing the paperwork—was also relatively easy. The snakeheads secured exit visas by bribing PRC officials, and once out of China, the émigrés waited in safe houses in cities like Hong Kong or Bangkok while the snakeheads procured the travel documents necessary for their entry into the United States. Fake passports would be created by professional forgers, bought as stolen goods on the black market, or obtained from corrupt officials in North America.

For some émigrés, the wait was long and agonizing. One man from Fujian province said he was locked in a motel basement for six months in Bangkok before the smugglers placed him and others on a tiny boat headed for Africa, en route to the United States. Another immigrant, a farmer, was forced to hide in a pigsty for months in rural Thailand before the snakeheads flew him to Frankfurt and then Miami.

The actual journey was the most difficult part of all. With no one single route to the United States, Chinese illegal aliens could arrive from all directions, by air, sea, or land. A review of internal INS documents revealed Chinese smuggling rings in countries like Australia, Japan, Guam, Brazil, Spain, and Russia. Sometimes the Chinese were flown directly into the United States, and in the early 1990s about one in five illegal Chinese aliens entered the United States by plane. But a much safer strategy was to fly the Chinese immigrant into Canada or Mexico instead. Once in Canada, the immigrant could hide in the airport bathroom, flush his documents down the toilet, and then claim political asylum. After his release by immigration authorities, he could sneak over the border with counterfeit papers, hide in the trunk of a car, or travel by boat, inflatable raft, or snowmobile to New York State. Immigrants could also slip across the border from Mexico, in refrigerated trucks or tourist buses.

Most of the time, the Chinese illegal aliens were required to make the journey across water and land. Many hid aboard Taiwanese fishing boats or cargo ships that sailed for Central America, or traveled by rail to cities with lax or corrupt security, such as Moscow or Budapest. Some immigrants endured long train rides to Eastern Europe, during which they subsisted on scanty meals of rice and nuts, then attempted to cross the border into Western European countries. This might involve climbing mountains and swimming across rivers. "It is arduous and taxing—many don't make it," Beng Chew, a London solicitor, told a reporter in June 2000. "Last year, I heard one woman in her early 30s died from exhaustion in the mountains. Some of the others didn't want to leave her but the agent insisted that they carry on."

The dangers of the journey equaled or surpassed what nineteenth-century Chinese émigrés endured. Smuggling often entailed lethal conditions, such as boats made of rotting, crumbling wood; illegal Chinese aliens have described trips in which they were forced to bail water out of sinking ships. In one case, crew members abandoned a disabled vessel and considered dynamiting it with hundreds of passengers on board. In July 1995, the U.S. Coast Guard discovered 147 illegal aliens from China on a fishing boat that one American authority called "the most incredibly screwed-up, rusted-out vessel I've ever seen." The immigrants had squeezed into a room no larger than the width of two cars. Contaminated water filled the hold, and the air was fetid because the portholes were covered with plywood.

Not surprisingly, the journey for some Chinese ended in the morgue. In June 1993, the *Golden Venture,* a ship with more than 260 illegal Chinese passengers, ran aground two hundred yards from Rockaway Peninsula near New York City. The crew urged the immigrants to jump overboard and swim for shore. So close to reaching their America, the Chinese took a last risk. Ten drowned, while hundreds of others were rescued by the New York City police, the Immigration Service, and the Coast Guard. Some

Chinese émigrés died in Europe, which presumably many saw as a way station to the United States. In 1995, eighteen Chinese died of asphyxiation in a sealed trailer en route to Hungary. The following year, five Chinese corpses were discovered in a truck crossing the Austrian border. In the summer of 2000, authorities found one of the most grisly human smuggling tragedies yet: fifty-eight Chinese suffocated in a giant refrigerator of rotting tomatoes in Dover, England. When officials swung open the doors, they were met by the putrid stench of decay, and two survivors reaching out with torn bloody fingers, gasping, *"Bang wo! Bang wo!"* (Help me! Help me!)

The most frightening voyages occurred within sealed cargo containers on freight ships. Some illegal immigrants were literally boxed in for weeks, enduring the entire trip in near-darkness. Some were given a certain measure of comfort, such as fans, mattresses, and cell phones, while others arrived "awash in human waste," in conditions so filthy that immigration authorities had to don hazardous materials gear before entering. Many survived on starvation-level food and water rations: one Chinese boy who spent twelve days and nights in a cargo container said he had eaten nothing but water and crackers during the entire journey. He and his fellow passengers huddled under blankets on a mattress, used plastic bags as toilets, and played poker by flashlight to while away the time.

By early 2000, American immigration authorities found that smugglers had turned to hard-topped shipping containers. As U.S. immigration officials grew more aggressive—using dogs to sniff out humans in cargo containers—so did the smugglers, who invented even more daring tactics. In Los Angeles, investigators found fifteen Chinese stowaways in a hard-topped container with two doors cut in the sides. The smugglers had camouflaged the doors with epoxy and paint, attached hinges inside the container, and created ventilation systems and escape hatches with fans and car batteries. The danger of a hard-topped container is that stowaways can be entombed alive. If there are no secret doors, the Chinese have to wait until the snakeheads cut open a door—or slowly suffocate to death.*

Often the greatest threat to the Chinese emigrants was the snakeheads themselves. One twenty-four-year-old Fujianese who spent four months crossing the Pacific in a freighter said the smugglers withheld food and water from all females who refused to have sex with them. Another man reported a case in which the crew gave female passengers drinking water spiked with sleeping pills in order to rape them. On a rickety fishing boat intercepted by the U.S. Coast Guard in 1995, authorities discovered signs of severe mental and physical abuse among the 147 Chinese on board. The crew had sexually assaulted many of the male passengers, including boys as young as ten, forcing them to endure oral and anal intercourse, even group masturbation sessions. By the end of the trip, some were so seriously traumatized that they considered suicide.

Most Chinese, however, survived the journey—only to find that the worst was still to come. The snakeheads hid migrants in "safe houses" as they awaited payment from relatives for the journey. During their stay, the enforcers often charged exorbitant rates for basic necessities like food and water so that their debt would increase. Illegal aliens reported being charged a hundred dollars for a single international phone call.

Although many Chinese immigrants signed IOUs sealed with their own blood, upon arrival some were shackled and handcuffed to metal bed frames or heavy objects, kept in basements without light, and fed a little rice gruel. If their relatives were unable to pay in time, the smugglees might be doused in icy water, beaten, and starved. In 1991, the FBI broke into a Brooklyn apartment and found a Chinese

---

*Of course, the Chinese are not the only people who used desperate means to enter the country. Immigration officials can recite accounts of many nationalities employing extreme measures to get into the United States, such as strapping themselves to the landing gear of airplanes, where they might fall or freeze to death, or even cramming themselves into suitcases, in hopes of making it into American airports undetected.

man handcuffed to a bed, scarred with cigarette burns, and bludgeoned by crowbars. In 1994, the police arrested eight gangsters from Fuzhou who had chained prisoners to a ceiling and tortured them by yanking out their fingernails and thrusting red-hot irons into their backs. One woman whose family could not pay on time was raped and assaulted for months, an ordeal that left her paralyzed. Some Chinese reported being so abused in captivity that they grew desensitized to violence and lost all emotion. As one described his experience in the hands of the snakeheads, "After being there for a period of time, I had no sense of fear anymore because being punished became a daily routine."

The snakeheads often promised aspiring migrants that "they can make a fortune—maybe a million dollars—in two, three or five years," according to Yu Shuing, a spokesperson at the Chinese embassy in Washington. The reality was quite different. Without the government protection legal status afforded, Chinese laborers were at the mercy of their employers, and typically they found menial work through Chinatown employment agencies, jobs such as dishwasher, waiter, or factory worker. Reluctant to pay minimum wage when they could hire a Chinese illegal alien for half the amount, some sweatshop owners paid no wages to workers at all: when a manufacturing contract was completed, the owner would shut down the operation and move elsewhere. As a result, some Chinese bitterly regretted moving to America. "To tell you the truth, I feel like garbage in the United States," a construction worker said. "Here, we sleep on the floor, and we work like slaves . . . Those living with me in the same apartment cry all the time."

Overinflated rents worsened their misery. During the 1980s and 1990s, illegal Chinese aliens poured into Chinatowns just as businessmen from Taiwan and Hong Kong, jittery about political developments in Asia, invested their capital in American real estate. The result was a frenzy of speculation and soaring rents,* which pressured Chinatown

---

*A 1986 study conducted by the Real Estate Board of New York exposed shockingly high prices: in a community where rents were once lower than in Harlem, the cost of retail space on Chinatown's Canal Street surpassed even that on Wall Street.

sweatshop owners to slash payments to workers even further. In New York, Chinese laborers routinely worked twelve hours a day in unventilated garment shops with broken sprinkler systems and padlocked metal gates barring the fire escapes, conditions rivaling those in the ill-fated Triangle Shirtwaist factory, where a fire destroyed 146 lives in 1911.

After work, many Chinese aliens came home to dingy, crowded apartments, often rat-infested, dungeon-like basements with exposed rusty pipes, live wires, and asbestos. Instead of taking a private room, many rented bunk space—often little more than two-by-fours—for ninety dollars a month, and shared the cost with other illegal immigrants by sleeping in shifts. "Most of our villagers considered America heaven," K. T. Yang, president of the United Fujian American Association told a reporter in New York. "And they're now forced to live in hell."

Despite these hardships, the frugal living habits of these illegal Chinese aliens—such as sharing crowded apartments and eating at the restaurants that employed them—enabled many to clear their financial obligations within a few years. According to Ko-lin Chin, by the early twenty-first century Chinese smugglees typically worked off their debt to the snakeheads in four years, with the majority obtaining their green cards or U.S. citizenship within five or six years of their arrival. "They are hard-working and ambitious, which is why they are here," Chin said. "Sooner or later, most will find a way to legalize their status."

Over time, he noted, some of these naturalized Chinese Americans have become highly successful, opening their own take-out restaurants, garment factories, renovation companies, groceries, and other small businesses. "They now drive Mercedes-Benzes and own million-dollar homes," Chin said of several Chinese he had surveyed as illegal aliens years before. "Most don't have a lot of formal education or skills—you wouldn't see them in computers—but they are good entrepreneurs. Americans don't realize how creative they can be."

But unforeseen events could thwart even the best-laid plans, and during the first critical years in the United States—the years when illegal aliens struggled feverishly to pay off their debt—the opportunities for their extortion were endless. Snakeheads were known to threaten relatives of immigrants, hoping to squeeze more money out of them, even if they were not behind on their payments. "If smugglers want the money, they say they will kill the males and sell the girls into a brothel," one illegal Chinese alien said. In 1995, Chinese debt collectors kidnapped Gao Liqin, a thirty-eight-year-old immigrant seamstress, from her home in Queens, New York. The abductors woke her family in Fujian with a phone call in the middle of the night, demanding $38,000 in ransom. Weeping into the phone, Gao Liqin made desperate pleas to her parents to cooperate. But by sending their daughter to the United States, the Gao family still owed a $30,000 debt, and they could not raise the money. The kidnappers cut off her finger, stuffed her head into a plastic bag, gang-raped her, strangled her with a telephone cord, and crushed her skull by hitting her over the head with a TV set. Amazingly, this killing did not deter other members of the Gao family from planning to travel to America. "If you work hard and stay out of trouble, usually you are fine," her brother said. "We had bad luck."

Many illegal aliens believed that eluding the snakeheads was impossible. "You can hide for a few years, maybe a year or two, but you can't for a lifetime," said Wang Libin, a passenger on the ill-fated *Golden Venture* who was granted political asylum because of his activism during the 1989 pro-democracy movement in China. However, he still owed money to the smugglers. "You have friends, these friends have friends, you have family. They will find you. There's no way to hide."

As a result, many victims dared not report snakehead crimes to the authorities. For even if they did, neither the police nor the INS would have the manpower, time, or money to crack down on the underground world of Chinese smugglers. Nor did officials have any incentive to do so.* During the 1990s, critics charged that neither the

---

*American police have been known to commit anti-Chinese hate crimes. In January 1987, New York City police officers appeared at the doorstep of a Chinatown

U.S. government nor the People's Republic of China enforced their immigration laws because the American garment industry relied on or exploited illegal Chinese aliens, and the mainland Chinese economy benefited from overseas remittances.

Given these unfavorable conditions, then, why did the Chinese continue to come? For those considering emigration, the prospect of their being exploited was only half of the equation. The other half was how their families would benefit from remittances sent home. During the 1990s, the fruits of émigré labor transformed entire regions in China, studding the Fuzhou landscape with mansions. Many were elegant stone houses with traditional moon gates and round windows; others were cheap, gaudy replicas of European castles, sparkling with pink or gold tiles, resembling the architecture of Las Vegas and Disneyland. Some were six stories tall, complete with elevators, swimming pools, luxury cars, and satellite dishes. Within these ostentatious homes, occupants wore gold jewelry and carried cell phones— flashy displays of wealth that provoked envy among neighbors and inspired others to emigrate.

Like suburban bedroom communities, these Chinese neighborhoods were filled with wives and children, except the men were working not in a nearby city but on another continent. By the end of the 1990s, so many wives were left behind in Fujian province that their home villages were known as "widow villages." Some "widows" built mansions piecemeal. Looming over rice paddies were half-constructed

---

apartment to investigate charges that the occupants had illegal access to cable TV. When the Wongs, a Chinese couple, asked to see a warrant, the police apparently broke down the door, yelling, "Why don't you Chinese go back to China?" and struck both of them. (Mrs. Wong, hit in the face with handcuffs, later required twelve stitches.) They later sued the police department and settled for $90,000. In January 1991, a New York City policeman pulled over Zhong Guoqing for running a red light. But Zhong, a Chinese émigré, failed to understand the officer's demand to see his registration, which so enraged the cop ("Are you a wise guy?" he asked) that he handcuffed Zhong and pounded his head. Zhong was wounded so severely that he spent the night in the hospital and suffered the partial loss of vision in one eye.

palatial homes, some with bare concrete inside, awaiting fresh infusions of cash from the United States. They evoked memories of the fortresses in Toishan, built by relatives of the earliest Chinese immigrants. Indeed, the people of Fujian were repeating a pattern from the nineteenth century—impoverished, overworked Chinese émigrés laboring under conditions of near-slavery in the United States, supporting families who lived like gentry in China. By the end of the twentieth century, a culture of leisure had already settled among the young in Fujian province. Everyone knew that laborers who earned $40 a month in China could make $2,000 in the United States. "So no one in the village works before they go to America," one immigrant's wife told a reporter. "There's no point."

In many areas, even the wives and mothers were missing. Some villages have been reduced to "ghost towns," as one scholar put it, "populated only by old people caring for very young children whose parents are working in garment factories on the Lower East Side of Manhattan and the Chinese takeout restaurants scattered across the 50 states." Because these communities lost their most productive adults—almost all men and women between the ages of eighteen and forty-five—child care responsibilities fell primarily on the shoulders of doting but aged grandparents. In 1999, the *New York Times* reported that female garment workers were paying a $1,000 fee, plus airfare, to have their infants safely delivered from New York Chinatown to their families in Fujian. So while some of the most affluent Americans were importing Chinese babies for adoption, many of the poorest Chinese women were shipping their babies—U.S. citizens by American birth—back to their home villages, to join the ranks of a new Chinese aristocracy.

Many illegal aliens felt the money was worth the risk, the heartbreak, and the fractured families. Some believed their children would ultimately benefit from the arrangement: "I am sacrificing myself to bring happiness to my family," one Chinese worker said. Others groped toward an elusive but enticing vision of future paradise. "Look at your salary," Fuzhou native Cho Li Muwang told an

American reporter after two failed attempts to leave China. "If you can go to some other place, even very far away, across the ocean, and work the same, but make ten times more money, would you go? What about twenty times more? What about one hundred times more? Would you go?"

CHAPTER TWENTY

An Uncertain Future

> *My grandfather came to this country from China nearly a*
> *century ago and worked as a servant. Now I serve as gov-*
> *ernor just one mile from where my grandfather worked.*
> *It took our family one hundred years to travel that mile.*
> *It was a voyage we could only make in America.*
>
> —Governor Gary Locke of Washington State,
> the first Chinese American governor in the
> United States, January 28, 2003

My book chronicles only the past and present journey of the Chinese in America, not where their story will go from here. Each new generation must rediscover history in the light of new events, and so it must be left to future scholars to continue the narrative.

Instead, I can only close this book with a fervent hope: that readers will recognize the story of my people—the Chinese in the United States—not as a foreign story, but a quintessentially American one.

From the moment the Chinese set foot on American soil, their dreams have been American dreams. They scrambled for gold in the dirt of California. They aspired to own their own land and businesses, and fought to have their children educated in American schools alongside other American children. Like most immigrant groups, they came here fleeing war and famine, persecution and poverty. And like the descendants of other immigrant groups, their children have come to call the United States home.

The America of today would not be the same America without the achievements of its ethnic Chinese. Generation after generation, they worked to build the American nation to its present level of greatness. Some fought in the Civil War and built the railroad that welded the country together. Their early struggles for justice created new foundations of law later used by the civil rights movement. They built America's earliest rockets and helped win the cold war. In Silicon Valley and elsewhere, their contributions helped establish and maintain U.S. supremacy in the information age. Today, they are dispersed in every profession imaginable: as inventors, teachers, authors, doctors, engineers, lawyers, CEOs, social workers, accountants, architects, police chiefs, firefighters, actors, and astronauts.

But sadly, despite this long legacy of contribution, many Chinese Americans continue to be regarded as foreigners. "Go back where you came from" is a taunt most new immigrants have faced at some point. As one put it, "Asian Americans feel like we're a guest in someone else's house, that we can never really relax and put our feet up on the table." Accents and cultural traditions may disappear, but skin tone and the shape of one's eyes do not. These features have eased the way for some to regard ethnic Chinese people as exotic and different—certainly not "real" Americans. Thus the Americanization of Chinese Americans has been overshadowed by the convenient but dishonest stereotypes in the mass market, which portray them as innately and irreversibly different from their fellow Americans.

What, in human terms, is the impact of such divisiveness? It's a native-born Californian, a West Covina city council member, being told over the phone, "Funny, you don't sound like a Wong. You sound so *American*." It's the virtual absence of Chinese American doctors on medical TV dramas, when in actuality one in every six medical doctors in the United States is Asian American. It's a famous Chinese American movie star with good reviews in serious work reporting that she and her colleagues are always asked by studios to "don our accents and use our high kicks à la Jackie Chan or a Bond girl." It's the decision of the Mattel toy company not to release an Asian Barbie doll in their year 2000 fantasy collection of future female American presidents, even though white, black, and Hispanic dolls are included. ("People like Asian-American dolls in costumes, not as president," notes Berkeley professor Elaine Kim. "This tells us how we are thought of.")

In June 1999, Ted Lieu, a United States Air Force captain who grew up in Ohio and attended college in California, wrote the following for the *Washington Post*:

"Are you in the Chinese Air Force?" the elegantly dressed lady sitting next to me asked. For a moment I was left speechless. We were at an awards dinner and I was proudly wearing my blue United States Air Force uniform, complete with captain's bars, military insignia, and medals. Her question jarred me and made me realize that even Air Force blue was not enough to reverse her initial presumption that people with yellow skin and Asian features are somehow not Americans. I wish this was just an isolated incident. Unfortunately, too many people today still view Asian Americans as foreigners in America . . . As an officer in the United States Air Force, one day I may be called to give my life to my country. It would be a shame if some people still question what I mean when I say "my country."

Scratch the surface of every American celebrity of Chinese heritage and you will find that, no matter how stellar their achievements, no matter how great their contribution to U.S. society, virtually all of them have had their identities questioned at one point or another.

Connie Chung, the second woman in American history to co-anchor a network nightly news broadcast, survived an unwelcoming newsroom atmosphere. Being one of the few women was bad enough, but as she adds, "In those early days at CBS, '71 to '76, people were saying 'Yellow Journalism'—little remarks that were clearly racist." But as late as 1990, Cliff Kincaid, a radio host in Washington, D.C., would call her "Connie Chink."

Maya Lin, now the most famous female architect in the United States, was viciously attacked when, as a Yale undergraduate in 1980, she won a nationwide contest to design the Vietnam Veterans Memorial in Washington, D.C. "How can you let a gook design this?" some veterans asked. "How did it happen that an Asian-American woman was permitted to make a memorial for American men who died fighting in Asia?"*

After her novel *The Joy Luck Club* became a literary blockbuster, author Amy Tan had to struggle to get it produced in Hollywood. Before the movie was released, one film executive complained to Chris Lee, the Chinese American president of Columbia TriStar, that there were "no Americans" in *The Joy Luck Club*. Lee retorted, "There are Americans in it. They just don't look like you."†

At the 1998 Olympics, when U.S. figure skater Michelle Kwan finished second after her teammate Tara Lipinski, the headlines on MSNBC read, "American beats Kwan." Many Chinese Americans were distressed that the media automatically considered Kwan a foreigner when in fact she had been born, reared, and trained in the United

---

*Lin later noted her loyalty and patriotism to the United States. "If you ask, I would identify myself as Chinese American," she wrote in *Art in America* in 1991. "If I had to choose one thing over the other, I would choose American. I was not born in China, I was not raised there, and the China my parents knew no longer exists . . . I don't have an allegiance to any country but this one, it is my home."

†*The Joy Luck Club* interwove Tan's family history with the fictional stories of four American women and their immigrant Chinese mothers. No other novel by an Asian American writer had achieved such success in the history of publishing—it topped the *New York Times* best-seller list and sold 4.5 million copies by 1997. The film appeared in 1993, directed by Wayne Wang and based on a screenplay co-written by Tan and Ron Bass.

States. Four years later, this error was repeated after Kwan lost the gold medal to Sarah Hughes. In a secondary headline, the *Seattle Times* announced, "American outshines Kwan, Slutskaya in skating surprise."

In 1998, when Matt Fong, a California state treasurer, ran for the U.S. Senate, reporters asked him which country he would support if China and the United States went to war. Fong was a fourth-generation American and the son of March Fong Eu, the first Asian American woman to serve as a California secretary of state. He lost the race and later told *Time* magazine, "There is a subtle stereotyping and racism below the surface."

In May 2001, David Wu, the first Chinese American ever elected to the U.S. House of Representatives, was stopped when he tried to enter the Department of Energy in Washington, D.C. "Most strikingly I was asked a couple of times whether I am a U.S. citizen or not," Wu later said. "This was both after I showed my congressional ID and after Ted Liu [Wu's congressional aide] showed him his staff ID."

In 2001, Elaine Chao, a Harvard Business School graduate who had served as chairman of the Federal Maritime Commission and assistant secretary of transportation, made history as the first Chinese American to accept a Cabinet position when President George W. Bush named her secretary of labor. When her critics attacked her business ties with China, her husband, Senator Mitch McConnell (R-Ky.) saw "subtle racism," "yellow fever," and xenophobic attitudes in the media.

Time and again, the question is posed within the Chinese American community: How many hoops do we have to jump through to be considered "real" Americans?

These episodes of racism do not occur by accident, in a vacuum. Nor do they arise solely on the basis of physical differences. Throughout American history, and indeed the history of most societies, the ruling class has carefully exploited differences in race and ethnicity as a mechanism of control—as a convenient smokescreen to make their own control more palatable. Racism has often divided and diminished

American labor—by thwarting the union of white and colored workers to help them win on issues that affect them all—and has enabled
the government to expand its scope of authority during emergencies,
such as economic depression, or war. At such times, entire ethnic
groups can be vilified and sacrificed as scapegoats to rally other people behind a leader's solution. Such was the fate of the Chinese in
America on the eve of the exclusion era.

As this book neared completion, anti-Chinese sentiment rose
again, in a resurgence of hatred reminiscent of the pre-exclusion days.
This time, it derived its energy from popular fear of sweeping international forces: the globalization of the economy and the rise in power
and prestige of the People's Republic of China.

At the dawn of the third millennium, China emerged, both economically and militarily, as a global superpower. Chinese industrial
and technological development rushed forward at such breathtaking
speed that some economic experts anointed the twenty-first century
as the "Chinese century."* In September 2001, China joined the
World Trade Organization, signifying its full legitimacy in the international marketplace and resuscitating fears that American jobs
would be lost to Chinese hordes willing to work for very little. At the
same time, the decline of the former Soviet empire stoked American
fears about China's armed forces, which command the third largest
nuclear arsenal in the world as well as the greatest military in Asia.
Washington has wavered between depicting China as our newest trad-

*Foreign correspondents and academics have also observed the coming of age of a
new generation of Chinese "superkids" or "little emperors"—the fruit of China's
one-child policy—for whom no sacrifice or expense was too great for their parents to
provide with the best education possible. The American press noted the presence of
musical and mathematical prodigies in Chinese kindergartens, of Chinese high school
students scoring triple 800s on the Graduate Record Examination. China watchers
predicted that the twenty-first century would soon witness a Chinese renaissance of
genius in science, literature, and the arts, matching or perhaps even surpassing the
United States.

ing partner and market and, with the demise of the Soviet bloc, as the successor enemy in the post–cold war era.*

A telling incident occurred in April 2001, when a Chinese fighter jet over the South China Sea, apparently flying too close to an American navy spy plane on a routine U.S. surveillance mission, caused the American pilot to take sudden evasive action, resulting in a midair collision. The Chinese pilot was killed and the Chinese government detained the twenty-four American crew members of the spy plane after they made an emergency landing on China's Hainan Island. After eleven days of tense negotiations and a carefully worded apology from the United States, the PRC released the crew, but by that time the Chinese American community had suffered a fierce backlash from their fellow Americans. Patrick Oliphant, a Pulitzer Prize–winning cartoonist, published a shocking caricature of a Chinese man, complete with buck teeth and thick glasses, serving cat gizzards. The *National Review* complained that the Chinese "put MSG in everything" and claimed, "if my dog were a member of the American crew Jiang Zemin would have eaten him by now."

During the spy plane crisis, recalls Theresa Ma, a Chinese American chemist in Lincoln, Nebraska, a neighbor approached her and asked, "Why don't you go to China to bring our men home?" This neighbor could not figure out the difference between Chinese Americans and Chinese foreign nationals—despite the fact that many Chinese Americans were U.S. citizens whose families had lived here for generations.

---

*For example, in October 2000, the Republicans ran a television commercial suggesting that electing Al Gore for president might result in nuclear annihilation by the People's Republic of China. The commercial claimed that China had "the ability to threaten our homes with long-range nuclear warheads" because the Clinton-Gore administration "sold" out the nation's security "to Communist Red China in exchange for campaign contributions." The advertisement featured a little white girl plucking daisy petals as she counted backward. Her counting was abruptly followed by the countdown for a missile, and then a nuclear explosion. "Don't take a chance," the commercial warned. "Please vote Republican." This TV ad was a remake of the

Some members of the media recommended the mass dismissal or expulsion or even imprisonment of the entire Chinese American community. In Springfield, Illinois, two radio deejays urged the boycott of all Chinese American restaurants, suggested that all Chinese Americans be shipped out of the country, and telephoned people with Chinese last names to harass them. A Fox News host called for Chinese employees to be fired from the national laboratories. A national talk-show host demanded that Chinese Americans be interned by the federal government, as the Japanese Americans were during World War II.*

Surveys have demonstrated the depth of anti-Chinese sentiment. A 2001 Gallup poll found that more than 80 percent of Americans viewed the PRC as "dangerous." In another poll, a national telephone survey commissioned by the Committee of One Hundred and the Anti-Defamation League of 1,216 randomly selected adult Americans, close to half thought that Chinese Americans "passing secrets to the Chinese government is a problem." Almost a third believed Chinese

---

well-criticized 1964 "Daisy" commercial, made for President Lyndon Johnson and implying that the views of his opponent, Barry Goldwater, would lead to an atomic war. The "Daisy" remake provoked a furor in the Chinese American community, which accused the Republican Party of playing the "yellow peril" card.

*Even newspaper editors openly indulged in anti-Chinese stereotypes. In April 2001, Amy Leang, a Chinese American college senior, began an internship at the *ASNE Reporter*, a publication of the American Society of Newspaper Editors, during its convention in Washington, D.C. Assigned to photograph the performance of a comedy troupe during the convention's opening reception, Leang watched, to her surprise, a crudely racist skit about U.S.-Chinese relations. What was particularly disturbing was that the audience for the skit comprised those who represented themselves as leaders among American editors. As she later wrote, "White males impersonated a Chinese official and his translator. The official sported a black wig and thick glasses and spoke fake Chinese. 'Ching ching chong chong,' the man shouted as he gestured wildly. What was disturbing was not just the fact that this was happening, but that hundreds of editors, my future bosses, were laughing. I felt myself swallowed by all the loud laughter. Each time the 'Chinese' voice became more jarring, the editors would laugh even harder. Despite feeling humiliated, I finished the job and turned in my pictures. The next morning, I woke up crying."

Americans were more loyal to the PRC than to the U.S. And in the political arena, Chinese and other Asian Americans stood out as the most unpopular candidates of all. Among those surveyed, more people felt reluctant to vote for an Asian American president than for a woman, an African American, or a Jewish American.

For the Chinese American community, these polls confirmed many of their worst fears—that their acceptance was linked to the ever-shifting relations between the United States and China rather than to their own particular behavior. It was sobering to consider that, more than a century after passage of the Chinese Exclusion Act, they were still perceived by many to be strangers in their own country.

The anti-Chinese backlash engendered much soul-searching and debate within the Chinese American community. The late 1990s and early 2000s saw endless, frantic discussions on how to prove one's loyalty to the United States, or whether to confront these attitudes with organized protests. Some immigrants began to blame themselves for being too complacent—for immersing themselves in their careers and families, and not braving the risks of participation in affairs of the larger world. On Internet chat groups and in public forums, they openly questioned whether they had been giving the right message to the next generation. Was it, perhaps, short-sighted to discourage their children from careers in the media and the arts, careers that could influence public perception of Chinese Americans, in favor of the more anonymous fields of science and technology? Could the putative security offered by such fields have been nothing more than an illusion? Were they wrong to warn their children to avoid politics? Could their own memories of repressive regimes in Asia have nudged them toward a safe haven of political apathy in the United States?

The national hostility to Chinese Americans also provoked high-profile discussions among community leaders and prominent activist groups such as the Organization of Chinese Americans, the Committee of One Hundred, and 80/20.* Some advocated bloc-vote strategies to give the community greater political clout; others discussed devoting more resources to public relations and philanthropy; still others encouraged ethnic Chinese to drape American flags over their windows. Like so many other immigrants, Chinese Americans knew they had made a genuine, permanent contribution to the United States, a place they now called home. They wanted to create a future where honoring one's heritage, and embracing one's country patriotically, would not be considered conflicting desires.

Though there was often much disagreement about the best route to take, no one doubted that some kind of collective political action was needed. As David Ho, the renowned AIDS researcher and *Time*'s Man of the Year in 1996, reminded other Chinese Americans, "We need our Jesse Jacksons and Al Sharptons to scream bloody murder when an injustice is carried out against our community."

This had to be done not only for themselves, but for the future of their children. American-born Chinese youths were also eloquently voicing their concerns about the difficulty and confusion inherent in growing up a minority, and the triple pressures weighing on them: the pressure to excel, the pressure to become white, and the pressure to embrace their ethnic heritage. Some felt they had to work harder, to perform twice as well as whites and be content with half the rewards. Others confessed embracing racial shame, trying to obliterate their Chinese heritage. While in many instances this rejection meant dating only whites and forfeiting the language and traditions of their ances-

---

*The Organization of Chinese Americans (OCA) is a Washington, D.C.–based civil rights lobbying group founded by Kung Lee Wang in 1973. The Committee of One Hundred (C100) is a nonpartisan organization of prominent Chinese Americans, designed to promote Sino-American relations and address crucial issues within the Chinese American community. The intent of the 80/20 initiative, organized by S. B. Woo, a Chinese American physicist and former lieutenant governor of Delaware, is to persuade 80 percent of the registered Asian American voters to support a single endorsed presidential candidate, the person most likely to provide policy benefits for the ethnic Asian community.

tors, in extreme cases it extended to surgically altering their eyelids to look more Caucasian. Yet others took the opposite tack, befriending and dating only other Chinese Americans, traveling to China to find spouses, or exploring their identity through genealogical research programs in China.

When it comes to fighting racism, no easy solutions exist. Perhaps the best hope for change lies in education, coupled with greater participation in the American democratic process. The future of Chinese Americans will depend on their ability to reclaim their voices—their ability to speak out, make their presence felt, and break out of the model-minority mold that has permitted others to define and dictate the form and extent of their success. Their obligations are no different from those of all Americans. We must exercise both our rights and responsibilities as patriotic citizens: voting and running for office, engaging in dialogue with lawmakers, airing our political opinions in the broader media, exposing systemic abuse and injustice within the government and other institutions. It is not enough to make a speech or just wave a flag, though—we need to make firm challenges to our government and ourselves to honor the civil liberties of all Americans. It is our right as Americans, our privilege, and our responsibility.

Only when American society is truly empowered by education and committed to respect for the human rights of all will it attain the confidence to see race and culture for what it is—a dynamic, ever-changing life force. The future is impossible to predict, but I believe the definition of "Chinese America" itself will grow more complex with time. Already the lines between the ethnic Chinese and other groups are blurring. The Chinese in the United States marry other Asians in record numbers, and the concept of "Chinese American" may be replaced by a new racial identity: "Asian American." Meanwhile, marriages between Chinese Americans and non–Asian Americans have produced new generations that resist easy labels. Indeed, for some, ethnic identity has become a matter of personal choice as much as indisputable racial appearance or heritage.

Take, for instance, the actor Cy Wong. His great-grandfather migrated from Cuba to Louisiana in 1867 to work as an indentured plantation laborer. After fulfilling the term of his contract, he remained in the American South and married a Creole woman. His son, Cy Wong's grandfather, married a mixed-race Native American woman of Choctaw and black ancestry, and Wong's father married a woman of Chickasaw and black descent. Wong, president of the Chinese Historical Association of Southern California, acknowledges that some people have difficulty accepting his Chinese identity. "From time to time, I have had to deal with prejudices, especially from some African Americans," he wrote in the *Los Angeles Times*. "They'll say, 'well, you may look a little Chinese, but you're still black.' I'm not denying that my pigmentation is dark, but the true color of a man is what's on the inside." When asked, "Who are you, and where are you from?" Cy Wong responded, "I am a descendant of an African native, a Chinese native, and a native American Indian. But *my* nativity is American. I fought for America. I spent six years for America in the Navy. I am a true American."

And then there is Lisa See, author of *On Gold Mountain*, whose great-great-grandfather, a Chinese herbalist, came to America in 1867. With her freckles, pale skin, and red hair, See does not look Chinese, but she has many stories to tell about her Chinese ancestors on the western frontier. Even though her great-grandmother, grandmother, and mother were all white, Lisa See grew up culturally Chinese, spending much of her childhood in her family's antique store in Los Angeles Chinatown. As an adult, she was astonished to find that others did not view her as a Chinese American. "Many of the Chinese people I interviewed talked about Caucasians as *lo fan* and *fan gway*, as white people, 'white ghosts,' " See wrote. "Often someone would say, by way of explanation, 'You know. She was a Caucasian like you.' They never knew how startling it was for me to hear that, because all those years in the store and going to those wedding banquets, I thought I was Chinese. It stood to reason, as all those people were my relatives. I had never really paid much attention to the fact that I had red hair like my [maternal] grandmother and the rest of them had straight black hair . . . Though I don't physically look Chinese, like my grandmother I am Chinese in my heart."

Once the rare exception, multiethnic Americans like Cy Wong and Lisa See are rapidly becoming the norm. Between 1969 and 1989, the number of children born to Chinese-Caucasian couples more than tripled. In 2000, scholars estimated that there were some 750,000 to 1 million multiracial Asian Americans in the United States.*

Mixed-race Americans of Chinese heritage have also achieved celebrity status, pushing the issue of their ethnicity into the spotlight. Tiger Woods, the world-famous golfer, has described himself as "Cablinasian" to embrace his white, black, Indian, Thai, and Chinese roots. And in Hollywood, a growing number of stars—Keanu Reeves, Russell Wong, Meg Tilly, Kelly Hu, Tia Carrere, and Phoebe Cates among them—are part Chinese.†

While some racially mixed Americans have retained their Chinese culture, others have taken on a brand-new identity. Many children of white-Chinese unions are now calling themselves "Hapa," a word that originated in Hawaii to describe the children of white merchants and native Hawaiians. Later, it referred to those with half-white, half-Japanese heritage, and now it is commonly used to describe all mixed-race people of some Asian ancestry. Hapa organizations have proliferated on college campuses such as Stanford, Berkeley, Harvard, Cornell, and the University of Washington. Indeed, Hapas are now

---

*Interracial marriages soared after 1967, when the Supreme Court in *Loving* v. *Virginia* declared all anti-miscegenation laws unconstitutional. Before the ruling, it was still illegal for white people to marry out of their race in sixteen states, but the landmark Supreme Court decision helped spawn an interracial baby boom.
†In the past, only a few Eurasian actors achieved stardom, and they were typically cast as Asian, not white. The two most famous Hapa stars were Bruce Lee, who popularized Chinese martial arts in films like *Enter the Dragon,* and Nancy Kwan, immortalized for her roles in *The World of Suzie Wong* and *Flower Drum Song.*

coming into their own as a political force and a burgeoning social movement: Hapa conferences, a Hapa magazine (*MAVIN*), and Hapa social clubs. Universities even offer courses in Hapa history.

As Hapas grow in number, they are asserting their freedom to celebrate the richness of their heritage, as are other multiethnic individuals. In the year 2000, for the first time in American history, the U.S. government permitted people to acknowledge their mixed-race heritage on the census by checking more than one box. When Cy Wong filled out his census form, he drew arrows to three boxes to emphasize his black, Chinese, and Native American lineage, and then wrote "Tri-ethnic and American" in the margin.

These trends provoke new questions: What is racial identity? Who gets to decide it? The government? The experts? Or the people themselves?

Though some find it convenient to see race as solid blocs of humanity, easily organized and controlled by bureaucracies on the basis of shared interests, the reality of individual life defies such neat compartmentalization. In reality, race is—and has always been—a set of arbitrary dividing lines on a wide spectrum of color, blending, almost imperceptibly, from one shade to the next.

Perhaps one day we will rediscover a basic truth—that while identity may be shaped and exploited by the powerful, its essence belongs, ultimately, to the individual. America was founded on this concept, but has never achieved its ideal.

Our founding fathers articulated a dream of creating a unique form of government, a democracy that would protect from the tyranny of the majority the rights of the minority, down to the individual. Unfortunately, this dream was, and continues to be, a far cry from the realities of American life. Despite their lofty rhetoric, many of the authors of the Constitution and the Bill of Rights owned slaves and did not believe that their privilege of freedom extended to women, minorities, or even non-landowners. And tragically, over the past two centuries, this country—in its dealings with blacks, Native Americans, and other ethnic groups—broke faith with the promise of these founding documents. Consequently, the history of America, like the history of so many other countries, has been one long struggle with group identity, an ongoing struggle, with an ever-unclear outcome.

The subjugation of individual rights to the group, leading inevitably to ultranationalism, has long been a cause and justification for war and genocide across the planet. It was to escape the oppression of group identity—the burden of racial antagonisms, inherited by blood—that thousands of Chinese and other immigrants abandoned the homes of their ancestors, for unknown futures in a strange land. Only time can tell if their journey will have been successful. This will depend entirely on whether America can continue to evolve toward the basic egalitarian concept upon which it was founded—"that all men are created equal, that they are endowed by their Creator with certain unalienable Rights, that among these are Life, Liberty, and the pursuit of Happiness." For it was the haunting, elusive dream that such a place really existed that first drew many of the Chinese to American shores.

NOTES

Chapter One. The Old Country: Imperial China in the Nineteenth Century

For nineteenth-century eyewitness descriptions of China, see Mrs. J. F. Bishop (Isabella L. Bird), *The Yangtze Valley and Beyond: An Account of Journeys in China, chiefly in the province of Szechuan and among the Man-Tze of the Somo Territory* (London: John Murray, Albemarle Street, 1899); Robert Fortune, *A Residence Among the Chinese; Inland, on the Coast and at Sea* (London: J. Murray, 1856); Robert Fortune, *Three Years of Wandering in the Northern Provinces of China, including a visit to the tea, silk and cotton countries: with an account of the agriculture and horticulture of the Chinese, new plants, etc.* (London: J. Murray, 1847); John Scarth, *Twelve Years in China; The People, the Rebels, and the Mandarins; By a British Resident* (Edinburgh: Thomas Constable and Company, 1860); Bayard Taylor, *A Visit to India, China and Japan; In the Year 1853* (New York: G. P. Putnam, 1862).

13   **60 million *liang* of silver:**   Jacques Gernet, *A History of Chinese Civilization,* translated by J. R. Foster (Cambridge, England, and New York: Cambridge University Press, 1982), pp. 530–31.

14   **Lin confiscated 20,000 chests of opium:**   Gernet, p. 537.

15   **"Should I break his nose or kill him":**   Paul Carus, "The Chinese Problem," *Open Court XV* (October 1901), p. 608, as cited in Robert McClellan, *The Heathen Chinee: A Study of American Attitudes Toward China, 1890–1905* (Columbus: Ohio State University Press, 1971), pp. 88–89.

17   **Guangdong credit crisis in 1847:**   Madeline Y. Hsu, *Dreaming of Gold, Dreaming of Home: Transnationalism and Migration Between the*

United States and South China, 1882–1943 (Stanford, Calif.: Stanford University Press, 2000), p. 25.

17   **a hundred thousand laborers found themselves unemployed:**   Ibid., p. 25.

17   **a Chinese resident in California wrote a letter:**   *San Francisco Chronicle*, July 21, 1878.

19   **"Swallows and magpies":**   Marlon K. Hom, "Rhymes Cantonese Mothers Sang," *Chinese America: History and Perspectives 1999* (Brisbane, Calif.: Chinese Historical Society of America, 1999), p. 63.

Chapter Two. America: A New Hope

20   **23 million people:**   Clyde A. Milner II, Carol A. O'Connor, and Martha A. Sandweiss, eds., *The Oxford History of the American West* (New York: Oxford University Press, 1994), p. 814.

20   **430 million:**   Jonathan D. Spence, *The Search for Modern China* (New York: W. W. Norton, 1990), p. 210.

20   **towns of more than 2,500 people:**   Clyde A. Milner II, Carol A. O'Connor, and Martha A. Sandweiss, p. 814.

21   **Population statistics for Paris and London:**   Adna Ferrin Weber, *The Growth of Cities in the Nineteenth Century: A Study in Statistics* (Ithaca, N.Y.: Cornell University Press, 1963), p. 450.

21   **a mere six cities in the United States had more than 100,000 people:**   Robert Sobel and David B. Sicilia, *The Entrepreneurs: An American Adventure* (Boston: Houghton Mifflin, 1986), p. 119.

21   **New York population in mid-nineteenth century:**   Adna Ferrin Weber, p. 450.

21   **Description of New York and Brooklyn:**   Ruth Barnes Moynihan, Cynthia Russett, and Laurie Crumpacker, eds., *Second to None: A Documentary History of American Women* (Lincoln: University of Nebraska Press, 1993), p. 209.

21   **Information on Irish and German immigrants:**   Roger Daniels, *Coming to America: A History of Immigration and Ethnicity in American Life* (New York: HarperPerennial, 1990), pp. 129, 146.

22   **Life expectancy data on China and the United States:**   James I. Lee and Wang Feng, *One Quarter of Humanity: Malthusian Mythology and Chinese Realities* (Cambridge, Mass.: Harvard University Press, 1999), p. 54; Michael Haines, "The Population of the United States, 1790–1920," in Stanley L. Engerman and Robert E. Gallman, eds., *The Cambridge Economic History of the United States* (Cambridge and New York: Cambridge University Press, 1996–2000), p. 159; Michael R. Haines, "Estimated Life Tables for the United States, 1850–1910," *Historical Methods* 31:4 (Fall 1998).

23–24   Life in American Midwest: M. H. Dunlop, *Sixty Miles from Content-ment: Traveling in the Nineteenth-Century American Interior* (New York: HarperCollins, 1995); Catherine Reef, *An Eyewitness History: Working America* (New York: Facts on File, 2000), p. 7.

24   **"people were settling right under his nose":**   Lillian Schlissel, *Women's Diaries of the Westward Journey* (New York: Schocken, 1982), p. 20.

25   **Statistics on American Indians:**   Clyde A. Milner II, Carol A. O'Con-nor, and Martha A. Sandweiss, p. 175; Howard Zinn, *A People's History of the United States: 1492–Present* (New York: HarperCollins, 1999; first Perrenial Classics edition, 2001), p. 125.

26   **On the number of Chinese before gold rush:**   Him Mark Lai, "The United States," in Lynn Pan, ed., *The Encyclopedia of the Chinese Over-seas* (Cambridge, Mass.: Harvard University Press, 1999), p. 261.

26   **Information on Afong Moy; "monstrously small":**   *New York Times,* November 12, 1834.

27   **Barnum exhibit; twenty thousand spectators:**   John Kuo Wei Tchen, "Staging Orientalism and Occidentalism: Chang and Eng Bunker and Phineas T. Barnum," *Chinese America: History and Perspectives 1996* (Brisbane, Calif.: Chinese Historical Society of America, 1996), p. 119.

27   **A "double-jointed Chinese dwarf Chin Gan":**   John Kuo Wei Tchen, *New York Before Chinatown: Orientalism and the Shaping of American Culture* (Baltimore: Johns Hopkins University Press, 1999), p. 97.

27   **Details on Chang and Eng Bunker:**   John Kuo Wei Tchen, "Staging Orientalism and Occidentalism, pp. 93–131; Ruthanne Lum McCunn, "Chinese in the Civil War: Ten Who Served," *Chinese America: History and Perspectives 1996;* John Kuo Wei Tchen, *New York Before China-town,* pp. 106–13, 134–42; Irving Wallace and Amy Wallace, *The Two* (New York: Simon & Schuster, 1978).

Chapter Three. "Never Fear, and You Will Be Lucky": Journey and Arrival in San Francisco

29   **"Americans are very rich people":**   Diane Mei Lin Mark and Ginger Chih, *A Place Called Chinese America* (Dubuque, Iowa: Kendall/Hunt Publishing Company, 1982; Organization of Chinese Americans, 1993), p. 5.

30   **three-quarters of a million Chinese men:**   Robert J. Schwendinger, "Investigating Chinese Immigrant Ships and Sailors," in Genny Lim, ed., *The Chinese American Experience: Papers from the Second National Conference on Chinese American Studies (1980),* p. 16. An estimated 250,000 Chinese were shipped to Cuba and 87,000 to Peru between 1847 and 1874, according to Laura L. Wong, "Chinese Immigration and Its

Relationship to European Development of Colonies and Frontiers," in
Genny Lim, ed., *The Chinese American Experience*, p. 37.

30   **"without a danger of being hustled":**   H. F. MacNair, *Modern Chinese
History: Selected Readings* (Shanghai: Commercial Press, 1927), pp.
409–10; Jack Chen, *The Chinese of America* (New York: Harper and
Row, 1980), p. 21.

30–31   **Description of coolie trade—the kidnappings and South American
conditions:**   Lynn Pan, *Sons of the Yellow Emperor: A History of the
Chinese Diaspora* (New York: Kodansha America, 1994), pp. 67–69;
Madeline Y. Hsu, *Dreaming of Gold, Dreaming of Home*, p. 34; John
Kuo Wei Tchen, *New York Before Chinatown*, pp. 49–50. Tchen
describes how American shipbuilders created the slave ships used for the
coolie trade, and that the guano harvested by the Chinese fertilized the
topsoil of Maryland tobacco plantations.

32   **forty dollars in gold:**   Thomas W. Chinn, H. Mark Lai, and Philip P.
Choy, eds., *A History of the Chinese in California: A Syllabus* (San Francisco: Chinese Historical Society of America, 1969), pp. 14–15; William
Speer, *An Humble Plea* (San Francisco, 1856), p. 7. According to historian Haiming Liu, the trip cost $40–$60 and it took 35 to 45 days to
travel from Guangdong to California. (Haiming Liu, "Between China
and America: The Trans-Pacific History of the Chang Family," Ph.D.
dissertation, University of California, Irvine, 1996.)

32   **Travel conditions over Pacific:**   Jack Chen, *The Chinese of America*, p.
23; Sylvia Sun Minnick, *Samfow: The San Joaquin Chinese Legacy*
(Fresno, Calif.: Panorama West Publishing, 1988), p. 8; Liping Zhu, *A
Chinaman's Chance: The Chinese on the Rocky Mountain Mining Frontier* (Niwot: University Press of Colorado, 1997), p. 24.

32   **"The food was different":**   Lee Chew, "Life Story of a Chinaman," p.
289, as cited in Ronald Takaki, *Strangers from a Different Shore: A History of Asian Americans* (New York: Little, Brown, 1989; reprinted by
Penguin Books, 1990), p. 68.

33   *Libertad:*   Jack Chen, p. 23.

34   **Description of San Francisco before the gold rush:**   J. Hittel, *A His-
tory of the City of San Francisco and Incidentally of California* (San
Francisco: A. L. Bancroft and Company, 1878), pp. 398–400; Edward
Kemble, "Reminiscences of Early San Francisco," in Joshua Paddison,
ed., *A World Transformed: Firsthand Accounts of California Before the
Gold Rush* (Berkeley, Calif.: Heyday Books, 1999), pp. 309, 315.

34   **Description of San Francisco in 1848:**   Christopher Lee Yip, "San Francisco's Chinatown: An Architectural and Urban History," Ph.D. dissertation in architecture, University of California, Berkeley, 1985, p. 11;
Joshua Paddison, ed., *A World Transformed: Firsthand Accounts of California Before the Gold Rush*, p. 311; David E. Eames, *San Francisco Street
Secrets* (Baldwin Park, Calif.: Gem Guides Book Company, 1995), p. 51.

34   **boom town of thirty thousand:** David E. Eames, p. 44.

34   **46 gambling halls, 144 taverns, and 537 places that sold liquor:** Ibid., p. 48.

35   **"worthy of an Empress":** Lucius Morris Beebe, *San Francisco's Golden Era* (Berkeley, Calif.: Howell-North, 1960), p. 12.

35   **Women were scarce:** David E. Eames, p. 44.

35   **92 percent of California was male:** Clyde A. Milner II, Carol A. O'Connor, and Martha A. Sandweiss, *The Oxford History of the American West*, p. 815.

35   **"Every man thought every woman in that day a beauty":** Curt Gentry, *The Madams of San Francisco: An Irreverent History of the City by the Golden Gate* (Garden City, N.Y.: Doubleday, 1964), p. 33.

35   **Information on brothels:** Mary Ellen Jones, *Daily Life on the Nineteenth-Century American Frontier* (Westport, Conn.: Greenwood Press, 1998), p. 152.

36   **five murders every six days:** David E. Eames, p. 66.

36   **"Committee of Vigilance" history:** Ibid., pp. 68–78.

36   **Description of San Francisco culture:** Ibid., p. 66.

37   **more than half of the San Francisco population was foreign-born:** Julie Joy Jeffrey, p. 143.

Chapter Four. Gold Rushers on Gold Mountain

38   **Information on Chinese costumes:** Edward Eberstadt, ed., *Way Sketches; Containing Incidents of Travel Across the Plains, From St. Joseph to California in 1850, With Letters Describing Life and Conditions in the Gold Region by Lorenzo Sawyer, Later Chief Justice of the Supreme Court of California* (New York, 1926), p. 124, as cited in Gunther Barth, *Bitter Strength: A History of the Chinese in the United States 1850–1870* (Cambridge, Mass.: Harvard University Press, 1971), p. 114.

39   **"allow a couple of Americans to breathe in it":** Gunther Barth, p. 114; *San Francisco Herald*, November 28, 1857.

39   **"wonderfully clean":** J. D. Borthwick, *Three Years in California, 1851–1854* (Edinburgh: Blackwood and Sons, 1857 [also Oakland, Calif.: Biobooks, 1949]), p. 44; Benson Tong, *Unsubmissive Women: Chinese Prostitutes in Nineteenth Century San Francisco* (Norman and London: University of Oklahoma Press, 1994), p. 13.

39   **"They are quiet":** Vardis Fisher and Opal Laurel Holmes, *Gold Rushes and Mining Camps of the Early American West* (Caldwell, Idaho: The Caxton Printers, Ltd., 1990), p. 272.

39   **"It was a mystery":** Ibid., p. 262.

39   **forty-pound nugget:** Pauline Minke, "Chinese in the Mother Lode (1850–1870)," thesis, California History and Government Adult Education, 1960, Asian American Studies Library, University of California at Berkeley, p. 27. (Later published as book—San Francisco: R and E Research Associates, 1974.)

40   **240-pound nugget:** Ibid., p. 27.

40   **friendly Shoshone and Bannock Indians:** Liping Zhu, *A Chinaman's Chance*, p. 28.

40   **water wheel:** Sucheng Chan, *Asian Americans: An Interpretative History* (New York: Twayne Publishers [imprint of Simon & Schuster], 1991), p. 29.

40   **Tin mining:** David Valentine, "Chinese Placer Mining in the United States: An Example from American Canyon, Nevada," in Susie Lan Cassel, ed., *The Chinese in America: A History from Gold Mountain to the New Millennium* (Walnut Creek, Calif.: Alta Mira Press, 2002), p. 40.

40   **Yuba River:** Isaac Joslin Cox, *Annals of Trinity County* (Eugene, Ore.: John Henry Nash of the University of Oregon, 1940), p. 210, as cited in Pauline Minke, p. 26.

40   **irrigation ditch from the Carson River to Gold Canyon:** *Origins & Destinations: 41 Essays on Chinese America / A Joint Project of Chinese Historical Society of Southern California and UCLA Asian American Studies Center* (Los Angeles: Chinese Historical Society of Southern California and UCLA Asian American Studies Center, 1994), p. 113; Jack Chen, p. 256.

40   **"wailings of a thousand lovelorn cats":** Charles Dobie, *San Francisco's Chinatown* (New York and London: D. Appleton-Century Company, 1936), p. 42, as cited in James L. Boyer, "Anti-Chinese Agitation in California, 1851–1904: A Case Study on Traditional Western Behavior," master of arts thesis, San Francisco State College, p. 112.

41   **"About every third Chinaman runs a lottery":** John Hoyt Williams, *A Great and Shining Road: The Epic Story of the Transcontinental Railroad* (Lincoln: University of Nebraska Press, 1989), p. 99.

41   **"We don't know and don't care":** Vardis Fisher and Opal Laurel Holmes, *Gold Rushes and Mining Camps of the Early American West*, p. 262.

41   **"He assaulted me without provocation":** Diane Mei Lin Mark and Ginger Chih, *A Place Called Chinese America*, p. 6.

41   **Information on Joaquin Murieta:** Pauline Minke, *Chinese in the Mother Lode*, pp. 34–35.

42   **"their presence here is a great moral and social evil":** Diane Mei Lin Mark and Ginger Chih, p. 32.

42   **"tide of Asiatic immigration":** Roger Daniels, *Asian America: Chinese and Japanese in the United States Since 1850* (Seattle: University of Washington Press, 1988), p. 35. Original citation: John Bigler, Governor's Special Message, April 23, 1852, p. 4.

42   **Commutation tax:** Charles J. McClain, "California's First Anti-
      Chinese Laws," *Chinese America: History and Perspectives 1995* (Bris-
      bane, Calif.: Chinese Historical Society of America, 1995), p. 91.

42   **Taxes:** Otis Gibson makes reference to a 1876 statement by the Chi-
      nese Six Companies which complained that the Chinese paid taxes on
      personal property, the foreign miner's tax, $200,000 in annual poll taxes,
      and more than $2 million in duties to the Custom House of San Fran-
      cisco. Otis Gibson, *The Chinese in America* (reprint edition, New York:
      Arno Press, 1979; original published in 1877 by Hitchcock & Walden in
      Cincinnati), p. 321.

42   **barred from the city hospital:** Robert J. Schwendinger, "Investigating
      Chinese Immigrant Ships and Sailors," *The Chinese American Experi-
      ence: Papers from the Second National Conference, Chinese American
      Studies (1980)*, p. 21.

43   **Information on foreign miner's tax:** Cheng-Tsu Wu, ed., *"Chink!" A
      Documentary History of Anti-Chinese Prejudice in America* (New York:
      World Publishing Company, 1972), pp. 4, 11; Charles J. McClain, "Cali-
      fornia's First Anti-Chinese Laws," p. 91; Chen-Yung Fan, "The Chinese
      Language School of San Francisco in Relation to Family Integration and
      Cultural Identity," Ph.D. dissertation in education, Duke University,
      1976, p. 44.

43   **"I had no money to keep Christmas with":** Charles Dobie, p. 50, as
      cited in James Boyer, p. 119.

43   **tied the Chinese to trees:** Pauline Minke, p. 46.

43   **"I was sorry to have to stab the poor fellow":** Vardis Fisher and Opal
      Laurel Holmes, p. 261; Charles Dobie, p. 50.

43   **runners to sprint from one village to the next:** Pauline Minke, p. 47.

43   **Maidu Indians:** Gunther Barth, p. 145.

44   **"no black or mulatto person":** Charles J. McClain, "California's First
      Anti-Chinese Laws," p. 100.

44   **"same type of human species":** Ibid., pp. 101, 140. The full text of
      Murray's opinion can be found in Cheng-Tsu Wu, ed., *"Chink!,"* pp.
      3–43.

44   **"soon see them at the polls":** Charles J. McClain, "California's First
      Anti-Chinese Laws," p. 101. Also, *People* v. *Hall* case file, October 1,
      1854, California State Archives, Sacramento.

44   **"Any failing to comply":** Diane Mei Lin Mark and Ginger Chih, *A
      Place Called Chinese America*, p. 32.

45   **In El Dorado County, white miners torched Chinese tents:** Victor
      G. and Brett de Bary Nee, *Longtime Californ': A Documentary Study of
      an American Chinatown* (New York: Pantheon, 1972, 1973), p. 37.

45   **"opened the way for almost every sort of discrimination against the
      Chinese":** Elmer Clarence Sandmeyer, *The Anti-Chinese Movement in*

California (Urbana: University of Illinois Press, 1991; original edition published in 1939), p. 45.

45   **picked over abandoned claims:** The historical record suggests that the Chinese miners were extremely thorough. As one contemporary observed, "When a Chinaman gets through going over the diggings with a comb, there ain't enough gold left to fill a bedbug's mouth." Nelson Chia-Chi Ho, "Portland's Chinatown: The History of an Urban Ethnic District," in Paul D. Buell, Douglas W. Lee, and Edward Kaplan, eds., *The Annals of the Chinese Historical Society of the Pacific Northwest* (The National Trust for Historic Preservation, 1984), p. 31.

45   **Ah Sam:** Autobiography of Charles Peters, pp. 143–45, as cited in Gunther Barth, *Bitter Strength,* p. 116.

45   **dilettante ancestors:** For example, interview with Rodney Chow, #149, Southern California Chinese American Oral History Project.

45   **Wong Kee:** Sue Fawn Chung, "Destination: Nevada, the Silver Mountain," *Origins & Destinations: 41 Essays on Chinese America,* p. 119.

46   **First ship to sail from Canton:** H. Brett Melendy, *Chinese and Japanese Americans* (New York: Hippocrene Books, 1984), p. 15; Hubert Howe Bancroft, *History of California,* Vol. 7 (San Francisco: The History Company, 1890), p. 336.

46   **"two or three 'Celestials' ":** *San Francisco Star,* April 1, 1848.

46   **325 Chinese arrived:** Ronald Takaki, *Strangers from a Different Shore: A History of Asian Americans* (New York: Little, Brown, 1989; reprinted by Penguin Books, 1990), p. 79.

46   **450 in 1850:** Ibid., p. 79.

46   **90 percent quickly moved to rural mining camps:** Laverne Mau Dicker, *The Chinese in San Francisco: A Pictorial History* (New York: Dover Publications, 1979), pp. 355–370, as cited in Qingsong Zhang, "Dragon in the Land of the Eagle: The Exclusion of Chinese from U.S. Citizenship, 1848–1943," Ph.D. dissertation, University of Virginia, 1994, p. 196.

46   **Information on "little China" in San Francisco:** Christopher Lee Yip, "San Francisco's Chinatown: An Architectural and Urban History," Ph.D. dissertation in architecture, University of California at Berkeley, 1985, pp. 85, 90–94; Chin-Yu Chen, "San Francisco's Chinatown: A Socio-Economic and Cultural History, 1850–1882," Ph.D. dissertation in history, University of Idaho, 1992, p. 27; Curt Gentry, *The Madams of San Francisco,* p. 55.

47   **more than 2,716 new immigrants:** Chin-Yu Chen, p. 29.

47   **by 1852 the number had jumped to more than twenty thousand:** Ibid., p. 29.

47   **gathering of some three hundred Chinese:** *San Francisco Daily Alta California,* December 10, 1849.

48   **Description of Chinese restaurants:** Christopher Lee Yip, pp. 144–46; Otis Gibson, *The Chinese in America,* pp. 70–71; Chin-Yu Chen, p. 95.

48   **"The best eating houses":**   William Shaw, *Golden Dreams and Waking Realities* (1851), as cited in Jack Chen, *The Chinese of America*, p. 57.

48   **chop suey:**   National Public Radio, *All Things Considered* transcript 2320-9, August 29, 1996; Robert Cross, "Chop Suey: Alive and Selling Well in American Restaurants; Beginnings of the Cuisine Lost, but Popularity Remains High," *Chicago Tribune*, February 11, 1988.

49   **twelve dollars for a dozen shirts:**   Jack Chen, p. 58.

49   **four months:**   Ibid., p. 58.

49   **Wah Lee:**   Paul Siu, *The Chinese Laundryman: A Study in Social Isolation* (New York: New York University Press, 1987), p. 46.

49   **curio stores:**   J. D. Borthwick, *Three Years in California* (Oakland, Calif.: Biobooks, 1948), p. 61, as cited in Chin-Yu Chen, pp. 28–29.

49   **"mere shells":**   *San Francisco Daily Alta California*, November 22, 1853, as cited in Christopher Lee Yip, p. 86.

49   **$200 a month:**   *The Oriental*, as cited in Chin-Yu Chen, p. 28.

50   *Gold Hills News:*   *Gold Hills News*, May 4, 1868, in Chin-Yu Chen, pp. 28, 41.

50   **"It is a little singular":**   Edward C. Kemble, *A History of California Newspapers 1846–1858. Reprinted from the Supplement to the Sacramento Union of December 25, 1858* (Los Gatos, Calif.: Talisman Press, 1962), p. 161.

50   **from a prefabricated kit:**   L. Rodecap, "Celestial Drama in the Golden Hills," *California Historical Quarterly*, 23:2 (June 1944), p. 101, as cited in Christopher Lee Yip, p. 149.

50   **"two or three months are generally consumed":**   Otis Gibson, *The Chinese in America*, pp. 78–79.

51   **prominent place in the memorial procession:**   Theodore Hittel, *History of California*, Vol. 4 (San Francisco: N. J. Stone, 1898), pp. 98–99, as cited in Charles J. McClain, "California's First Anti-Chinese Laws," *Chinese America: History and Perspectives 1995*, p. 88.

51   **Mayor John Geary:**   *San Francisco Daily Alta California*, May 12, 1851, p. 2.

51   **"China Boys will yet vote at the same polls":**   *San Francisco Daily Alta California*, May 12, 1851, as cited in Victor Low, *The Unimpressible Race: A Century of Educational Struggle by the Chinese in San Francisco* (San Francisco, California: East/West Publishing Company, 1982), p. 2.

51   **"Many have already adopted your religion as their own":**   Mary Roberts Coolidge, *Chinese Immigration* (New York: Henry Holt, 1909), p. 55. Also in Victor Low, p. 2.

51   **"morally a far worse class":**   *San Francisco Daily Alta California*, May 21, 1853, p. 2, as cited in Victor Low, pp. 2–3. Also in H. Brett Melendy, *Chinese and Japanese Americans*, p. 30.

52   **"How long, sir":**   Qingsong Zhang, Ph.D. dissertation, 1994, p. 46.

Chapter Five. Building the Transcontinental Railroad

55 **Eight hundred laborers:** Tzu-Kuei Yen, "Chinese Workers and the First Transcontinental Railroad of the United States of America," Ph.D. dissertation, St. John's University, 1976, p. 34.

55 **"unsteady men, unreliable":** David Haward Bain, *Empire Express: Building the First Transcontinental Railroad* (New York: Viking, 1999), p. 208.

55 **close to fifty thousand:** John Hoyt Williams, *A Great and Shining Road: The Epic Story of the Transcontinental Railroad* (Lincoln: University of Nebraska Press, 1989), p. 95.

55 **hired fifty Chinese anyway:** Tzu-Kuei Yen, p. 33.

56 **"I will not boss Chinese!":** Thomas W. Chinn, H. Mark Lai, and Philip P. Choy, eds., *A History of the Chinese in California: A Syllabus* (San Francisco: Chinese Historical Society of America, 1969), p. 44.

56 **four feet ten . . . and weighed 120 pounds:** Stephen E. Ambrose, *Nothing Like It in the World* (New York: Simon & Schuster, 2000), p. 150.

56 **race of people who had built the Great Wall of China:** John Hoyt Williams, pp. 96–97; Lynne Rhodes Mayer and Kenneth E. Vose, *Makin' Tracks: The Story of the Transcontinental Railroad in the Pictures and Words of the Men Who Were There* (New York: Praeger, 1975), p. 27.

56 **"quiet, peaceable, patient":** Southern Pacific Relations Memorandum, *The Chinese Role in Building the Central Pacific*, January 3, 1966. Also Charles Nordhoff, *California, A Book for Travelers and Settlers* (New York, 1873), pp. 189–90. Both cited in Thomas W. Chinn, H. Mark Lai, and Philip P. Choy, p. 45.

56 **"dregs" of Asia:** Tzu-Kuei Yen, pp. 40–42.

56 **"I like the idea":** William Deverell, *Railroad Crossing: Californians and the Railroad, 1850–1910* (Berkeley: University of California Press, 1994), p. 15. Also Stephen E. Ambrose, p. 243.

57 **Central Pacific recruitment tactics:** David Haward Bain, *Empire Express*, p. 331. Charlie Crocker hired a Chinese artist to engrave the recruitment information onto woodblocks and printed 5,000 handbills, which were posted in China and California.

57 **"inherent and inalienable right of man":** Erika Lee, "Enforcing and Challenging Exclusion in San Francisco: U.S. Immigration Officials and Chinese Immigrants, 1882–1902," *Chinese America: History and Perspectives 1997* (Brisbane, Calif.: Chinese Historical Society of America, 1997), p. 3.

57 **transported by riverboat to Sacramento:** Stephen E. Ambrose, p. 161.

57 **organized into teams of about a dozen:** David Haward Bain, p. 221.

57 **foreman:** Thomas W. Chinn, H. Mark Lai, and Philip P. Choy, p. 44.

57   special ingredients like cuttlefish: Lynne Rhodes Mayer and Kenneth E. Vose, *Makin' Tracks*, p. 32.

57   slept in tents: Thomas W. Chinn, H. Mark Lai, and Philip P. Choy, p. 45.

57   employ more than ten thousand Chinese men: Sucheng Chan, *Asian Americans: An Interpretative History* (New York: Twayne Publishers, 1991) p. 30.

57   "persecuted not for their vices":   Stephen E. Ambrose, p. 153.

58   "always outmeasured the Cornish miners":   Charlie Crocker's testimony, November 25, 1876. Bancroft Library, University of California at Berkeley. Crocker also said of the Chinese, "They are very trusty; and they are very intelligent, and they live up to their contracts."

58   "I think we were paying $35 a month and board to white laborers": cited in David Haward Bain, p. 222.

58   "damned nagurs":   David Haward Bain, p. 222.

58   driving the Chinese off the job: Tzu-Kuei Yen, p. 36.

58   ten barrels of gunpowder: John Hoyt Williams, p. 115.

59   handheld drills: Neill C. Wilson and Frank J. Taylor, *Southern Pacific: The Roaring Story of a Fighting Railroad* (New York: McGraw-Hill, 1952), p. 18.

59   porphyritic rock: John Hoyt Williams, p. 115.

59   seven inches a day: Ibid.; Lynne Rhodes Mayer and Kenneth E. Vose, p. 40.

59   a million dollars for each mile of tunnel: Tzu-Kuei Yen, p. 126.

59   several shifts of men: Tzu-Kuei Yen, p. 129; Neill C. Wilson and Frank J. Taylor, p. 19.

59   nitroglycerin: Neill C. Wilson and Frank J. Taylor, p. 18. Also, John Hoyt Williams, p. 133.

59   an ancient method used to create fortresses: Stephen E. Ambrose, p. 156.

60   salt beef, potatoes, bread: Lynne Rhodes Mayer and Kenneth E. Vose, p. 32.

60   fresh boiled tea: Ping Chiu, *Chinese Labor in California, 1850–1880: An Economic Study* (Madison: State Historical Society of Wisconsin for the Department of History, University of Wisconsin, 1963), p. 49; Lynne Rhodes Mayer and Kenneth E. Vose, p. 32.

60   "not having acquired the taste of whiskey":   Tzu-Kuei Yen, p. 35.

60   "a sort of hydrophobia":   John Hoyt Williams, p. 98. Original citation: Pamphlet by B. S. Brooks, *The Chinese in California*, San Francisco, possibly 1876. Bancroft Library, University of California at Berkeley.

60   thirty-foot drifts: John Hoyt Williams, p. 130.

60   "Homeric winter":   John Hoyt Williams, p. 143.

60   eighty feet high: Lynne Rhodes Mayer and Kenneth E. Vose, p. 52.

60   Power snowplows: Tzu-Kuei Yen, p. 123.

60   **Sheds:** Lynne Rhodes Mayer and Kenneth E. Vose, p. 52.

60   **horses broke the icy crust:** John Hoyt Williams, p. 143; Original cita-
        tion: George Kraus, *High Road to Promontory* (Palo Alto, Calif.: Amer-
        ican West Publishing Company, 1969), p. 148.

60   **Norwegian postal worker:** John Hoyt Williams, p. 144.

60   **carved a working city under the snow:** John Hoyt Williams, pp.
        143–44. Also Wesley S. Griswold, *A Work of Giants* (New York:
        McGraw-Hill, 1962), pp. 191–92.

61   **"a gang of Chinamen":** *Dutch Flat Enquirer,* December 25, 1866, as
        cited in Thomas W. Chinn, H. Mark Lai, and Philip P. Choy, p. 45.

61   **corpses still standing erect:** Ronald Takaki, *Strangers from a Different
        Shore,* p. 86; *Railroad Record,* October 31, 1867, p. 401, as cited in John
        Hoyt Williams, p. 161.

61   **Landslides:** John Hoyt Williams, p. 115.

61   **Melting snow:** Tzu-Kuei Yen, p. 121.

61   **plummet to 50 degrees below zero:** Tzu-Kuei Yen, p. 132.

61   **soar above 120:** John Hoyt Williams, p. 208.

61   **twelve-hour shifts:** Tzu-Kuei Yen, p. 37.

61   **on Sundays:** *Origins & Destinations: 41 Essays on Chinese America,*
        p. 125.

61   **two-thirds those of white workers:** Tzu-Kuei Yen, p. 111.

61   **a fourth those of white foremen:** Tzu-Kuei Yen, p. 130.

61   **allocation for feed for horses:** Ibid., p. 130.

62   **endured whippings:** Ibid., p. 38; Stephen E. Ambrose, p. 241. The his-
        torical record suggests that Strobridge had difficulty viewing the Chinese
        as human beings. "I used to quarrel with Strobridge when I first went
        in," Crocker told a biographer. "Said I, 'Don't talk so to the men—they
        are human creatures—don't talk so roughly to them.' Said he, 'You have
        got to do it, and *you* will come to it; you cannot talk to them as though
        you were talking to gentlemen, because they are not gentlemen. They are
        about as near brutes as they can get.' " (David Haward Bain, p. 208.)

62   **brink of bankruptcy:** John Hoyt Williams, p. 181; Tzu-Kuei Yen,
        p. 28.

62   **two thousand Chinese in the Sierras walked off the job:** Thomas W.
        Chinn, H. Mark Lai, and Philip P. Choy, p. 45.

62   **a list of demands:** Tzu-Kuei Yen, pp. 130–31; Thomas W. Chinn, H.
        Mark Lai, and Philip P. Choy, p. 46. According to Chinn, Lai, and Choy,
        the workers demanded a raise to forty dollars a month and a reduction of
        work to ten hours in the open and eight hours in the tunnels.

62   **circulated . . . a placard:** Tzu-Kuei Yen, pp. 130–31.

62   **an attempt to recruit ten thousand recently freed American blacks:**
        John Hoyt Williams, p. 181.

62   **cut off the food supply:** John Hoyt Williams, p. 181.

Notes

Notes

62 **strike lasted only a week:** Tzu-Kuei Yen, pp. 39, 130–31.

62 **raise of two dollars a month:** Ping Chiu, p. 47

62 **"If there had been that number of whites in a strike":** Stephen E. Ambrose, p. 242.

63 **Description of Irish harassment and Chinese retaliation:** Tzu-Kuei Yen, pp. 143–44.

63 **ten miles of track a day:** David Haward Bain, p. 639.

63 **wager $10,000:** Stephen E. Ambrose, p. 348. A witness to the competition raved about the Chinese, "I never saw such organization as this; it is just like an army marching across over the grounds and leaving a track built behind them." (Stephen E. Ambrose, p. 350.)

63 **690 miles of track:** "Condition of the Union Pacific Railroad." Letter from the Secretary of the Interior, Transmitting Report of Isaac N. Morris, one of the Commissions appointed to examine the unaccepted portions of the Union Pacific Railroad. June 3, 1876, Referred to the Committee on the Pacific Railroad. June 20, 1876, Ordered to be printed. Forty-fourth Congress, 1st Session, House of Representatives, Ex. Doc. No. 180.

63 **1,086 miles:** Ibid.

64 **one thousand Chinese railroad workers died:** An estimated 1,200 Chinese died out of 10,000 to 12,000 Chinese workers. (*The Asian American Almanac*, p. 46; Connie Young Yu, "Who Are the Chinese Americans?," in Susan Gall, managing ed., and Irene Natividad, executive ed., *The Asian American Almanac: A Reference Work on Asians in the United States* [Detroit: Gale Research, 1995]; Lynne Rhodes Mayer and Kenneth E. Vose, 28.) *The Harvard Encyclopedia of American Ethnic Groups*, p. 219, gives the figure of 12,000 to 14,000 Chinese workers. William Chew, a descendent of a transcontinental railroad worker, found through his research that on average for every two miles of track laid, three Chinese laborers died in accidents (*Salt Lake Tribune*, May 11, 1999).

64 **twenty thousand pounds of bones:** Lynn Pan, *Sons of the Yellow Emperor: A History of the Chinese Diaspora* (New York: Kodansha America, 1994), p. 55.

64 **journey back to the Sierra Nevada to search for the remains of their colleagues:** Connie Young Yu, "John C. Young, A Man Who Loved History," *Chinese America: History and Perspectives 1989* (San Francisco: Chinese Historical Society of America, 1989), p. 6.

64 **excluded from the ceremonies:** Sucheng Chan, *Asian Americans*, p. 31.

64 **laid off most of the Chinese workers:** Ibid., p. 32.

64 **refusing to give them even their return passage:** Ibid.

64 **retained only a few hundred:** Ibid., p. 32.

64 **converted boxcars:** *Origins & Destinations: 41 Essays on Chinese America*, p. 129.

418Notes

Chapter Six. Life on the Western Frontier

66   whites were paid seven dollars a day, the Chinese only two dollars or less: Leigh Bristol-Kagan, "Chinese Migration to California, 1851–1882: Selected Industries of Work, the Chinese Institutions and the Legislative Exclusion of a Temporary Work Force," Ph.D. dissertation in history and East Asian languages, Harvard University, 1982, p. 38.

66   "shaking, toothless wrecks": Edwin Clausen and Jack Bermingham, *Chinese and African Professionals in California: A Case Study of Equality and Opportunity in the United States* (Washington, D.C.: University Press of America, 1982), p. 14.

67   austere Chinese work ethic all but disappeared: Madeline Y. Hsu, *Dreaming of Gold, Dreaming of Home*, p. 42.

67   "when the ships occasionally cannot [sail]": Madeline Y. Hsu, p. 42.

67   "simple, reverential, and thrifty": Zhiqiu Pan, *Ningyang Cundu (Ningyang deposited letters)* (Toishan: n.p., 1898), as cited in Madeline Y. Hsu, p. 40.

68   "In a flash": Ibid.

68   "various charities are everywhere": Madeline Y. Hsu, pp. 41–42.

68   beheaded some seventy-five thousand suspected participants: Jack Chen, p. 16.

69   clashes killed two hundred thousand people: Madeline Y. Hsu, p. 27.

70   "red-haired, green-eyed foreign devils": R. David Arkush and Leo O. Lee, eds., *Land Without Ghosts: Chinese Impressions of America from the Mid-Nineteenth Century to the Present* (Berkeley and Los Angeles: University of California Press, 1989), p. 16; Lee Chew, "The Life Story of a Chinaman," in Hamilton Holt, ed., *The Life Stories of Undistinguished Americans* (New York: J. Pott, 1906), p. 285.

70   "[A]s we walked along the streets": "Life History and Social Document of Mr. J. S. Look," Seattle, August 13, 1924 by C. H. Burnett, p. 1. Major Document 182, Box 27, Survey of Race Relations, archives of the Hoover Institution on War, Revolution and Peace, Stanford University. (The hair color, clothes, and courtship rituals of white Americans provoked the most interest among Chinese immigrants, judging from their memoirs.)

70   "barbarian women": R. David Arkush and Leo O. Lee, p. 34.

70–71 "cacophony of dingdang noises": Ibid., p. 34.

71   "a great bother": Ibid., pp. 35–36.

71   "ritual of touching lips together": Ibid., p. 38.

71   "requires making a chirping sound": Ibid., p. 38.

72   only one in ten California farm laborers was Chinese: Betty Lee Sung, *The Story of the Chinese in America* (New York: Collier, 1971), pp. 35–36. Carey McWilliams, *California, the Great Exception* (New York: Current Books, 1949), p. 152.

72 **one in two:** Ibid.

72 **almost nine in ten:** By 1886, the Chinese comprised 85.7 percent of the California agricultural force. Susan Auerbach, *Encyclopedia of Multiculturalism*, Vol. 2 (New York: Marshall Cavendish, 1994), p. 372.

72 **two-thirds of the vegetables:** Jack Chen, *The Chinese of America*, p. 84; *Origins & Destinations*, p. 437.

72 **reclamation of the Sacramento–San Joaquin delta:** C. D. Abbott, a landowner who employed Chinese laborers, asserted that "white men refused to work up to their knees in the water, slime and filth"; Sandy Lydon, *Chinese Gold: The Chinese in the Monterey Bay Region* (Capitola, Calif.: Capitola Book Company, 1985), p. 286.

73 **left the Chinese behind, to scream out at passing ships:** Julian Dana, *The Sacramento: River of Gold* (New York: Farrar and Rinehart, 1939), pp. 160–64, as cited in Sucheng Chan, "The Chinese in California Agriculture, 1860–1900," in Genny Lim, ed., *The Chinese American Experience: Papers from the Second National Conference on Chinese American Studies (1980)*, p. 71.

73 **"tule shoe":** Sylvia Sun Minnick, *Samfow: The San Joaquin Chinese Legacy* (Fresno, Calif.: Panorama West Publishing, 1988), p. 69; Jack Chen, p. 87.

73 **two or three dollars an acre:** Tzu-Kuei Yen, p. 103.

73 **seventy-five dollars an acre:** Ibid.

73 **hundreds of millions:** The value of Chinese labor to the construction of the railroad and the reclamation of the tule land was estimated to be $289,700,000 in 1876–1877 dollars. Thomas W. Chinn, H. Mark Lai, and Philip P. Choy, eds., *A History of the Chinese in California: A Syllabus* (San Francisco: Chinese Historical Society of America, 1969), p. 56. Also Jeff Gillenkirk and James Motlow, *Bitter Melon: Inside America's Last Rural Chinese Town* (Seattle: University of Washington Press, 1987), p. 9.

73 **lice and fleas:** Robert A. Nash, "The 'China Gangs' in the Alaska Packers Association Canneries, 1892–1935," *The Life, Influence and the Role of the Chinese in the United States, 1776–1960*, Proceedings/Papers of the National Conference held at the University of San Francisco, July 10, 11, 12, 1975, sponsored by the Chinese Historical Society of America (San Francisco: Chinese Historical Society of America, 1976), p. 273.

74 **more than three thousand Chinese:** Thomas W. Chinn, H. Mark Lai, and Philip P. Choy, p. 42. By 1881, 3,100 Chinese cannery workers were employed by Columbia River canneries.

74 **"Only Chinese men were employed in the work":** Rudyard Kipling, *From Sea to Sea: Letters of Travel* (Garden City, N.Y.: Doubleday, 1923), pp. 33–34, as cited in Chris Friday, *Organizing Asian American Labor: The Pacific Coast Canned-Salmon Industry, 1870–1942*, p. 25.

74 **"not so much like men":** Chris Friday, p. 30.

74   "as with the whip":   Ibid., p. 40.

74   debone up to two thousand fish: Ibid., p. 30.

74   "the Iron Chink":   Ibid., p. 84.

75   special four-dollar-a-month fishing license: Jack Chen, p. 100; Arthur
        F. McEvoy, *The Fisherman's Problem: Ecology and Law in the California
        Fisheries, 1850–1980* (Cambridge, England: Cambridge University Press,
        1986), pp. 112–14.

75   withhold fishing licenses: Arthur F. McEvoy, pp. 112–13; Sylvia Sun
        Minnick, p. 74.

75   almost a quarter of all of the Chinese: Ronald Takaki, *Strangers from
        a Different Shore: A History of Asian Americans* (New York: Little,
        Brown, 1989; reprinted by Penguin Books, 1990), p. 79.

76   Description of San Francisco in the 1870s: Roger W. Lotchin, *San
        Francisco, 1846–1856: From Hamlet to City* (Urbana and Chicago: Uni-
        versity of Illinois Press, 1997), p. xxxvii.

76   "narrow, revoltingly dirty":   Ibid., p. xxxviii.

77   nearly half of the labor force in the city's four major industries: Ben-
        son Tong, *Unsubmissive Women*, p. 76.

77   80 percent of the workers in woolen mills: Jack Chen, p. 111. Accord-
        ing to Jack Chen, 80 percent of the shirtmakers in San Francisco were
        also Chinese.

77   90 percent of the cigar makers: Stephan Thernstrom, ed., Ann Orlov,
        managing ed., Oscar Handlin, consulting ed., *Harvard Encyclopedia of
        American Ethnic Groups* (Cambridge, Mass.: Belknap Press of Harvard
        University, 1980), p. 219.

77   had five thousand highly successful Chinese businessmen: Otis Gib-
        son, *The Chinese in America*, p. 59.

77   owned half the city's cigar factories: Ping Chiu, *Chinese Labor in
        California*, p. 122.

77   eleven out of twelve slipper factories: Chin-Yu Chen, "San Fran-
        cisco's Chinatown," p. 86; Jack Chen, p. 113; Thomas W. Chinn, H.
        Mark Lai, and Philip P. Choy, p. 51.

77   gleaming with crystal, porcelain, and ivory: Lynn Pan, *Sons of the
        Yellow Emperor*, p. 102.

77   "It is no uncommon thing to find":   Otis Gibson, p. 54.

78   "there were so many of us":   "Life History and Social Document of
        Mr. J. S. Look," Seattle, August 13, 1924, by C. H. Burnett, p. 1.

78   crates found on the street: Victor G. and Brett de Bary Nee, *Longtime
        Californ': A Documentary Study of an American Chinatown* (New York:
        Pantheon, 1972), p. 70.

78   slept in shifts: Ibid., p. 69.

78   "scarcely a single ray of light":   Otis Gibson, p. 54.

78   Description of Chinatown informal government: Victor G. and
        Brett de Bary Nee, pp. 64–66.

78–79   served as unofficial ambassadors: Chin-Yu Chen, p. 35.

79   own guild in San Francisco: Jack Chen, p. 28.

79   Kong Chow Association: Christopher Lee Yip, "San Francisco's Chinatown: An Architectural and Urban History," Ph.D. dissertation in architecture, University of California at Berkeley, 1985, p. 37.

79   split into two groups: Ibid., p. 37.

79   offices in prominent neighborhoods: Ibid., p. 94.

79   Description of services of the Six Companies: Chin-Yu Chen, pp. 34, 37.

79   house of worship: B. Lloyd, *Lights and Shades in San Francisco* (San Francisco: A. L. Bancroft and Company, 1876), pp. 272–74; Pauline Minke, "Chinese in the Mother Lode (1850–1870)," thesis, California History and Government Adult Education, 1960, Asian American Studies Library, University of California at Berkeley.

80   Description of funerals and burials: Linda Sun Crowder, "Mortuary Practices in San Francisco Chinatown," *Chinese America: History and Perspectives 1999*, pp. 33–46; Sylvia Sun Minnick, *Samfow*, p. 292; B. Lloyd, p. 367, and *San Francisco Daily Alta California*, September 1, 1868, April 4, 1868, and June 1, 1867, as cited in Christopher Lee Yip, pp. 109–13. As late as 1992, 1,300 sets of bones were still warehoused in San Francisco for future shipment to China (Chin-Yu Chen, p. 18); Sandy Lydon, *Chinese Gold*, pp. 131–32.

81   "Tonight we pledge ourselves":   Lynn Pan, p. 20.

81   Description of *mui tsai*:   Judy Yung, *Unbound Feet: A Social History of Chinese Women in San Francisco* (Berkeley: University of California Press, 1995), pp. 37–39.

81   "death was all around them":   Elizabeth Cooper, *My Lady of the Chinese Courtyard* (New York: Frederick A. Stokes, 1914), pp. 13–14, as cited in Benson Tong, p. 18.

82   "Mother was crying":   Victor and Brett de Bary Nee, p. 84.

82   "grand, free country":   "Story of Wong Ah So." Major Document 146, Box 26, Survey of Race Relations, Hoover Institution of War, Revolution and Peace, Stanford University. Wong Ah So was later rescued by Donaldina Cameron, converted to Christianity, learned how to read and write English, and married a Chinese merchant in Boise, Idaho. In 1933, she wrote to Cameron to report that one of her daughters would graduate from the University of Washington, where she was studying bacteriology.

82   "devil American prison":   Benson Tong, *Unsubmissive Women*, p. 57.

82   Quick-witted girls managed to escape their fate: Ibid., pp. 58–59.

83   audiences that included police officers: Ibid., p. 69.

83   a Chinese theater or even a Chinese temple: Ibid., p. 70.

83   Description of parlor houses and cribs: Stephen Longstreet, ed., *Nell Kimball: The Life As an American Madam by Herself* (New York:

Macmillan, 1970), pp. 226–27; Herbert Ashbury, *The Barbary Coast: An Informal History of the San Francisco Underground* (New York: Alfred A. Knopf, 1933), pp. 174–76; Judy Yung, pp. 27–30.

83   **"Two bittee lookee":**   Judy Yung, *Unbound Feet*, p. 29.

84   **both feet frozen:**   Huping Ling, *Surviving on the Gold Mountain: A History of Chinese American Women and Their Lives* (Albany: State University of New York Press, 1998), p. 57.

84   **"Chiney ladies":**   Ibid., p. 57.

84   **nailed shut inside a crate:**   Ibid., p. 57

84   **leased them out to local garment factories to sew by day:**   Ibid., p. 59.

84   **"beats and pounds them with sticks of fire-wood":**   Otis Gibson, p. 156.

84   **acid thrown in her face:**   Benson Tong, p. 142.

84   **swallowing raw opium:**   Judy Yung, p. 33.

85   **average brothel employed nine women:**   Huping Ling, p. 59.

85   **annual profit of $2,500:**   Lucie Cheng Hirata, "Free, Indentured, Enslaved: Chinese Prostitutes in Nineteenth-Century America," *Signs: Journal of Women in Culture and Society*, Autumn 1979. As cited in Judy Yung, p. 30.

85   **paid $40 in insurance:**   Otis Gibson, p. 137.

85   **"Yut Kum consents to prostitute her body":**   Benson Tong, p. 201. Original citation: *Congressional Record*, 43rd Cong., 2d sess., March 1875, 3, pt. 3:41.

86   **frightening them to tears:**   Otis Gibson, p. 208.

86   **writs of habeas corpus:**   Victor G. and Brett de Bary Nee, p. 88.

86   **"search the whole house":**   Ibid., p. 88.

86   **sticks of dynamite:**   Benson Tong, p. 185.

86   **ascending to the rooftops:**   Lynn Pan, p. 104. For additional sources on Donaldina Cameron, see Mildred Crowl Martin, *Chinatown's Angry Angel: The Story of Donaldina Cameron* (Palo Alto: Pacific Books, 1977); Peggy Pascoe, *Relations of Rescue: The Search for Female Moral Authority in the American West, 1874–1939* (New York: Oxford University Press, 1990); Carol Green Wilson, *Chinatown Quest: One Hundred Years of Donaldina Cameron House 1874–1974* (San Francisco: California Historical Society, 1974); Sarah Refo Mason, "Social Christianity, American Feminism, and Chinese Prostitutes: The History of the Presbyterian Mission Home, San Francisco, 1874–1935," in Maria Jaschok and Suzanne Miers, eds., *Women and Chinese Patriarchy: Submission, Servitude and Escape* (Hong Kong: Hong Kong University Press, 1944); Laurence Wu McClain, "Donaldina Cameron: A Reappraisal," *Pacific Historian*, Fall 1985.

86   **sophisticated system of alarm bells:**   "Statement of Chun Ho, Rescued Chinese Slave Girl, at the Presbyterian Rescue Home, Miss Cameron,

Matron, in the Matter of Investigation into Chinese Highbinder Societies," p. 9. File 55374/876, Box 360, Entry 9, Record Group 85, National Archives, Washington, D.C.

86   **fifteen hundred Chinese women were rescued:**   Judy Yung, p. 35.

86   **"to better her condition":**   Huping Ling, p. 24.

87   **"gaze upon the countenance of the charming Ah Toy":**   Curt Gentry, *Madams of San Francisco: An Irreverent History of the City by the Golden Gate* (Garden City, N.Y.: Doubleday, 1964), p. 52.

87   **three months short of her hundredth birthday:**   Judy Yung, *Unbound Feet*, p. 34.

87   **Description of Suey Him's life:**   Ibid.

87   **those keeping house grew from 753 in 1870 to 1,145 in 1880:**   Huping Ling, p. 61.

88   **Story of Polly Bemis:**   Huping Ling, p. 79; Benson Tong, p. 22; Vardis Fisher and Opal Laurel Holmes, *Gold Rushes and Mining Camps of the Early American West* (Caldwell, Idaho: The Caxton Printers, Ltd., 1990), pp. 273–74.

88   **Descriptions of abductions of wives by highbinders:**   Benson Tong, p. 172.

88   **"She would either have to marry one of them men or go back to China":**   Major Document #154, Box 26, Survey of Race Relations, Hoover Institution on War, Revolution and Peace, Stanford University.

89   **physicians in San Francisco lobbied to exclude Chinese prostitutes:**   *The Chinese Hospital of San Francisco* (Oakland: Carruth and Carruth, 1899), p. 1; *San Francisco Chronicle*, July 1, 1871; California Department of Public Health, *First Biennial Report of the State Board of Health of California for the Years 1870 and 1871* (San Francisco: D. W. Gelwicks, 1871), p. 46. All three cited in Benson Tong, *Unsubmissive Women*, p. 105.

89   **"death-houses":**   Benson Tong, p. 106.

89   **"stretched on the floor of this damp, foul-smelling den":**   Ibid., p. 107.

90   **"My father traveled all over the world":**   *Origins & Destinations: 41 Essays on Chinese America*, p. 83.

90   **"When I came to America as a bride":**   Rose Hum Lee, *The Growth and Decline of Chinese Communities in the Rocky Mountain Region* (New York: Arno Press, 1978), p. 252.

91   **"Now and then the women visit one another":**   Sui Seen [Sin] Far, "The Chinese Woman in America," *Land of Sunshine*, January 1897, p. 62.

92   **a few hundred Chinese families lived in America, and perhaps one thousand Chinese children:**   Otis Gibson, *The Chinese in America*, p. 318.

Chapter Seven. Spreading Across America

93   **63,199 Chinese:**   1870 U.S. Census. For Chinese census statistics in the
        United States for the nineteenth century, see Thomas W. Chinn, H. Mark
        Lai, and Philip P. Choy, eds., *A History of the Chinese in California: A
        Syllabus* (San Francisco: Chinese Historical Society of America, 1969),
        p. 19, table II.

93   **99.4 percent:**   1870 U.S. Census. Table II in Thomas W. Chinn, H.
        Mark Lai, and Philip P. Choy gives the statistic of 62,831 Chinese in the
        western states in 1870. Very few Chinese lived in the East Coast or Mid-
        west during this era. Officially there was only one Chinese person in the
        entire state of Illinois in 1870, a number that grew to 209 by 1880. Some
        of the few Chinese in the Midwest had migrated from East Coast cities,
        not the West Coast. (Douglas Knox, "The Chinese American Midwest:
        Migration and the Negotiation of Ethnicity," unpublished paper. Also
        Adam McKeown, "Chinese Migrants Among Ghosts: Chicago, Peru and
        Hawaii in the Early Twentieth Century," Ph.D. dissertation in history,
        University of Chicago, 1997, p. 241.)

93   **78 percent—in California:**   1870 U.S. Census. According to table II in
        Thomas W. Chinn, H. Mark Lai, and Philip P. Choy, 49,277 Chinese
        lived in California in 1870.

94   **"come to the conclusion that we Chinese are the same as Indians and
        Negroes":**   Lai Chun-chuen, Remarks of the Chinese Merchants of San
        Francisco on Governor Bigler's Message, translated by W. Speer, Ban-
        croft Library, University of California at Berkeley, as cited in Charles J.
        McClain, "California's First Anti-Chinese Laws," *Chinese America:
        History and Perspectives 1995* (Brisbane, Calif.: Chinese Historical Soci-
        ety of America, 1995), p. 102.

94   **King Weimah:**   Gunther Barth, *Bitter Strength*, p. 145.

95   **"If the Chinese were allowed to vote":**   Eric Foner, *Reconstruction:
        America's Unfinished Revolution, 1863–1877* (New York: Harper and
        Row, 1988), p. 447.

95   **federal court decision:**   Cheng-Tsu Wu, ed., "*Chink!,*" p. 14.

96   **"Emancipation has spoiled the Negro":**   "The Coming Laborer," *Vicks-
        burg Times*, June 30, 1869, as cited in James W. Loewen, *The Mississippi
        Chinese: Between Black and White* (Prospect Heights, Ill.: Waveland Press,
        1988; originally published by Harvard University Press, 1971), pp. viii, 22.

96   **"Give us five million":**   Eric Foner, pp. 419–20.

96   **Tye Kim Orr:**   Andrew Gyory, *Closing the Gate: Race, Politics, and the
        Chinese Exclusion Act* (Chapel Hill: University of North Carolina Press,
        1998), p. 31.

96   **Information on Cornelius Koopmanschap:**   Andrew Gyory, p. 31.
        Also, Gunther Barth, pp. 191–95.

97   "All Chinese make much money in New Orleans if they work": Lynn Pan, *Sons of the Yellow Emperor*, pp. 53–54.

97   "nice rooms and very fine food": Ibid.

97   the arrival of about two thousand Chinese in the South: Sucheng Chan, *Asian Americans*, p. 82.

97   some 250 Chinese men came as employees of the Houston & Texas Central Railroad: Ibid., p. 82.

97   a thousand Chinese arrived in Alabama: Ibid., p. 82.

97   staged a strike to protest the whipping: Lucy M. Cohen, "George W. Gift, Chinese Labor Agent in the Post–Civil War South," *Chinese America: History and Perspectives 1995* (Brisbane, Calif.: Chinese Historical Society of America, 1995), p. 174.

97   attempted to lynch a Chinese agent: *Jackson Weekly Clarion*, November 20, 1873, as cited in James W. Loewen, p. 31.

97   shot and killed Chinese: Ibid.

98   Information about bilingual interpreters: Lucy M. Cohen, *Chinese in the Post–Civil War South: A People Without a History* (Baton Rouge: Louisiana State University Press, 1984), p. 83.

98   press charges against their employers: Lucy M. Cohen, "George W. Gift, Chinese Labor Agent in the Post–Civil War South," p. 74.

98   U.S. authorities halted Chinese labor recruitment: Ibid., p. 159.

99   By 1915, scarcely a single plantation: Powell Clayton, *The Aftermath of the Civil War in Arkansas* (New York: Neale, 1915), p. 214, as cited in James W. Loewen, p. 31.

100   Information on strike in North Adams: Andrew Gyory, pp. 39–41.

100   first manufacturer in American history: Andrew Gyory, p. 60.

101   "A large and hostile crowd": *The Nation*, June 23, 1870, p. 397.

101   "No scabs or rats admitted here": Andrew Gyory, p. 41.

101   "there can be nowhere a busier, more orderly group of workmen": *Harper's New Monthly Magazine*, December 1870, p. 138, as cited in Ronald Takaki, *Strangers from a Different Shore*, p. 98.

101   "labored regularly and constantly": William Shanks, "Chinese Skilled Labor," *Scribner's Monthly*, Vol. 2, September 1871, pp. 495–96, as cited in Ronald Takaki, p. 98.

101   Information on James B. Hervey: Ronald Takaki, p. 99; Gunther Barth, pp. 203–6; Renqiu Yu, *To Save China, to Save Ourselves: The Chinese Hand Laundry Alliance of New York* (Philadelphia: Temple University Press, 1992), pp. 9–10. Arthur Bonner, *Alas! What Brought Thee Hither? The Chinese in New York 1800–1950* (Cranbury, N.J.: Associated University Presses, 1997), pp. 26–27, 30–32.

101   "shows a manifest attempt to revive the institution of slavery": Roger Daniels, *Asian America: Chinese and Japanese in the United States Since 1850* (Seattle: University of Washington Press, 1988), p. 42.

102   10 percent wage reduction: Ronald Takaki, p. 98.

102   "more and more like their white neighbors":   Renqiu Yu, p. 9.

102   discharged all of them: Arthur Bonner, p. 32.

102   peddling and candy making: John Kuo Wei Tchen, *New York Before Chinatown*, pp. 77, 81, 227, 233–35.

102   748 Chinese lived in Manhattan: Ibid., p. 225.

102   two thousand Chinese laundries: Renqiu Yu, p. 8.

103   five Chinese youths: Thomas E. LaFargue, *China's First Hundred: Educated Mission Students in the United States 1872–1881* (Pullman: Washington State University Press, 1987), p. 166.

103   Ah Lum: Carl T. Smith, "Commissioner Lin's Translators," *Chung Chi Bulletin*, no. 42, June 1967.

103   Information on Yung Wing: Yung Wing, *My Life in China and America* (New York: Henry Holt and Company, 1909); Jack Chen, *The Chinese of America*, pp. 177–78.

103   "foreign intercourse with China":   Yung Wing, p. 2.

104   "I wanted the utmost freedom of action":   Yung Wing, p. 35.

104   "Knowledge is power":   Yung Wing, p. 50.

105   decapitation of seventy-five thousand people: Jack Chen, p. 16.

105   "If I were allowed to practice my profession":   Yung Wing, p. 60.

106   "the best time to serve their homeland":   Timothy Kao, "Yung Wing (1828–1912): The First Chinese Graduate from an American University." Paper presented during "Chinese Pioneer Scholars in the Nineteenth-Century U.S.: A Little-Known Aspect of the Chinese Diaspora" conference, Yale University, September 21, 1998, p. 2.

106   adapting to New England life: Ibid., p. 4.

106   played American sports: Ibid., p. 3.

107   Information on Tang Guoan, Tang Shaoyi, and Zhan Tianyou: Ibid., p. 6.

109   Lue Gim Gong: Ruthanne Lum McCunn, *Chinese American Portraits: Personal Histories 1828–1988* (San Francisco: Chronicle Books, 1988), pp. 33–39; Ruthanne Lum McCunn, "Lue Gim Gong: A Life Reclaimed," *Chinese America: History and Perspectives 1989*, pp. 117–35.

110   "With few or no Chinese women available":   Lucy M. Cohen, *Chinese in the Post–Civil War South*, p. 176.

110   outnumbered Irish male arrivals two to one: Roger Daniels, *Coming to America*, p. 142.

110   *Harper's Weekly*:   *Harper's Weekly*, October 3, 1857, as cited in Gunther Barth, p. 210.

110   most owners of Chinese boarding houses were married to either Irish or German women: *New York Times*, June 20, 1859.

111   "handsome but squalidly dressed young white girl":   *New York Times*, December 26, 1873, as cited in Ronald Takaki, p. 101.

111 **Edward Harrigan:** John Kuo Wei Tchen, *New York Before China-town*, pp. 127, 219–20. Original citation: Edward Harrigan papers, Manuscripts and Archives section, New York Public Library.

111 **Store windows:** John Kuo Wei Tchen, *New York Before Chinatown*, p. 128.

111 *Yankee Notions: Yankee Notions*, March 1858, as cited in John Kuo Wei Tchen, *New York Before Chinatown*, p. 124–27.

111 **even "whiter" than most of their neighbors:** *New York World*, January 30, 1877, as cited in John Kuo Wei Tchen, *New York Before Chinatown*, p. 229.

112 **"young and pretty Irish girl":** *New York Sun*, February 16, 1874.

112 **Story about Charles Sun:** Interview with Paul Siu in Douglas Knox's unpublished paper, "The Chinese American Midwest: Migration and the Negotiation of Ethnicity."

113 **only state in the union:** Lucy M. Cohen, *Chinese in the Post–Civil War South*, p. 2.

113 **"little half-breed children":** John Kuo Wei Tchen, *New York Before Chinatown*, p. 228.

114 **Information on the two sons of Yung Wing (Morrison and Bartlet Yung):** Provided by Yung Wing's grandson, Frank Yung, in his correspondence with the author.

114 **"pass for what he wants":** Lucy M. Cohen, *Chinese in the Post–Civil War South*, p. 170.

114 **"That made me angry":** Ibid., p. 171.

115 **"I have come from a race":** Edith Maud Eaton (pseudonym Sui Sin Far), "Leaves from the Mental Portfolio of an Eurasian," *Independent*, January 21, 1909.

115 **"Why is my mother's race despised?":** Ibid.

Chapter Eight. Rumblings of Hatred

116 **Information on the depression in the 1870s:** Victor G. and Brett de Bary Nee, *Longtime Californ'*, pp. 46–47.

117 **one Chinese and two whites for every job:** Victor Low, *The Unimpressible Race*, p. 29; Ronald Takaki, *Strangers from a Different Shore*, p. 105.

118 **"In the factories of San Francisco":** John Todd, *The Sunset Land* (Boston: Lee and Shepard, 1870), p. 283.

118 **History of poem "The Heathen Chinee":** Ronald Takaki, pp. 104–5; Arthur Bonner, *Alas! What Brought Thee Hither? The Chinese in New York 1800–1950*, pp. 33–34.

119 **"In all our knowledge":** Arthur Bonner, pp. 33–34.

119 **Cubic Air law:** Otis Gibson, *The Chinese in America*, pp. 361–62; Ori-

gins & Destinations, pp. 57–58; San Francisco Board of Supervisors, order no. 939, as cited in Cheng-Tsu Wu, ed., *"Chink!,"* pp. 65–66 (see also pp. 13–14).

119   **"like brutes":**   Otis Gibson, pp. 361–62.

119   **"queue ordinance":**   Diane Mei Lin Mark and Ginger Chih, *A Place Called Chinese America,* p. 33; Cheng-Tsu Wu, ed., *"Chink!,"* p. 14.

120   **"sidewalk ordinance":**   Diane Mei Lin Mark and Ginger Chih, p. 33.

120   **two dollars a quarter:**   Ibid.; Otis Gibson, p. 282.

120   **Congress deliberately withheld the right of the Chinese to naturalize:** Roger Daniels, *Asian America,* p. 43.

121   **"the Chinks are shootin' ":**   Stephen Longstreet, *All Star Cast: An Anecdotal History of Los Angeles* (New York: Thomas Y. Crowell, 1977), p. 80.

121   **"American blood had been shed":**   Stephen Longstreet, p. 80.

121   **"Hang them! Hang them!":**   Ibid.

121   **highly respected Chinese doctor:**   C. P. Dorland, statement delivered at the Historical Society of Southern California, January 7, 1894, as cited in Cheng-Tsu Wu, ed., *"Chink!,"* p. 151.

121   **"The little fellow was not above twelve years of age":**   David Colbert, ed., *Eyewitness to the American West: From the Aztec Empire to the Digital Frontier in the Words of Those Who Saw It Happen* (New York: Viking, 1998), p. 172.

122   **some ten million acres:**   Sucheng Chan, *Asian Americans,* p. 31. The number of acres granted ranged from nine to eleven million, depending on how they were counted.

122   **"WE WANT NO SLAVES OR ARISTOCRATS":**   Roger Daniels, *Asian America,* p. 38.

123   **less than 2 percent of the patients:**   Otis Gibson, *The Chinese in America,* p. 364.

123   **more than 35 percent:**   Ibid., p. 364.

123   **harbored more Europeans at public expense:**   Ibid., p. 22.

123   **"chasing a phantom":**   Ibid., p. 23.

123   **Dr. Arthur Stout:**   John Hoyt Williams, *A Great and Shining Road,* p. 95. Also, Stuart Creighton Miller, *The Unwelcome Immigrant: The American Image of the Chinese, 1785–1882* (Berkeley and Los Angeles: University of California Press, 1969), p. 161. Arthur Stout's pamphlet, *Chinese Immigration and the Physiological Causes of the Decay of the Nation,* asserted that syphilis and "mental alienation" were Chinese characteristics.

123   **American Medical Association:** Stuart Creighton Miller, p. 163.

123   **"Even boys eight and ten years old":** Ibid.

123   **"Anglo-Saxon Blood":** Ibid., pp. 164, 237. Original citation: Mary Santelle, "The Foul Contagious Disease. A Phase of the Chinese Question.

How the Chinese Women Are Infusing a Poison into the Anglo-Saxon Blood," *Medico-Literary Journal*, I (November 1878), pp. 4–5.

123   "the result of thousands of years of beastly vices":   Stuart Creighton Miller, p. 163.

124   huge quantities of bowie knives: Otis Gibson, p. 306.

124   sixty pistols: Otis Gibson, p. 306.

124   the Chinese Six Companies issued a manifesto: Otis Gibson, p. 300.

124   severe drought: Victor Low, *The Unimpressible Race*, p. 40.

124   output was reduced to a third: Ibid., p. 40.

125   ten thousand unemployed men: Ibid., p. 40.

125   "Before I starve in a country like this":   Andrew Gyory, *Closing the Gate*, p. 115.

125   "tear the masks from off these tyrants":   Ibid., p. 113.

125   suggested exterminating the Chinese population: Betty Lee Sung, *The Story of the Chinese in America*, p. 43.

126   "A while ago it was the Irish":   Robert Louis Stevenson, *The Amateur Emigrant* (London: Chatto and Windus, 1895), p. 131, as cited in Lynn Pan, *Sons of the Yellow Emperor*, p. 93.

126   "running the gauntlet":   Otis Gibson, p. 50.

126   "They follow the Chinaman":   Ibid., p. 51.

126   "When I first came":   "Life History and Social Document of Andrew Kan," Seattle, Washington, August 22, 1924, by C. H. Burnett, p. 2. Major Document 178, Box 27, Survey of Race Relations, Hoover Institution on War, Revolution and Peace, Stanford University.

126   "We were simply terrified":   Huie Kin, *Reminiscences* (Peiping, 1932), p. 27, as cited in Ronald Takaki, p. 115.

127   "I remember as we walked along the street":   "Life History and Social Document of Mr. J. S. Look," August 13, 1924. Major Document 182, Box 27, Survey of Race Relations, Hoover Institution on War, Revolution and Peace, Stanford University.

127   shot to death five Chinese farm workers: Victor G. and Brett de Bary Nee, p. 22; Andrew Gyory, p. 94.

127   ten thousand agitators: Lynn Pan, p. 95.

127   "On to Chinatown!":   Andrew Gyory, p. 96.

128   "Even CHINAMEN":   Ibid., p. 98.

128   hired a Chinese man just to walk in and out of his factory: Andrew Gyory, p. 99.

128   hired white men to masquerade as Chinese: Ibid.

128   greeted with cries of "Chinamen!":   Ibid.

128   "So we will serve every Chinaman":   Ibid.

128   "Any officer, director, manager":   Victor G. and Brett de Bary Nee, p. 53. Also Cheng-Tsu Wu, ed., *"Chink!" Anti-Chinese Prejudice in America* (New York: World Publishing Company, 1972), pp. 14, 69. The

original citation in *"Chink!"* is *Criminal Laws and Practice of California* (A. L. Bancroft and Company, 1881). The constitution also prevented the Chinese from voting: "Natives of China, along with idiots, insane persons, and persons convicted in infamous crimes or the embezzlement of public money, shall never exercise the privilege of electors in this state."

128   **mass exodus:**   Andrew Gyory, p. 177. Newspaper coverage of exodus includes *New York Times*, March 6, 1880, and *St. Louis Globe Democrat*, March 5, 1880.

129   **former president Ulysses S. Grant:**   Andrew Gyory, pp. 186–87.

Chapter Nine. The Chinese Exclusion Act

130   **Quotes from the debate in Congress:**   Can be found in Andrew Gyory, *Closing the Gate*, pp. 224–44.

132   **"one of the most infamous and tragic statutes":**   Ibid., p. 258.

132   **mass anti-Chinese rally in Seattle issued a manifesto:**   Sucheng Chan, *Asian Americans*, pp. 50–51; Ruthanne Lum McCunn, *Chinese American Portraits: Personal Histories 1828–1988* (San Francisco: Chronicle Books, 1988), p. 48.

133   **kicked down doors, dragged the occupants outside:**   Ruthanne Lum McCunn, p. 48; Lorraine Barker Hildebrand, *Straw Halls, Sandals and Steel* (Tacoma: Washington State American Revolution Bicentennial Commission, 1977), pp. 49–59.

133   **two men died from exposure:**   Ruthanne Lum McCunn, p. 49.

133   **one merchant's wife went insane:**   Lorraine Barker Hildebrand, p. 50. According to Lum May's statement about his wife, "From the excitement, the fright, the losses we sustained through the riot she lost her reason. She was hopelessly insane and attacked people with a hatchet or any other weapon if not watched ... she was perfectly sane before the riot."

133   **the secretary of war dispatched troops to Seattle:**   Doug Chin, "The Anti-Chinese Movement," *The International Examiner*, January 6, 1982.

133   **"special tax":**   Ruthanne Lum McCunn, p. 51.

133   **beating up several Chinese:**   Ibid.

133   **Information about the second Seattle riot:**   *Harper's Weekly*, March 6, 1886; Lorraine Barker Hildebrand, pp. 69–74.

133–34 **Information about the Rock Springs massacre and indemnities:**   Judy Yung, *Unbound Feet*, p. 21; R. David Arkush and Leo O. Lee, *Land without Ghosts*, p. 57; Tzu-Kuei Yen, pp. 153–62; Craig Stori, *Incident at Bitter Creek: The Story of the Rock Springs Chinese Massacre* (Ames: Iowa State University Press, 1991).

134   **Chen Lanbing:**   *New York Times*, September 10, 1880, as cited in R. David Arkush and Leo O. Lee, p. 59; Kim Man Chan, "Mandarins in

America: the Early Chinese Ministers to the United States, 1878–1907," Ph.D. dissertation, University of Hawaii, 1981, p. 127.

134–35   **Information on Snake River Massacre:**   David H. Stratton, "The Snake River Massacre of Chinese Miners, 1887," in Duane A. Smith, ed., *A Taste of the West: Essays in Honor of Robert Athearn*, p. 124, as cited in Roger Daniels, *Asian America*, p. 64.

135   **Scott Act:**   Cheng-Tsu Wu, ed., "*Chink!*," pp. 82–85.

135   **Twenty thousand Chinese:**   Huping Ling, *Surviving on the Gold Mountain*, p. 2; Betty Lee Sung, *The Story of the Chinese in America*, p. 54; Cheng-Tsu Wu, ed., "*Chink!*," p. 16.

135   **State Department . . . ignored him:**   Betty Lee Sung, p. 54.

136   **"unwise, impolitic, and injurious":**   Roger Daniels, *Asian America*, p. 57.

136   **"it could not be alleged":**   Ibid.

136   **"considers the presence of foreigners":**   *Washington Post*, June 19, 1999.

136   **"residing apart by themselves":**   Ibid.

136   **"strangers in the land":**   Ibid.

136   **Geary Act:**   Victor Low, *The Unimpressible Race: A Century of Educational Struggle by the Chinese in San Francisco* (San Francisco: East/West Publishing Company, 1982), p. 75; Betty Lee Sung, p. 55; Cheng-Tsu Wu, p. 16; Jack Chen, *The Chinese of America*, p. 162.

136   **A Chinese consul urged his countrymen not to register:**   Betty Lee Sung, p. 55; Erika Lee, "Enforcing and Challenging Exclusion in San Francisco: U.S. Immigration Officials and Chinese Immigrants, 1882–1905," *Chinese America: History and Perspectives 1997* (Brisbane, Calif.: Chinese Historical Society of America, 1997), p. 9.

137   *Fong Yue Ting* v. *United States:*   Sucheng Chan, *Asian Americans*, pp. 91–92.

137   *Lem Moon Sing* v. *United States:*   Ibid., pp. 91–92.

137   **"almost next to impossible to prove the birth":**   Erika Lee, p. 7.

137   **Wong Kim Ark:**   Charles Park, "American by Birth: One Hundred Years Ago, a Chinese American Man Won the Right for All American Born People to Claim U.S. Citizenship," *A* magazine, March 31, 1998.

138   **"acts of Congress or treaties have not permitted":**   Ibid.

139   **Information on the burning of Honolulu Chinatown:**   Sucheng Chan, p. 57; L. Eve Armentrout, "Conflict and Contact Between the Chinese and Indigenous Communities in San Francisco, 1900–1911," *The Life, Influence, and the Role of the Chinese in the United States, 1776–1960.* Proceedings, papers of the national conference held at the University of San Francisco, July 10, 11, 12, 1975, sponsored by the Chinese Historical Society of America (San Francisco: The Chinese Historical Society of America, 1976), pp. 56–57.

139   **Wong Wai:**   *Wong Wai* v. *Williamson* (1900).

140   Information on the attempt to destroy San Francisco Chinatown: Sucheng Chan, p. 57; L. Eve Armentrout in *The Life, Influence, and the Role of the Chinese in the United States, 1776–1960*, pp. 57–59.

140   "We helped build your railroads": Petition to President Wilson of the United States, June 1914. File 53620/115 A, Entry 9, Box 229, Record Group 85, National Archives, Washington, D.C.

141   "reduced to the status of dogs in America": Silas K. C. Geneson, "Cry Not in Vain: The Boycott of 1905," *Chinese America: History and Perspectives 1997* (Brisbane, Calif.: Chinese Historical Society, 1997), p. 30; editorial, "The U.S. Government to Extend the Exclusion Agreement, Part 6," *Chung Sai Yat Po*, April 2, 1904.

141   *United States* v. *Ju Toy:* Silas K. C. Geneson, p. 29.

141   "final and conclusive": Ibid., p. 29.

142   "to order an alien drawn, quartered and chucked overboard": Ibid., p. 29.

142   725 of 7,762 Chinese: Ibid., p. 29.

142   rejection rate rose to one in four: Ibid., p. 29.

142   "even the old monks": R. David Arkush and Leo O. Lee, p. 58.

143   some $30 million to $40 million worth of trade: Betty Lee Sung, p. 65.

143   90,000 cases of fuel monthly to 19,000: Silas K. C. Geneson, pp. 40–41.

143   difficult to even give away free cigarettes: Consul General Julius Lay to Acting Secretary of State Francis Loomis, September 28, 1905, Foreign Service, Despatches of United States Consuls in Canton, 1790–1906, Washington, D.C. National Archives microfiles, as cited in Silas K. C. Geneson, p. 34.

143   Theodore Roosevelt issued an executive order: Silas K. C. Geneson, p. 36.

143–44 29 percent of the certificates: Ibid., p. 37.

144   "Much trouble has come": Ibid., p. 36.

144   8,031 Chinese: Erika Lee, "Enforcing and Challenging Exclusion in San Francisco: U.S. Immigration Officials and Chinese Immigrants, 1882–1905," *Chinese America: History and Perspectives*, p. 3.

144   dropped to 279: Ibid., p. 3.

144   in 1885, 22: Ibid., p. 3.

144   a total of ten Chinese people: Ibid., p. 3.

144   103,620 to 85,341: U.S. Census.

144   "They would stab through the rice": Judy Yung interview with Mr. Chew, file 20, "Angel Island Oral History Project," Asian American Studies Library, University of California at Berkeley.

145   "My cousin and I": K. H. Wong, *Gum Sahn Yun (Gold Mountain Men)* (San Francisco: Fong Brothers, Inc., 1987), p. 187.

145   "It seemed not more than several minutes": Gladys Hensen, *Denial of Disaster* (San Francisco: Cameron and Company, 1990), p. 26.

145   "They carried their bundles":   *Chung Sai Yat Po*, May 10, 1906.

145   robbed by the soldiers: *San Francisco Chronicle*, June 10, 1906, and April 29, 1906, as cited in Erica Y. Z. Pan, *The Impact of the 1906 Earthquake in San Francisco's Chinatown* (New York: Peter Lang Publishing, 1995), pp. 43 and 54.

145   ordered by these soldiers to perform physical labor: *San Francisco Chronicle*, June 10, 1906.

146   "shoot to kill":   Erica Y. Z. Pan, p. 53.

146   "high railroad officials":   *San Francisco Chronicle*, April 29, 1906.

146   "the National Guard":   Gordon Thomas and Max Witts, *The San Francisco Earthquake* (New York: Stein and Day, 1971), p. 259.

146   Between 1855 and 1934:   Stanford Lyman, *Chinese Americans* (New York: Random House, 1974), p. 110.

147   the ratio of Chinese sons to daughters: Betty Lee Sung, p. 99.

147   "if the stories told in the courts":   U.S. Treasury Department, Annual Report 1903, p. 98, as cited in Madeline Y. Hsu, *Dreaming of Gold, Dreaming of Home,* p. 75. The quote in the report comes from p. 51 in "Report of Proceedings of a Chinese-Exclusion Convention," which was held in San Francisco, November 21–22, 1901.

147   "overrun with vermin":   Silas K. C. Geneson, "Cry Not in Vain," p. 29.

147   "a race of pigs":   Ibid.

147   Description of Angel Island: Him Mark Lai, Genny Lim, and Judy Yung, *Island: Poetry and History of Chinese Immigrants on Angel Island, 1910–1940* (Seattle: University of Washington Press, 1991).

147   "prevalent among aliens from oriental countries":   Ibid., p. 13.

147   some 175,000 Chinese immigrants: Ester Wu, "Chinese Immigrants Remember Detention at Angel Island," *Dallas Morning News*, May 21, 2000.

148   75 to 80 percent: Unpublished paper given to author by Bob Barde, Academic Coordinator of the Institute of Business and Economic Research at Berkeley.

148   "dumped together as so many animals":   "The History and Problem of Angel Island," p. 3. Major Document #150, Box 26, Survey of Race Relations, Hoover Institution on War, Revolution and Peace, Stanford University.

148   "There is no privacy whatsoever":   Ibid., p. 1.

148   "veritable firetrap":   Letter from the Special Immigration Inspector in Meredith, New Hampshire, to the Commissioner General of Immigration in Washington, D.C., August 21, 1915. File 53438-54, Box 208, Entry 9, Record Group 85, National Archives, Washington, D.C.

149   pitched a tent for him: Ibid.

149   "a prison with scarcely any supply of air or light":   Letter from L. D. Cio to F. S. Brockman, July 19, 1913, p. 2. File 53620/211, Entry 9, Box 230, Record Group 85, National Archives, Washington, D.C.

149 "cattle": Letter from J. C. Huston, American Consul in Charge at American Consulate General in Tientsin, China, to the Secretary of State, April 10, 1923. File 53620/115C, Entry 9, Box 229, Record Group 85, National Archives, Washington, D.C.

149 customary for the Chinese to eat only twice a day: Letter, Office of the Commissioner, Chinese Division in Boston, Massachusetts, to Commissioner General of Immigration, June 5, 1915. No. 2513, File 53775-139 and 139 A, Box 235, Entry 9, Stack Area 17W3, Row 2, Compartment 17, Shelf 1, Record Group 85, National Archives, Washington, D.C.

149 angry demonstrations in the dining room: Him Mark Lai, Genny Lim, and Judy Yung, *Island*, p. 19. In an oral history interview, Law Shee Low described the food served at Angel Island: "The bean sprouts were cooked so badly you wanted to throw up when you saw it. There was rice but it was cold . . . The food was steamed to death; it smelled bad and tasted bad. The vegetables were old and the fatty beef was of poor quality. They must have thought we were pigs." Judy Yung, *Unbound Voices: A Documentary History of Chinese Women in San Francisco* (Berkeley: University of California Press, 1999), p. 216.

149 post a sign in Chinese: Him Mark Lai, Genny Lim, and Judy Yung, *Island*, p. 19.

149 troops to Angel Island: Ibid.

150 "Is your house one story or two stories": Betty Lee Sung, p. 102.

150 "There are many cases": "Life History and Social Document of Mr. J. S. Look," Seattle, August 13, 1924, by C. H. Burnett." p. 3. Major Document #182, Box 27, Survey of Race Relations, Hoover Institution on War, Revolution and Peace, Stanford University.

151 tiny windowless closet three feet square: *Origins & Destinations*, p. 82.

151 "calm down": Ibid., p. 82.

151 "chopsticks slaying case": Case 4139/11-29, Record Group 85, National Archives, Pacific Sierra Region, San Bruno, California.

151 Leong Bick Ha: Yen Le Espiritu, *Asian American Women and Men: Labor, Laws and Love* (Thousand Oaks, Calif.: Sage Publications, 1997), p. 55.

151 "Wait till the day I become successful": Him Mark Lai, Genny Lim, and Judy Yung, *Island*, p. 94.

151 "Leaving behind my writing bush": Ibid., p. 84.

152 "Now poor Wong Fong": Letter, Collector of Customs, Port of San Francisco, to Mr. H. A. Ling, Attorney, August 21, 1895, National Archives, Pacific Sierra Region, San Bruno, California. Given to author from the personal files of Neil Thomsen, archivist at NARA San Bruno.

152 Information on Elsie Sigel murder: Arthur Bonner, *Alas! What Brought Thee Hither? The Chinese in New York 1800–1950*, pp. 120–22.

153   draperies to be removed from each room, stall, and both: *Providence Daily Journal,* June 25, 1909, and *Providence Sunday Journal,* June 20, 1909, as cited in *Origins & Destinations,* p. 423.

153   90 percent of such raids: Letter written on behalf of United Chinese Association of Ohio and the Chinese Merchants Association of Cleveland, Ohio, to William B. Wilson, Secretary of Labor, March 30, 1916. File 53775/139, Entry 9, Box 235, Record Group 85, National Archives, Washington, D.C.

153–54 Description of arrests and imprisonment: Petition to President Wilson, stamped June 1, 1914. File 53620-115A, Box 229, Entry 9, Stack Area 17W3, Row 2, Compartment 1, Shelf 6, Record Group 85, National Archives, Washington, D.C.

154   "solitary, dark confinement":   "Report of the Special Committee in Charge of the Investigation of the Treatment of Chinese Residents and Immigrants by U.S. Immigration Officers." By the Special Committee appointed by the Chinese Chamber of Commerce and Chinese-American League of Justice of Los Angeles, California, January 4, 1913. File 53620/115, Entry 9, Box 228, Record Group 85, National Archives, Washington, D.C.

154   "unfit for the transportation of cattle":   Ibid.

155   "This business had been going on for a number of years":   Letter to the Attorney General, December 16, 1917. File 54184/138, Box 259, Entry 9, Record Group 85, National Archives, Washington, D.C.

155   as much as $100,000 a year: *San Francisco Examiner* news clip, October 1917. File 54184/138B, Box 259, Entry 9, Record Group 85, National Archives, Washington, D.C.; Valerie Natale, "Angel Island 'Guardian of the Western Gate,'" *Prologue: Quarterly of the National Archives Record Administration* 30:2 (Summer 1998).

155   charging $1,400:   Valerie Natale, "Angel Island 'Guardian of the Western Gate.'"

155   Description of the extent of Immigration Service corruption: Letter, John Densmore to the Secretary of Labor, May 1, 1919. File 54184/138-B, Box 259, Entry 9, Record Group 85, National Archives, Washington, D.C; Valerie Natale, "Angel Island 'Guardian of the Western Gate.'"

155   discharge of some forty people: Letter, John Densmore to Alfred Hampton, Assistant Commissioner-General of Immigration, May 14, 1917, National Archives. Also, research of Bob Barde, academic coordinator of the Institute of Business and Economic Research, University of California, Berkeley, provided to author.

156   "May 27 10:20 p.m. Chink called McCall":   Page 16, "Copy of Complete Telephone Conversations; May 23, 1917 to July 4, 1917. Inclusive." File 54184/138B, Box 259, Entry 9, Record Group 85, National Archives, Washington, D.C.

156   **Chen Ke:** Renqiu Yu, p. 23.

156   **"Whenever my mother would mention it":** Donald Dale Jackson, "Behave Like Your Actions Reflect on All Chinese," *Smithsonian*, February 1991.

Chapter Ten. Work and Survival in the Early Twentieth Century

158   **Biographical details on Kang Youwei, Liang Qichao, and Sun Yat-sen:** See Eugene Anschel, *Homer Lea, Sun Yat-sen and the Chinese Revolution* (New York: Praeger, 1984); Michael Gasster, *Chinese Intellectuals and the Revolution of 1911: The Birth of Modern Radicalism* (Seattle: University of Washington Press, 1969); Jane Leung Larson, "New Source Materials on Kang Youwei and the Baohuanghui: The Tan Zhangxiao (Tom Leung) Collection of Letters and Documents at UCLA's East Asian Library," *Chinese America: History and Perspectives 1993;* Jung-Pang Lo, ed., *K'ang Yu-wei: A Biography and a Symposium* (Tucson: University of Arizona Press, 1967); L. Eve Armentrout Ma, *Revolutionaries, Monarchists and Chinatowns: Chinese Politics in the Americas and the 1911 Revolution* (Honolulu: University of Hawaii Press, 1990); Franklin Ng, "The Western Military Academy in Fresno," *Origins & Destinations: 41 Essays on Chinese America;* Young-tsu Wong, "Revisionism Reconsidered: Kang Youwei and the Reform Movement of 1898," *Journal of Asian Studies*, August 1992; Robert Worden, "A Chinese Reformer in Exile: The North American Phase of the Travels of K'ang Yu-wei, 1899–1909," Ph.D. dissertation, Georgetown University, 1971.

161   **1913 Alien Land Act:** Sandy Lydon, *Chinese Gold*, pp. 408–11.

162   **"The whites treated us Chinese like slaves":** Jeff Gillenkirk and James Motlow, *Bitter Melon: Inside America's Last Rural Chinese Town* (Seattle: University of Washington Press, 1987) p. 89.

162   **Lum Yip Kee:** Lynn Pan, *Sons of the Yellow Emperor*, p. 73.

162   **Chun Afong:** Ibid., p. 73.

162   **Thomas Foon Chew:** J. C. Wright, "Thomas Foon Chew: Founder of Bayside Cannery," in Gloria Sun Hom, ed., *Chinese Argonauts: An Anthology of the Chinese Contributions to the Historical Development of Santa Clara County* (San Jose, Calif.: Foothill Community College, 1971), pp. 20–41; Thomas W. Chinn, *Bridging the Pacific: San Francisco Chinatown and Its People* (San Francisco: Chinese Historical Society of America, 1989), pp. 105–7; Eric A. Carlson, "Fortunes in Alviso," *Metro*, April 12–18, 2001, p. 15.

162   **Chin Lung:** Ruthanne Lum McCunn, *Chinese American Portraits: Personal Histories 1828–1988* (San Francisco: Chronicle Books, 1988), pp. 89–97. For more details on his life, see Sucheng Chan, *This Bitter-*

sweet Soil: The Chinese in California Agriculture, 1860–1910 (Berkeley and Los Angeles: University of California Press, 1986), pp. 206–12.

163 **roughly a quarter of all Chinese workers:** Out of 45,614 Chinese, 11,438 worked in restaurants. *Asians in America: Selected Student Papers,* Asian American Research Project, University of California at Davis, Working Publication #3, p. 31.

163 **Chow mein:** Imogene L. Lim and John Eng-Wong, "Chow Mein Sandwiches: Chinese American Entrepreneurship in Rhode Island," *Origins & Destinations,* pp. 417–35; Peter Kwong, *The New Chinatown* (New York: Hill and Wang, 1987, first edition, and 1996, revised edition), p. 34.

163 **David Jung:** *Chicago Tribune,* February 17, 1988.

164 **"as a rule Caucasians":** Tan Fuyuan, *The Science of Oriental Medicine, Diet and Hygiene* (Los Angeles, 1902), p. 11, as cited in Haiming Liu, "Between China and America," Ph.D. thesis provided to author, p. 96.

164 **Hu Yunxiao:** Haiming Liu, p. 89.

164 **ran advertisements in English-language newspapers:** Ibid., p. 94.

164 **twenty-eight Chinese herb doctors:** International Chinese Business Directory Co., Inc., Wong Kin, President, *International Chinese Business Directory for the World for the Year 1913* (San Francisco, 1913). As cited in Haiming Liu, p. 90.

164 **Chang Yitang:** Haiming Liu, pp. 97–99.

165 **believes he invented those credentials:** Louise Leung Larson, *Sweet Bamboo: Saga of a Chinese American Family* (Los Angeles: Chinese Historical Society of Southern California, 1990), p. 19.

166 **"The [more] he was arrested":** Ibid., p. 71.

166 **Joe Shoong:** Thomas W. Chinn, *Bridging the Pacific,* pp. 185–86; "Joe Shoong, Chinese Merchant King, Dies," *San Francisco Chronicle,* April 15, 1961; Ronald Takaki, *Strangers from a Different Shore,* p. 252.

166 **"the richest, best-known Chinese businessman":** *Time,* March 28, 1938, p. 56.

166 **Ray Joe:** Oral history conducted by Sam Chu Lin and provided to author.

166 **"I sleep on two trucks pulled together for bed":** Ibid.

167 **kept a stick in their stores:** James W. Loewen, p. 33.

167 **earn on average twice the white median income:** Ibid., p. 53.

168 **almost 30 percent of all employed Chinese worked in laundries:** Betty Lee Sung, *The Story of the Chinese in America* (New York: Collier, 1971), p. 188.

168 **out of a total of 45,614 Chinese workers, 12,559 were laundry people:** *Asians in America: Selected Student Papers.* Asian American Research Project, University of California at Davis, Working Publication #3, p. 31.

168 **scrub board, soap, and an iron:** Betty Lee Sung, p. 190.

168   **"In the old days, some of those fellows were really ignorant":**   Paul C. P. Siu, *Chinese Laundryman: A Study of Social Isolation* (New York: New York University Press, 1987), p. 52.

168   **charged at least 15 percent less:**   Interview with Danny Moy, New York Chinatown History Project, archived in Museum of Chinese in the Americas, 70 Mulberry Street, New York City.

169   **"My father used to joke":**   Judith Luk oral history interview with Tommy Tom, assistant manager of Wah Kue wet wash, January 9, 1981, New York Chinatown History Project, Museum of Chinese in the Americas, New York.

169   **"I heard that some of them used a string to hang a piece of bread from the ceiling":**   Renqiu Yu, *To Save China, to Save Ourselves*, p. 26.

169   **"In China in the old days":**   Interview with Loy Wong, April 26, 1982, New York Chinatown History Project, Museum of Chinese in the Americas, New York.

169   **"became like balls":**   Ruthanne Lum McCunn, p. 155.

169   **in the thirty-eight years she worked in a laundry, she left it only three times:**   Yen Le Espiritu, *Asian American Women and Men*, p. 38.

169–70   **"Some of these old-timers":**   James Dao interview with Andy Eng, manager of the Wing Gong laundry, New York Chinatown History Project, Museum of Chinese in the Americas.

170   **enjoyed an astounding 90 percent literacy rate:**   Renqiu Yu, p. 38.

170   *yishanguan:*   Renqiu Yu, p. 28.

170   **1920s correspondence between Hsiao Teh Seng:**   Translated by Paul C. P. Siu and archived in the Ernest Burgess Papers, Regenstein Library Special Collections, University of Chicago. An excellent description of these letters can be found in Adam McKeown, "Chinese Migrants Among Ghosts: Chicago, Peru and Hawaii: The Early Twentieth Century," Ph.D. dissertation in history, University of Chicago, 1997, pp. 80–86.

172   **L. C. Tsung's *The Marginal Man*:**   Jack Chen, *The Chinese of America*, pp. 158–59.

Chapter Eleven. A New Generation Is Born

173   **100,686 men and 4,779 women:**   1880 U.S. Census.

173   **seven Chinese men for every Chinese woman:**   Diane Mei Lin Mark and Ginger Chih, *A Place Called Chinese America*, p. 173. According to the 1920 U.S. Census, there were 53,891 Chinese males and 7,748 Chinese females.

174   **only about one hundred fifty Chinese women:**   *Origins & Destinations*, p. 89.

174   **not a single Chinese woman:**   Victor G. and Brett de Bary Nee, *Longtime Californ'*, p. 25; Jack Chen, *The Chinese of America*, p. 176.

175   **"My parents wanted us to become professionals"**: Interview with
       Herbert Leong, interview #141, Southern California Chinese American
       Oral History Project, sponsored by the Asian American Studies Center
       at the University of California, Los Angeles, and the Chinese Historical
       Society of Southern California.

175   **"You can make a million dollars"**: Victor G. and Brett de Bary Nee, p.
       151.

175   **"baboons"**: Victor Low, *The Unimpressible Race,* p. 15.

175   shut down a public school for Chinese children: Victor Low, p. 14.

175   **segregate Asians, American Indians, and blacks**: Ibid., pp. 20–21. For
       instance, the 1864 School Law stated, "Negroes, Mongolians, and Indians
       shall not be admitted into the public schools; provided, that upon the
       application of the parents or guardians of ten or more such colored chil-
       dren, made in writing to the Trustees of any such district, said Trustees
       shall establish a separate school for the education of Negroes, Mongolians,
       and Indians, and use the public school funds for the support of the same."

176   **new California state law granted separate public education for blacks
       and Indians**: Ibid., pp. 26–27.

176   **Chinese children were the only racial group to be denied a state-
       funded education**: Victor Low, pp. 37, 49.

176   **"the association of Chinese and white children"**: Judy Yung,
       Unbound Feet, p. 48.

176   **"filthy or vicious habits"**: Victor Low, p. 50.

176   **"dangerous to the well-being of the state"**: Ibid., p. 60.

176   rather go to jail: Ibid., p. 61.

177   adopted a resolution: Ibid., p. 61.

177   **punish the board members with contempt citations**: Ibid., p. 63.

177   **"urgency provision"**: Ibid., p. 66.

177   **"May you Mr. Moulder"**: Ibid., p. 71. The letter, dated April 8, 1885,
       was published in the *San Francisco Daily Alta California* newspaper on
       April 16, 1885.

177   Lum Gong: James Loewen, pp. 65–68; Sucheng Chan, p. 58.

177   **A few Chinese American children managed to find ways to attend
       Caucasian schools**: In places like San Jose, California, and Hawaii,
       Chinese American children were integrated into white schools. There,
       the law stipulated that they could attend white schools as long as no
       white parents complained. Darlene T. Chan, "San Jose's Old Chinatown,
       Heinlenville, 1850–1930: A Historical Study," Ph.D. dissertation in edu-
       cation, University of San Francisco, 1994, p. 26.

178   **a group of white parents at Washington Grammar School**: Victor
       Low, pp. 109–10.

178   **a Chinese boy graduated at the top of his class**: Author interview with
       Sam Chu Lin, November 2002; Cheng-Tsu Wu, ed., *"Chink!,"* p. 147.

179   "I remember rushing home from school":   Ruthanne Lum McCunn, *Chinese American Portraits*, p. 133.

179   Bernice Leung: Interview with Bernice Leung, interview #137, Southern California Chinese American Oral History Project.

179   "I was brought up purely Caucasian":   Huping Ling, *Surviving on the Gold Mountain*, p. 78. Original citation: Arthur Dong, *Forbidden City, U.S.A.*, color video, 56 minutes, 1989, in *The American Experience*.

179   "There was endless discussion":   Victor Wong, "Childhood II," in Nick Harvey, ed., *Ting: The Caldron: Chinese Art and Identity in San Francisco* (San Francisco: Glide Urban Center, 1970), p. 71.

180   "We have never lived in Chinatown":   "Interview with Lillie Leung," by Wm. C. Smith, Los Angeles, August 12, 1924. Major Document #76, Box 25, Survey of Race Relations, Hoover Institution on War, Revolution and Peace, Stanford University.

180   "Well, you read all right":   "Story of a Chinese College Girl," p. 4, Major Document 54, Box 24, Survey of Race Relations, Hoover Institution on War, Revolution and Peace, Stanford University. Also Judy Yung, *Unbound Voices*, p. 301.

180   "In grade school I was fairly successful":   Interview conducted October 13, 1924, in Los Angeles, unnamed participant. Major Document #233, Box 28, Survey of Race Relations, Hoover Institution on War, Revolution and Peace, Stanford University.

180   "When we came to the study of China":   Ibid.

181   "Mother watched us like a hawk":   Oral history interview with Alice Sue Fun, in Judy Yung, *Unbound Voices*, p. 269.

181   "a lot of housework":   Ibid.

181   "When we grew up":   Grace Pung Guthrie, *A School Divided: An Ethnography of Bilingual Education in a Chinese Community* (Hillsdale, N.J.: Lawrence Erlbaum, 1985), p. 63.

182   Some fifty Chinese-language elementary schools and a half dozen Chinese-language high schools: Haiming Liu, p. 19.

182   "an ordeal that I grew to hate":   Louise Leung Larson, *Sweet Bamboo*, p. 65.

182   "totalitarian attitude":   Interview with Rodney Chow, interview #149, Southern California Chinese American Oral History Project. Sponsored by the Asian American Studies Center at the University of California, Los Angeles, and the Chinese Historical Society of Southern California.

183   "It was not that I was entirely unwilling to learn":   Pardee Lowe, *Father and Glorious Descendant* (Boston: Little, Brown, 1943), p. 140.

183   "I had to learn the Chinese language":   "Interview with Mrs. C. S. Machida," by Wm. C. Smith, Los Angeles, August 13, 1924. Major Document #73, Box 25, Survey of Race Relations, Hoover Institution on War, Revolution and Peace, Stanford University.

183 almost all of the Chinese American children in San Francisco: Judy Yung, *Unbound Feet*, p. 151.

184 very first Boy Scout troop: Thomas W. Chinn, *Bridging the Pacific: San Francisco Chinatown and Its People* (San Francisco: Chinese Historical Society of America, 1989), pp. 122–25.

184 "Take it all in all": Victor Low, pp. 112–13.

185 "It is almost impossible to place a Chinese or Japanese": Betty Lee Sung, p. 236.

185 "You Chinee boy or Jap boy?": Pardee Lowe, *Father and Glorious Descendant* (Boston: Little, Brown and Company, 1943), pp. 191–92.

186 "Everywhere I was greeted with perturbation": Ibid., pp. 146–47.

186 " 'Sorry,' they invariably said": Ibid., p. 147.

186 "Recently two friends of mine": "Life History and Social Document of Fred Wong," p. 6. Date and place given on document, August 29, 1924, Seattle, Washington. Survey of Race Relations, Hoover Institution on War, Revolution and Peace, Stanford University.

187 a Los Angeles bank: Interview with Clarence Yip Yeu, interview #102, Southern California Chinese American Oral History Project.

187 "Don't you have an accent?": Victor Low, p. 170.

187 Information on Frank Chuck: Connie Young Yu, *Profiles in Excellence: Peninsula Chinese Americans* (Palo Alto, Calif.: Stanford Area Chinese Club, no date listed, possibly 1986), pp. 19–23.

188 Information on Chan Chung Wing; "found it very difficult to defend my clients": Lillian Lim, "Chinese American Trailblazers in the Law," unpublished paper presented at the Sixth Chinese American Conference, July 9–11, 1999.

189 graduate from high school in numbers equal to Chinese boys: Judy Yung, *Unbound Feet*, pp. 126–27.

189 refused to finance her college education: Jade Snow Wong, *Fifth Chinese Daughter* (original publication, Seattle: University of Washington Press, 1945; reprint edition, 1997), p. 109.

189 a total of four Chinese female students: Huping Ling, p. 45.

189 not until the 1920s that the San Francisco public school system began hiring female Chinese schoolteachers: Judy Yung, *Unbound Feet*, p. 129.

190 Chinatown Telephone Exchange: Ibid., p. 139.

191 Alice Fong Yu: Ibid., p. 129; Thomas W. Chinn, *Bridging the Pacific*, pp. 236–38.

191 Information on Martha, Mickey, and Marian Fong: Judy Yung, *Unbound Feet*, p. 131.

191 Faith So Leung: Ibid., p. 133. Also Thomas W. Chinn, *Bridging the Pacific*, pp. 187–89.

191 Dolly Gee: Judy Yung, *Unbound Feet*, pp. 138–39.

192   **Information on Bessie Jeong:** Interview with Bessie Jeong, interview
       #157, Southern California Chinese American Oral History Project;
       "Story of a Chinese Girl Student," Major Document #5, Box 24, Survey
       of Race Relations, Hoover Institution on War, Revolution and Peace,
       Stanford University; Judy Yung, *Unbound Feet,* pp. 131–33, 142, 165–66.

193   **"My parents wanted to hold onto the old idea":** "Interview with Lil-
       lie Leung," by Wm. C. Smith, Los Angeles, August 12, 1924. Major Doc-
       ument #76, Box 25, Survey of Race Relations, Hoover Institution on
       War, Revolution and Peace, Stanford University.

193   **"spooning":** Judy Yung, *Unbound Feet,* p. 166.

193   **One San Francisco ABC couple:** Description of Daisy Wong Chinn
       and Thomas W. Chinn in Judy Yung, *Unbound Feet,* p. 167.

194   **founded Pi Alpha Phi:** *A* magazine, February/March 1995, p. 14.

194   **Sigma Omicron Pi:** Judy Yung, *Unbound Feet,* p. 128.

194   **"Chinese Collegiate Shuffle!":** Ronald Riddle, *Flying Dragons, Flow-
       ing Streams: Music in the Life of San Francisco's Chinese* (Westport,
       Conn.: Greenwood Press, 1983), p. 145, as cited in Huping Ling, p. 104.

194   **"our parents always preached":** Diane Mark and Ginger Chih, *A
       Place Called Chinese America,* p. 86.

195   **Expatriation Act of 1907:** Judy Yung, *Unbound Feet,* pp. 168–69.

195   **1922 Cable Act:** Sucheng Chan, "The Exclusion of Chinese Women,"
       in Chinese Historical Society of America, *Chinese America: History and
       Perspectives 1994,* p. 124.

195   **"My Most Embarrassing Moment":** Interview with Yu-Shan Han,
       interview #152, Southern California Chinese American Oral History
       Project.

195   **"Chinese women who are born here are regular flappers":** "Mr. Mar
       Sui Haw," Seattle, Washington, by C. H. Burnett, August 28, 1924, p. 11.
       Major Document #244, Box 29, Survey of Race Relations, Hoover Insti-
       tution on War, Revolution and Peace, Stanford University.

196   **"It is not right for Chinese man born in China":** "Life History and
       Social Document of Andrew Kan," Seattle, Washington, August 22,
       1924, by C. H. Burnett, p. 12. Major Document #178, Box 27, Survey of
       Race Relations, Hoover Institution on War, Revolution and Peace, Stan-
       ford University.

196   **"Don't get married in the United States!":** Lee family oral history
       project, 1991, p. 21, as cited in Erika Lee, "The Chinese American Com-
       munity in Buffalo, New York 1900–1960," honors thesis at Tufts Univer-
       sity, 1991.

196   **did not want any of their offspring to marry outside their own
       dialect:** Interview with Rodney H. Chow, interview #149, Southern
       California Chinese American Oral History Project.

196   **Milton L. Barron surveyed 97 Chinese marriages:** Milton L. Barron,

People Who Intermarry (Syracuse, N.Y.: Syracuse University Press, 1946), pp. 11–19, as cited in Betty Lee Sung, *The Story of the Chinese in America*, p. 258.

197   **"foreign devil child":**   Judy Yung, *Unbound Feet*, p. 170.

197   **"disapprove very much":**   Tye Leung Schulze, "Ting," in Louise Schulze Lee private collection, as cited in Judy Yung, *Unbound Feet*, p. 170.

198   **killing or wounding more than seven thousand people:**   Him Mark Lai, "Roles Played by Chinese in America During China's Resistance to Japanese Aggression and During World War II," *Chinese America: History and Perspectives*, 1997, p. 76.

Chapter Twelve. Chinese America During the Great Depression

201   **"I remember wearing sneakers with holes in them":**   Interview with Lillian Louie, p. 4, New York Chinatown History Project, Museum of Chinese in the Americas.

202   **2,300, or 18 percent:**   Judy Yung, *Unbound Feet*, p. 183.

202   **22 percent:**   Ibid.

202   **"During the Depression":**   Interview with Mark Wong, in Victor G. and Brett de Bary Nee, *Longtime Californ'*, p. 168.

202   **"tens of thousands of Chinese laundry men":**   *Chinese Nationalist Daily*, April 24, 1933, p. 1, as cited in Renqiu Yu, *To Save China, to Save Ourselves*, p. 35.

202   **3,200 members:**   Renqiu Yu, p. 55.

203   **Lillian Lee Kim story:**   Lillian Lee Kim, "An Early Baltimore Chinese Family: Lee Yick You and Louie Yu Oy," *Chinese America: History and Perspectives 1994* (Brisbane, Calif.: Chinese Historical Society of America, 1994), pp. 155–74.

203   **"thoroughly modern":**   Ronald Takaki, *Strangers from a Different Shore*, p. 247.

204   **"the looks that made China's beauties so fascinating":**   Judy Tzu-Chun Wu, "The Loveliest Daughter: A Melting Pot of the East and the West," *Journal of Social History*, Fall 1997, p. 7.

204   **almost one-fifth of the city's tourist trade:**   Ronald Takaki, p. 248.

204   **"Make tourists WANT to come":**   Ibid., p. 249.

204   **pulling rickshaws for white sightseers:**   Interview with Rodney H. Chow, interview #149, Southern California Chinese American Oral History Project. In Los Angeles, China City opened in 1938 but burned down the following year. Later, it was rebuilt but was again destroyed by fire in 1949. Source: Asian American Studies Center at the University of California, Los Angeles, and the Chinese Historical Society of Southern California, *Linking Our Lives: Chinese American Women of Los Angeles*

(Los Angeles: Chinese Historical Society of Southern California, 1984), p. 16.

204 guides warned visitors to hold hands: Betty Lee Sung, p. 130.

204 "opium-crazed": Ronald Takaki, p. 251.

205 "a joint stock company": Adam McKeown, "Chinese Migrants Among Ghosts," p. 284.

205 Information on Forbidden City: Huping Ling, *Surviving on the Gold Mountain*, pp. 119–20; Judy Yung, *Unbound Feet*, pp. 202–3; author interviews with Chinatown residents.

205 suggested having naked girls jump out of a cake: Gloria Heyung Chun, *Of Orphans and Warriors: Inventing Chinese American Culture and Identity* (New Brunswick, N.J.: Rutgers University Press, 2000), p. 35.

206 "Every day and all year round": Letter to *New York Times*, October 1, 1922, from S. J. Benjamin Cheng, a Columbia University student, as cited in Arthur Bonner, *Alas! What Brought Thee Hither?*, p. 107.

206 "I never saw an underground tunnel": Victor G. and Brett de Bary Nee, p. 71.

206 so that chickens could be raised there: Interview with Rose Wong, interview #80, Southern California Chinese American Oral History Project.

206 "We hated them!": *The Life and Times of Lung Chin: A Story of New York Chinatown*, manuscript in folder labeled "Chinatown 19[15]–? Restaurants, Tongs, Opium, Sports, basketball, social culture," Museum of Chinese in the Americas.

207 "the great and evil man": Cheng-Tsu Wu, ed., "*Chink!*," pp. 136–38. Original citation: Sax Rohmer, *The Return of Dr. Fu-Manchu* (New York: McKinlay, Stone and MacKenzie, 1916).

207 "green eyes gleamed upon me": Ibid.

209 "You're asking me": *Los Angeles Times*, July 12, 1987.

209 "Because I had been the villainess": *Hollywood Citizen News*, 1958, as cited in Judy Chu, "Anna May Wong," in Emma Gee et al., eds., *Counterpoint: Perspectives on Asian America* (Los Angeles: Asian American Center, University of California at Los Angeles, 1976), p. 287.

210 did little more than provide exotic background: Interview with Lillie Louie, interview #135, Southern California Chinese American Oral History Project.

210 Information on Tom Gubbins: Interviews with Eddie E. Lee (#17), Gilbert Leong (#19), Mabel L. Lew (#22), Lillie Louie (#35), Bessie Loo (#38), Ethel Cannon (#64), and Gim Fong (#89), Southern California Chinese American Oral History Project.

210 "the closest we would ever get to China": Louise Leung, "Night Call in Chinatown," *Los Angeles Times Sunday Magazine*, July 26, 1936, pp. 3–4.

211 **"the older people, they were always talking about going back home":** Victor Wong, "Childhood II," in Nick Harvey, ed., *Ting: The Caldron*, p. 70.

211 **"If your uncle comes back to America":** Letter, Sam Chang to Tennyson Chang, January 4, 1925, as cited in Haiming Liu, unpublished manuscript, p. 205; *Origins & Destinations*, p. 260.

211 **more than 90 percent of their placements:** Hsien-ju Shih, "The Social and Vocational Adjustments of the Second Generation Chinese High School Students in San Francisco," Ph.D. dissertation, University of California, Berkeley, 1937, p. 72. As cited in Gloria Heyung Chun, *Of Orphans and Warriors*, p. 17.

211 **"Father used to tell me":** Interview with James Low, in Victor G. and Brett de Bary Nee, p. 169.

212 **"Oh, you couldn't get a job":** Grace Pung Guthrie, *A School Divided*, p. 35.

212 *Chung Sai Yat Po* **openly urged young Chinese Americans:** Haiming Liu, p. 20.

212 **dreaming about going "back" to China:** Interview with Rodney H. Chow, interview #149, Southern California Chinese American Oral History Project.

212 **75 percent of the attendees:** *Chinese Digest,* July 3, 1936, p. 14.

212 **"ever since I can remember":** Robert Dunn, "Does My Future Lie in China or America?," *Chinese Digest,* May 15, 1936.

213 **"built on the mound of shame":** Kaye Hong, "Does My Future Lie in China or America?," *Chinese Digest,* May 22, 1936.

213 **The careers of Robert Dunn and Kaye Hong:** Gloria Heyung Chun, p. 31.

213 **one in five ABCs migrated to work in China:** Gloria Heyung Chun, *Of Orphans and Warriors*, p. 26; Judy Yung, *Unbound Feet*, p. 159.

214 **Recruitment of ABCs by organizations in China:** Gloria Heyung Chun, p. 26.

214 **Information on Flora Belle Jan:** Judy Yung, *Unbound Feet*, pp. 143, 169.

Chapter Thirteen. "The Most Important Historical Event of Our Times": World War II

216 **some 250,000 casualties:** Jonathan D. Spence, *The Search for Modern China* (New York: W. W. Norton, 1990), p. 447.

216 **locals simply starved to death:** Madeline Y. Hsu, *Dreaming of Gold, Dreaming of Home,* p. 179.

217 **pawned first their jewelry and furniture:** Ibid.

217 **at least 150,000 Toishanese—about one in four—had either died or disappeared:** Ibid., p. 180. Also June Y. Mei, "Researching Chinese-

American History in Taishan: A Report," in Genny Lim, ed., *The Chinese American Experience: Papers from the Second National Conference in Chinese American Studies (1980)*, p. 58. As James Low recalled of those years, "I saw other families starve during the Japanese war and World War II. The mothers had used all the money for gambling, for jewelry, for eating." (Victor G. and Brett de Bary Nee, *Longtime Californ'*, p. 173.)

217   **distributed thousands of English-language flyers:** Renqiu Yu, *To Save China, to Save Ourselves*, pp. 101–2.

217   **fewer than ninety planes in safe working condition:** Iris Chang, *Thread of the Silkworm* (New York: Basic Books, 1995), p. 31.

217   **two thousand in the Japanese military:** Ibid.

217   **aviation schools or clubs:** Him Mark Lai, "Roles Played by Chinese in America During China's Resistance to Japanese Aggression and During World War II," *Chinese America: History and Perspectives 1997* (Brisbane, Calif.: Chinese Historical Society of America, 1997), pp. 79–81.

218   **Information on Ouyang Ying and Katherine Cheung:** Judy Yung, *Unbound Feet*, p. 162.

218   **Stanley Lau:** Ibid., p. 99.

218   **Clifford Louie:** Ibid., p. 98.

218   **thirty-nine Chinese sailors:** Ibid., p. 110.

218   **demonstrated in front of the *Spyros*:** Judy Yung, *Unbound Feet*, p. 241.

218   **"spattered with blood and tears":** *Chung Sai Yat Po*, December 19, 1938, as cited in Judy Yung, *Unbound Feet*, p. 242.

219   **"100 percent opposed to passing the picket line":** Judy Yung, *Unbound Feet*, p. 242.

219   **"Rice Bowl" parties:** Huping Ling, *Surviving on the Gold Mountain*, p. 107; Judy Yung, *Unbound Feet*, pp. 239–40.

219   **American Bureau for Medical Aid to China:** This organization, with the support of prominent Caucasian Americans, provided more than $10 million worth of aid to China during the war. Madame Chiang served as the honorary chair of the bureau. The archival papers of ABMAC are available in Columbia University's Rare Book and Manuscript Library.

219   **blood bank in New York:** Huping Ling, p. 108.

220   **relief-fund boxes on their counters:** Renqui Yu, pp. 101–2.

220   **garment workers sewed thousands of winter garments:** Judy Yung, *Unbound Feet*, p. 244.

220   **collecting tin cans, foil, and other scrap metal:** Florence Gee, "I am an American—How can I help win this war?," *Chinese Press*, May 15, 1942, as cited in Ronald Takaki, *Strangers from a Different Shore*, p. 373.

220   **$20 million for the Chinese War Relief Association:** Him Mark Lai, "Roles Played by Chinese in America During China's Resistance to Japanese Aggression and During World War II," p. 94.

220 **$25 million:** Him Mark Lai, "China and the Chinese American Community," *Chinese America: History and Perspectives 1999*, p. 6.

220 **about 75,000 at the start of the 1930s:** 1930 U.S. Census (74,954 Chinese). Also Diane Mark and Ginger Chih, *A Place Called Chinese America*, p. 179.

220 **$300 for every Chinese in the country:** Him Mark Lai, "Roles Played by Chinese in America During China's Resistance to Japanese Aggression and During World War II," p. 94.

220 **some gave almost every cent:** Renqiu Yu, p. 100.

220 **Montgomery Hom:** Author interview with Montgomery Hom in Los Angeles.

221 **percentage of U.S.-born Chinese Americans surpassed:** L. Ling-chi Wang, "Politics of Assimilation and Repression: History of the Chinese in the United States, 1940 to 1970," unpublished manuscript, Asian American Studies Collection, Ethnic Studies Library, University of California at Berkeley, p. 288.

223 **"hardworking, honest, brave":** Sucheng Chan, *Asian Americans: An Interpretative History* (Boston: Twayne, 1991), p. 121.

223 **"Virtually all Japanese are short":** *Time*, December 22, 1941, p. 33.

224 **used jujitsu:** Interview with Rodney Chow, interview #149, Southern California Chinese American Oral History Project.

224 **carried identification cards:** Judy Yung, *Unbound Feet*, p. 250; Jules Archer, *The Chinese and the Americans* (New York: Hawthorne Books, 1976), p. 106. It appears that the Chinese embassy also issued identification cards for people of Chinese ethnicity in the United States. One such card can be found in File #5608-505, Box 2168, Accession #58734, Stack Area 17W3, Row 13, Compartment 15, Shelf 1, Record Group 85, National Archives, Washington, D.C. The card reads: "Chinese Embassy Washington, D.C. Chinese Identification Card. The bearer of this CHINESE Identification card, whose photograph appears heron, is a member of the CHINESE race."

225 **Yu-shan Han:** Interview with Yu-shan Han, interview #152, p. 19, Southern California Chinese American Oral History Project.

225 **"You damn Jap":** Judy Yung, *Unbound Feet*, p. 256.

225 **Citizens Committee to Repeal Chinese Exclusion:** Diane Mark and Ginger Chih, p. 98; Harry H. L. Kitano and Roger Daniels, *Asian Americans: Emerging Minorities* (Englewood Cliffs, N.J.: Prentice Hall, 1988), p. 38.

225 **"enemies of the American people":** H. Brett Melendy, p. 28.

226 **first Chinese woman and second woman ever invited to address a joint session of Congress:** Mur Wolf, "Madame Chiang Kai-shek; Week of August 14, 2000; Mayling Soong, who became Madame Chiang Kai-Shek, is the Wellesley Person of the Week." Wellesley College 125th

Anniversary Person of the Week. Office for Public Information, Wellesley College.

226   "Goddamnit, I never saw anything like it": *Time*, March 1, 1943, p. 23.

227   "To men of our generation": Charlie Leong quote, in Victor and Brett de Bary Nee, *Longtime Californ'*, pp. 154–55. For a description of Leong's life, see Sandy Lydon, p. 483. A journalism graduate of San Jose State College and Stanford University, Leong was the first Chinese American editor of a college newspaper and the first Asian American to join the San Francisco Press Club.

227   Colonel Won-Loy Chan: Author interview with Montgomery Hom, documentary filmmaker of *They Served with Pride*.

228   15,000 to 20,000 Chinese served in the military: Thomas Chinn, ed., *Bridging the Pacific*, p. 147; Him Mark Lai, "Roles Played by Chinese in America During China's Resistance to Japanese Aggression and During World War II," p. 99; Judy Yung, *Unbound Feet*, p. 252. (About 13,499, or 22 percent, of adult Chinese men enlisted in the army. Source: Ronald Takaki, p. 374; Gloria Chun, p. 44.)

228   20 percent of the Chinese population: Him Mark Lai, "Roles Played by Chinese in America During China's Resistance to Japanese Aggression and During World War II," p. 99.

228   8.6 percent: Ibid., p. 99.

228   40 percent: Yen Le Espiritu, *Asian American Women and Men: Labor, Laws and Love*, p. 50.

228   "New York's Chinatown cheered itself hoarse": Rose Hum Lee, "Chinese in the United States Today: The War Has Changed Their Lives," *Survey Graphic*, October 1942, p. 4444.

228   "I remember Sunday, December 7th, vividly": Richard V. Lee, M.D., "A Brief Lee Family History," paper presented at the conference on Yung Wing and the Chinese Educational Mission, 1872–1881, at Yale University, September 28–29, 2001.

229   "I had never felt so happy and proud": Gloria He-Yung Chun interview with David Gan, former soldier with the U.S. Army. Gloria He-Yung Chung, *Of Orphans and Warriors*, p. 85.

229   asked if they were part of the Chinese army: Christina M. Lim and Sheldon H. Lim, "In the Shadow of the Tiger: The 407th Air Service Squadron, Fourteenth Air Force, CB1, World War II," *Chinese America: History and Perspectives 1993*, p. 27.

229   "goddamn Chink": Peter Phan, "Familiar Strangers: The Fourteenth Air Service Group; Case Study of Chinese American Identity During World War II," *Chinese America: History and Perspectives 1993*, p. 85.

229   all his possessions thrown out the window: Ibid.

229   "I was told that 'no Chinaman will ever fly in my outfit' ": Oral history interview with William Der Bing in 1979, in Diane Mei Lin Mark and Ginger Chih, *A Place Called Chinese America*, p. 96.

230 **"I was so damn surprised":** Peter Phan, "Familiar Strangers," *Chinese America: History and Perspectives 1993*, p. 87.

230 **Gordon P. Chung-Hoon:** "Navy Names Destroyer to Honor Rear Adm. Chung-Hoon," Department of Defense press release, October 10, 2000; "Navy Ship Named for Isle World War II Hero," Associated Press, October 12, 2000.

231 **"China is your home":** Peter Phan, "Familiar Strangers," *Chinese America: History and Perspectives 1993*, p. 78.

231 **Nationalist soldiers marching in straw sandals:** Ibid., p. 91.

231 **John Chuck:** Ibid., p. 90.

231 **"behind time":** Ibid., p. 93.

232 **"Except for the uniforms":** Christina M. Lim and Sheldon H. Lim, "In the Shadow of the Tiger," *Chinese America: History and Perspectives 1993*, p. 62.

233 **Information on Air WACs:** Author interview with Judith Bellafaire, Ph.D., curator of the Women in Military Service for America Memorial, Inc., January 27, 2003; Judith Bellafaire, "Asian-American Servicewomen in Defense of the Nation," 1999 article available online from http://www.womensmemorial.org/APA.html and included in the Women in Military Service for American Memorial exhibit, Arlington National Cemetery, Arlington, Virginia; Rudi Williams, "Asian Pacific American Women Served in World War II, Too," American Forces Press Service, May 1999.

233 **Helen Pon Onyett:** Judith Bellafaire, "Asian-American Servicewomen in Defense of the Nation"; Huping Ling, *Surviving on the Gold Mountain*, p. 120.

234 **as long as the marriage had occurred before May 26, 1924:** Roger Daniels, *Asian America*, pp. 96–97.

234 **only about sixty Chinese women a year:** *Origins & Destinations: 41 Essays on Chinese America*, p. 89; Roger Daniels, *Asian America*, p. 97.

234 **male-female ratio was three to one:** Yen Le Espiritu, *Asian American Women and Men*, p. 55.

234 **almost six thousand Chinese American soldiers:** Ibid.

234 **One soldier on leave flew to China:** Rose Hum Lee, "The Recent Immigration Chinese Families of the San Francisco–Oakland Area," *Marriage and Family Living* 18 (1956), pp. 14–24. As cited in Huping Ling, p. 114.

234 **80 percent of all new Chinese arrivals:** Peter Kwong, *The New Chinatown*, p. 20.

234 **an average of two births a day:** L. Ling-chi Wang, "Politics of Assimilation and Repression," p. 284.

234 **many had to sleep in the hallways:** Author interview with Him Mark Lai, March 16, 1999, San Francisco.

234 **soared from 77,000 to 117,000:** Yen Le Espiritu, p. 55.

Chapter Fourteen. "A Mass Inquisition": The Cold War, the Chinese
    Civil War, and McCarthyism

237   fewer than one in four survived: J. A. G. Roberts, *A Concise History
       of China* (Cambridge, Mass.: Harvard University Press, 1999), p. 239.

238   "its readiness to conclude":   *A Decade of American Foreign Policy:
       Basic Documents, 1941–49*, prepared at the request of the Senate Com-
       mittee on Foreign Relations by the Staff of the Committee and the
       Department of State. Washington D.C.: Government Printing Office,
       1950, produced online by the Avalon Project at Yale Law School: http://
       www.yale.edu/lawweb/avalon/wwii/yalta.htm

240   "When a Chinese with some influence":   Murray A. Rubinstein, ed.,
       Taiwan: A New History (Armonk, N.Y.: M. E. Sharpe, 1999), p. 284.

240   10,000 billion Chinese dollars: Tiejun Zhang, *Chu Ran Meng Jue Lu*,
       vol. 2 (Taipei, Taiwan: Xue Yuan Publishers, 1974), p. 211.

240   factor of 85,000:   Leslie Chang, *Beyond the Narrow Gate: The Journey
       of Four Chinese Women from the Middle Kingdom to Middle America*
       (New York: Dutton, 1999), pp. 18–19.

240   63 million yuan: Leslie Chang, p. 19.

240   "eight hundred cases of notes":   Stella Dong, *Shanghai, 1842–1949*
       (New York: William Morrow, 2000), p. 282.

241   Houston businessman: L. Ling-chi Wang, "Politics of Assimilation
       and Repression," p. 306.

241   scarcely enough to buy a postage stamp: Ibid., p. 307. During this
       era, my maternal grandfather had received an advance from the Nation-
       alist government to write a book for the political department of the Chi-
       nese air force. By the time he finished writing the book and withdrew the
       money from the bank, the advance was worth less than the price of a
       shirt. (Tiejun Zhang, p. 212.)

241   1.5 million troops: J. A. G. Roberts, *A Concise History of China*,
       p. 250.

243   five thousand foreign Chinese intellectuals marooned: Peter Kwong,
       The New Chinatown, p. 59; Ronald Takaki, *Strangers from a Different
       Shore*, p. 417; Kitano and Daniels, *Asian Americans*, p. 42; Ting Ni, "Cul-
       tural Journey: Experience of Chinese Students of the 1930s and the
       1940s," Ph.D. dissertation in history, Indiana University, April 1996, p.
       142.

243   4,675:   Ting Ni, p. 81.

243   "We joked about getting gold-plated":   Author interview with Linda
       Tsao Yang.

244   "We came to a fork in our lives":   Ibid.

244   more than 2,500 Chinese students lacked basic funds: *Time*, Febru-
       ary 28, 1949.

245   **more than $8 million:**   The Committee on Educational Interchange Policy, *Chinese Students in the United States, 1948–1955* (New York, 1956), as cited in Ting Ni, pp. 24, 94.

245   **"Guomingdang-hired goon squad":**   L. Ling-chi Wang, p. 394.

246   **"Communist bandits":**   Ibid.

246   **"understanding" between the races:**   Gloria Heyung Chun, p. 84.

248   **bugged the headquarters of the Chinese Hand Laundry Alliance:**   Renqiu Yu, p. 191.

249   **white mob tore apart a Chinatown restaurant:**   L. Ling-chi Wang, p. 333.

249–50 **subpoenaed several staff members of the *China Daily News:***   Renqiu Yu, *To Save China, to Save Ourselves*, p. 187.

250   **Information on Eugene Moy:**   Renqiu Yu, p. 188; Andrew Hsiao, "100 Years of Hell-Raising," *Village Voice*, June 23, 1998; L. Ling-chi Wang, pp. 439, 443; Him Mark Lai, "China and the Chinese Community: The Political Dimension," *Chinese America: History and Perspectives 1999*, p. 11.

250   **interrogated Tan Yumin:**   Renqiu Yu, p. 191.

250   **"The FBI guy shouted back":**   Ibid., p. 187.

250   **"fantastic system":**   Kitano and Daniels, *Asian Americans*, p. 43.

251   **"destroy that system":**   L. Ling-chi Wang, p. 425.

251   **J. Edgar Hoover:**   L. Ling-chi Wang, p. 406; Roger Daniels, *Asian America*, p. 305.

251   **"Only once before in modern times":**   L. Ling-chi Wang, p. 423.

251   **"'criminal conspiracy'":**   Report from Drumwright on visa fraud. File 122.4732/12-955, Location 250/1/05/05, Box 720, Record Group 59, National Archives, Washington, D.C; L. Ling-chi Wang, pp. 422, 423. Wang provides an excellent summary of Drumwright's charges.

251   **"Chinatown was hit like an A-bomb fell":**   Ibid., p. 418.

252   **"mass inquisition":**   Ibid., p. 422. It should be noted that during the Korean War, the Chinese American community lived under the threat of mass incarceration. In 1952, the federal government allocated $775,000 to establish six internment camps, in the states of California, Arizona, Pennsylvania, Oklahoma, and Florida. (L. Ling-chi Wang, p. 368.)

252   **ten thousand Chinese confessed:**   Ronald Takaki, p. 416.

253   **some 120 Chinese intellectuals were detained:**   Yelong Han, "An Untold Story: American Policy Towards Chinese Students in the United States," *The Journal of American–East Asian Relations*, Spring 1993. As cited in Ting Ni, p. 25.

253   **Biographical details on Tsien Hsue-shen:**   Iris Chang, *Thread of the Silkworm* (New York: Basic Books, 1995).

256   **"That this government permitted this genius":**   "Made in the U.S.A.?," *60 Minutes*, October 27, 1970, CBS Archives.

256 **Information on Cameron House in the 1950s:** Author interview with Harry Chuck at Cameron House, March 17, 1999.

257 **"many of my peers strove to be all-American":** Judy Yung, *Unbound Feet*, p. 287.

257 **passed an anti-gambling law:** Ben Fong-Torres, *The Rice Room: Growing Up Chinese-American: From Number Two Son to Rock'n'Roll* (New York: Plume, 1995), p. 53.

257 **New York State Housing Survey:** L. Ling-chi Wang, p. 515.

257 **Information on William Chew:** Author interview with Bill Chew; Chew's unpublished manuscript in his private collection.

258 **the "Chinese Rockefeller of Hawaii":** Burt A. Folkart, "Known as 'Chinese Rockefeller' of the Islands; Hawaii Multimillionaire Chinn Ho Dies," *Los Angeles Times*, May 14, 1987.

258 **Information on Delbert Wong:** Interview with Delbert Wong, interview #59, Southern California Chinese American Oral History Project; Sam Chu Lin, "Historical Society Commemorates WWII 50th Anniversary," *Asian Week*, November 11, 1994; K. Connie Kang, "From China to California, a Six-Generation Saga: One Family's Milestones and Challenges Tell the Story of a Changing World," *Los Angeles Times*, June 29, 1997; Lillian Lim, "Chinese American Trailblazers in the Law."

258 **Median family income of $6,207:** Betty Lee Sung, p. 128.

259 **$5,660:** Ibid., p. 128.

259 **ruled unconstitutional the real estate convenants:** Ben Fong-Torres, p. 52. Yet many of the social barriers would remain. When future Nobel laureate C. N. Yang tried to purchase a house in Princeton, New Jersey, in 1954, the seller abruptly returned his down payment, telling Yang that the transaction would hurt his business. (Zhenning Yang, *Forty Years of Learning and Teaching* [Hong Kong: Sanlian Publishing House, 1985], pp. 11–12.)

259 **moved in furtively:** Rodney Chow interview, interview #149, Southern California Chinese American Oral History Project.

259 **"The first night, they broke my windows":** Interview with Lancing F. Lee, Southern California Chinese American Oral History Project.

260 **"the only Asian family":** Interview with Alice Young, *Nightline*, ABC News, June 28, 1999.

260 **nationwide study recorded twenty-eight American cities with Chinatowns:** Betty Lee Sung, *The Story of the Chinese in America*, p. 144.

260 **fallen to sixteen:** Ibid., p. 144.

Chapter Fifteen. New Arrivals, New Lives: The Chaotic 1960s

263 **seventy thousand people:** Nicholas D. Kristof, "Hong Kong, Wary of China, Sees Its Middle Class Fleeing," *New York Times*, November 9, 1987.

264   **only a token 105 Chinese:**   H. Brett Melendy, *Chinese and Japanese Americans,* p. 66.

264   **Thanks to special legislation:**   For details of the Refugee Relief Act of 1953 and legislation for immigrants with special skills, see L. Ling-chi Wang, "Politics of Assimilation and Repression: History of the Chinese in the United States, 1940–1970," unpublished manuscript, Asian American Studies Collection, Ethnic Studies Library, University of California at Berkeley.

264   **threw up barbed wire:**   Betty Lee Sung, pp. 92–93.

264   **presidential directive:**   Victor G. and Brett de Bary Nee, *Longtime Californ',* p. 254.

264   **some fifteen thousand Chinese refugees:**   Betty Lee Sung, p. 93.

265   **"no basis in either logic or reason":**   John F. Kennedy, *Public Papers of the Presidents of the United States* (Washington, D.C.: U.S. Government Printing Office, 1964), pp. 594–97.

265   **Statistics and political quotes regarding the Hart-Celler Act, or 1965 Immigration Act:**   "Three Decades of Mass Immigration: The Legacy of the 1965 Immigration Act," *Immigration Review,* No. 3–95, September 1995.

266   **Lillian Sing:**   Testimony of Lillian Sing, "Chinese in San Francisco—1970." Employment Problems of the Community as Presented in Testimony Before the California Fair Employment Practice Commission, December 1970, p. 15. As cited in Stanford Lyman, *Chinese Americans,* p. 143.

266   **1969 San Francisco Human Rights Commission:**   Victor G. and Brett de Bary Nee, pp. 302–3; Cheng-Tsu Wu, ed., *"Chink!,"* p. 241.

267   **"It's really amazing how the Chinese exploit themselves":**   Ronald Takaki, *Strangers from a Different Shore,* p. 428. "Here we are like the disabled," one Chinese woman said of immigrant vulnerability. "We're deaf because we cannot understand the language. We're dumb because we cannot speak it. We're blind because we cannot read it. And we're lame because we cannot find our way around." (Ruthanne Lum McCunn, *Chinese American Portraits,* p. 151.)

267   **"Your father has to work a long time":**   M. Elaine Mar, *Paper Daughter* (New York: HarperCollins, 1999), p. 98.

267   **"We each slept on a small piece of plywood":**   Grace Pung Guthrie, *A School Divided,* p. 71.

268   **greatest tuberculosis rate in the country:**   Victor G. and Brett de Bary Nee, p. xxv; L. Ling-chi Wang, p. 509.

268   **highest suicide rate:**   Victor G. and Brett de Bary Nee, pp. xxv, 260.

268   **labor in sweatshops for at least eight to ten hours a day:**   Victor Low, *The Unimpressible Race,* p. 143.

268   **"They work half the night":**   Ibid., p. 144.

268   "It began with the newcomers getting hassled": Bill Lee, *Chinese Playground: A Memoir* (San Francisco: Rhapsody Press, p. 1999), pp. 64–65.

269   "It was payback time": Ibid., p. 5.

269   Dressed in black from head to toe: Stanford Lyman, *Chinese Americans*, p. 163; Bill Lee, *Chinese Playground*, p. 128.

269   "delinquency was too clinical a word": Ben Fong-Torres, *The Rice Room*, p. 193. The worst outbreak of gang violence occurred on September 4, 1977, when three masked men armed with shotguns and automatic weapons burst into the Golden Dragon restaurant in San Francisco Chinatown and fired randomly on customers, killing five people and wounding eleven.

269   asked for a community clubhouse: Chiou-Ling Yeh, "Contesting Identities: Youth Rebellion in San Francisco's Chinese New Year Festival, 1953–1967," in Susie Lan Cassel, ed., *The Chinese in America: A History from Gold Mountain to the New Millennium*, p. 336.

270   "They have not shown that they are sorry": *East/West*, March 13, 1968, as cited in Chiou-Ling Yeh, "Contesting Identities," p. 336.

270   "Some of these kids are talking about getting guns and rioting": Ibid., p. 337.

270   Inter-Collegiate Chinese for Social Action: Ibid.

270   Concerned Chinese for Action and Change: Ibid., p. 338; L. Ling-chi Wang, p. 576; Nick Harvey, ed., *Ting: The Caldron*, p. 101.

270   "I knew to expect stories about China": Ben Fong-Torres, p. 59.

271   "I was nine years old when the letters made my parents, who are rocks, cry": Maxine Hong Kingston, *The Woman Warrior: Memoirs of a Girlhood Among Ghosts* (New York: Alfred Knopf, 1976; Vintage international edition, 1989), p. 50.

271   "The aunts in Hong Kong": Ibid., p. 50.

272   "PIG INFORMERS DIE YOUNG": Ben Fong-Torres, p. 209.

273   "It seems obvious": Supreme Court opinion, delivered by Justice Douglas. *Lau v. Nichols*, No. 72-6530, Supreme Court of the United States, 414 U.S. 56, Argued December 10, 1973, Decided January 21, 1974.

273   Third World Liberation Front: Nick Harvey, ed., *Ting: The Caldron*, p. 103; William Wei, *The Asian American Movement* (Philadelphia: Temple University Press, 1993).

274   Red Guard Party: Nick Harvey, ed., *Ting: The Caldron*, p. 103; Stanford Lyman, *Chinese Americans*, p. 165.

274   I Wor Kuen: Lori Leong, *East Wind* magazine 1:1 (1982); author interview with Corky Lee, November 2002; Rocky Chin, "New York Chinatown Today: Community in Crisis," in Amy Tachiki, Eddie Wong, Franklin Odo, and Buck Wong, eds., *Roots: An Asian American Reader*.

A Project of the UCLA Asian American Studies Center (Regents of the University of California, 1971).

275   **"the blushing dawn of ethnic awareness"**:   Gish Jen, *Mona in the Promised Land* (New York: Vintage, 1996), p. 3.

275   **" 'You know, the Chinese revolution was a long time ago' "**:   Ibid., p. 118.

276   **Fred Ho**:   Wei-hua Zhang, "Fred Ho and Jon Jang: Profiles of Two Chinese American Jazz Musicians," *Chinese America: History and Perspectives 1994* (Brisbane, Calif.: Chinese Historical Society of America, 1994), pp. 175–99.

276   **Grace Lee Boggs**:   Grace Lee Boggs, *Living for Change: An Autobiography* (Minneapolis: University of Minnesota Press, 1998).

277   **"Afro-Chinese Marxist"**:   Frank H. Wu, *Yellow: Race in America Beyond Black and White* (New York: Basic Books, 2002), p. 331.

277   **"Through sheer will"**:   Letter, Louis Tsen to Grace Lee Boggs, May 22, 1996, in Grace Lee Boggs, *Living for Change*, p. xv.

277   **Information on the social rise of the Chinese in the South** comes from James W. Loewen, *The Mississippi Chinese: Between Black and White* (Prospect Heights, Ill.: Waveland Press, 1988, 1971).

278   **Black civil rights leaders asked Chinese grocers for financial donations**:   Ibid., p. 171.

278   **Sam Chu Lin**:   Author interview with Sam Chu Lin.

279   **"I didn't go to the Chinese dances"**:   James W. Loewen, p. 160.

279   **Sam Sue**:   Joann Faung Jean Lee, *Asian American Experiences in the United States: Oral Histories of First to Fourth Generation Americans from China, the Philippines, Japan, India, the Pacific Islands, Vietnam and Cambodia* (Jefferson, N.C.: McFarland & Company, 1991), pp. 3–9.

281   **"I had the impression that anything I wanted, I could get"**:   Carter Wiseman, *I. M. Pei: A Profile in American Architecture* (New York: Harry N. Abrams, 1990), p. 32.

281   **"I had heard that there was discrimination against Chinese"**:   Dr. An Wang with Eugene Linden, *Lessons: An Autobiography* (Boston: Addison-Wesley, 1986), p. 32.

281   **"Frankly the United States seemed a lot like China to me"**:   Ibid., p. 33.

281   **"Science is the same the world over"**:   Ibid., p. 31.

281   **started Wang Laboratories in 1951 with only $600**:   Ibid., p. 75.

281   **took his company public in 1967**:   Charles Kenney, *Riding the Runaway Horse: The Rise and Decline of Wang Laboratories* (Boston: Little, Brown, 1992), p. 48.

281   **Chin Yang Lee**:   Author interview with Chin Yang Lee; Heidi Benson, "C. Y. Lee, Fortunate Son: Author of the Enduring 'Flower Drum Song' Is Grateful for 'Three Lucks in My Life,' " *San Francisco Chronicle*, September 18, 2002.

281   **Tsung-Dao Lee and Chen-ning Yang:** *New York Times*, January 15, 1957.

282   **Chien-Shiung Wu:** *New York Times*, February 18, 1997; *The Guardian*, May 13, 1997.

282   **Shing-Shen Chern:** *McGraw-Hill Modern Scientists and Engineers*, (New York: McGraw-Hill, 1980), p. 201.

282   **Chia-Chiao Lin:** Chia-Chiao Lin and Frank H. Shu, "On the Spiral Structure of Disk Galaxies," *Astrophysical Journal*, no. 140, 1964; "On the Spiral Structure of Galaxies II: Outline of a Theory of Density Waves," *Proceedings of the National Academy of Sciences*, no. 55, 1966.

282   **Tung-Yen Lin:** MaryLou Watts, "Prestressed Concrete Pioneer T. Y. Lin Named Cal's Alumnus of Year," *CM (Construction Management) Magazine*, March 16, 1995; David Pescovitz, "Berkeley Engineers Changing Our World," Lab Notes: Research from the College of Engineering, University of California, Berkeley, vol. 2, issue 6, August 2002; "Builder of Bridges: Alumnus of the Year T. Y. Lin," *California Monthly*, December 1994; files and correspondence from T. Y. Lin to author; "Top People in the Past 125 Years," *Engineering News-Record* 243:9, p. 27; "Famed Structural Engineer T. Y. Lin Named Cal Alumni Association's Alumnus of the Year," *Business Wire*, December 19, 1994.

282   **Min-Chueh Chang:** Amy Zuckerman, "M. C. Chang," *Worcester Magazine*, July 27, 1988; *Times* (London), June 14, 1991; *New York Times*, June 7, 1991; Roy O. Greep's comments at the memorial service for Min-Chueh Chang, October 10, 1991; letter from Isabelle C. Chang, widow of Min-Chueh Chang, to author, July 6, 1999. According to Ms. Chang, her husband was nominated for the Nobel Prize six times.

Chapter Sixteen. The Taiwanese Americans

283   **"number three" choice:** Murray A. Rubinstein, ed., *Taiwan: A New History* (Armonk, N.Y.: M. E. Sharpe, 1999), p. 299.

283   **between one million and two million refugees:** Franklin Ng, p. 10.

285   **"desolate place both in literary and cultural terms":** Anna Chennault, *The Education of Anna* (New York: Times Books, 1980), p. 92.

286   **about two thousand students were leaving Taiwan:** Ronald Skeldon, ed., *Reluctant Exiles? Migration from Hong Kong and the New Overseas Chinese* (Armonk, N.Y.: M. E. Sharpe, 1974), p. 45.

286   **T. V. Soong:** Leslie Chang, *Beyond the Narrow Gate*, p. 18; Stella Dong, *Shanghai, 1842–1949*, p. 288; Him Mark Lai, "China and the Chinese American Community: The Political Dimension," *Chinese America: History and Perspectives 1999*, p. 10.

287   **U.S. News and World Report:** *U.S. News and World Report*, July 24, 1995.

287   suspended all national-level elections: Murray A. Rubinstein, ed.,
       Taiwan: A New History, p. 326.

287   "the period of Communist rebellion":   Ibid., p. 327.

288   reign of "White Terror":   Ibid., pp. 145, 330.

288   "By grade school":   Author interview of Dick Ling, December 27, 2000.

289   "That student got into deep, *deep* trouble":   Author interview of Carl
       Hsu, February 28, 2001.

289   "You couldn't even buy vacuum tubes then":   Author interview of
       Ching Peng, December 27, 2000.

291   Sayling Wen: Sayling Wen and Chin-chung Tsia, *Taiwan Experience:
       How Taiwan Transformed Herself from Economic Difficulty to Economic
       Boom* (Taipei, Taiwan: Locus Publishing Company, 1998), pp. 24–25.

291   40 percent of Taiwan's income: Murray A. Rubinstein, ed., *Taiwan: A
       New History,* p. 328.

291    $100 million: Ibid., p. 325.

291   "Turn your living room into a factory":   Sayling Wen and Chin-
       chung Tsia, p. 58.

292   The story of Taiwan's economic miracle: Murray A. Rubinstein, ed.,
       Taiwan: A New History, p. 374; Chun-Chieh Huang and Feng-fu Tsao,
       eds., *Postwar Taiwan in Historical Perspective* (Bethesda: University
       Press of Maryland, 1998).

293   "In schools, teachers taught us about the task":   Sayling Wen and
       Chin-chung Tsia, p. 45.

295   "White people all looked alike":   Author interview with Ying-Ying
       Chang.

296   "the sight of a hot dog":   Cai Nengying, "Lu Meizhufu huajiachang (A
       Housewife Staying in America Talks About Household Matters)," in
       Huang Minghui, ed., *Lu Mei Sanji (Notes on Staying in America)* (Taipei:
       Zhengwen, 1971), pp. 34–35. As cited in R. David Arkush and Leo O.
       Lee, *Land without Ghosts,* p. 219.

297   dared not spend even a few cents: Interview with Cheng-Cheng
       Chang in Palo Alto, California.

297   "As I grew up in Taiwan":   E-mail from Albert Yu to author, March
       13, 2000.

298   Huang Qiming: Him Mark Lai, "China and the Chinese American
       Community: The Political Dimension," *Chinese America: History and
       Perspectives 1999,* p. 15.

298   Chen Yuxi: Ibid., p. 15.

298   only one in four students returned: Ronald Skeldon, ed., *Reluctant
       Exiles?,* p. 45.

299   Chia-ling Kuo: Chia-ling Kuo, "The Chinese on Long Island: A Pilot
       Study," *Phylon* 31:28 (1970), pp. 80–89, as cited in Ting Ni, "Cultural
       Journey," p. 185.

299   "I would not let those ignorant people bother me":   Chia-ling Kuo, p. 286; Ting Ni, pp. 186–87.

299   "great majority of Chinese- and Japanese-Americans":   "Orientals Find Bias Is Down Sharply in U.S," *New York Times,* December 13, 1970, as cited in Cheng-Tsu Wu, ed., "*Chink!,*" p. 220.

300   Biographical information on Chang-Lin Tien: Kate Coleman, "Reluctant Hero," *San Francisco Focus,* December 1996.

303   Biographical information on David Lee: Author interview of David Lee.

305–6   "Orientals are inordinately industrious":   James W. Chinn, *East/West,* December 2, 1970, as cited in Cheng-Tsu Wu, ed., "*Chink!,*" pp. 231–37.

306   one in four Chinese American men sixteen years or older: L. Ling-chi Wang, "Politics of Assimilation and Repression," p. 472. By 1970, one-fourth of Chinese American men had college degrees, which was twice the national average. (Him Mark Lai, in *Encyclopedia of the Chinese Overseas,* p. 266.)

306   only 55 percent of that of white men: Ibid., p. 472.

306   five Asian American health inspectors: Cheng-Tsu Wu, ed., "*Chink!,*" pp. 215, 232, 233.

307   "he presumably lacked the ability to deal with the public":   Thomas Yang Chin and Shirley Takemorei, *Third World News,* December 7, 1970. As cited in Cheng-Tsu Wu, ed., "*Chink!,*" p. 232.

307   "I suppose you like to play the lotteries like all good Chinese":   Cheng-Tsu Wu, ed., "*Chink!,*" p. 237. Original citation: Kai M. Lui, letter, *East/West: The Chinese American Journal,* September 1, 1970.

307   "Oriental women had been trained to be subservient":   Frank Quinn, Fair Employment Practices Commission hearing transcript, December 10, 1970, p. 38.

307   only 2.5 percent: Pauline L. Fong, "The Current Social and Economic Status of Chinese American Women," paper presented at the National Conference on Chinese American Studies, October 9–11, 1980, San Francisco.

307   "In fact, the better educated we became":   Judy Yung, *Unbound Feet,* p. 288.

308   in-house study at Bell Labs: Author interview of Carl Hsu, co-founder of 4A, Asian Americans for Affirmative Action; "The Founding of 4A," *4A Newsletter* 1:1 (January 1979); correspondence of Ron Osajima, co-founder of 4A, to author, February 18, 2001; "Request for a Comparison Study of White Males and Asian Americans," Bell Labs memorandum, July 22, 1977.

308   "Most of us had very deep fears about retribution":   Author interview with Carl Hsu.

309   **"worse than the betrayal of a loyal ally"**:   *New York Times*, January 5, 1981; Anna Chennault, *The Education of Anna*, p. 242.

309   **"Mr. President"**:   Anna Chennault, p. 236.

310   **"During Watergate, we didn't understand why Nixon had to resign"**: Jennie Yabroff, "Stranger in a Strange Land," *Salon*, October 17, 1997.

Chapter Seventeen. The Bamboo Curtain Rises: Mainlanders and Model Minorities

312   **"the news filled me with such euphoria"**:   Jung Chang, *Wild Swans: Three Daughters of China* (New York: Simon & Schuster, 1991), p. 495.

313   **partly or completely illiterate**:   Jasper Becker, *The Chinese* (New York: Free Press, 2000), p. 210.

314   **"study abroad fever"**:   Leo A. Orleans, *Chinese Students in America: Policies, Issues and Numbers* (Washington, D.C.: National Academy Press, 1988), p. 28.

314   **doubled the immigration slots**:   Lynn Pan, *Sons of the Yellow Emperor*, p. 276.

315   **more than 80,000 PRC intellectuals**:   *Los Angeles Times Magazine*, March 25, 1990; Jing Qiu Fu, "Broken Portraits: The Dilemma of Chinese Student Leaders in the U.S. After the Tiananmen Square Incident," master's thesis, Asian American Studies, University of California at Los Angeles, 1999, p. 1.

315   **freed Deng Jiaxian**:   Ting Ni, pp. 190–91.

315   **Yuan Jialiu**:   Ibid., p. 190.

316   **Yuan's family**:   Ibid., p. 190.

316   **roughly half the Chinese foreign students**: Dr. An Wang with Eugene Linden, *Lessons: An Autobiography* (Boston: Addison-Wesley, 1986), p. 42.

316   **"regret in their eyes"**:   Author interview of Linda Tsao Yang.

316   **Let Keung Mui**:   Interview with Let Keung Mui by Se Wai Mui, his son. Manuscript entitled "Our Lives, Our Stories, Our Neighborhood. Vol. V. Oral Histories compiled by the students of the class. Our Neighborhood: The Lower East Side Experience. Seward Park High School, June 1988," New York Chinatown History Project, Museum of Chinese in the Americas.

317   **"Why would one person need so many lights?"**:   Liu Zongren, *Two Years in the Melting Pot* (San Francisco: China Books and Periodicals, 1988), p. 16.

317   **"A hundred dollars"**:   Ibid., p. 20.

318   **"I liked *E.T.*"**:   Ibid., p. 20.

318   **wealthiest one percent of Americans**:   James D. Torr, ed., *The 1980s* (San Diego: Greenhaven Press, 2000), p. 54.

318   **four hundred richest Americans:**   Ibid.

319   **"Many of Detroit's corporate heads":**   Ronald Takaki, "Who Killed Vincent Chin?," in Grace Yun, ed., *A Look Beyond the Model Minority Image* (New York: Minority Rights Group, 1989), pp. 26–27.

320   **"In Detroit, the bumper stickers say it all":**   Ibid., p. 27.

320   **"What kind of law is this?":**   Ronald Takaki, *Strangers from a Different Shore*, p. 482.

321   **"Three thousand dollars can't even buy a good used car":**   Ibid.

321   **"I don't understand how this could happen in America":**   Ibid.

321   **"My blood boiled":**   Ibid., p. 484.

321   **"The killing of Vincent Chin happened in 1982":**   Ibid., p. 483.

321   **Additional sources on Vincent Chin:**   Sucheng Chan, *Asian Americans*, pp. 176–78; Christine Choy and Renee Tajima, *Who Killed Vincent Chin?*, color documentary, 90 minutes, 1988.

322   **Sources on the Jim Loo murder:**   Sucheng Chan, p. 178; United States Commission on Civil Rights, *Civil Rights Issues Facing Asian Americans in the 1990s: A Report of the United States Commission on Civil Rights, February 1992*, pp. 26–28.

322   **"I don't like you because you're Vietnamese":**   Seth Effron, "Racial Slaying Prompts Fear, Anger in Raleigh," *Greensboro News and Record*, September 24, 1989.

323   **Chen Wencheng:**   Him Mark Lai, "China and the Chinese American Community: The Political Dimension," *Chinese America: History and Perspectives 1999*, p. 16; *Newsweek*, August 3, 1981; British Broadcasting Corporation, August 4, 1981.

323   **Henry Liu:**   For a detailed account and analysis of the events that led to the Liu murder, see David E. Kaplan, *Fires of the Dragon: Politics, Murder and the Kuomintang* (New York: Atheneum, 1992.)

324   **David Lam:**   Chris Rauber, "Tech Pioneer Signs On as CEO of Startup," *San Francisco Business Times*, May 9, 1997; "David Lam Joins Tru-Si Technologies, Inc. as Chairman of the Board," *Business Wire*, April 28, 1999; interview with David Lam by Joyce Gemperlein and Sandra Ledbetter for the Tech Museum of Innovation's "The Revolutionaries" series, a joint project with the *San Jose Mercury News* in 1997.

324   **David Wang:**   Author interview of David Wang; *Applied Matters*, April 1993; Kristin Huckshorn, "If It's Here, It Must Be History; Smithsonian Enshrines 1987 Chip Machine," *San Jose Mercury News*, March 4, 1993.

324   **John Tu and David Sun:**   Michael Lyster, "$1 Billion and Counting," *Orange County Business Journal*, January 1–7, 1996; "Doing the Right Thing," *The Economist*, May 20, 1995; Greg Miller, "Memory Makers," *Los Angeles Times*, October 16, 1995.

324   **Pehong Chen:**   "8 of 9 Newbies to Forbes 400 Super-Rich List Are

Asians," *Business Times*, September 20, 2000; "Code Warriors: The Forbes 400," *Forbes*, October 9, 2000.

324 **Charles Wang:** Dan Barry, "Computer Mogul Refines His Game; Facing Rough Times, Charles Wang Tries a New Style," *New York Times*, February 4, 1997; John Teresko, "The Magic of Common Sense: How CEO Charles Wang Took Software Maker Computer Associates from Start-up to $3.5 Billion," *Industry Week*, July 15, 1996; Amy Cortese, "Sexy? No. Profitable? You Bet. Software Plumbing Keeps Computer Associates Hot," *Business Week*, November 11, 1996.

324 **"ethnoburbs":** Wei Li, "Building Ethnoburbia: The Emergence and Manifestation of the Chinese Ethnoburb in Los Angeles' San Gabriel Valley," *Journal of Asian American Studies*, February 1999.

325 **"Say I am Chinese":** *Origins & Destinations*, pp. 220–21.

325 **more than one-third of Monterey Park's population:** *San Diego Union Tribune*, January 10, 1999.

325 **more than one-quarter in the nearby communities:** Ibid.

325 **largest suburban concentration of ethnic Chinese:** Wei Li, "Anatomy of a New Ethnic Settlement: The Chinese Ethnoburb in Los Angeles," *Urban Studies* 35:3 (1998), p. 480.

325 **"I feel like I'm in another country":** Mark Arax, "Selling Out, Moving On," *Los Angeles Times*, April 12, 1987.

325 **"I feel like a stranger in my own town":** Ibid.

325 **"Will the Last American":** "English Spoken Here, OK?," *Time*, August 25, 1985; Ronald Takaki, *Strangers from a Different Shore*, p. 425.

325 **Anti-Chinese jokes:** Timothy Fong, *The First Suburban Chinatown: The Remaking of Monterey Park, California* (Philadelphia: Temple University Press, 1994), p. 71.

326 **vandals attacked Chinese-owned movie theaters:** Ibid., p. 69.

326 **"First it was the real estate people":** Timothy Fong, p. 48; Andrew Tanzer, "Little Taipei," *Forbes*, May 1985, p. 69.

327 **"HOW TO BE A PERFECT TAIWANESE KID":** Franklin Ng, *The Taiwanese Americans* (Westport, Conn.: Greenwood Press, 1988), p. 42.

328 ***Newsweek* ran a favorable article:** Martin Kasindorf with Paula Chin in New York, Diane Weathers in Washington, Kim Foltz in Detroit, Daniel Shapiro in Houston, Darby Junkin in Denver, and bureau reports, "Asian Americans: A 'Model Minority,'" *Newsweek*, December 6, 1982.

328 ***MacNeil/Lehrer* . . . and *NBC Nightly News:*** Ronald Takaki, *Strangers from a Different Shore*, p. 474.

328 *60 Minutes:* "The Model Minority," *60 Minutes*, CBS, February 1, 1987.

329 **MIT, UCLA, and UCI nicknames:** Ronald Takaki, *Strangers from a Different Shore*, p. 479; Frank H. Wu, p. 48.

329   **"Orient Express":** Dana Y. Takagi, *The Retreat from Race: Asian American Admissions and Racial Politics* (New Brunswick, N.J.: Rutgers University Press, 1992 and 1998), p. 60.

329   **"What do you think I am, Chinese?":** Frank H. Wu, *Yellow: Race in America Beyond Black and White,* p. 48.

329   **"I am NOT a Chinese American electrical engineer":** Lynn Pan, *Sons of the Yellow Emperor,* p. 278.

329   **"I had never been around so many Asian faces":** Phoebe Eng, *Warrior Lessons: An Asian American Woman's Journey into Power* (New York: Pocket Books, 1999), p. 91.

329   **"Stop the Yellow Hordes":** Ronald Takaki, *Strangers from a Different Shore,* p. 479.

330   **East Coast Asian Student Union:** Dana Y. Takagi, *The Retreat from Race,* pp. 26–27.

330   **Information on Princeton, Brown, Stanford and Harvard:** Ibid., pp. 27–29, 30, 33, 39, 41–42, 67, 69.

330   **5 percent to 20 percent:** Ibid., p. 21.

330   **40 percent of the entering freshman class:** Wallace Turner, "Rapid Rise in Students of Asian Origin Causing Problems at Berkeley Campus," *New York Times,* April 6, 1981.

331   **fell 21 percent:** Dana Y. Takagi, *The Retreat from Race,* p. 25.

331   **"a red light went on":** Linda Mathews, "When Being Best Isn't Good Enough: Why Yat-Pang Au Won't Be Going to Berkeley," *Los Angeles Times Magazine,* July 19, 1987.

331   **shocked to discover that Berkeley had turned away students with perfect GPAs:** Dana Y. Takagi, *The Retreat from Race,* pp. 94, 109.

331   **Yat-Pang Au:** *Los Angeles Times Magazine,* July 19, 1987; Tamara Henry, "UC Revises Admissions Policies Amid Protests," Associated Press, as printed in the *Los Angeles Times,* December 10, 1989; *Los Angeles Times Magazine,* July 19, 1987.

332   **"I don't hold it against them":** *NBC Nightly News,* July 26, 1989.

332   **found UCLA guilty of bias:** Dana Y. Takagi, *The Retreat from Race,* p. 9.

332   **Lowell High School:** Huping Ling, *Surviving on the Gold Mountain,* p. 171; *Seattle Times,* March 26, 1996; *Asian Week,* March 22, 2000; *San Francisco Examiner,* November 8, 1999, November 25, 1999, January 8, 2000.

333   **"Asian applicants are competing with white applicants":** *Daily Californian,* October 8, 1987, as cited in Dana Y. Takagi, *The Retreat from Race,* p. 9.

333   **"never been based on meritocratic standards":** *A* magazine, October/November 1995, p. 87.

Chapter Eighteen. Decade of Fear: The 1990s

336 "individuals from any country who express fear of persecution": Marlowe Hood, "Dark Passage; Riding the Snake," *Los Angeles Times Magazine*, June 13, 1993.

336 "political suicide": Jing Qiu Fu, "Broken Portraits," p. 45.

336 "make Chinese intellectuals as scapegoats": Ibid., p. 42.

336 "China will definitely change": Ibid., p. 55.

336 Chinese Student Protection Act: Him Mark Lai, "China and the Chinese American Community: The Political Dimension," *Chinese America: History and Perspectives 1999*, p. 19.

337 "No sane person": Ronald Skeldon, ed., *Reluctant Exiles? Migration from Hong Kong and the New Overseas Chinese* (Armonk, N.Y.: M. E. Sharpe, 1974), p. 166.

337 70 percent of Hong Kong's government doctors: Ibid., p. 35.

337 some 15 to 19 percent of Hong Kong émigrés: Ibid., p. 31.

337 605 Hong Kong residents: Ibid., p. 103.

337 estimated 1.5 million Canadian dollars: Ibid., p. 32.

338 soared from twenty thousand: Ibid., pp. 30, 103.

338 in excess of $30,000: Ibid., p. 55.

339 "empty wife": Ibid., p. 11.

339 Jimmy Lai, Ronnie Chan, Frank Tsao, Tung Chee-hwa: Evelyn Iritani, "The New Trans-Pacific Commuters," *Sacramento Bee*, February 9, 1997.

340 found it difficult to adjust: Ronald Skeldon, ed., *Reluctant Exiles?*, p. 171.

340 "Hong Kong is a place which is famous for its materialistic glamour": Alex C. N. Leung, *Bulletin of the Hong Kong Psychological Society*, No. 28–29, January–July 1992, p. 139.

341 "He starts gambling and smoking": Ronald Skeldon, ed., *Reluctant Exiles?*, p. 173.

341 "his marriage, his children": Alex C. N. Leung, p. 142.

343 "You may be the best in your class": Min Zhou, " 'Parachute Kids' in Southern California: The Educational Experience of Chinese Children in Transnational Families," *Educational Policy* 12:6 (November 1998).

343 some thirty thousand to forty thousand Taiwanese students: Helena Hwang and Terri Watanabe, "Little Overseas Students from Taiwan: A Look at the Psychological Adjustment Issues," master's thesis, University of California at Los Angeles, 1990; Chong-Li Edith Chung, "An Investigation of the Psychological Well Being of Unaccompanied Taiwanese Minors/Parachute Kids in the United States," Ph.D. dissertation in counseling psychology, University of Southern California, December 1994, p. 1.

344   **approximately ten thousand of them:**   S. Y. Kuo, *Research on Tai-wanese Unaccompanied Minors in the United States* (Taipei: Institute of American Culture, Academia Sinica), as cited in Chong-Li Edith Chung, p. 1.

344   **allowances of $4,000 or more a month:**   Min Zhou, " 'Parachute Kids' in Southern California."

344   **162 Taiwanese adolescents:**   Chong-Li Edith Chung, pp. x, 87, 88.

344   **"It looks happy on the outside":**   Min Zhou, " 'Parachute Kids' in Southern California."

345   **about $15,000 a year:**   Ibid.

345   **about $40,000:**   Ibid.

345   **"If they're going to dump me here":**   D. Hamilton, "A House, Cash and No Parents," *Los Angeles Times*, June 24, 1993, p. A16.

345   **"work hard, to focus":**   Min Zhou, " 'Parachute Kids' in Southern California."

345   **fax them copies of report cards:**   Ibid.

346   **detonated a homemade bomb:**   Min Zhou, " 'Parachute Kids' in Southern California."

346   **charged with arms smuggling:**   Ibid.

346   **San Marino school district:**   Chong-Li Edith Chung, p. 47.

346   **Kuan Nan "Johnny" Chen:**   Jeff Wong, " 'Parachute Kids': Latchkey Kids with Cash Vulnerable to Trouble," Associated Press, May 15, 1999; *NBC Nightly News*, January 9, 1999.

346–47 **two out of three abductions:**   *San Diego Union-Tribune*, January 10, 1999.

347   **nine out of ten:**   Associated Press, May 15, 1999.

347   **About 80 percent:**   Min Zhou, " 'Parachute Kids' in Southern California."

347   **paid $19,000 each:**   Maggie Farley, "Shanghai Youths Test Welcome Mat in US," *Los Angeles Times*, May 3, 1999, p. A1.

347   **"In China, we can have only one child":**   Ibid.

Chapter Nineteen. High Tech vs. Low Tech

349   **40 percent of the country's assets:**   Edward N. Wolff, "Recent Trends in Wealth Ownership," a paper for the Conference on Benefits and Mechanisms for Spreading Asset Ownership in the United States, New York University, December 10–12, 1998; Edward N. Wolff, *Top Heavy: The Increasing Inequality of Wealth in America and What Can Be Done About It* (New York: New Press, 1996); "A Scholar Who Concentrates . . . on Concentrations of Wealth," *Too Much*, Winter 1999.

349   **lost 80 percent of their net worth:** Edward N. Wolff, "Recent Trends in Wealth Ownership," table 2, "The Size Distribution of Wealth and Income, 1983–1997."

351   **Sources on Jerry Yang:** *A* magazine, June/July 2000, p. 10. "Yahoo," (chapter 10), in David Kaplan, *The Silicon Boys and Their Valley of Dreams* (New York: William Morrow, 1999); "Jerry Yang Yahoo! Finding Needles in the Internet's Haystack," (chapter 6), in Robert H. Reid, *Architects of the Web: 1,000 Days That Built the Future of Business* (New York: John Wiley, 1997).

352   **Sources on Morris Chang:** Author interview with Morris Chang, March 17, 2000; Mark Landler, "The Silicon Godfather: The Man Behind Taiwan's Rise in the Chip Industry," *New York Times,* February 1, 2000.

353   **capped the program at 65,000 visas a year:** *Denver Post,* June 18, 2000.

353   **115,000 in 1998:** Sara Robinson, "High-Tech Workers Are Trapped in Limbo by I.N.S.," *New York Times,* February 29, 2000.

353   **195,000:** Ibid.

354   **"white-collar indentured servitude":** Ibid.

354   **Swallow Yan:** Author correspondence with Swallow Yan, July 2000; *The Scientist,* May 29, 2000.

355   **"Blue Team":** Robert G. Kaiser and Steven Mufson, " 'Blue Team' Draws a Hard Line on Beijing: Action on Hill Reflects Informal Group's Clout," *Washington Post,* February 22, 2000.

356   **Christopher Cox:** The three-volume report, commonly referred to as the "Cox Report on Chinese Espionage" (March 1999), is an unclassified version of the Final Report of the United States House of Representatives Select Committee on U.S. National Security and Military/Commercial Concerns with the People's Republic of China, a Top Secret report issued on January 3, 1999. For details on how the report misused my research, see Perla Ni, "Rape of Nanking Author Denounces Cox Report: Iris Chang Tells Conventioneers That Her Research Was Misused," *Asian Week,* June 3, 1999. Jonathan S. Landreth, "Arrested for Spying? Or for Being Chinese? Author Iris Chang on Dr. Tsien Hsue-Shen," *Virtual China News,* December 23, 1999.

357   **"a paper with Chinese writing on it":** Norman Matloff, "Democracy Begins at Home," *Asian Week,* July 14, 1995.

357   **"yellow high-tech peril":** Sarah Lubman and Pete Carey, "False Spying Charges Have Happened Before: Valley Chinese-Americans Complain Allegations Have Destroyed Careers," *San Jose Mercury News,* June 23, 1999.

358   **"It happened so fast":** Correspondence from Chih-Ming Hu to author.

358   **"When I went to high-tech company job interviews":** Ibid.

358 **"I was scared":** Jonathan Curiel, "Widespread Support for Jailed Scientist: Chinese Americans Eager to Help Lee," *San Francisco Chronicle,* January 10, 2000.

358 **"I was 100 percent innocent!":** Chih-Ming Hu, March 16, 1999.

359 **indicted him for allegedly transferring nuclear secrets:** Vernon Loeb and David Vise, "Physicist Lee Indicted in Nuclear Spy Probe," *Washington Post,* December 11, 1999.

359 **fifty-nine counts:** *The New Yorker,* October 2, 2000.

359 **more than 260 agents:** Vernon Loeb and David Vise, "Physicist Lee Indicted in Nuclear Spy Probe," *Washington Post,* December 11, 1999. Two hundred FBI agents were used just to watch Lee twenty-four hours a day.

359 **548 addresses:** Vernon Loeb, "Ex-Official: Bomb Lab Case Lacks Evidence," *Washington Post,* August 17, 1999.

359 **passed it with flying colors:** Robert Scheer, "Was Lee Indicted, and Not Deutch? Spy scandal: Look closer and you can see the politics behind the case," *Los Angeles Times,* February 8, 2000.

360 **"Do you think the press prints everything that's true?":** Unclassified transcript of FBI interview 004868-004950.

360 **"Do you know who the Rosenbergs are?":** Wen Ho Lee with Helen Zia, *My Country Versus Me: The First-Hand Account by the Los Alamos Scientist Who Was Falsely Accused of Being a Spy* (New York: Hyperion, 2001), p. 81. Also, transcript of FBI interview 004868-004950.

360 **"for my convenience, not for any espionage purposes":** Wen Ho Lee with Helen Zia, p. 122. For more details, see pp. 119–22, 323–26.

361 **blew a sheaf of documents:** William J. Broad, "Files in Question in Los Alamos Case Were Reclassified," *New York Times,* April 15, 2000.

361 **reclassified the downloaded PARD files:** Ibid. It is not illegal to copy PARD files, nor is it a security violation.

361 **Deutch had actually removed top-secret files:** Daniel Klaidman, "The Nuclear Spy Case Suffers a Meltdown," *Newsweek,* August 30, 1999.

361 **seventeen thousand pages of documents:** James Risen, "CIA Inquiry of Its Ex-Director Was Stalled at Top, Report Says," *New York Times,* February 1, 2000.

361 **"alien resident" housekeeper:** Robert Scheer, "CIA's Deutch Heedlessly Disregarded Security," *Los Angeles Times,* February 29, 2000.

361 **neither encryption nor a secure phone line:** Ibid.

361 **important memory cards:** Ibid.

361 **deleting more than a thousand files:** *New York Times,* February 1, 2000.

362 **refused to give interviews:** Ibid.

362 **"three crimes we knew were sure-fire violations":** Bill Gertz, "Pentagon Probe Targets Deutch," *Washington Times,* February 17, 2000.

362   **recommended Nora Slatkin:** James Risen, "Deutch Probe Looks at Job," *New York Times*, February 12, 2000.

362   **"Deutch can get away with anything":** Ling-chi Wang, "Wen Ho Lee & John Deutch: A Study of Contrast and Failure of Leadership," public electronic mail statement, February 9, 2002.

363   **"Deutch is a leading member":** Robert Scheer, "Was Lee Indicted, and Not Deutch? Spy scandal: Look closer and you can see the politics behind the case," *Los Angeles Times*, February 8, 2000.

363   **"built on thin air":** "U.S. Lacks Evidence in China Spy Probe, Ex-Aide Says," Reuters News Report, August 17, 1999.

363   **shackled in chains:** "Amnesty International Protests Solitary Confinement, Shackling of Dr. Wen Ho Lee," public statement of Amnesty International, August 16, 2000; Hendrik Hertzberg, "In Solitary," *The New Yorker*, October 2, 2000.

363   **"While Deutch has been coddled":** Robert Scheer, "CIA's Deutch Heedlessly Disregarded Security"; "Spy Scandal: Scientist Wen Ho Lee Is Being Treated Unfairly, Especially as Compared to the Former Intelligence Chief," *Los Angeles Times*, February 29, 2000.

363   **"This case stinks":** "Wen Ho Lee Reportedly Makes a Deal," Associated Press, September 11, 2000.

363   **Fang Lizhi:** *San Jose Mercury News*, February 2, 2000; George Koo, "Deutch Is Sorry; Lee Is in Jail," *San Francisco Examiner*, February 8, 2000.

363   **Plato Cacheris:** James Glanz, "Scientific Groups Complain About Treatment of Weapons Scientist," *New York Times*, March 7, 2000.

363   **worked out a plea bargain:** James Sterngold, "Wen Ho Lee Will Plead Guilty to Lesser Crime at Los Alamos," *New York Times*, September 10, 2000; Marcus Kabel, "U.S., Wen Ho Lee Reach Plea Agreement," Reuters, September 11, 2000.

364   **"terribly wronged":** Wen Ho Lee with Helen Zia, p. 2.

364   **"embarrassed our entire nation":** "Lee Free; Federal Judge Apologizes," Associated Press, September 13, 2000; Vernon Loeb, "Physicist Lee Freed With Apology: U.S. Actions 'Embarrassed' Nation, Judge Says," *Washington Post*, September 14, 2000, p. A1.

364   **"the FBI has been investigating a crime":** *San Francisco Chronicle*, August 26, 2001.

364   **Eddie Liu:** E-mail from Eddie Liu, March 14, 1999.

364   **"China's spying, they say":** Vernon Loeb, "China Spy Methods Limit Bid to Find Truth, Officials Say," *Washington Post*, March 21, 1999.

365   **mysterious $700 withdrawal:** Robert Schmidt, "Crash Landing: The New York Times shook the government with its articles on Chinese nuclear-missile espionage. But six months after fingering Wen Ho Lee as a spy, the paper said, in effect, never mind," *Brill's Content*, November 1999.

365   "suspiciously congratulatory": Ibid.

365   "We've got to remember": *Los Angeles Times*, May 21, 1999.

365   "He doesn't distinguish between Chinese foreign nationals": Annie Nakao, "Spy Scandal Hurts Asian Americans," *San Francisco Examiner*, May 26, 1999.

366   "The problem is guilt by racial association": Ibid.

366   laptop computer out to be repaired: Author interview with Brian Sun.

366   "The Lab treated me as a suspect": Lawrence Livermore National Laboratory in-house report given to author.

366   "interested obsessively": Vernon Loeb, "Espionage Stir Alienating Foreign Scientists in U.S.; Critics of Distrust Fear a Brain Drain," *Washington Post*, November 25, 1999.

367   "The term going around now": Andrew Lawler, "Silent No Longer: 'Model Minority' Mobilizes," *Science*, November 10, 2000, p. 1072.

367   "subjective, arbitrary and capricious": Lawrence Livermore National Laboratory in-house report given to author. The study was conducted by Dick Ling, Joel Wong, Kalina Wong, and several Asian American scientists who wished to remain anonymous. Officials at the laboratory have criticized the study as unreliable because not all Asian American employees were included. "We have never claimed that our studies are absolutely correct since LLNL refused to release the list of APIAs (Asian Pacific Islander Americans) for our studies," Dick Ling wrote to the author. "We have compiled the APIA list through personal knowledge and employees' last names."

367   earned as much as $12,000 less: Ibid.

367   15 to 20 percent: Ibid.

367   "the same appropriate yardsticks": Ibid.

367   "Subconsciously, you become the enemy": Author interview with Lawrence Livermore scientist, December 27, 2000.

368   "In hindsight, there are some things I might have done differently": Wen Ho Lee with Helen Zia, p. 327.

368   not one single Chinese graduate student: Dan Stober, "Lee Case Leaves Ethnic Chinese Shunning Lab Jobs," *San Jose Mercury News*, February 20, 2000.

368   half of the ten finalists: Ibid.

368   class action lawsuit: James Glanz, "Weapons Labs Close to Settling a Bias Lawsuit," *New York Times*, March 26, 2000.

369   the largest group of foreign students: Vernon Loeb, "Espionage Stir Alienating Foreign Scientists in U.S.; Critics of Distrust Fear a Brain Drain," *Washington Post*, November 25, 1999.

369   about half of all foreign scientists with doctorates: Ibid.

369   not one of the twenty-four applicants was American: Ibid.

369   **Feng Gai:** Ibid.

369   **"felt his every move would be monitored":** David Pines, "Why Science Can't Be Done in Isolation," *Newsweek*, September 27, 1999.

370   **shrink the population to 700 million:** Jasper Becker, p. 235.

371   **"Owing to the current political situation":** Kay Johnson, "The Revival of Infant Abandonment in China," in Amy Klatzkin, ed., *A Passage to the Heart: Writings from Families with Children from China* (St. Paul, Minn.: Yeong and Yeong Book Company, 1999), p. 224.

371   **"In a dim room":** Jurgen Kremb, "Der Kinder-Gulag von Harbin," *Der Spiegel*, No. 37, September 11, 1995, as cited in Human Rights Watch, *Death by Default: A Policy of Fatal Neglect in China's State Orphanages* (New York, Washington, Los Angeles, London, Brussels: Human Rights Watch, 1996), p. 68.

371   **two hundred children:** *A* magazine, June/July 1997, p. 35.

371   **donate $3,000:** Richard Tessler, Gail Gamache, and Liming Liu, *West Meets East: Americans Adopt Chinese Children* (Westport, Conn.: Bergin and Garvey, 1999), p. 39.

372   **"China's Market in Orphan Girls":** *New York Times Magazine*, April 11, 1993.

372   **more than thirty-three thousand infants:** According to Families with Children from China, in the fiscal year 2002 there have been 33,637 adoptions from China to the United States since 1985.

372   **42.7 years:** Richard Tessler, Gail Gamache, and Liming Liu, p. 70.

372   **65 percent:** Ibid.

372   **$15,000 to $20,000:** Interview with Jean H. Seeley, September 23, 1999; Richard Tessler, Gail Gamache, and Liming Liu, pp. 39, 42.

372   **$70,000-to-$90,000 range:** Richard Tessler, Gail Gamache, and Liming Liu, p. 70.

373   **"She spent eight months in purgatory":** Christine Kukka, "The Labor of Waiting," in Amy Klatzkin, ed., *A Passage to the Heart*, pp. 19–20.

373   **"I thought that if I got a child":** Shanti Fry, "Surviving Waiting Parenthood: Some Completely Useless Advice from One Who's Been There," in Amy Klatzkin, ed., *A Passage to the Heart*, p. 3.

373   **"Say good-bye to China":** Jean H. Seeley, "Adventures in Adoption" essay, in correspondence between Jean H. Seeley and author.

373   **"Why are you kissing that child?":** Martha Groves, "Why Are You Kissing That Child?," in Amy Klatzkin, ed., *A Passage to the Heart*, p. 264.

374   **"a chink baby":** Richard Tessler, Gail Gamache, and Liming Liu, p. 149.

374   **"Couldn't get a white one, huh?":** Ibid.

374   **"killed a lot of your cousins":** Ibid.

374   **gifts from the birth parents:**   *A* magazine, June/July 1997, p. 36.

374   **"You're mean":**   John Bowen, "The Other Mommy in China," in Amy Klatzkin, ed., *A Passage to the Heart,* p. 311.

374   **"we shop at Asian markets":**   Richard Tessler, Gail Gamache, and Liming Liu, p. 141.

374   **"Lo Mein":**   Richard Tessler, Gail Gamache, and Liming Liu, p. 114.

375   **"I began to see children and their 'differences' in a new light":**   Patty Cogen, "I Don't Know Her Name, But I'd Like to Enroll Her in Preschool," in Amy Klatzkin, ed., *A Passage to the Heart,* p. 166.

375   **200 million to 250 million people:**   Ling Li, "Mass Migration Within China and the Implications for Chinese Emigration," and Jack A. Goldstone, "A Tsunami on the Horizon: The Potential for International Migration," in Paul J. Smith, ed., *Human Smuggling: Chinese Migrant Trafficking and the Challenge to America's Immigration Tradition* (Washington, D.C.: Center for Strategic and International Studies, 1997), pp. 34, 58.

375   **"That's why I left in a hurry":**   Ko-lin Chin, *Smuggled Chinese: Clandestine Immigration to the United States* (Philadelphia: Temple University Press, 1999), p. 23.

375   **"In China today":**   *Los Angeles Times,* June 13, 1993.

376   **"Those friends and relatives would all want money from you":**   James W. Gin, oral history interview, Southern California Chinese American Oral History Project.

376   **$22,204, compared to $370:**   *Newsday,* June 21, 1993.

376   **"Everyone went crazy":**   *Sing Tao Daily,* December 2, 1996, as cited in Ko-lin Chin, p. 9.

377   **Estimates range from ten thousand to one hundred thousand:**   Ko-lin Chin, p. 6.

377   **"It's like trying to pin jello to a wall":**   Brian Duffy, "Coming to America," cover story, *U.S. News and World Report,* June 21, 1993, p. 27.

377   **survey conducted by Ko-lin Chin:**   Alex Tizon, "The Rush to 'Gold Mountain': Why Smuggled Chinese Bet Everything on a Chance to Live and Work in the U.S.," *Seattle Times,* April 16, 2000.

377   **among the forty billionaires:**   Ibid.

377   **Almost six thousand Chinese crewmen:**   L. Ling-chi Wang, "Politics of Assimilation and Repression," p. 272. He cites the number of 5,834, given by an annual report of the U.S. Immigration Service.

378   **"During the Cultural Revolution":**   Ko-lin Chin, p. 24.

378   **"I was victimized under the one-child policy":**   Ibid., p. 24.

378   **"I heard that everything was so nice in America":**   Ibid., p. 14.

378   **"Before I came, I thought America was a very prosperous country":**   Ibid., p. 25.

378   **"going to America as going to heaven":**   Ibid., p. 24.

378   "For us, it doesn't mean freedom":   Paul J. Smith, ed., *Human Smuggling*, p. xii.

378   up to $8 billion a year: Associated Press, January 28, 2000.

378    $60,000 to $70,000:   Shawn Hubler, "The Changing Face of Illegal Immigration Is a Child's," *Los Angeles Times,* January 31, 2000.

379   locked in a motel basement: *Allentown Pennsylvania Morning Call,* August 2, 1993.

379   forced to hide in a pigsty: Ko-lin Chin, p. 52.

379   review of internal INS documents: Author's visit to Immigration and Naturalization Service headquarters in Washington, D.C.

379   one in five illegal Chinese: *Asia, Inc.,* May 1993.

379   Description of smuggling activities from Canada or Mexico: Kenneth Yales, "Canada's Growing Role as a Human Smuggling Destination and Corridor to the United States," in Paul J. Smith, *Human Smuggling,* pp. 156–168; Ko-lin Chin, "Safe House or Hell House? Experience of Newly Arrived Undocumented Chinese," in Paul J. Smith, *Human Smuggling,* p. 169.

380   "It is arduous and taxing":   *Sunday Telegraph* (London), June 25, 2000.

380   rotting, crumbling wood: Malcolm Glover and Lon Daniels, "Smuggler Main Ship Hunted on High Seas," *San Francisco Examiner,* June 3, 1993, p. 1.

380   bail water out of sinking ships: Ko-lin Chin, p. 71.

380   considered dynamiting it: Ibid., p. 71.

380   "the most incredibly screwed-up":   Jan Ten Bruggencate, "147 Illegals Endured a Ship of Ghouls," *Honolulu Advertiser,* August 23, 1995.

380   *Golden Venture:*   *Newsweek,* June 21, 1993; *Seattle Times,* April 16, 2000.

381   died of asphyxiation in a sealed trailer: *Sunday Telegraph* (London), June 25, 2000.

381   five Chinese corpses: Ibid.

381   fifty-eight Chinese suffocated: Ibid.

381   fans, mattresses, and cell phones: Kim Murphy, "Smuggling of Chinese Ends in a Box of Death, Squalor," *Los Angeles Times,* January 12, 2000.

381   "awash in human waste":   Chelsea J. Carter, "More Chinese Illegal Immigrants Arrive in Shipping Containers," Associated Press, April 10, 2000.

381   twelve days and nights: *Los Angeles Times,* January 24, 2000.

381   fifteen Chinese stowaways: Scott Sunde, "Chinese Smugglers Switch to New Tactics," *Seattle Post-Intelligencer,* February 10, 2000.

382   strapping themselves to the landing gear: Michelle Malkin, "Dying to Be an American," *Washington Times,* January 18, 2000, p. A12.

382   **withheld food and water from all females:** *New York Post*, June 24, 1993; Ko-lin Chin, *Smuggled Chinese*, p. 74.

382   **water spiked with sleeping pills:** Ko-lin Chin, *Smuggled Chinese*, p. 74.

382   **sexually assaulted many of the male passengers:** Anthony M. DeStefano, "Chinese Turned into Sex Slaves," *Newsday*, August 23, 1995, as cited in Paul J. Smith, *Human Smuggling*, p. 11; *Honolulu Advertiser*, August 23, 1995.

382   **charged a hundred dollars for a single international phone call:** Ko-lin Chin, "Safe House or Hell House?," in Paul J. Smith, ed., *Human Smuggling*, p. 180; Ko-lin Chin, *Smuggled Chinese*, p. 104.

382   **signed IOUs sealed with their own blood:** *Honolulu Advertiser*, August 23, 1995.

382   **shackled and handcuffed:** Ko-lin Chin, in Paul J. Smith, ed., pp. 183–84.

382   **FBI broke into a Brooklyn apartment:** Peter Kwong, *The New Chinatown*, pp. 179–80.

383   **eight gangsters from Fuzhou:** Ibid., pp. 184–85.

383   **raped and assaulted for months:** Ko-lin Chin, *Smuggled Chinese*, p. 110.

383   **"After being there for a period of time":** Ko-lin Chin, in Paul J. Smith, ed., *Human Smuggling*, p. 187.

383   **"they can make a fortune":** *Seattle Post-Intelligencer*, January 12, 2000.

383   **some sweatshop owners paid no wages:** *Downtown Express*, June 21, 1993.

383   **"To tell you the truth":** Ko-lin Chin, *Smuggled Chinese*, pp. 130–31.

383   **surpassed even that of Wall Street:** Ronald Skeldon, ed., *Reluctant Exiles?*, p. 262; L. Ling-chi Wang, "Politics of Assimilation and Repression," p. 515.

384   **broken sprinkler systems:** Alan Finder, "Despite Tough Laws, Sweatshops Flourish," *New York Times*, February 6, 1995, p. A1.

384   **ninety dollars a month:** Peter Kwong, *The New Chinatown*, p. 180.

384   **"Most of our villagers considered America heaven":** Dan Barry, "Chinatown Fires May Stem from a Hoax to Get Housing," *New York Times*, November 29, 1995.

384   **typically worked off their debt to the snakeheads in four years:** Author interview with Ko-lin Chin, January 8, 2003.

384   **"They are hard-working and ambitious":** Ibid.

384   **"They now drive Mercedes-Benzes":** Ibid.

385   **"If smugglers want the money":** Alex Fryer, "Chinese Stowaways in America," *Seattle Times*, January 23, 2000.

385   **Gao Liqin:** Seth Faison, "Brutal End to an Immigrant's Voyage of Hope," *New York Times*, October 2, 1995, p. A1; Randy Kennedy, "Murder Charges Sought in Immigrant's Slaying," *New York Times*, September 21, 1995.

385   "If you work hard and stay out of trouble":   *New York Times*, October 2, 1995.

385   "You can hide for a few years":   Ashley Dunn, "After the Golden Venture, the Ordeal Continues," *New York Times*, June 5, 1994.

385   "You have friends":   Ibid.

386   cheap, gaudy replicas of European castles: Antoaneta Bezlova, "Town Is Changed as Chinese Seek Fortunes Abroad," *USA Today*, February 16, 2000; Interpress Service, January 24, 2000; *Los Angeles Times*, June 21, 1993.

386   wore gold jewelry and carried cell phones: Marlowe Hood, "Sourcing the Problem: Why Fuzhou?," in Paul J. Smith, ed., *Human Smuggling*, p. 82.

386–87 half-constructed palatial homes: *Seattle Times*, April 16, 2000; Elisabeth Rosenthal, "Despite High Risk, Chinese Go West; Emigrants Pay Snakehead Smugglers to Get to the Promised Land," *International Herald Tribune*, June 27, 2000.

387   "So no one in the village works":   *International Herald Tribune*, June 27, 2000.

387   "populated only by old people":   Marlowe Hood, "Sourcing the Problem: Why Fuzhou?," in in Paul J. Smith, ed., *Human Smuggling*, p. 80.

387   paying a $1,000 fee, plus airfare, to have their infants safely delivered: Somini Sengupta, "Squeezed by Debt and Time, Mothers Ship Babies to China," *New York Times*, September 14, 1999.

387   "I am sacrificing myself to bring happiness to my family":   Ko-lin Chin, *Smuggled Chinese*, p. 18.

387   "Look at your salary":   *Seattle Times*, April 16, 2000.

Chapter Twenty. An Uncertain Future

390   "Asian Americans feel like we're a guest in someone else's house": Mia Tuan, *Forever Foreigners or Honorary Whites? The Asian Ethnic Experience Today* (New Brunswick, N.J.: Rutgers University Press, 1998), p. 4.

390   astronauts: In 2003, the two Chinese American astronauts active in the National Aeronautics and Space Administration were Dr. Leroy Chiao and Dr. Edward Tsang Lin. In 1985, Dr. Taylor Wang flew on STS-51B Challenger, the first operational Spacelab mission.

390   "Funny, you don't sound like a Wong":   Author correspondence with Ben Wong, West Covina City Council member, December 2000.

390–91 one in every six medical doctors: *Nightline*, ABC News, June 28, 1999.

391   "don our accents":   Author correspondence with Rosalind Chao.

391   "People like Asian-American dolls in costumes":   *A* magazine, August/September 2000, p. 10.

391   **"Are you in the Chinese Air Force?":** Ted W. Lieu, "A Question of Loyalty," *Washington Post*, June 19, 1999.

392   **"In those early days at CBS":** Author interview with Connie Chung, August 28, 2000.

392   **"Connie Chink":** *Civil Rights Issues Facing Asian Americans in the 1990s*, p. 44.

392   **"How can you let a gook design this?":** *Maya Lin—A Strong Clear Vision*, 105-minute documentary, written and directed by Freida Lee Mock, produced by Freida Lee Mock and Terry Sanders, American Film Foundation.

392   **"How did it happen that an Asian-American woman was permitted":** Franklin Ng, "Maya Lin and the Vietnam Veterans Memorial," in *Chinese America: History and Perspectives 1994*, p. 214.

392   **"There are Americans in it":** Howard Chua-Eoan, "Profiles in Outrage: America Is Home, but Asian Americans Feel Treated as Outlanders with Unproven Loyalties," *Time*, September 25, 2000, p. 40; *A* magazine, summer 1994, p. 24.

392   **"American beats Kwan":** Joanne Lee, "Mistaken Headline Underscores Racial Assumptions," *Editor & Publisher*, April 25, 1998, p. 64.

393   **"American outshines Kwan":** *Seattle Times*, February 22, 2002; *ESPN The Magazine*, May 1, 2002.

393   **which country he would support:** *Los Angeles Times*, March 2, 2000; *Time*, September 25, 2000, p. 40.

393   **"There is a subtle stereotyping":** *Time*, September 25, 2000.

393   **"Most strikingly I was asked a couple of times":** Al Kamen, "DOE Trips on Security Blanket," *Washington Post*, May 25, 2001; Sam Chu Lin, "Rep. Wu Refused Entry to Energy Department," article provided by Lin during correspondence with author. ("I just find that incredibly ironic," David Wu said of the incident, "because I was going down there at their invitation to try to help them with their Asian Pacific American Heritage celebration.")

393   **"subtle racism":** Roxanne Roberts, "An Asian American Gala, with the Emphasis on American," *Washington Post*, May 11, 2001.

395   **"the ability to threaten our homes with long-range nuclear warheads":** Leslie Wayne, "Infamous Political Commercial Is Turned on Gore," *New York Times*, October 27, 2000.

395   **Patrick Oliphant:** Cartoon on April 9, 2001, syndicated by Andrews McMeel Universal. Letter of complaint from Victor Panichkul, national president of Asian American Journalists Association, to John P. McMeel, chairman of Andrews McMeel Universal, April 11, 2001.

395   **"put MSG in everything":** Jonah Goldberg, "Back to Realpolitik; Out with Hysterics," *National Review*, April 4, 2001.

395   **"Why don't you go to China":** Correspondence from Theresa Ma to author, September 22, 2001.

396   **In Springfield, Illinois:** William Wong, "A Great Wall of Unease; In Spy Plane's Wake, Crude Jokes and Racist Stereotypes Make Chinese Americans Queasy," *San Francisco Chronicle*, April 18, 2001.

396   **Fox News host:** Statement by George M. Ong, president of the Organization of Chinese Americans, April 11, 2001.

396   **interned by the federal government:** Statement by Larry Golden, professor of Political Studies and Legal Studies, University of Illinois at Springfield.

396   **"The official sported a black wig":** Amy Leang, "Walk, Not Just Talk the Talk," *ASNE Reporter,* April 2001; Lloyd Grove, "Regrets, No Apology," *Washington Post,* April 13, 2001.

396   **80 percent of Americans viewed the PRC as "dangerous":** *Business Week,* April 16, 2001.

396   **national telephone survey:** Sonya Hepinstall, "Survey: Chinese Americans Still Have a Long Way to Go," Reuters, April 25, 2001. (The study, commissioned by the Committee of One Hundred in collaboration with the Anti-Defamation League, was conducted by Marttila Communications Group and Yankelovich in 2001.)

398   **David Ho's quote:** *Time,* September 25, 2000, p. 40.

400   **Information about Cy Wong:** Author interview with Cy Wong.

400   **"From time to time":** Cy Wong, "East Meets South: Cy Wong, the Great-Grandson of a Chinese Immigrant, Traveled to Louisiana to Research His Colorful History," *Los Angeles Times,* September 26, 1993.

400   **"Many of the Chinese people I interviewed":** Lisa See, *On Gold Mountain* (New York: St. Martin's Press, 1995; Vintage, 1996), p. xx.

401   **number of children born to Chinese-Caucasian couples more than tripled:** Joyce Nishioka, "U.C. Berkeley Hosts Hapa Conference," *Asian Week,* May 26, 1999, p. 8.

401   **some 750,000 to 1 million multiracial Asian Americans in the United States:** Janet Dang and Jason Ma, "HAPAmerica: The Coming of Age of Hapas Sets the Stage for a New Agenda," *Asian Week,* April 19, 2000.

401   **Information on Hapa movement:** *Asian Week,* June 10, 1998, and April 19, 2000.

402   **drew arrows to three boxes:** Author interview with Cy Wong.

ACKNOWLEDGMENTS

Only when a book is finally finished—when one is left staring at towers of banker's boxes stuffed with thousands of documents—does an author truly comprehend the degree to which she is indebted to others. I was blessed to have the cooperation of many wonderful people during this long and fascinating journey.

My deep gratitude goes to Susan Rabiner, my literary agent, for her superb judgment and her firm, unwavering confidence in this book right from the very beginning. She brought this project to Viking Penguin, where Caroline White and Wendy Wolf refined the narrative with their brilliant editing and meticulous attention to detail. I want to thank not only these two editors but other members of the Viking Penguin staff for their consummate professionalism: Yen Cheong, Carolyn Coleburn, Clifford Corcoran, Kate Griggs, Claire Hunsaker, Hilary Redmon, Nancy Resnick, Kim Taylor, and Grace Veras, among others. Carol Shookhoff, a line editor who carefully scrutinized the manuscript, also deserves special mention.

Within the historical profession, it was a great privilege to know Him Mark Lai, a scholar of rare and admirable spirit, a man whom I consider to be the father of Chinese American studies. Like many others, I stand in complete awe of his encyclopedic knowledge and tireless dedication to his life's work. His mastery of both Chinese- and English-language sources has enabled him to pioneer this field as a historical discipline, and this book, largely a synthesis of previous research, rests on the foundation of his knowledge. Him Mark Lai spent several hours with me to discuss the broad outlines and themes of Chinese American history, and I treasured our conversations immensely.

L. Ling-chi Wang, head of the ethnic studies department at the University of California at Berkeley, veteran activist, and a spokesman for the Rape of Nanking Redress Coalition, steered me to his excellent research on Chinese

American history in the Asian American Collection of Berkeley's Ethnic Studies Library. At various academic conferences over the years, I learned much from his discussions of Chinese America in the context of the political struggle for American civil liberties. Always at these forums, I was both inspired by him and honored to be associated with him, because of his passionate commitment to Asian American scholarship and the future of human rights.

In Washington, D.C., John Taylor, a friend and cherished fixture at the National Archives for more than half a century, was one of the best allies an author could hope for. Compassionate and knowledgeable, profoundly wise and endlessly helpful, John Taylor played a special role in helping me research this book, just as he did for my first two books, and my research benefited from his vast experience.

I was lucky to have the help of other important experts as I gathered source materials. Roger Daniels e-mailed me his extensive bibliography of references. Suellen Cheng and her husband, Munson Kwok, at the Museum of Chinese American History (now renamed the Chinese American Museum of Los Angeles) assisted me in countless ways as I conducted research in the museum archives and oral history collection. Peggy Spitzer Christoff graciously showed me her database of case files from the National Archives in Chicago, which traced the lives of Chinese immigrants in the Midwest. Douglas Knox generously shared with me his unpublished paper based on research conducted at the University of Chicago. Neil Thomsen, formerly with the National Archives Records Administration at San Bruno, gave me copies of the most intriguing historical documents he had found during his long career there. Wei Chi Poon, the Asian American Studies Collection specialist at Berkeley's Ethnic Studies Library, helped me immeasurably in the early stages of my research and handled all of my inquiries with her cheerful and efficient manner. Bruce Nichols at the Immigration and Naturalization Service opened his voluminous files for my review. My friend Marian Smith, a historian for the INS, not only offered insightful commentary as this book evolved, but deciphered for me the mysteries of outdated immigration indexing systems, which gave me access to records at the National Archives that had not been ordered for decades. Victor Mar of the Chinese Historical Society of Greater San Diego sent me a short biography of Ah Quin—a nineteenth-century merchant—and photocopies of Ah Quin's handwritten diary, which exceed 1,500 pages. Lack of space prevented inclusion of Ah Quin in this book, but it was stunning for me to see, in the pages of this diary, Ah Quin's remarkable transformation, first from cook to servant, and then from labor recruiter to capitalist.

The perspective of other writers and journalists also strengthened this book. Amy Tan and Connie Chung were generous with their time when I interviewed them. Novelist May-lee Chai, whom I had befriended during our days at the Associated Press, shared her beautifully written editorials and heartfelt opinions on Chinese America, ethnic profiling, and the mixed-race experience. Sam Chu

Lin, a broadcast pioneer in the Chinese American community, made copies for me of the audiotape and film interviews he had conducted with his family, which greatly enriched this book as well as my understanding of the Chinese in the South. I will always remember our spirited discussions on Chinese American history, along with his bittersweet and often humorous reminiscences of his youth in Mississippi. Best-selling author Edward Epstein offered memorable conversations and wise counsel as I launched into this project. Helen Zia, civil rights activist and author of *Asian American Dreams,* provided an insider's perspective on the gradual evolution of the Chinese American community as a modern political force. As the co-author of *My Country Versus Me,* an autobiography of Wen Ho Lee, Helen Zia also gave me the rare opportunity to sit down with Dr. Lee at a private dinner, to learn more about his ordeal in the hands of the U.S. government.

Certain individuals and institutions deserve special thanks for their timely response to requests for information: the Arizona Historical Society; Kevin O'Sullivan at AP Wide World News; the California State Library; Ellen Halteman, librarian at the California State Railroad Museum; the Chinese Historical Society; Clarence Chu of the Dai Loy Museum in Locke, California; Valerie Zars at Getty Images/Hulton Archive; Sally Stassi at the Historic New Orleans Collection; Elena S. Danielson and Ronald M. Butaloff at the Hoover Institution Library and Archives; the Idaho State Historical Society; Michael Shulman at Magnum Photos; the Museum of Chinese in the Americas (MoCA); the Oregon Historical Society; Murray Lee, curator of Chinese American history in the San Diego Chinese Historical Museum; the University of Washington archive; and Robert Fisher, collections manager of the Wing Luke Asian Museum.

Closer to home, my part-time assistants, Connie Amarel and Carol Lagorio, typed thousands of facts into my database and transcribed my taped interviews during the research phase of this book. I can never thank them enough for their hard work.

Other people offered invaluable suggestions, or assisted in ways too numerous to recount here: Steven Aftergood, Shirley Awana, Bob Barde, Ralph Bennett, Ronnie Chan, Gilbert Chang, Kuo-hou Chang, Morris Chang, Pamela Chang, Wen-hsuan Chang, Rosalind Chao, Anna Chennault, William Chew, Ko-lin Chin, Christine Choy, Frank Cowsert, Kent Dedrick, Ignatius Ding, Stella Dong, Phoebe Eng, Bernadine Chuck Fong, Kenneth Fong, Scott Forsythe, Dina Gan, Gloria Hom, Genevieve Hom-Franzen, Tony Hsieh, Carl Hsu, Chih-ming Hu, Kaimeng Huang, Liberty Huang, Liwen Huang, Susana Huang, Victor Hwang, Kay Johnson, Herb and Diana Kai, Joseph M. Kamen, Paula Kamen, Amy Orfield Kohler, George Koo, Stewart Kwoh, Peter Kwong, Ann Lau, Amy Leang, Corky Lee, C. Y. Lee, Robert Lee, Jennie F. Lew, Ronald Lew, Marvin Lewis, Christina Li, Dick Ling, Sara Lippincott, Haiming Liu, Dale Louie, Steve Louie, Sonia Mak, Barbara Masin, Barbara Morgenroth, James Motlow, Willard H. Myers, Franklin Ng, Patrick O'Connor, Ron Osajima, Ching

Peng, Wena Poon, Richard Rongstad, Lisa See, Jean H. Seeley, Charles Shao, Charlie Sie, Lillian Sing, Betty Lee Sung, C. B. Sung, Julie Tang, Douglas Wachter, Anna Wang, David Wang, Dorothy Wang, Tow Wang, Jim Weaver, Priscella Wegers, Eugene Wei, Ben Wong, Cy Wong, Joel Wong, Jeannie Woo, S. B. Woo, Carolyn Wu, Judy Wu, Stephen Wunrow, Noelle Xi, Swallow Yan, Jeff Yang, Linda Tsao Yang, John Yee, Alice Young, Renqiu Yu, Frank Yung, Karen Yung, Richard Yung, and Nancy Zhang.

Without the support and encouragement of my family, this book would not have been possible. My husband, Brett, gave me his wisdom, patience, and love— the hallmarks of his character that have nurtured and sustained me for more than a decade. My brother, Michael Chang, read a portion of the manuscript before publication and offered his unique perspective. Many thanks go to my uncle Shau-yen Chang, for narrating in vivid detail the story of my family's escape from mainland China during the 1949 Communist revolution; my uncle Cheng-cheng Chang, for his recollections of immigrant student life in the United States during the 1960s; and my uncle S. G. Tyan, for kindly lending me Chinese-language literature on the subject of high-tech development in Taiwan. Finally, I owe a debt of gratitude to my parents, whom I can never repay. They were the ones who first made me proud to be Chinese American.

INDEX

Larson, Louise Leung, 165, 182
Lau, Stanley, 218
laundrymen, 48–49, 120, 138n–139n, 168–72, 202, 220
Lau v. *Nichols,* 273
Lawrence Livermore National Laboratory, 367
lawyers, 188
Lea, Homer, 159
League of Nations, 215
Leang, Amy, 396n
Leaves from the Mental Portfolio of an Eurasian (Eaton), 115
Lee, Ang, 310
Lee, Bill, 268–69
Lee, Bruce, 401n
Lee, Chin Yang, 281
Lee, Clarence, 228
Lee, Dai-ming, 251
Lee, David, 303–5
Lee, Lancing F., 259
Lee, Richard, 228
Lee, Rose Hum, 228
Lee, Tsung-Dao, 281–82
Lee, Wallace, 196
Lee, Wen Ho, 359–64, 368
Lee, Yan Phou, 70, 228n
Lee Chew, 57
legal action by Chinese, 136, 137–38, 138n–139n, 141, 176–77, 252, 273, 368. *See also* activism of Chinese Americans; *specific cases*
legislation, anti-Chinese. *See also* immigration laws; *specific laws:* in California, 43–45, 75, 119–20, 128, 176n; China's response to, 142–43; Chinese responses to, 137–38, 140; lapsing of, 259; in New York City, 202; in San Francisco, 138n–139n
Lem Moon Sing v. *United States,* 137
Leon, William, 152–53
Leong, Charlie, 227
Leong Bick Ha, 151n
Let Keung Mui, 316–17
Leung, Alex, 340–41
Leung, Bernice, 179
Leung, Faith So, 191
Leung, Hugh, 145
Leung, Lillie, 180, 193
Leung, Louise, 210–11
Leung, Tom, 165–66
Leung, Tye, 197

Li, Wei, 324
Liang Qichao, 158–59
Liang Tun-yen, 106n
Lieu, Ted, 391
Lim, Harry, 232
Lin, Chia-Chiao, 282
Lin, Sam Chu, 278–79
Lin, Tung-Yen, 282
Ling, Dick, 288, 289
Ling Sing, 43
LinkExchange, 352n
Lin, Maya, 392
Lin Zexu, 14, 103
Liu, Henry, 323
Liu Haiming, 164
Liu Zongren, 317
Locke, Gary, 389
Loewen, James W., 167, 279
London, Jack, 162
Lone Mountain Cemetery, 80
Long Island (New York), 299
Long March (1934), 237
Loo, Bessie, 210
Loo, Jim, 322
Look, J. S., 78, 127, 151
Los Alamos National Laboratory, 359–60, 369
Los Angeles, 75, 121, 137, 154, 196
Los Angeles Survey of Race Relations (1924), 151, 193
Los Angeles Times, 210, 331, 345, 363, 400
Louie, Clifford, 218
Louie, Lillian, 201
Loving v. *Virginia,* 401n
Low, Charlie, 205
Low, James, 211–12
Lowe, Pardee, 183, 185–86
Lowell High School, 332–33
Luce, Henry, 226
Lue Gim Gong, 109
Luh, Raymond, 357
Lum Gong, 177
Lum Yip Kee, 162
Lung Chin, 206

Ma, Theresa, 395
MacArthur, Douglas, 248, 249
Macao, 30, 103
McCarran-Walter Act, 264
McCarthyism, 247–48
McConnell, Mitch, 393
McCunn, Ruthanne Lum, 87

B.C. 0005528049 20240822